Slave Genealogy of the Roulhac Family

French Masters and the Africans They Enslaved

Roy L. Roulhac

Text Copyright © 2012 Roulhac Family Association, Inc.
All Rights Reserved

ISBN: 1478275847
ISBN 13: 9781478275848

Cover photograph: Portrait of a middle age African American man dressed in a suit and bow tie. He is identified as "Uncle Caesar," a slave owned by Mrs. Joseph B. G. Roulhac of Hillsborough, North Carolina. Image is dated ca. 1880 (Tintypes). For Caesar's story, see Chapter 2: *Slave History of Joseph B. G. Roulhac and Catherine Roulhac.* Reprinted with permission of the North Carolina Collection, University of North Caroline at Chapel Hill.

Back cover author photograph, Dale Rich.

Table of Contents

Acknowledgements ix
Foreword xi
Prologue xv
Introduction xxxv

Part I – Slave Genealogy
Chapter 1
    Psalmet Gregoire Roulhac and his Descendants 2
Chapter 2
    John Gregoire Roulhac and his Descendants 69
Chapter 3
    Francis Leonard Gregoire de Roulhac and his Descendants 97

Part II – The March to Freedom
Chapter 4
    Civil War Pension Records of African Descended Roulhacs 117
Chapter 5
    Back to Africa: Roulhacs in Liberia 147
Chapter 6
    We've Come This Far By Faith:
    The Roulhac Family Association 191
Appendix 1: Memoir of the Gregoire de Roulhacs in France 259

Appendix 2: Memoir of Francis Leonard Gregoire Roulhac 277

Appendix 3: Jackson County FL Marriage (Roulhac Grooms, 1866 – 1910) 139 297

Appendix 4: Jackson County, FL Marriages (Roulhac Brides) 1848 - 1925140 301

Appendix 5: Roulhacs in the 1870 US Federal Census (Partial List) 303

Appendix 6: List of Emigrants to Liberia, November 11, 1869 309

Appendix 7: List of Emigrants to Liberia, November 5, 1870 315

Appendix 8: Roulhac 1918 World War I Draft Registrants 323

Appendix 9: Roulhac World War II Enlistments 329

Appendix 10: Roulhac Cemetery – Marianna, FL145 333

Appendix 11: Charter Members - Roulhac Family Association, Inc. 333

Index 335

End Notes 355

To Roulhac ancestors who eluded slave traders, died during the Middle Passage and endured inhumane treatment during chattel slavery, Jim Crow and segregation to make our reality possible.

The trans-Atlantic slave trade, uniquely characterized by individuals of the same or similar ethnicities enslaving each other, resulted in the export of approximately 12 million Africans to the United States, South America and the Caribbean. Merchants often inspected slaves to assess their skills, perceived physical strength, suicidal tendencies and rebelliousness, which varied by ethnic group. From the collection of Dale Rich, Courtesy Library of Congress.

The "Door of No Return" at Goree Island, off the coast of Dakar, Senegal, is one of many along West Africa's coast through which slaves, stolen from their home and scattered throughout the American and Caribbean Diaspora, passed. In 2009, President Barack Obama and his family visited Ghana's Cape Coast Castle, symbolically passed through its "door of no return" and then back though the door. The door was then renamed, the "Door of Return." Photograph courtesy Sharon Jordan Holley, pictured.

Acknowledgements

This project would have been impossible without the help of many individuals I encountered during more than forty years of research and those who assisted during the final stages of producing this publication. Special thanks to the Sue Tindel and Robert Earl Standland who made my visits to the basement of the Jackson County, Florida Courthouse productive. Cassandra Spratling, Raymond Davis, Johnella Frazier and Kenyatta Wright read early drafts and provided thoughtful suggestions for improvement. Thanks to Dale Rich for sharing compelling images from his Freedom Seekers Exhibit. I am indebted to my colleague Sarah Robichaud and my daughter Dr. Sheryl McGriff for meticulously reading and editing the specification ready manuscript. Any typos, grammatical errors and omissions that remain are solely my own. Finally, my gratitude is extended to the members of the Roulhac Family Association for their continuing support and interest in preserving and documenting the Roulhac history for future generations.

Foreword

Many books have been written about slavery — particularly the enslavement of Africans during the Transatlantic Slave Trade — from historical fiction, to non-fiction, to science fiction. These books have included the impact of slavery on individuals in slave narratives and biographies, and on the world in text and reference books. Yet, you'd be hard pressed to find a book as unique as Roy Roulhac's *Slave Genealogy of the Roulhac Family*. Unlike many books where African American authors trace their genealogy by relying primarily on oral histories and census records, Roy was fortunate enough to find a treasure – a memoir written by one of three French brothers who enslaved African descended Roulhacs – that greatly aided his ability to trace in roots to colonial North Carolina and document his ancestors' sojourn through slavery into the Civil War, Reconstruction and repatriation.

Upon arriving in America seeking to capitalize on trade with the colonist, the brothers maintained their privileged status by both marrying into affluent families that accumulated their wealth from slave labor, and then themselves becoming slave owners. Some members of the Roulhac family became "speculators" who bought and sold enslaved Africans in Wake County, North Carolina and drove them, like cattle, to Mississippi.

While stories of slavery through various mediums illustrate the dichotomy in the slave industry between the enslaved and their enslavers, *Slave Genealogy* reveals in an enslaver's own words the contemptuous attitude whites had toward their "slaves" who worked and lived in deplorable conditions. Roy makes excellent use of the memoirs to document the relationship between the white Roulhacs and those they enslaved, many who adopted the Roulhac surname, with varied spellings, after their liberation. The memoirs, Roy points out, include very little information about the French Roulhacs' practice of enslavement. However, through marriage and probate records, he was able to uncover how they and families they married created their wealth on the backs of those they enslaved. He also reveals the enslavers' own afflictions; disorder rarely documented in other works. One can only conclude that the enslaver's position in society also caused them to suffer, although not to the extremes of those they oppressed.

With the extensive use of slave schedules, pension records, marriage, death and birth records, wills and other official records, *Slave Genealogy* is an exemplary work that places the self-determination of former "slaves" front and center of a story they were excluded from in the memoirs of their owners. Even more appealing is the connection *Slave Genealogy* makes between the men who were enslaved on Roulhac plantations and those who joined the Civil War to fight for their liberation and to men, women and children who boarded ships to Liberia during the American Colonization Society's racist attempt to rid the country of free blacks by sending them "back to Africa." Private Lewis Rolack's decade-long pursuit for equality in obtaining an adequate pension after finding himself unable to work because of poor health is a particular compelling story to look for in part two of the book. When his application was finally approved for partial disability, he did not relent. His tenacity to increase his pension to the maximum amount allowed by the Pension Acts benefited him and his family for many years after he died.

It is a great honor to write this foreword for Judge Roy Roulhac's second book for more reasons than one. That he asked me is the first, considering we haven't known each other very long. I met Roy in the summer of 2011 at a friend's dinner party. Our brief encounter left me with a lasting impression. The little I heard from him that night spoke volumes. He was certainly a man with a story worth being told. A story that can be found in the pages of this exceptional work.

Secondly, Roy has entrusted such a valuable project into the hands of a newspaper editor. Book writing/editing and news writing/editing can be worlds apart. In news writing, the writer/reporter has to tell a story in as few words possible – subject/verb. Not so with literature and scholarly research. The more, the better. Short subject-verb sentences need to be elaborated upon, stretched out to tell the story, paint a visual, so that readers can enter into the author's narrative, whether fiction or non-fiction. So it was, with this work it wasn't looking at what to cut but where to elaborate. I appreciated the challenge.

Lastly, and most importantly, the story of the Roulhacs, while very similar to many African American families whose ancestors endured and persevered through enslavement, is not like one I've read before in slave anthologies and other works on U.S. slavery. Roy, intentionally, details the slave genealogy of his ancestors' enslavers. The documentation of births, marriages, deaths and transference of wealth in the white Roulhacs' wills, bills of sales, census records, slave schedules, mortgages, contracts of hire, newspaper accounts and unpublished material of the French families' memoirs, not only illuminates ways that those enslaved by the Roulhacs were dismissed and recorded as property — along with animals and furniture – but also discloses, the triumphs of those who escaped to some modicum of freedom in the Civil War and then later participated in their own governance during Reconstruction. Most impressive, however, is the story of those who left America, Africa-bound after their liberation.

Readers, whether Roulhacs, African Americans or of any other ethnicity can easily reflect on their own heritage in this documentation of despair and triumph. *Slave Genealogy of the Roulhac Family* not only tells a story of a family of victors — individuals who did not idly accept what most during their time concluded as their fate of oppression but played a significant role in their liberation — it also includes the personal triumph of one individual, its author, who not knowing the legacy from which he came, survived and thrived through his own self-determination. In this work, Roy picks up and continues the tradition of passing down history to his own descendants and those of the Roulhac lineage.

    Zenobia Jeffries
    Editor, The Michigan Citizen
    Detroit, MI

Prologue

"The social upheavals of the two world wars, the Great Depression, and the spread of the automobile have made it both possible and necessary for the Negro to move away from his former isolation of the rural plantation. The decline in agriculture and parallel growth of industry have drawn large numbers of Negroes to urban centers and brought about a gradual improvement in their economic status. New contacts had led to a broadened outlook and new possibilities for education advance. Once plagued with a tragic sense of inferiority resulting from the crippling effects of slavery and segregation, the Negro has now been driven to reevaluate himself. He has come to feel that he is somebody. With this new sense of somebodiness and self-respect, a new Negro has emerged with a new determination to achieve freedom and human dignity whatever the cost may be.

Martin Luther King, Jr.

July 19, 1962

Dr. Martin Luther King, Jr. spoke these words half a century ago on a hot summer day at an all white Washington, D.C. private social club. It marked the first time that a black man would speak formally at the National Press Club's regular weekly luncheon. It was just one of many doors of racial discrimination the civil rights leader would knock down, although membership in the club itself was still very much segregated.[1] Like many old boys' clubs of that time, the

National Press Club was a bastion of white male privilege. If blacks were inside, they were there to cook, clean or serve. They were barely seen and rarely heard. Still, for many black men, those jobs were held in high esteem. They were often passed down from one generation to another. Having a job that didn't require getting dirty carried a degree of dignity, no matter how menial the work. Dressed meticulously in white shirts, black clip-on bowties, white waiter jackets and black trousers, black men went about their duties with a sense of pride and their heads held high. I was one of those Negro men, one of those new Negroes of whom Dr. King spoke. I had landed a job as a waiter at the National Press Club just one month prior to Dr. King's speech. There was - and still is, however, one major distinction between me and the Negroes Dr. King described. I've always had a sense of somebodiness. I was 19 years old and had left my home state of Florida searching for an opportunity. As a black boy growing up during the age of Jim Crow, in a very small rural town in Florida's panhandle and picking cotton in sweltering sun, I'd never found anything particularly sunny about the sunshine state. Hence, my reason for heading north, as far away as I could.

The north, I found, suited me. The right kind of place for a young man like me. Independent. Bold. Daring. Confident. I suspect my esteem came from the adults in my life - my parents, mentors and teachers. My mother always bolstered my self-esteem by reinforcing the notion that although we lacked material wealth we were just as good as anyone else. Still there was always my own self-determination, which sustains me still. As a child, I had two favorite pastimes. One was climbing an old oak tree in the backyard of our home on Oak Street in Marianna, the county seat of Jackson County, Florida. I would settle as close to the top as my legs could carry me. I would watch the clouds float by and dream about a more prosperous future. When I wasn't in that tree, I'd hang out on Lafayette Street, the main thoroughfare in downtown Marianna, and watch cars and trucks go by. A glance at vehicles' license plates informed me the drivers were from someplace far away. I would imagine going to that far away place, although for me, far away didn't denote geographical distance alone. It was an existence where my dark brown skin did not limit what I could do, have and become. Early on I made up my mind that I would work in a profession that required me to wear a suit and tie. Attire that required, no, commanded respect. I didn't know what. I just knew I was a suit and tie man; a man to be respected. Yet, I understood the ticket to gaining respect had to be stamped with an education. So I became a standout student, earning top grades and leadership positions that would pave my path to success. I did this while having to work, sometimes three jobs to help my family make ends meet.

Those aspirations born in that oak tree so many years ago would eventually bear more fruit than I could ever imagined. My college degrees, the first after nine years of part-time study, led to successful careers in law as a state and federal administrative law judge and in business. I have also travelled the globe, visiting numerous countries on five continents. My journeys, both professional and personal, led me to a path I never considered in my youth. In recent years, however, my most meaningful travels have been through the pages of history books, archival documents and census records in search of my ancestors and those of Roulhac Family Association members, who were once classified as "property" and whose hopes continue to be fulfilled through our lives and those of future generations.

Like many African Americans, Alex Haley's 1978 publication of *Roots: The Saga of an American Family* and the subsequent mini-series ignited a hunger for my own family history. The idea of my actually knowing — finally, my African ancestry, excited me. Initially, I believed I too would trace my roots to some village on the continent of Africa, just like Haley. But gradually what came to matter more was passing on the legacy of my enslaved ancestors, who overcame unspeakable conditions as the property of whites to themselves being property-owners of land, homes and businesses, and ultimately becoming a proud people. I wanted my only child, Sheryl McGriff; my three grandsons Rallien, Aaron and Daniel; great grandsons James and Corey and generations of Roulhacs to come to know their ancestors with more than a rudimentary knowledge of their lives as enslaved Africans, or so-called slaves. I wanted them to have a familial appreciation for their ancestors surviving and thriving to make a way for me and for them.

Four Generations: Back, L to R – Daniel McGriff, Roy, Aaron McGriff, Rallien Johnson; Front – Barbara Johnson, Corey Allen, James Allen, Sheryl McGriff and Sharee Johnson, 2012, NC.

I was born, Roy Lee Roulhac, during World War II to J. Y. and GeHazel Gibson Rolack in Marianna, Florida, a town of 5,200. Just nine years before my birth, Claude Neal, a black man accused of raping and murdering a white girl, was lynched and his naked body put on public display in an oak street on the courthouse square, two blocks from the shotgun house where I was born. Although legal slavery had ended almost a century before, as in most other Southern states, many things remained the same in the small town of Marianna, particularly, the oppression of blacks. My first job was picking cotton with my mother. I would get up with her before the sun and wait in front of our house, hoping to be among the first picked up by the three-quarter ton truck that rumbled through the unpaved Negro quarters in the shadows of downtown Marianna every morning looking for cotton pickers. Being among the first meant being able to scoot into the back under the tarp draped over the truck's bed to gain shelter from the rain or fierce winds that could deplete one's energy — and spirit, even before the cotton-picking began. I was about 10 years old. I, like all the other pickers, earned three cents a pound or three dollars if I picked 100 pounds, which my mother frequently achieved. I never came close.

During the 18 years of my childhood in Jackson County, my family lived in at least a dozen different shotgun houses, including two in Greenwood, a rural farm community eight miles north of Marianna, where my father was born. Most of my pre-school years were spent in one of Marianna's oldest neighborhoods that at various times was referred to as "tin pan alley," "jailhouse bottom" and "baby land" - a likely reference to the untrained neighborhood midwife who assisted the community's pregnant black ladies who were denied admission to the county's only segregated hospital. The densely populated three-square block community's two main unpaved streets, St. Clair and Chipola, were on hills that sloped southward to the Louisville and Nashville Railroad tracks. I was born at 53 St. Clair Street near the top of the hill across the street from the city jail whose inmate population was primarily black men. The Chipola River, with its mullets and catfish that were frequently the main part of our meals, was a few streets down a hill to the east. Two blocks north ran Lafayette Street (Highway 90) that extends from Jacksonville, Florida's northeastern border west to California. The courthouse and a parking area for horse-drawn wagons that brought farmers and sharecroppers into town on Saturdays to shop and socialize around the courthouse square were within two blocks. I enjoyed those Saturdays. I got a chance to see my relatives from Greenwood, McChapel and Pope Chapel, communities in the country as they made their weekly visits to socialize, shop and reconnect with kin who had left share-cropping and farming for opportunities "in town". Some, including my grandfather Lucius Roulhac, who I rarely saw, to reward me for doing well in school, would give me a nickel; just enough to buy a Baby Ruth or a RC cola.

58 Chipola Street, Marianna, Florida. One of my many shotgun homes.

In Jackson County the races lived separate and apart. The bus and train stations featured "colored" and "whites only" signs on waiting rooms, toilet doors and above water fountains. Although there were no signs posted on the sitting areas surrounding the courthouse, intuitively, blacks and whites congregated in separate quarters of the square. Entering front doors of homes and businesses outside the black community was strictly forbidden. The balconies in the Gem and Ritz movie theaters were reserved for blacks and concession stand counters within the downstairs lobbies were strictly off limits to us. Many homes in the black community did not have electricity or indoor plumbing until the mid-1950s. There were separate schools for black and white students and new textbooks were unheard of in schools attended by blacks.

In 1957, the year I started ninth grade at Jackson County Training School (JCTS), my parents entered into a land contract to buy a three room house at 1205 Oak Street on the west side of town, shortening by a mile the distance my brother Sylvester and me would have to walk to school. For the next four years, we walked with my father to the school, where despite his accidental blindness in 1952 and marginal education, operated a fresh roasted peanut vending stand. My mother, who managed to earn a sixth grade education, spent her time nurturing my brother, four nephews – William, James, Freddie and Toney - and me while working as a $3-a-day maid when she would find work. As the oldest child still at home, I was expected to do what I could to help out. In addition to my chores at home, I had three part-time jobs. Every Monday night, I walked or rode my bicycle to the Elks Club, approximately two miles away, to wash dishes and assist Earl White, the cook, in the kitchen by shredding cabbage for coleslaw. After school on Tuesdays and Thursdays, I cleaned the Selective Service office in downtown Marianna. On Saturdays, I raked leaves and helped the maid, Roberta Wilson, clean the home of Ralph Daffin, the son of a local banker and, as I later discovered, a descendant of the French Roulhacs who had enslaved my ancestors. Still, on the rare occasions when neither work, school or hanging out demanded my time, I was up in that oak tree behind that house, dreaming of that far away suit and tie future.

Front – Toney; 2nd row, left to right: William, Freddie and James; Back – Roy and Sylvester

My social life centered on school and church. I attended two Baptist churches (Buckhorn in Greenwood and St. Luke in Marianna—my daddy's people's home churches) and three African Methodist Episcopal churches (McChapel, my mother's home church; St. James, our church in town; and Pope Chapel, the church my grandfather, Lucius Roulhac, attended). Church had a powerful impact on my life. "Getting religion" was an important rite of passage for black children growing up in the South. Children in rural communities or those like me whose parents lived in the town but had been raised in the "country" and still had family and church ties there, upon turning 12 years old, were expected to attend revival meetings. They were expected to sit on the mourners' bench — the pew closest to the pulpit in the center of the church - until the Holy Ghost moved them to accept Jesus Christ as their Lord and Savior. Revival, which usually lasted for a week during the summer, was a time for reflection. You couldn't even go outside to play or enjoy the social activities with other saved children or those not yet twelve until you were moved to accept Christ. I sat unmoved on the mourner's benches at McChapel and St. Luke for two straight summers before I confessed my religion. Needless to say, I eagerly accepted the responsibility of this rite of passage from adolescence to adulthood and following the practice of my saved cousins in the "country", I told my religion to anyone in my neighborhood willing to spare a minute of hand shaking and foot stomping.

But the church was my salvation in other ways. It was one of the places where I learned responsibility and encouraged by mentors Virgil L. Elkins and Roberta M. Pressley, began public speaking. That oratorical talent also transferred to the classroom. Each Friday the school had an all-class assembly and each grade rotated organizing and presenting a program of songs, skits and speeches. Frequently, I gave a dramatization of *The Creation*, by Jacksonville, Florida born James Weldon Johnson, the author of *Lift Every Voice and Sing*, the Negro National Anthem. One of my first major speeches was about Richard Allen, the founder of the African Methodist Episcopal Church. I was in the eleventh grade by then and my presentation earned me second place in a state oratorical contest at Edward Waters College in Jacksonville and fourth in the national competition at Mother Bethel A.M.E. Church in Philadelphia, Pennsylvania. I travelled to Philadelphia with the Edward Waters College Glee Club outfitted in suit, hat and overcoat given to me by supporters at St. James back in Marianna. Until the national competition, I had never left Florida. It was then, among these talented college students that I was convinced that an education could take me places. Most importantly, that fourth place finish earned me a one-year scholarship to Edward Waters College, where I was elected freshman class vice-president.

While in high school, I was class and student council, a member of the honor society and salutatorian of my graduating class. However, these accomplishments were not without some major challenges. At 17, I became a teenage father. My daughter Sheryl was born in the fall of my senior year. But this was a period of great emotional distress for me, although not nearly to the extent that my 16-year-old classmate Barbara Jean Thompson endured. In those days, embarrassed teenage mothers were forced to drop out of school and often times sent away to live with relatives. Barbara, the JCTS marching band's drum major, dropped out and moved to Atlantic Highlands, New Jersey to live with her father. She returned to Marianna shortly before Sheryl's birth and attended night school while raising her. With the support of her family and a few years later her husband Robert Johnson, who adopted Sheryl into his family, Barbara not only earned a high school diploma, but also secured undergraduate and graduate degrees from Florida A&M University and Troy State College, respectively, and had a stellar career as an elementary school teacher in Jackson County schools. Without a doubt, the decision by Barbara's mother, Ora Mae Dickens, not force us into marriage played a significant role in the potential for us to "make something of ourselves".

Graduating from high school was a major accomplishment, not just for me but also for my entire family. I was the first of any of my direct ancestors to do so. It was a giant stepping-stone toward a life of opportunities they never imagined and no doubt an underpinning securing my armor of "somebodiness." The AME church scholarship and the college's work-study program made it possible for me to complete my freshman year at Edward Waters College. By the end of my freshman year, however, I had no money to continue my education full-time. So I decided I would follow the path of some of my older high school classmates and go to Ocean City, Maryland to find summer work in the resort city's hotels and restaurants.

Roy completes the first step in search of suit and tie future

I never made it to Ocean City. One of my college professors, Joseph D. Paige, persuaded me to join his family and him in Washington, D.C. He was leaving Edward Waters College to teach in the science department at Howard University and pursue a doctoral degree at American University. I was happy for the chance to go and figured I could get a job, complete my education at Howard and continue to chase my dream of a suit and tie job.

That journey "up-north" began in earnest only after I returned to Marianna to gain my parents approval and blessings. It was not an easy decision, but my parents believed that the prospect of my obtaining an education outweighed the loss of the material and emotional support I provided to my four nephews, my brother and them. So I, with some trepidation, packed my suitcase and left Florida with little money but with lots of determination to fulfill that suit and tie dream. I may not have had money, but thanks to Mamie Cooper one of my high school teachers, I knew how to type and had public speaking and leadership skills honed at church and on school podiums that would serve me well.

The next stop was Washington, D.C., where I met fellow southerners LeRoy Washington, Robert Hilliard and Earnest C. Withers, Jr., the son of noted Memphis, Tennessee-based civil rights Photographer Earnest C. Withers. Their friendship and encouragement greatly assisted in my transition for rural to big city life. In June 1962, within a few weeks of my arrival in D.C., I was referred by and the Haberman Employment Agency to the National Press Club where I was hired as a waiter. I was paid 60 cents an hour and tips that ranged from 10 to 20 cents. On a good week, I made $35, barely enough for food and shelter. The black clip-on bowtie, white shirt, black pants and white waiters jacket was not the businessman's suit I aspired to, but it was a start. It was clear to me that while I may not have been immediately moved on that mourner's bench many years before, someone was praying for me. On my first day of work I learned Press Club waiter positions were usually passed down from father to son or through close connections.

I was proud that my name was on the schedule to work Tuesday, July 19, 1962. I considered myself fortunate that I would be part of a historic moment. I heard Dr. King, as he calmly expounded on his dream of a nation where all men had an equal opportunity for success. It didn't matter that day whether I received any tips from the white men in that smoke-filled dining room. I was thrilled just to be there. Dr. King's speech filled me with hope that the day was near when the Negroes' long struggle for dignity, justice and full citizenship would be won. On a more personal level, the speech reinforced the teachings of my parents, teachers and mentors who made me believe that with determination, a good education and an equal chance, I could fulfill my dream of becoming the suit and tie man I envisioned in the oak tree back home. I reflected that day on my parents, who had been driven in the 1940s from the "country" in search of unskilled labor positions in an increasingly industrialized South. Dr. King's message lifted my spirits. I knew I was on my way to escaping a life of sharecropping, farm labor and domestic work that had sustained my ancestors. After his speech, other waiters and me eagerly shook Dr. King's hand and I got his autograph, which he carefully scribbled on the back of the employment agency business card I still carried in my wallet.[2]

Dr. Martin L. King, Jr., at the National Press Club, July 19, 1962, a day after his release from jail in Albany, GA. Reprinted by arrangement with the Heirs to the Estate of Martin Luther King, Jr., c/o Writers House as agent for the proprietor, New York, NY. Copyright 1963 Martin Luther King, Jr., copyright renewed 1991 Coretta Scott King.

Four months later, I was anxious to do better. I knew there was no way I could go to college on the meager wages my waiter job paid. Although I took pride in my work and was grateful for having a means to support myself and help my family back home, I quit my job and signed up for the United States Army. My plan was to use my GI Bill to pay for my education. I would finally get my degree. I was unaware of America's escalating involvement in the Vietnam War. Within weeks of completing requirements for my induction, I received a job offer to work for the federal government as a medical abstract clerk in the medical records department at Freedman's Hospital on Howard University's campus. The $3,820 annual salary with healthcare, sick leave, vacation time and participation in a retirement system was one step closer to my suit and tie dream job. There I figured I could work myself up the career ladder, while going to school part-time. But I had signed up for the Army. Fortunately, I knew the manager back at one of my several after school jobs, Marianna's draft board. She remembered the good job I'd done cleaning that office and respected my hard-earned accomplishments since leaving Marianna. When I telephoned her and explained my predicament, I was able to convince her to cancel my voluntary enlistment.

My exemption from military service was short-lived, however. Nineteen sixty-four was the beginning of a steady increase in the military draft which reached its highest level in 1973. Therefore, I joined a growing number of potential draftees who opted to enlist in the National Guard. Successful completion of Officer Candidate School enhanced my military pay as a lieutenant rather than a private in a military police unit. I continued to work as a clerk at Freeman's Hospital. I started classes at Howard as planned. However, the university offered too few night classes for me to complete my education there in a reasonable time so I transferred to Southeastern University in D.C., without understanding the consequence of attending an unaccredited college. I also knew in order to pursue my dreams, I would have to look further than the now defunct university.

Prologue

I moved to Detroit in 1968, chasing greater economic opportunity and a chance to graduate from an accredited college. The timing of my move to Detroit in March 1968 was perfect. A 30-day delay in leaving would have meant the certain activation of my D.C. National Guard military police unit during the riots that followed Dr. King's April 15 murder in Memphis. In Detroit, which a year earlier had experienced one of the country's deadliest race riots, I immediately began working at the Urban Adult Education Institute as an administrative assistant for Dr. Paige, the former professor at Edward Waters College who facilitated my moved to Washington, while continuing to pursue my bachelor's degree at Wayne State University.

To my total dismay, none of my numerous credits from Southeastern, the non-accredited university I had attended part time for four years were accepted by Wayne State. Except for 32 credit hours I earned at Edward Waters College and 16 at Howard University, seven years out of high school, I had to begin my college education anew. Two years later, in December 1970, my six-year military obligation ended and I graduated from Wayne State with a degree in business management..

Despite having my degree and sending out many resumes, I was unable to find a job in 1970 corporate America. I suspect the large Afro hairstyle I wore at the time didn't fit the mold. But I refused to let my suit and tie dreams die. While pondering our futures over cocktails at Foster's, a popular after work hangout in downtown Detroit, Eddie Martin, a friend and fellow Floridian, suggested that I enroll in law school. I didn't know what I'd do with a law degree; I just knew my oak-tree inspired journey was not meant to end at unemployment. While working full time, I took night classes at the University of Detroit Law School. In 1975, after four years, I received my law degree, becoming the second Jackson County African American to graduate from law school.

As fate would have it, my mother, who at great sacrifice had be my biggest nurturer made her transition eight months before I earned my undergraduate degree and was not there to share my joy. But at her funeral, for the first time, I met my nine-year-old daughter Sheryl. With the support and encouragement of her mother and stepfather, Sheryl and me commenced a special, loving and considering the psychological impact of our meetings, a sometimes-challenging relationship. Happily, Sheryl and her family relocation to Detroit in 1995 provided an opportunity for us to form a closer familial bond. Like her mother Barbara and me, Sheryl recognized the importance of education and instilled that value in her three sons who are all third-generation college graduates! Sheryl lives directly across the street from my home and recently completed her doctorate in educational leadership in higher education and is the Dean of Career Education at my law school alma mater, the University of Detroit Mercy.

Even before graduating law school, I held several law-related positions, working as Michigan State Senator Jack Faxon's Legislative Assistant in Lansing – 90 miles from Detroit - and as a legal assistant in the law department at Detroit Edison. After graduation, I worked for a short period in the Juvenile Division of the Wayne County Prosecutor's Office and in private practice. In the fall of 1976, I worked as Federal Congressional District Coordinator in President Jimmy Carter's campaign in Gary, East Chicago and Hammond, Indiana. I had hoped the influence of my well-connected friends in Washington and my service in the campaign would land me a job somewhere in the federal government in Washington where I would have eagerly returned. But that did not happen. After the election, I returned to Michigan and within a few months began what has become a 35-year career as a state and federal administrative law judge.

My attraction to leadership posts, born from speaking in school and rural churches, has not waned. Over the years, I have served in several leadership positions within various bar-related and community associations. I have been president of the Michigan Association of Administrative Law Judges, the State Bar of Michigan's Administrative and Labor Law Sections, the Association of Black Judges of Michigan and the Fred Hart Williams Genealogical Society. My service with the genealogical society turned my interests toward home;

to Marianna where my family's journey in this country had taken them.

I had never given much thought to my personal history until I moved to Washington, D.C., where I was often asked how a dark-skinned "colored boy," with no apparent French features, ended up with a French surname. I didn't know. I'd never thought my surname was unusual, nor did I give attention to the name being of French origin. In fact, when I was growing up, I had no idea my surname was French! The Roulhac name was rather common. It was more prevalent than "Smith" or "Jones." Large numbers of families and institutions bearing that name could be found throughout Jackson County and neighboring Washington, Gadsden and Bay counties. There was Roulhac High School, a school for "colored" students in neighboring Washington County, and Roulhac Cemetery and Roulhac Street in Marianna. Moreover, JCTS, the segregated school I attended did not offer foreign language classes.[3] Moreover, in Jackson County and throughout the South, "Roulhac," pronounced "Roo-lack" in French, is pronounced "Row-lack," with complete disregard for the long "u" or the silent "h" throughout the South. But in D.C., to avoid appearing ignorant about such a personal matter, I made up a bogus but plausible response: My ancestors had been enslaved in Louisiana where the first African slaves were brought by the French army during the 1710 Spanish War of Succession. It took me over 20 years to discover how wrong I was.

I was inspired to look for my pre-Civil War ancestors in 1981. I discovered the dilemma of documenting the lives of my ancestors who, while possessed of the same human characteristics as all people, were at the same time legally classified as chattel property. Considered inferior, they were bought, sold, hired out, mortgaged and deprived of all human rights. They were prohibited from voting, learning to read or write, and marrying. Further, no official record of their births, marriages and deaths were required or maintained. Thus, to identify my pre-Civil War ancestors I needed to search for the Europeans who oppressed and enslaved them and follow their migration patterns. Combining my legal and genealogical research skills, I began what has become a thirty-year obsession to discover the truth about my ancestors.

During my first trip to Washington's Library of Congress in 1982, I discovered the microfilm of the 1894 *Genealogical Memoir of the Roulhac Family in America*. Over a century later, the *Memoir*, penned by a Frenchman, Francis Leonard De Gregoire Roulhac, three years before his death in 1852, would become my most significant resource.4 I ordered the microfilm and could barely wait for it to arrive. When it came a few weeks later, I rushed to Wayne State University's Purdy Library, made paper copies and immediately read all of its 108 pages in one sitting. I was disappointed that the *Memoir* only made veiled references to the Roulhac family's involvement in the slave trade, although slavery was at the heart of the social and economic fabric of the south and of their own lives and livelihood. Nevertheless, the *Memoir* was the beginning of a search that would connect me to my ancestors.

The best chance African Americans have in discovering their enslaved ancestors before 1870, when the federal censuses first included all blacks by name, was for the enslaver to die before the Civil War ended and leave a record of the property, including their enslaved Africans, and their disposition. After five years of searching, I had almost given up on ever finding any antebellum record of my ancestors.

The Jackson County Courthouse basement has become one of my first stops whenever I visit my hometown. On this particular winter day in 1986, while browsing through Deed Book D for transactions related to Roulhacs, on page 258 I happened upon an entry for John Gray Roulhac's 1858 probate record. When I opened the 130-year-old record detailing the disposition of his estate, the information of those fragile pages was a startling reminder of my ancestors' reality. There they were - my great-great grandparents Nero and Nelly Roulhac and their children, which included my great-grandfather - on the same-yellowed pages as ox carts, bay horses and sorrel colts, priced down to the penny, for quick sale..

Prologue

The Jackson County Courthouse. The County, named after Andrew Jackson, Florida's first military governor, was created in 1822. It covers 954 square miles in Florida's panhandle. The courthouse square served as a popular Saturday gathering place for blacks until 1962 when the elevated lawn was eliminated during the courthouse's renovation. In 1934, twenty-three year old Claude Neal's mutilated body was hung from an oak tree on the northeast corner of the courthouse the morning after he was lynched in Greenwood, a rural community eight miles north of Marianna. Courtesy, Brewer Studios, Marianna.

My great-great grandmother Nelly, age 46, was valued at $483.33, slightly less than the $500 assigned value of John Gray Roulhac's seven mules. Nelly's son, my great-grandfather, ten-year-old Fayton, was priced at $600, just over twice as much as his 106 stock hogs. Nelly and Fayton were among the 37 slaves owned by John Gray Roulhac. My ancestors were valued at $4,491.65, about 20% of the $24,32.38 appraised value of all of John's slaves. John's slaves accounted for over 85% of the $28,976.30 appraised value of his entire estate. Roulhac Family Association member Greg Frazier, a certified public accountant, using the consumer price index and an exponential regression methodology, calculated the 2011 value of John Gray Roulhac's 37 enslaved Africans as $3,862,552.74!

Prologue

Thankfully, the slave experience, with its legally sanctioned dehumanizing intent, did not rob Roulhac ancestors of their humanity. Meeting my forefathers through the pages of history transformed academic knowledge about slavery into an intimate acquaintance that both pained me, knowing the horrific conditions they endured, and filled me with pride learning that they, among the strong that survived the Middle Passage, fought valiantly to improve their lot and keep their family—my family—together despite oppressive conditions. I come from a line of survivors!

Introduction

This book is part of an ongoing effort to document and preserve the history of Roulhacs of African descent and to add our story to the American narrative on slavery and race. It is an attempt to rediscover challenges and victories and pass them to our children and grandchildren so they may be inspired by and benefit from them. We stand on the shoulders of our ancestors who labored under extreme adverse conditions devoid of opportunities that we too often take for granted. We owe it to them to tell their story.

This publication is divided into two parts. Each chapter in Part I includes an annotation of the genealogical sketches contained in the 1894 *Genealogical Memoir of the Roulhac Family in America* of three brothers and their heirs who owned slaves, fought in the Civil War or played an active role in the Reconstruction era politics of suppression and violence. Added to their histories are wills, bills of sales, census records, slave schedules, mortgages, contracts of hire, probate records, newspaper accounts and other previously unpublished material. The greater part of the *Memoir* was written in 1849 by Francis Leonard De Gregoire and updated and published in 1894 by his great-niece, Helen M. Prescott. It documents the history of the Gregoire de Roulhacs from the Middle Ages to 1890s and memorializes the lineage and migration patterns of brothers – Psalmet Gregoire Roulhac Dethais (1752 – 1808); John Gregoire de Roulhac (1758 – 1810) and Francis Leonard Gregoire de Roulhac (1765 – 1852) – who settled in North Carolina between 1777 and 1793. In France, the Gregoire de Roulhacs were wealthy, influential and part of the French aristocracy with a coat of arms to demonstrate their nobility. Two, Psalmet and John, arrived in North America during the American Revolution when the colonists were engaged in armed conflict with the British to free themselves from the tyranny of taxation without representation.

The uncovered documents highlight the family's participation in chattel slavery, drawing attention to how enslaved Africans were passed down from generation to generation as an inheritance along with pieces of furniture, land and animals, and in some instances hired out to others, mortgaged or sold. The documents demonstrate the dichotomous relationship between the French enslavers and the Africans they oppressed, and also disclose elements of their own suffering, including their suicidal tendencies. Ultimately, they reveal a more complete story about the French Roulhacs during the antebellum period and their unrelenting post-Civil War efforts to maintain their legally sanctioned and what they believed to be their God-given superior and privileged status. Additionally, the annotations provide a glimpse into the struggles and triumphs of the Africans they enslaved.

Chapter 1 details the slave genealogy of Psalmet Roulhac and five generations of his descendants. In 1790, when the first U.S. Federal Census was taken, Psalmet who had only been in the country for 13 years and did not speak English when he arrived, enslaved 11 Africans. Although he was only 54 years old when he died in 1808, he had amassed over 1,300 acres of land and enslaved 30 Africans during his 31 years in America. He bequeathed to his wife and children his property, including those whom he enslaved. Psalmet's only son, John Maule Roulhac, was the beneficiary of considerable wealth from both his father and his mother's brother. As fate would have it, none of Psalmet's descendants would carry the Roulhac surname. However, a practice developed of adding "Roulhac" as the middle name of both male and female descendants. John Maule, whose inheritance from his father was dependent upon his compliance with stringent instructions for completing his education and entering into an apprenticeship, committed suicide. Psalmet's daughter Mary Jane Roulhac married a doctor, Horace Ely, from New England and relocated to Jackson County, Florida, where their son, Francis Roulhac

Ely, became one of the County's largest slave owners. One of her grandsons married the Florida's Confederate Governor John Milton's daughter. Psalmet's daughter Elizabeth and her descendants continued his legacy in the Georgia counties of Clinton, Jones, Clay, McIntosh and Muscogee, by marrying into well-known slave merchant families as the Slades, Roses, Blounts and Gignilliats.

Chapter 2 recounts the slave history of John Gregoire Roulhac, who in 1888, eight years after settling in North Carolina, married Psalmet's sister-in-law, Jamina Maule, who owned 440 acres of land and six Africans. Five years later, she drowned her young son and committed suicide as did her only other child, William Maule Roulhac. John Gregoire later married Frances Gray, of the prominent Gray family of Bertie County, North Carolina. Most of John and Frances Gray Roulhac's descendants, like Psalmet's, were heavily involved in exploiting the labor of those they enslaved to create and preserve wealth for their heirs. Their son Joseph B.G. Roulhac married Catherine Ruffin, the daughter of Thomas Ruffin, a large slave owner, justice and chief judge of the North Carolina Supreme Court, who authored one of the most controversial decisions on the relationship between slaves and their masters. Joseph settled in Wake County, North Carolina, where he became a speculator who, with his partner, bought slaves and shipped them to Mississippi. Joseph's sister, Frances called Fannie, never married, but unlike most women of the day, maintained a large enslaved population. Many of Fanny's slaves escaped to join the Civil War and others, after the War, emigrated to Liberia. Another son, John Gray Roulhac, with his father's inheritance, joined his uncle Horace Ely in Jackson County, Florida, where by 1850 he was the fourth largest owner of enslaved Africans. He enslaved my ancestors on his North Carolina and Florida plantations.

Chapter 3 details the slave history of Francis Leonard Gregoire Roulhac. He initially emigrated from France to Haiti where he was the overseer and manager of coffee and sugar plantations before his dreams of wealth and security were interrupted by the only successful slave revolt. Fearing for his safety, he abandoned the Island and after a stay in France shorten by the impact of the French Revolution on his noble and aristocratic family, obtained a forged passport to join his brothers in antebellum North Carolina. There, after marrying his brother John's sister-in-law, he continued his enslavement of Africans in Montgomery and Rutherford County, Tennessee. In his last will, mindful of preserving the value of his estate, admonished his children to "never forget that bond servants ought to be treated with kindness and humanity as they are not brutes, but fellow creatures."

Part II, The March to Freedom, documents the African descended Roulhacs' efforts to free themselves from a legacy of repression where the power of the enslaver was absolute, and their struggle to redefine the U.S. Constitution's "We the people," to include themselves and their descendants. Chapter 4 is a summary of pension and military records of enslaved Roulhacs who escaped from plantations in North Carolina and Tennessee to fight with the Union Army and Navy to free themselves and future generations of African Americans from the horrors of slavery. Privates David Rolack and Joseph Rolacke, brothers, joined the 2nd North Carolina Volunteers (later designated as the 36th Regiment, U. S. Colored Troops), on the same day. Two Roulhac soldiers made the ultimate sacrifice and gave their lives for the freedom of others. Private John Rolac, "with hazel eyes, brown hair and a light complexion," was one of about a thousand Negro soldiers to serve in white regiments. He was captured during the Battle of Plymouth, North Carolina and imprisoned at Andersonville, Georgia, the most infamous of Confederate prisons, where he died, along with nearly 13,000 Union prisoners of malnutrition, exposure and disease. John Rolac was one of only 102 Negroes confined at Andersonville and the only known Negro soldier buried there.

Chapter 5 recounts the 1869 and 1870 migrations of North Carolina Roulhacs to Arthington, Liberia, in West Africa, where they sought a better life than they experienced during the near-slave oppression of Reconstruction. Their relocation to Africa was part of the American Colonization Society's effort, begun in 1816, to rid the country of freedmen who they believed were prone to incite the slave population to stage a successful uprising as had Africans in Haiti. Among the 160 former slaves to embark for Liberia on November 11, 1869, one hundred twenty-three were from North Carolina. The 12 emigrants on the voyage from Bertie County included three single mothers and their children. The ship's log included, 27-year-old Jane Roulhac sailed with her two children, 10-year-old Henrietta and four-year-old Nero.

Chapter 6 contains genealogies of some Roulhac Family Association members, who despite family histories of slavery and second-class citizenship, made valuable contributions to the development and progress of their communities.

Finally, the appendices in *Slave Genealogy* include the early history of the French Gregoire de Roulhacs; the complete memoir of Francis L. G. Roulhac; Jackson County Marriages, 1866- 1908; a partial list of Roulhacs in the 1870 Federal Censuses; a passenger lists of emigrants - including Roulhacs from North Carolina – who sailed to Liberia in 1869 and 1870; World War I Roulhac Draft Registrants; World War II Roulhac Enlistments; Roulhac Family Association's charter members and a survey of the Roulhac cemetery in Marianna.

PART I
Slave Genealogy

Gregoire de Roulhac Coat of Arms

Leon Kelly of Marianna, Florida, purchased this framed painting (in color) of the Coat of Arms of Gregoire de Roulhac branch of French Roulhacs at a garage sale while stationed in Gelnhausen, Germany in 1983. With the exception of the braided ribbon that separates the coronet from the field and the embellishment on the top of the field, it is identical to the coat of arms included in the 1894 *Genealogical Memoir of the Roulhac Family in America*. The Coat of Arms is described in the *Memoir* as follows: Gregoire on the right and Roulhac - on the left. Crest, as Earls coronet, or (gold). Gregoire – on the field, gules, (red) a lion rampant, or: border, an azure field, fleur-de-lis, or: Roulhac – on a field, azure, three stars, or, (silver); on a chief, gules, (red) a crescent, or: outlines and divisions, black. No motto.

Chapter 1

The early accounts of French Roulhacs portray them as upright, virtuous, honest and religious. They were well educated. From ages four to 11, the children were under the care of a tutor and forbidden to ramble the streets or mix with other children, even when they visited their relatives. At 12 years, the boys were sent to college and the girls to a nunnery. After six or seven years, they returned home for instruction in drawing, music dancing, fencing and embroidery or were prevailed upon to enter the Congregation of Oratoire, whose members were a body of public teachers. Roulhac family members not only attended, but also operated some of the early French colleges. The Gregoire de Roulhacs were judges, lawyers, teachers, and canons of collegial churches, doctors, nuns, ministers, government workers and enemies of the French Revolution. The father of the three brothers who migrated to America was the chief judge and mayor of Limoges, and an acquaintance of King Louis XVI's finance minister Turgot. Their oldest brother, who inherited their father's offices and titles, participated in Louis XVI's assembly of notables, an expanded version of the King's Council, and was a member of the National Assembly in 1789.

The three brothers who emigrated to the United States were seventh-generation members of the Gregoire de Roulhac branch of French Roulhacs. They were one of three branches of French Roulhacs – Roulhac, Marquis of Rasay and Roulhac de Roulhac. The Gregoire de Roulhacs were divided into many subdivisions, such as Faugeras, Dethias, Du Clasang, Du Ronvaix and Dupuisfaucher, which were given as proper names for country estates and to distinguish families coming from the same stock. Older branches of Roulhacs disowned the Gregoire de Roulhacs because they degraded their "noble blood" by adopting a mercantile life.

Appendix I contains a complete account of the early history of the French Roulhacs as described in the *Memoir of the Roulhac Family in America*.[5]

Psalmet Gregoire Roulhac and his Descendants[1]

The Lord took away everything because he had not used it for his glory.
First Generation: Psalmet Gregoire Roulhac

1.2 Psalmet Gregoire Roulhac Dethias *was born Oct. 30, 1752, at Limoges, Francis.*

"Although he moved in an humbler sphere than some of his brothers, he was no less qualified to adorn any situation where fortune might have placed him. He was enlightened, open, generous and liberal. Having ended his collegiate training, he entered the Congregation of the Oratoire and became a Professor of Belles, Lettres, and at one time President at Autun. The American Revolution taking place, speculations were entered into by many French commercial houses in the seaports. Amongst them was a house at Bordeaux of great credit and reputation, known under the name of Rainbau, Barmarius & Co., some principal partners of which were our townsmen. Psalmet was invited by them to become their agent in America, with very flattering prospects, as they had immense credit with

---

1 Note: The italicized text in this chapter and the next two represents unedited portions of the *Genealogical Memoirs of the Roulhac Family* as published in 1894 by Helen Prescott. The unitalicized text portions are my annotations.

the house of Beaumarchais, a banker in Paris. That same banker had for a long time large claims on the United States which were only settled many years after. The proposal appeared advantageous to a young man of very limited means, and his father calculating that should his son be successful, his younger brothers might find with him some day, a fair opening to make their way in the world, encouraged him to accept it. So as agent, Psalmet came to the United States, but not as a partner, as that house, which failed in a short time after, asserted to her creditors in France. Our father had wished him to become so, but he had refused to do it, until he should arrive in America and be able to judge for himself. In expectation of his becoming one of the firm his father advanced him a sum a money nearly equal to the portion which he knew he could leave to his younger children at his death, which sum he should not be charged with by his elder brother, in case he did not succeed in his doubtful enterprise.

Arrived in Boston, April 20, 1777, he saw early that he would involve himself irrevocably were he to sign the articles of co-partnership sent him from France, and he refused to do it, agreeing to act only as an agent. The country was torn by dissention and a civil war and the United States, without cash, was inundated with worthless paper currency. Many cargoes from France were consigned to him but a good part of these were taken at sea by British cruisers, or made the first port they could enter, after being left to the care of unworthy agents, as Psalmet could not be present in Boston, Philadelphia, Baltimore and Charleston at the same time. The consequence of all this was the failure of all those French houses that had entered into American speculations, the house of Rainbau, Barmarius & Co. being of the number. To their creditors they asserted that their partner, Roulhac, had immense sums in his hands and that he had become immensely rich, but the truth was, that he himself was reduced to beggary and great distress.

In a few years his health was impaired, his small means nearly gone, and his only resource was to purchase a small tract of land which was extremely poor and worn out, in Beaufort Co., N.C. To enable him to live until he could get a support from his farm, he obtained a small supply of dry goods and groceries from Dr. Savage of Richmond, Va., which he was to sell on commission. A party of Tories in his neighborhood, knowing him as a Frenchman and belonging to the adverse party, came one night disguised, seized and tied him, with his clerk, Tom Pilly, with ropes in his counting room, and left the store entirely naked, carrying away money, books, papers and even his wearing apparel. He was found the next morning safely secured and yet tied. A few days afterwards he had the good fortune, by the help of the militia in his vicinity, to recover the greatest part of his clothing and books, found in a swamp, but a large sum in certificates, which afterwards were assumed and funded by Congress, could not be found, as probably the ignorant villains might have taken them for waste paper and destroyed them as no account. A short time after this he married a Miss Maule, connected with some of the best and most respectable families in that part of the country, and retired at the same time to his far

Psalmet Roulhac and Anne Hare Maule[6] were married July 17, 1783, at Smiths Point, on Pamlico River, by Thomas Bonner, Esq. A copy of the marriage license and the plat of 100 acres of land, willed by her father, John Maule to his daughter, Anne, are still preserved; and also a quaint old letter written by Psalmet to his mother in France in 1786. In it he says:

> This country is less than ever adapted to commerce, whoever can accustom himself to a retired country life, may with a little industry, live at a small expense and even comfort. The country is susceptible of several productions unknown here, and to them I intend giving my attention. With time, vines and mulberries will yield very well. The plantation furnishes scarcely enough to live on and that is all. One must buy rum, sugar, coffee and tea, for obliged to live on salt meat the greater part of the year, these articles are almost a necessity, because of the unwholesome water they have here. Did I not pick cotton and flax, which we manufacture at home, I would not be in a state to have clothes, on account

of the exorbitant prices, and necessity obliges me to content myself with very little. When I married I had scarcely a pair of sheets and two or three old tablecloths. Our spinners have bettered us a little in this respect, for the demand for this species of linen is most urgent. My wife have been for ten years under the supervision of negligent executors, had scarcely a chemise, yet she was rich in land and Negroes, when I married her – you can judge of the rest. Happily I have now an opportunity to buy a dozen shirts from the sale of the effects of a recently deceased Frenchman. Besides living in the country and having seen too much of the world to despise luxurious garments, I am content with little and provided I can procure the most necessary for the house and enough to be genteel when I am obliged to go out, I wish nothing more. My wife joins with me in presenting you our humble respects. We cease not to make our prayers to Heaven for the tenderest and best of mothers. Be persuaded I pray you of their sincerity.

I have the honor to be, with the tenderest and most respectful attachment, your very humble and very obedient son, and my very dear mother's servant.

Roulhac

By economy he soon obtained a competency, and his house was a resort, often an asylum for unfortunate Frenchmen when they first came to America and that part of the country. He called it "The Hermitage." It was originally an old fort on Pamlico Sound, and built of bricks that were brought from England in 1721. It was a few miles from the town of Bath, formerly the capitol of the province, now reduced to a few dilapidated houses and an old Episcopal church, whose roof had caved in many years before. With him lived Moses Maule, his wife's brother, who was a very wealthy and hospitable man, entertaining much company for weeks and sometimes months together, hunting, fishing, and enjoying whatever amusements the *country afforded. On his death he left the greater part of his property to his sister's children. His tombstone was still standing in 1870 on the site of the old homestead at Maule's Point, and could be seen from boats on the river. Ann Maule Roulhac died at the age of twenty-nine, on Nov. 23, 1794, leaving four children. His brother says:* "Sometime after that, Psalmet addressed a widow lady of some property, and certainly much more gentle in her manners than the generality of women in that part of the country, but she was an accomplished coquette and led my brother by the nose, making him believe she was going to marry him. The day was even appointed and invitations given to his brother John and me to come on Christmas day, to the wedding. On the eve of that day, I, in company of his eldest daughter, about thirteen or fourteen years of age, went on. We had to ride ten or eleven miles in a most piercing, cold, north-west wind; then to cross Pungo river, about three miles; then ride five miles more and there wait for horses, which Psalmet was to send for us at the ferry, from Mrs. Jasper's, the name of his contracted. Seldom was I ever in such cold weather and, in crossing the river, the flying spray froze on our clothes. We had just arrived at the other ferry, where we found no horses, when Psalmet made his appearance to tell us to return as it was a "flash in the pan." As he was a true philosopher, he bore the disappointment and jokes of his acquaintances and friends, with gaiety and cheerfulness." *On Aug. 5, 1798, he was married again, by Thomas Alderson, to Elizabeth Barrow, (b. Oct. 24, 1754), widow of John Adams and Samuel Archbell. They had no children.*

"He attempted once to go to the legislature, and sat up as a candidate, when another Frenchman, M. Cabarus, who was very popular, having been often Speaker of the Lower House in Carolina, set up as a candidate for Congress. Both of them were defeated for no other crime than being foreigners. The Blount family, rich and influential, took a strong part against them, and were never forgotten for it by them. Never very robust, and living in one of the most unhealthy parts of North Carolina, Psalmet became subject, nearly every fall, to long intermittent bilious fevers, which sapped his constitution. He died at the age of fifty-four, Oct. 8, 1808, of a violent attack of influenza, which raged that year in the United States."

Slave History: Psalmet Roulhac, Ann Hare Maule and Elizabeth Barrow

Ann Hare Maule's family had a long history of slave ownership. Patrick Maule of Bath County, North Carolina, Ann Maule's grandfather, died in 1736. In his April 19, 1736 last will and testament, Patrick Maule bequeathed his 18 slaves, real estate, cattle and other property to his wife, three daughters and son, John Maule, Anne's father, as follows:[7]

> In the Name of God Amen, I, Patrick Maule, of Bath County, being in my right senses do make this my last will & testament, in manner & form following:
>
> I give to my loving wife, Elizabeth Maule, & to her assigns forever, the following Negroes, Viz: Angus, Hannah, Affrica, Robin, & London, to be delivered after the tar kilns are off & the crop finished; also, I give unto her the household furniture, except the eating spoon & five silver teaspoons. I give to my wife ... fifteen cows, their calves, ten four-year-old steers & two third parts of the hogs on my plantation at Rumney Marsh, also the young horse, the foregoing to be delivered after my interment. And further, I leave my plantation at Rumney Marsh to my wife during her natural life, with a dwelling house to be built for her by my executors, twenty foot long & sixteen foot wide; Also, I give unto my sd. wife full privilege for making tar & turpentine of my land on Jacks Creek during her natural life.
>
> I give & bequeath to my son, John Maule, his heirs & assigns forever, the following slaves, viz: Cesar, Farewell, Bina, Tom, Richards, Young Hannah. I give & bequeath to my son, John aforesd...my lands at Smiths

point, also my lands at Blunts Creek, also my saved lot in Bath town, all to him & to his heirs forever. Also, I give & bequeath to my son, John aforesd., two hundred acres of land adjacent to Roger Kenyons plantation, to him & his heirs forever. I give to my son John, fifteen cows, their calves, at Blunts Creek, with their increase.

I give to my daughter, Sarah Maule, the following slaves viz: Elleck, Great Tom, Peg, Andrew, & Kope; Also I give & bequeath to my daughter aforesd. & to her heirs forever, my land at Tranters Creek, also fifteen cows & calves with their increase.

I give & bequeath to my daughter, Mary Maule, the following slaves, Viz: Hector, Sue, Mustapha, & Dick; also, I give to my sd. daughter, Mary, & her heirs forever my lands on North Dividing Creeks; also my lands on Jacks Creek, also I give her fifteen cows & calves with their increase.

In 1774, when John Maule died, he left the following Last Will and Testament, leaving property to his children, including Anne and Moses Maule, Psalmet's wife and brother-in-law:[8]

In the Name of God Amen, I, John Maule, of Beaufort County and Province aforesaid, being in a very poor state of health but of sound & perfect mind & memory, do make this my last will and Testament in manner & form following, to-wit: After my decease my body to be decently inter'd at the discretion of my executors hereafter mentioned; my just debts and funeral expenses to be paid out of my estate, and the remainder part of my estate I dispose of as follows:

Imprimis, I lend the use of the manor plantation whereon I now live, to my beloved wife, Elizabeth Maule, with all the land belonging to the same, which was given to me by my father, Patrick Maule. During that time that she shall and will continue thereon, and after her death or removal from of the said plantation, I give & bequeath the said plantation and land, to my son, Moses Maule, to him & his heirs lawfully begotten forever.

I likewise give to my wife aforesd, seven Negroes, whose names are as follows: Donas, Tom, Cesar, Farewell, Hannah, Venus, and Bess. I likewise give her all my household furniture, and all my stock of cattle, except twenty cows & calves which is to be disposed of in manner hereafter first mentioned.

I likewise give her all my stock of hogs and sheep, and two horses, Jack and Lightfoot, to her and her heirs forever.

Item, I give further to my son, Moses Maule, six Negroes named as follows: Adam, Harry, Jem, Crees, Little ... and Phillis; I likewise give him all my right & titles to my mill on Blounts Creek, likewise, all the land that was given to me by my father, Patrick Maule, which joins the said mill, except the pine timber on two hundred acres of land that joins Walter Evetts line; and my will is that my executors shall make John Neal a deed for sd land; I also give him 4 cows and calves.

Item, I give to my daughter, Elizabeth Maule, my Quarter Plantation and lands thereunto belonging, which I bought of Moses Nevil, to her and the heirs of her body forever. I likewise give her the following Negros: Frinkalo, Gabe, Binah, Beck, Abigal, and Doll; also four cows & calves, to her and her heirs forever.

Item, I give to my daughter, Anne, one piece of land with the plantation that I bought of John Nevil, and also one tract of land which I purchased of William Morris and Katherine, his wife, containing 400 acres, to her and the heirs of her body forever; also, the following Negros, Ben, Asia, Sandy, Ede, & Celia; and also four cows and calves, to her and her heirs forever.

Item, I give to my daughter, Penelope, the lands I purchased of Susanna Waggonner, containing 640 acres, lying on Blounts Creek, and also 250 acres joining Wm. Morris's Land, to her and the heirs of her body forever. Also the following Negros, Quamans, Nell, Kate, Sid, & Dorcas; also four cows and calves, to her and her heirs forever.

Item, I give to my daughter, Jamina, 220 acres lying on the head of Blounts Creek wch. I purchased of Benjamin Fathree; also a tract of land lying on Nevels Creek which I bought of Jacob Giddings lying on Nevils Creek, and two hundred & thirty acres of land lying in Pitt County, to her and her heirs forever; also the following Negros, Pegg, Tony, Little Ben, Little Hannah, Rose and Kate, also four cows & calves, to her and her heirs forever.

My will is further that my executors cause to be finished my new house as soon as they conveniently can, and that they collect the debts due to me as soon as they can, and that they sell my half of a schooner belonging to me and Capt. Seth Doane, and the money arising therefrom, together with my ready money, be put to interest, and also the money arising out of the several legacy given to my children, except so much as shall be necessary to educate and support them, till they receive their estate, w'ch shall be at the age of twenty one years or marriage.

I further will, that if any of my before named children shall die in their minority, or before they receive their fortunes, that then their fortune shall be equally divided between the surviving ones, and likewise the increase of all the Negros given to them, shall be equally divided amongst them as they come to the age of twenty-one years or married as aforesaid; and also, all the remainder of my estate not mentioned shall be divided in the same manner, lands only excepted.

Lastly, I nominate and appoint my beloved brother-in-law, Moses Hare, my beloved and faithful friends, John Patten, Reading Blount, Junr., and Joseph Blount, all of the County aforesaid, to be my executors of this my Last Will and Testament and I hereby revoke all former wills made by me.

In Witness whereof, I have hereunto set my hand and seal, this 11th day of December, in the year of our Lord, one thousand, seven hundred and seventy-three.[9]

Psalmet and his children were among the beneficiaries of the estate of his brother-in-law, Moses Maule, who died in 1799. Moses' Last Will and Testament dated December 2, 1799, distributes his property as follows:[10]

In the name of God Amen. I Moses Maule, being sick of body but of sound disposing mind and memory calling to mind the uncertainties of this life and that it is appointed for all men once to die do make this my Last Will and Testament in manner and form following, viz:

Imprimis, I give and bequeath unto my nephew William Roulhac, son of my deceased sister Jamina Roulhac, the mill seat that I purchased of William Morris known by the name of Pattens Old Mill and three hundred acres of land adjoining to it for his heirs and assigns forever. I also give and bequeath to my said nephew William Roulhac five Negroes viz: Jim and Cate, his wife, Luie, Sue and Reilly. It is my will and desire that Mr. John Roulhac, the father of my said nephew, shall have the use and profits of the said property until my said nephew shall arrive to the age of twenty-one years and if the said Mr. John Roulhac should die before that period then it is my desire that my executors hereafter named shall take into their possess the said property and his and rent the same out for the sole use of my nephew aforesaid until he is of age and should my nephew William Roulhac die before he is twenty one years of age, then I give the aforesaid mill seat and lands to Mr. John Roulhac, his heirs and assigns forever, but should the said Mr. Roulhac die before my said nephew and my said nephew die before his is twenty one years of age, then I give the same mill seat and lands to my nephew John Maule Roulhac, his heirs & assigns forever.

Item: I give and bequeath to my said nephew John Maule Roulhac, son of my deceased sister Ann Roulhac, his heirs and assigns forever, one half of my mills together with one half of all my lands thereto belonging laying in several tracts and containing several hundred acres … also the plantation whereon I live and all the rest of the land I own in the counties of Beaufort and Hyde, excepting what I already have given away and the other half of my mills and half of my lands thereto belonging. I also give and bequeath unto my said nephew John Maule Roulhac all the remainder of my Negroes excepting, to wit, Jacob and Toney and all the rest of my personal property ... except my riding horse, bridle and saddle and watch.

Item: I will and bequeath unto my two nieces Elizabeth Roulhac and Jane Roulhac, daughters of my dec'd sister Ann Roulhac one thousand dollars each to be raised out of the property that I have given to my nephew John Maule Roulhac...

Item: I give and bequeath unto my nephew John Smith, son of my deceased sister Elizabeth Smith, five hundred dollars to be raised by my executor Psalmet G. Roulhac out of the property that I have above given to my nephew John Maule Roulhac to be paid to him on the death of his father Thomas Smith and not before...

Item: It is my will and desire that all my just debts be paid by my executors hereafter named out of the property that I given to my nephew John Maule Roulhac as aforesaid.

Item: I will and bequeath unto my cousin Mary Garish twenty five pounds a year for four years to be paid her by my executors out of the property I have given my nephew Maule Roulhac aforesaid in produce for the support of her family.

Item: I will and bequeath unto my friend William Harrahan one half of my mills together with one half of all my lands there unto belonging lying in several tracts and containing several hundred acres as reference to the deeds & patents will show with one half of my stock belonging to the mills the ... I give his heirs and assigns forever.

Item: I will and bequeath unto my friend William Massinpsey?? my Negro boy Toney...

Item: I give and bequeath unto my friend William Orrell, Senior my Negro fellow Jacob ...

Item: I will and bequeath unto Mrs. Ashley Harrahan my watch ...

Item: I give and bequeath unto my friend Andrew Greer my riding horse, bridle and saddle.

Item: I give and bequeath unto Psalmet G. Roulhac and Walter Harrahan, Senior all my right and title to Scotland Neck lands...

Item: It is my will and desire that if my nephew William Roulhac should die before he is twenty-one years of age or married that the Negroes I have given him as aforesaid shall go to his father John Roulhac but should the said Mr. John Roulhac die before my said nephew William and my said nephew William should die before he is twenty one or married, then I give the said five Negroes to my nephew John Maule Roulhac...

Item: it is my will and desire that if my nephew John Maule Roulhac should die before he is married or twenty-one years of age, then all his property that I have given him as aforesaid shall be equally divided between his two sisters, Elizabeth and Jane, aforesaid...

Lastly, I do nominate, constitute and appoint my friends Psalmet G. Roulhac and Walter Harrahan, Sr., executors to this my Last Will and Testament, revoking all others by me heretofore made. In witness I have hereunto set my hand, affixed my seal this 7th of Dec'r 1799.

Moses Maule (Seal)

In 1790, when the first U.S. Census was taken, Beaufort County, North Carolina, had a population of 951 free white males over sixteen; 926 free white males under sixteen; 1,826 free white females, 129 other free persons and 1,632 slaves. Fourteen years after arriving in America, Psalmet owned 19 slaves.[11] Ten years later, when the 1800 Federal Census was taken, Psalmet's enslavement of Africans had increased to 26.[12] Psalmet Roulhac died October 8, 1808. His January 21, 1805 Last Will and Testament, Psalmet reads in part as follows:

> I Psalmet Gregoire Roulhac of Beaufort County State of North Carolina being of sound & disposing mind and memory, do hereby make & ordain in my own hand writing this my Last Will & Testament, in manner and form following, to wit:
>
> 1st I lend unto my beloved wife Elizabeth, the use and occupancy of my manor plantation whereon I now live with all out lands … containing together by estimation four hundred sixty five acres more or less during her natural life. I also lend her during her natural life, the following Negro slaves, viz: Cato, Nell, Lem, Horace, Dinah and Old Ben which said slaves with their increase, if any, are after her decease to revert to and be divided, share and share alike between my three children. I further give & bequeath to my sd beloved wife Elizabeth the following Negro slaves: Dinah, Tip, Young Ben, Siloy & James…
>
> 2nd I give devise & bequeath unto my beloved son John Maule Gregoire Roulhac…my manor plantation…

after the decease of his mother-in-law …also the following Negro slaves: Caesar, Toney, Will, Mingo, Hannah, Cime, Chance, & Little Cato.

3rd In case my daughter Elizabeth Blount entirely & absolutely renounces the legacy left to her by the Last Will & Testament of Bezar Barroio, deceased, I give & devise unto her … one half of two tracts of land in Long Acre, one containing six hundred & forty acres which I bought of Edmond McKeil, Sheriff of Beaufort County, the other containing three hundred & twenty acres I purchased of Jno Kennedy also Sheriff of Beaufort, four hundred & eight acres being the half of the whole to be laid out and divided between her & her sister Mary Jane Roulhac in such manner agreeable to quantity & quality as to include one half of the tenable ground on sd two tracts … & should my sd daughter Elizabeth accept of & receive the aforesaid legacy I then in that case give & devise the sd one half of the sd lands to her sister Mary Jane Roulhac … I also give & bequeath unto my sd daughter Elizabeth Blount the following Negro slaves to wit: Young Pompey, Old Pompey, Celia, Sam, ___ and Wilsie…

4th I give, devise & bequeath unto my beloved Mary Jane Roulhac … the other half of my Long Acre land as prescribed in the preceding clause… I further give & bequeath to my sd daughter Mary Jane G. Roulhac the following slaves, viz, Mill, Cap, Frank, Quam, Mose, Ede, Wingood, Chloe & one bed bedstead & furniture to be delivered to her on the day of her marriage or when she attains the years of twenty one…

7th My will & desire is that if at the time of my decease any of my slaves are bound out to trades or put out for their victuals & clothes for any period of time they continue with their respective masters until their time is expired & as for the young ones who cannot be hired on account of their tender years, I desire that as many as may be fit to be put with good & poor people to rise them up for their victual & clothing rather than to remain with the mother & become a charge to my estate.

8th My will & desire is that my son John Maule G. Roulhac on the income of his own property above specified in the 6th clause of the present will be kept & supported distance from home at some university or some good academy in this State until he is at sixteen years of age. There to be instructed in religion & morality, the English grammar, the living languages, specifically French with as little mixture of Latin & Greek as possible, history, geography, mathematics, navigation & surveying. It is further my special will & desire that after he attains his sixteenth or seventeenth year at the discretion of my executors, hereafter named, whom I hereby constitute his guardian & whom I do solemnly & as he values my last blessing, I charge him to obey & respect as he would myself he be bound if possible out of town to some ___ & useful trade as millwright, wheelwright, turner carpenter, cabinet maker or such with some good experienced & moral workman until he attains the age of twenty or twenty one & should he before that term in any manner with his apprenticeship & lead an idle disorderly or vicious life, it is my special will & desire that the part of my estate, both real & personal with the profits, interest or increase thereof to which he is or may be entitled by the foregoing part of the foresaid will at the age of twenty one, shall wholly and solely remain in the hands of my executors, his guardians, until he attains the twenty fifth year of his age & not before shall he in that case have any right to claim the same or any part thereof.

Several generations of Africans were often enslaved on the same plantation as illustrated by this 1862 photograph of five generation of slaves on James Joyner Smith's Beaufort, South Carolina plantation. Photograph by Timothy O'Sullivan, Courtesy Library of Congress, Civil War Photograph Collection.

Elizabeth Barrow Roulhac, Psalmet's second wife, died less than a year after Psalmet. Her November 21, 1807 Last Will and Testament was probated in Hyde County, North Carolina, during the August 1809 term. She made the following distribution of her property:[13]

1st, I give and bequeath unto my beloved grandson William Barrow Adams three Negroes, viz, Jim, Tish, Ben. It is my desire that my son John Adams shall have the use and profits of the said Negroes until my said grandson shall arrive at the age of eighteen years. It is also my will and desire that if my aftersaid grandson, William Barrow Adams, should die before he is twenty-one years of age, then I give the aforesaid Negroes with their increase, if any, unto my son John Adams to him and his heirs forever. But should my son John Adams die before my said grandson William Barrow Adams, and my said grandson should die before he is twenty-one years of age, then I give the aforesaid Negroes unto his brothers or sisters or mother, if any, to them and their heirs forever.

No. 2, I give, devise unto my beloved son John Adams all the rest of my Negroes, all the remaining part of my estate both real and personal with all moneys or notes which I myself may be entitled to receive or obtain from my husband P.G. Roulhac's estate, whatever, to him and his heirs forever.

Second Generation: Issue of Psalmet G. Roulhac and Ann Maule Roulhac

2.1 Elizabeth Roulhac *(6) b. at the "Hermitage," Beaufort County, N.C., Oct. 4, 1786; m. May 14, 1803, at seventeen years of age, James Blount, son of Col. Edmund Blount and Judith Rhodes, of Washington County, N.C., b. June 28, 1780. Disliking her marriage with one of the hated Blounts, her father drew up a marriage contract, which did not please the young man. They lived in Plymouth, N.C., at Hickory Grove, a place, which his daughter described as a beautiful spot, until 1816, when they moved to Georgia, and settled in Blountsville, Jones Co. There he died, Dec. 12, 1820, leaving a widow and five children. She died Feb. 17, 1824*

[Author's note: Elizabeth died sometime after April 17, 1832, when she executed Last Will], *at Clinton, Ga. "She was a woman of great fortitude and firmness of character, adorning in an eminent degree all the Christian virtues."*

Slave History: Elizabeth Roulhac Blount and James Blount

Elizabeth Roulhac Blount inherited $1,000 upon the death of her uncle, Moses Maule who died in 1799, and 1,048 acres of land and six slaves from her father, Psalmet Roulhac, who died in 1808. When the 1820 Federal Census was taken in August 1820, four months before he died, James Blount owned 26 slaves. The wealth created by James Blount is displayed in his June 12, 1819, Last Will and the subsequent probate of his estate in Jones County, Georgia

> Item: I will & bequeath to my well beloved wife Elizabeth Blount one square of land lying on Big Cedar Creek in Jones County known by number 128, joining the lands of Mitchell Warnum & others which I bought of Charles Burford, Esq., containing two hundred two and a half acres, to her & her heirs forever. I also give my wife Elizabeth Blount the following Negro slaves, viz: Pompey & his wife Hannah, one young Negro man Sampson & a girl named Mary, one dark bay mare called Jim & one mule, her choice, two beds, bedsteads & furniture, one truck, her choice, six chairs, two sets of plow gear, one gig & harness, all the salt, sugar & coffee which may be in the house at the time of my decease, one cow & calf or yearling & one thousand dollars to be paid her in cash as soon as it can be collected by my executors, to be hereafter named. Also should my death take place in the fall of the year or winter one hundred bushels of cord & two thousand pounds of pork, or in like proportions from the time that event may take place. I also give her all the crock-

ery, china or glass ware which may be in the house at that time, one mahogany candle stand, one pine table and spinning wheel, one reel, 2 axes, 2 grub hoes & 2 weeding hoes & all the poultry, provided she should comply with a clause to be hereafter inserted respecting the lands which have descended to her by the death of her brother John Maule Gregoire Roulhac.

Item: I give & bequeath to beloved son John Maule Roulhac Blount the following Negro slaves, viz: Enoch, Sid, his wife [Lydda] & her three children, Lucy, Frank & Guernsey, to him & his heirs forever, also one hundred dollars in cash to be paid by his mother Elizabeth Blount for keeping & maintaining him two years from the sale of my property, at the discretion of my executors to be hereafter named. As my beloved wife Elizabeth hath in the sincerity of her heart informed me that she is now pregnant by me. I think it my duty to provide for the infant which may be born of her body. It is therefore my will & desire that should she have a son that he be called James after me & if a daughter Elizabeth after her mother & I do hereby allot & set off for said infant when born the following Negro slaves, viz: Wilson, Whitmel, Howard or Mike & Marina. Also a full share in the division of the monies arising from the sale of my property to be hereafter specified, three hundred dollars of which is to be paid my wife Elizabeth Blount for keeping & maintaining said infant should it live, in five equal annual installments after which time its support is to be taken from its own proper estat

In December 25, 1822, Thomas Hamilton, the executor of James Blount estate, made the following accounting of money due on January 1, 1822, or received for hiring Blount's former slaves out during the year: Pompey to Robert Woodall - $124 due as of January 1822; Sampson to Reason Gay - $100; Enoch to J. Carrington - $101; Wilson to John ___ $100; Whitmel to William Harrison - $81; Howard to William Harrison - $51.50; Celia to Richard Harris - $65; Mary to Dempsey Butler - $60; Marina to John Monk - $60; Lucy to Jack Goddard - $14; Lydda and her children Frank and Guernsey to Mrs. Blount - $8 and for the rent of Burford Plantation to Reason Gay - $201.

Elizabeth Roulhac Blount died February 17, 1824 at Clinton, Georgia. In her April Last Will, she left all of her property to her sons John M. Blount and Thomas Blount as follows:

> In the name of God, Amen, I Elizabeth Blount of the County of Jones and State of Georgia, knowing the uncertainty of life and believing in a remission of my sins, by the merits and meditation of Christ do make and declare this my last will and testament.
>
> I give and bequeath to my two sons John M. Blount & Thomas Blount, the following Negroes, Pompey, Hannah and Suck, to have and to hold to them and their heirs in equal division. Also I give and bequeath to my two sons John & Thomas and their heirs, share & share alike all my money, notes and demands of every description whatsoever. Lastly, I give to my said sons all and every other species of property of which I am possessed. In testimony whereof, I have hereunto set my hand and seal this the seventeenth of April 1832.
>
> Elizabeth Blount (Seal)
Test, Thomas B. Slade
Ann J. Slade[14]

4.3. Mary Jane Dumas Roulhac, b. at Beaufort County, NC in 1792; m. June 1811, Horace Ely, from Springfield, Mass. Being a Yankee, the match was opposed by her family, and her uncle, Francis, her guardian, drew up a marriage contract, which he readily agreed to. "He proved an industrious man and daring speculator, accumulating, apparently, an immense property, built vessels, sending them to sea with different kinds of produce belonging to the country, erecting mills, etc., with the appearance of great wealth for many years. At last broke, and all vanished, except the property of his wife." She died about 1835, when he moved to Marianna, Fla, and practiced medicine, having studied in Philadelphia. He m. 2nd, Mrs. Daffin, mother of his son-in-law, Wm. Daffin. He d. about 1850 [sic] (Author's note: He died in 1867].

Slave History: Mary Jane Roulhac and Horace Ely

Before Mary Jane Roulhac married Horace Ely, her inheritance included $1,000 from her uncle, Moses Maule, and eight slaves – Mill, Cap, Frank, Quam, Mose, Ede, Wingood and Chloe to be delivered to her upon her marriage, from her father, Psalmet Roulhac. However, before her marriage, the following marriage contract between Mary Jane Roulhac and Horace Ely was created:

> Whereas a marriage is intended to be shortly had and solemnized between Horace Ely, merchant, of the town of Plymouth, Washington County, State of North Carolina and Mary Jane Roulhac of Martin County, State aforesaid, be it known by

> This indenture made on the twenty-eighth day of May in the year of our Lord one thousand eight hundred and eleven between Mary Jane Roulhac and Horace Ely on one part and Francis Roulhac of the State of Tennessee on the other part, witnesseth, that in consideration of the marriage above mentioned, the said Mary Jane Roulhac has sold and delivered and

by these presents does sell and deliver the following Negro slaves, to wit: Milly, Rose, Penny, Jamia, ___ unto Francis Roulhac, his heirs, executor and assigns, in trust, and for such uses and __ and for such intent and purposes as are herein after mentioned …on behalf of Mary Jane Roulhac until the solemnization of the said intended marriage …and from after the solemnization thereof to the use on behalf of the said Mary Jane and Horace Ely, he the said Horace having a full and perfect right to enjoy and dispose of all the profits or hire arising or will arise from said Negro slaves or their future increase during the natural life of said Mary Jane and in case that the said Horace Ely should survive the said Mary Jane Roulhac, his intended wife, the said Mary Jane Roulhac agree then to the use on behalf of the said Horace Ely, his heirs and assigns forever and in case the said Mary Jane should survive the said Horace Ely her intended husband to the use on behalf of Mary Jane her heirs and assigns forever. In testimony whereof the parties to these presents have set their hands and seals the day and year first above written and sealed and delivered in the presence of us.

Francis Roulhac, J. Flowers

Within five months of Mary Jane and Horace Ely's marriage, slaves Penny and Milly were sold at a Sheriff's sale to Joseph B.G. Roulhac for $545 to satisfy a $1,208.49 debt owed by Horace Ely.

Bill of Sale

14 November 1831
State of North Carolina
Washington County

This indenture made this 14th November 1831 between Will M. Chesson, sheriff of Washington County on the first part and Joseph B.G. Roulhac on the second part, witnesseth.

> Whereas by virtue of a writ …filed from the County Court of Washington, tested at August term & No 20 Executor .. returnable at November term 1831 … at the instance of Tredwell Kisam?? against Horace Ely for the sum of one thousand two hundred & eight one dollars forty-nine cents together with the interest thereon accrued , delivered to me Will M. Chesson, sheriff of Washington County …. I proceeded … to sell at public auction, having first advertised in the manner presented by law, Negro slaves the property of Horace Ely, subject to a trust created by a marriage contract, viz: Milly, Ned, Nelly, ____, Bick, Penny, Joe, Cato, Quammie, Gabe, ____ & Dinah, and the said Negro slaves were purchased by Jos. B. G. Roulhac of the County of Bertie for the sum of five hundred and forty-five dollars being the highest bid made …Now I Will M Chesson sheriff of aforesaid by virtue of my office and for and in consideration of the same sum of five hundred & forty-five dollars to me in hand paid by the said Roulhac, the receipt whereof is hereby acknowledged, have bargained, sold and delivered and by these presents do … deliver unto the said Roulhac the above mentioned Negro slaves, to have & to hold the said Negroes unto the said Roulhac his executor, administrator and assigns forever …..

A few years later, Mary Jane wrote a letter to her children requesting that they allow her to dispose of the land and Negro slaves in which she and her husband had a life interest and which her husband had caused to be sold. The letter is set forth below:

Chapter 1

Plymouth NC Feb 12, 1834
To: Francis R. Ely, Ann L Armistead & Mary Jane Ely

My Dear Children

The marriage contract between myself and your father, certain Negroes were conveyed in trust to Francis [Leonard Gregoire] Roulhac, for your father's use and mine during our joint lives; on his death, to me for my life if I survived him; on my death to you, whether he survived me or not.

It is known to you that your father for reasons that seemed to him to justify it, sold some of the said Negroes some years ago for $540; whereby he came to be the debtor of Francis Roulhac, the trustee, for the value of the Negroes; and that to pay him, he conveyed the half of a certain tract of land in.... either to the said Francis Roulhac or to Joseph B. G. Roulhac, to be held in the room of the said Negro, upon the same trust and for the same uses.

It is also known to you that adversity overreached your father in the course of his business, and that his estate in the said land and Negroes have been sold by executor, and that Francis R. Ely is the purchaser of the land, and Jos B. G. Roulhac, the purchaser of the Negroes. It is apparent from the foregoing statement, that your father's estate in the said land and Negroes, purchased as aforesaid by Francis R. Ely and Joseph B.G. Roulhac, will terminate with his life or mine; that the use in the said land and Negroes will survive to me for my life if I survive him and that upon my death, the land and Negroes will belong in fee simple to you, my children, as tenants in common.

I need not call to your minds the present situation and future prospect of you, my children. Francis, it is known, is doing and likely to do well in the world by reason of property derived by him from his mother's relations as well as by his own conduct and circumstance. But it is otherwise with you my daughters. Your relations from whom Francis was benefitted, died before you were known, or they did not contribute to prosper you in the world. Your father's adversity and mine renders us unable to help you as we would; while your sex unfits you the business and bustle and hardships of life. Nor must I call to your minds the situation of your father who was once propertied of a large estate, accumulated chiefly by his exertions, but is now deprived of the whole of it, and in great adversity. Considering all things and considering also my own bad state of health, I cannot but feel great anxiety lest you my daughter and your father may not in the future succeed well in the world. While I am happy to have every reason to believe that you my son will always be in good and easy circumstances.

I have therefore to request that you my children, in whom the said land and Negroes are vested after my death, will permit me to dispose of them more suitable to the necessities of my family than they are disposed of by the marriage contract above mentioned. I make this request because I think I may value so much upon your regard for me and because (as you will observe) the property - which I would dispose of, was originally mine. I desire therefore that each of you will permit your father to have use, profit and enjoy the said lands and Negroes and the rents issues and profits thereof without consideration to be had to you, and without liability to account with you, during his life.

I desire that my son, at his father's death, will convey to my daughters for the consideration hereinafter named, his estate in the said Negroes; and that you my daughters for that consideration will convey to my son, your estate in the said land so that the whole of the land may belong to my son, and the whole of the Negroes to my daughters. To comply with this request will be a sacrifice of interest only on the part of my son, and not on the part of my daughters, for it is believed that his estate in the Negroes is of more value that theirs in the land. But the sacrifice is small, and I hope he will cheerfully make it when he comes to compare his situation in the world with theirs, to consider that the property - though vested in him by the marriage contract, was mine, and that is my request in behalf of his sisters, in order to prosper them in the world.

To comply with my request in behalf of your father, I am persuaded will be little or no sacrifice of interest to either of you. For not to mention his kindness to us all heretofore, and his present adversity, it is clear that the land and Negroes cannot be sold to pay any debts of his contracting; that he will keep them together; that he will work them to the best advantage; and that finally, when he dies, he can carry nothing with him, but must leave the land and Negroes and all he shall make to you my children. In confidence that if I have deserved anything during my life at your hands, it cannot be less than what I now ask; and that as my life has heretofore been devoted to your service, and not yours to mine, you cannot do less than to comply with these request, I am.

 Horace Ely, a physician, migrated to Jackson County, Florida in 1835. In 1840, he was living in neighboring Calhoun County and owned enslaved six Negroes.[15] At the end of the decade, Dr. Horace Ely, with others, received contracts to rebuild the Jackson County Courthouse, which had been destroyed by fire in 1848 and complete the construction of a bridge over the Chipola River. By 1850, Dr. Ely was operating a hotel in Marianna that provided lodging for some of the City's most prominent citizens including, lawyers J. J. Finley, William E. Anderson, Thomas Alexander and James F. McClellan; physician John Kizer; mail contractor Alfred B. Powell; printer William Sullivan, and barkeeper Joseph Comerford.[16] Horace Ely also owned 30 slaves – 24 in Jackson County[17] and six in neighboring Calhoun County.[18]

Horace Ely's slaves not only labored on his plantations, but he also hired them to others as shown in the following deed:

Deed of Hire

> This Indenture made this seventeenth day of June in the year of our Lord eighteen hundred and fifty-two between Levy Kent and Horace Ely and Benjamin G. Alderman, witnesseth:

> That the same Levy Kent in consideration of the covenants on the part of the said Horace Ely and Benjamin G. Alderman, hereinafter set forth and for the sum of Five dollars to him paid by the said Horace Ely and Benjamin G. Alderman, the receipt whereof is hereby acknowledged, doth bargain, sell, convey, confirm unto the said Horace Ely and Benjamin G. Alderman and the survivors of them and to their and his appointees and assigns, a Negro man named Bob, aged about thirty-one years. To have and to hold the said Negro unto them and the survivor and to their and his appointees and assigns, in trust, however, and to and for the following use and purpose, that is to say,

that they the said Horace Ely and Benjamin G. Alderman shall and will suffer and permit the said Negro man Bob, to continue at this trade and to use his own time in the same manner and upon the same terms that the said Levy Kent now permits him to do and to permit the said Negro to have all the assets he may make and earn over the sum of one hundred and fifty dollars which he is to pay annually to the said Horace Ely and Benjamin G. Alderman as wages for his time which said annual sum the said Horace Ely and Benjamin G. Alderman covenant to pay to the said Levy Kent during his life and to his executors or administrators after his death immediately upon the receipt thereof. And the said Levy Kent accounts that if the said Horace Ely and Benjamin G. Alderman should depart this life, the said Negro man surviving them that the said Levy Kent will execute another deed, the appointment of another person as trustee, to carry out the object of this Indenture which object is to secure and continue said Negro the same testament and employment he now enjoys and follows and that if the said Levy Kent, Horace Ely and Benjamin G. Alderman should depart this life before the said Negro, that the said Levy Kent's executors or administrators shall and will make such appointment of another trustee. And the said Horace Ely and Benjamin G. Alderman accept and take upon themselves the said trust and covenant to perform the same truly and faithfully and according to the tenor and true intent of this Indenture. In witnesseth whereof, the said parties have hereto set their hands and seals the day and year first above written.

Signed & sealed in presence of Levy Kent O. Bassett

Horace Ely, John Blaney, Benj. G. Alderman

In 1858, a Jackson County grand jury, concerned by the "too frequent" and "pernicious" practice of selling "even dry goods to Negroes in the absence of proper permission," Dr. Ely was indicted for "selling spirituous liquors, which were consumed where it was sold, without a license" to Negroes. In 1861, the grand jury speculated that the shanties owned by Dr. Horace Ely were among the principal depots for this traffic.[19]

By 1860, Horace Ely, 71, owned real estate and personal property valued at $8,000 and $3,000, respectively. He also enslaved nine Africans,[20] including Cato, an incarcerated 32-year-old "one-eyed Negro slave" who had been convicted of raping Susan Leonard, a prostitute, and sentenced to be hung on December 16, 1860. After two subsequent convictions and appeals, including a change of venue to Calhoun County, Cato was acquitted. Cato's defense team included, soon-to-be Confederate Governor John Milton and Attorney James F. McClellan.[21]

Although Horace Ely was over 70 years old when the Civil War started, he, along with most of Marianna's trained physicians, volunteered to fight with the "Cradle to Grave" home guard Confederate unit during the September 27, 1864 Battle of Marianna. Ely was captured and held prisoner at the courthouse. He was later paroled.

Chapter 1

Confederate Park Downtown Marianna
The monument pays tribute to Confederate home guard unit – mostly young boys and old men - who served in the September 27, 1864 Battle of Marianna. Lafayette Street is on the left.

Cato, who after the Civil War adopted the Ely surname, married Mary Horsley, April 29, 1866.[22] In the 1870 Jackson County, Florida census, he is enumerated as a 45-year-old mulatto farm laborer, born in North Carolina. He was living with a 45-year-old mulatto laundress, Mary Ely, and Henry Ely, a 15-year-old mulatto, both born in Georgia.[23] Cato resided a few dwellings from Republican Court Clerk John Q. Dickinson, a former Freemen's Bureau agent, who a year later would be murdered. Horace Ely's grandson, John Randolph Ely, was a prime suspect in Dickinson's murder.

5.4. John Maule, b. at "The Heritage," Nov. 23, 1794. He was at college when his father died, and knowing he was heir to a large estate, he refused to learn a trade, as his father had directed. Soon after coming of age, from ill health, his mind became affected and he shot himself. By his will, still preserved, his property was left to his nieces and nephews.

Slave History: John Maule Roulhac

John Maule Roulhac was very wealthy when he committed suicide. He inherited considerable property – several hundred acres of land in Beaufort and Hyde counties and slaves he inherited from his uncle Moses Maule and his father Psalmet Roulhac. As set forth in Psalmet's last will, John's inheritance was dependent upon his compliance with stringent instructions for completing his education and entering into an apprenticeship.

John Maule Roulhac executed the following as his Last Will and Testament on September 21, 1814:

Beaufort County, State of North Carolina[24]

> In the name of God, Amen, I, John M. Roulhac, of the County and State aforesaid, living in good health and sound and deposing mind and memory, thanks be to almighty God for the same, but calling to mind that mortality of my body and knowing that it is appointed for all men once to die, do this 21st day of September in the year of our Lord one thousand eight hundred and fourteen, make and publish this my Last Will and Testament in manner and format following.
>
> Item: I give and bequeath unto Edmund L. Blount, Ann Jacqueline Blount and Lavinia Blount, children of my well-beloved sister, Elizabeth Blount, wife of James Blount, the following property (viz): Old Negro Cinder, Young Negro Cinder, Chance, Cato, Nancy, Moses, Mitchell, Chloe, Old Cato, Nell, Toney, Bill, Mingo and Abigail to be equally divided between my nephew and nieces aforesaid, and also the monies arising from the hire of said Negroes, together will all the monies, bonds and notes now in the hands of my Guardian,

William Roulhac [Editor's note: William is the oldest son of Psalmet's brother, John Gregoire Roulhac, the second French brother to come to America.] so much of said monies, bonds and notes as may be necessary. It is my wish and desire that it be appropriated to the education of my nephew Edmund Blount and my nieces, Ann Jacqueline and Lavinia Blount, and the balance thereof, if any, to be equally divided between them and their heirs forever. It is understood that all my just debts are to be first satisfied and paid.

Item: I give and bequeath unto my nephew Francis [Roulhac] Ely the following Negroes (viz): Cesar, Jack, Harry, Old Ben and Sook, to him and his heirs forevItem: I give and bequeath unto my much esteemed relative William Roulhac, the following property, that is, Negroes Dempsey and Adam and also my horse bridle and saddle. It is understood that if William Roulhac should die without a lawful issue, it is my will and desire that the property hereby willed to him should devolve upon and be equally divided between my nephews Edmund L. Blount and Francis Ely and my nieces Ann J. Blount and Lavinia Blount, to them and their heirs forever.

Third Generation: Issue of Elizabeth Roulhac (2) and James Blount

6.1 Ann Jacqueline, (16) b. Feb. 15, 1805, in Washington Co., N.C. At an early age she showed a remarkable taste for literature, and in 1820 she was sent to be educated at the Moravian Seminary, Salem, N.C. Among the rigid disciplinarians of this school, she learned the lessons of industry and integrity, duty and self-sacrifice, which rendered her, in after life, a devoted, helpful wife, a loving, faithful mother, an earnest, conscientious teacher, and an active consistent Christian. Gifted with brilliant intellect, rare charm of manner, and great kindness of heart, she was well prepared for the high position which she afterwards so nobly filled. She m. Apr. 1, 1824, at Clinton, Ga., Thomas Bog [T. B.] *Slade, son of Gen. Jeremiah and Janet Bog Slade, he being of the sixth generation from Henry Slade, who came from England to the coast of North Carolina about 1650.*

T. B. Slade was born Jan. 20, 1800, in Martin Co., N.C. At the age of fifteen he was sent to the University at Chapel Hill, where he graduated in 1820 with the highest honors of his class. It is recorded of him that during his four years of collegiate life he never received a demerit, missed a recitation, or failed in a single duty. He practiced law with his father till 1824, when he moved to Georgia. In 1828 he abandoned the law and commenced his career as a teacher. He was one of the pioneers of female education in Georgia, and the good influence of himself and his wife, who always assisted him, runs like a thread of gold through many lives that bless our country. They both joined the Baptist Church, and he was ordained a minister of the Gospel in 1835, that he might preach to destitute churches, which he did gratuitously throughout his long life. He taught successfully in Clinton, Penfield, Macon, and Columbus, Ga.; thirty of his pupils forming the nucleus of the Wesleyan Female College, in the organization of which he assisted, and was chosen the first Professor of Natural Sciences. (This was the first college that ever gave diplomas to females). In 1842, Mr. Slade moved to Columbus, Ga., where, for thirty years, he was principal of a female institute of the highest grade and prosperity, although he was never known to ask for a pupil or to reject one because she was unable to pay. His wife was an active and efficient co-worker, the perfect union of strength and gentleness of character, making her presence a blessing and an example to all who knew her. A fitting climax to their long wedded life of usefulness, and therefore, happiness, was the celebration of their Golden Wedding in 1874, at which, besides many guests, nearly forty children and grandchildren were present. He d. in Columbus, Ga., May 5, 1882, in his eighty-third year, while she survived him nearly nine years, dying Feb. 12, 1891. "Two lives beautifully blended, as the rays of the setting sun, lighting and purpling the crystal clouds until sun and clouds are mingled in one mass of crimson beauty."

Chapter 1

Slave History: Anne Jacqueline Blount and T. B. Slade

According to the 1850 U.S. Census, fifty-year-old Thomas Slade was a schoolmaster in Columbus, Muscogee County, Georgia, living with his wife, Ann J., 10 children, and 29 girls ranging in age from 14 to 17 years. For a list of family members and students who resided at the school, see the 1850 Federal Census, Columbus, Muscogee, Georgia, p. 83. Thomas Slade, in addition to serving as a schoolmaster and Gospel preacher, owned eight slaves in 1850, including a 95-year-old blind female and two mulattoes.[25] He owned seven slaves in 1860.[26]

*7.2. **Edmond Sharpe Blount**, b. Sept. 10, 1806 in Washington Co., NC, d. Jan 18, 1822, in Clinton, [Jones Co.], GA.*

Edmond and his siblings Ann, Jacqueline and Lavinia were the beneficiaries of the estate of their uncle, John Maule Roulhac, in equal shares, of the following slaves in equal shares: Negro Cinder, Young Negro Cinder, Chance, Cato, Nancy, Moses, Mitchell, Chloe, Old Cato, Nell, Toney, Bill, Mingo and Abigail.

*8.3 **Lavina Elizabeth Blount**, (27) b. July 28, 1812 in Washington County, N.C.; educated at Salem, N. C.; m. in Clinton, Ga., Oct. 15, 1828, Simri Rose, b. Ma 28, 1799, in Branford, Conn. He was editor and proprietor for a long time of the "Macon Messenger," one of the first newspapers in Ga. He was one of the founders of Macon, of its early institutions and enterprises, but none remain a greater monument to this memory than the beautiful garden of graves, Rose Hill Cemetery, which he founded, planned and decorated with shrubs and flowers from every clime and that so appropriately bears his honored name. He d. in Macon, Ga., April 5, 1869. Mrs. Rose was gifted by nature with grace and ease of manners, which, with a confiding disposition, made her many friends among all classes of society. A true Christian spirit pervaded her life, and her acts of love and charity were far in advance of the age in which she lived. In every department of Christian work, her active mind and hands were ever ready to aid and comfort. The love of her own and her sisters'* *family for her was truly beautiful and only excelled by her lifelong devotion to that unselfish and appreciative sister. She d. at Ellicott City, Md., Oct. 23, 1883, and her remains were taken to Macon, and laid to rest by the side of her husband in Rose Hill Cemetery.*

Slave History: Lavina Elizabeth Blount and Simri Rose

Lavinia and her siblings Ann Jacqueline and Edmond were the beneficiaries, in equal shares, of the following slaves: Negro Cinder, young Negro Cinder, Chance, Cato, Nancy, Moses, Mitchell, Chloe, Old Cato, Nell, Toney, Bill, Mingo and Abigail.

In 1832, Simri Rose, Lavinia's husband, was allotted two parcels from what was considered "Cherokee Land," located in the northeastern part of Georgia, the only state to distribute parcels of land by lottery. Over 18,500 parcels were distributed. In 1860, he enslaved six persons in two slave houses.[27]

9.4. John Maul Roulhac, b. Feb. 13, 1816, in Blountsville, Jones County, GA, never married. He lived in India 14 years, in employment of the East India Co., where he amassed a fortune, unfortunately returning to America in time to join the Civil War and lose it all. He d. in Macon, Ga., Oct. 20, 1890.

10.5. Thomas Hamilton, (36) b. Nov. 27, 1819 in Blountsville, Jones County, GA; m. Aug. 10, 1837, at Macon, GA, Sarah Ross Clarke, b. May 7, 1819, daughter of M.D. Clarke and N. M. Norman. Her paternal grandmother was descended from the House of Stuarts of Scotland. After her death in 1848, he went to California, remained there several years, then visited some of the Isles of the sea and South America. Was living in Australia when the Civil War broke out, and he came home to enlist as a surgeon in the Southern Army. He now lives with his son, James, at Clear Water Harbor, FL.

Civil War History: Thomas Hamilton Blount

Thomas Blount served in Croft's Battery, Georgia Light Artillery (Columbus, Artillery) in the Confederate Army as an assistant surgeon.[28]

Issue of Mary J. D. Roulhac (4) and Dr. Horace Ely

11.1 Francis Roulhac, *(40) b. Sept. 1, 1812, in Plymouth, N.C.; m. May 1834, Frances Adelaide Randolph, only daughter of Samuel Randolph (b. in Va.) and Martha Ellis (b. in N.C.). They lived in Plymouth till about 1840, when they moved to Marianna, Fla. Here he was a very successful merchant and accumulated a large fortune; was a man of great hospitality and entertained his friends in princely style. He d. Jan. 5, 1858. His wife d. Sept. 6, 1880.*

Slave History: Francis Roulhac Ely and Frances Randolph Ely

In his 1814 Will, John Maule Roulhac bequeathed to Francis Roulhac Ely and his heirs Cesar, Jack, Harry, Old Ben and Sook. Twenty years later, in 1834, Francis Roulhac Ely and Joseph B.G. Roulhac entered into the following bill of sale:

Bill of Sale

Feb 4, 1834, Francis R. Ely to Jos. B.G. Roulhac

For amt purchase of 4 Negroes: Daniel, Henry, Lancashire & Ned - $980.00

Bal note due me on 1 Jan 1833 for hire of said Negroes for 1832 - $75.26

Bal on amount due on note for hire of said Negroes for 1833 – $66.50

Total $1,121.76

In the late 1830s, Francis Roulhac Ely and his wife, Frances Randolph Roulhac, relocated to Jackson County, Florida. Francis R. Ely is listed on the Jackson County, Florida, 1840 jury list and as a voter in Florida's first statewide election in 1845.[29] He owned and operated plantations on the Chipola and Chattahoochee Rivers and built a large antebellum home on West Lafayette Street in Marianna. Today that home is known as the Ely-Criglar House, is listed on the National Register of Historic Places and is owed by Ruth and Lawrence Kinsolving who in 2011 permitted the Roulhac Family Association to host part of its reunion activities there. Francis became one of the largest slave owners in Jackson County. The following two documents are illustrative of his extensive slave-trading activities:

Deed

This Indenture made and entered into this twenty sixth day of June in the year of our Lord eighteen hundred and forty seven by and between Walter S. C. Yonge of the one part and Francis R. Ely in his own right and as trustee and agent for John Thompkins and John A. Jacobs secretary of the Kentucky Institute of the Deaf and Dumb of the other part.

Witnesseth that the said Walter S. C. Young for and in consideration of the sum of one thousand six hundred dollars to him in hand paid by the said Francis R. Ely the receipt whereof is hereby acknowledged hath granted, bargained and sold and by these presents doth grant bargain, sell release ___ convey and confirm unto the said Francis R. Ely his heirs and assigns all those lots, tracts or parcels of land lying and being in Jackson County in the State of Fla, known and more particularly described as being lots numbered seventeen (17), eighteen (18), nineteen (19), twenty (20), twenty one (21) and twenty two (22) in the plat of the Town of Marianna; also the following slaves to wit: Hannah, aged about thirty-six years, Caroline, aged about seventy eight years and Chloe, aged about fifty years. To have and hold the aforesaid lots of land and the appurtenances thereunto belonging and the said slaves with their future increase unto the said Francis R. Ely, his heirs and assigns forever…

            Walter S. C. Yonge[30]

The State of Florida, Jackson County

Know all men by these present that I Amelia Yonge, wife of Walter S. C. Yonge, the grantor in the foregoing deed, do hereby relinquish and renounce unto Francis R Ely his heirs and assigns all my right, title and claim of dower in and to the premises in the said deed. In witnesseth whereof I have hereunto set my hand and affix my seal this twenty sixth day of June A.D. 1847.

Amelia Yonge[31]

               Mortgage

State of Florida, Jackson County

In consideration of Five Dollars to us in hand paid, the receipt where of is hereby acknowledged, we have this day sold and conveyed and do hereby sell and covey unto Francis R. Ely the following slaves to wit: Adeline, aged about nineteen years and Whit, aged about sixteen years, and we do hereby covenant and warrant and to defend the title to said slaves to the said Ely, against the lawful claims of all persons whatever. The slave conveyance is made as a mortgage to secure the payment of a note for five hundred and fifty-four dollars and fourteen cents made by J. J. Finley, payable to said Ely on order dated the 10th July 1847, and due on the first day of January 1850, to bear interest after due at the rate of 8 per cent per annum, which interest is to be paid annually – and it is also understood that the mortgage is intended to secure the payment to said Ely of any future advances or credits which he may give the said J. J. Finley until the mortgages shall be fully and wholly satisfied.

Witnessed our hand and seals this the 18th day of September 1847.[32]

J. J. Finley, M.M. Finley

On June 5, 1847, in his own capacity and as agent for the Kentucky Institute of the Deaf and Dumb, for $1,600, Francis R. Ely purchased from Walter S.C. Yonge, five lots (17 to 22) in Marianna and four slaves: Hannah, aged about 36 years; Caroline, about 78 years and Chloe, about 50.[33]

A few months later, September 18, 1847, J. J. Finley mortgaged two slaves Adeline, about 19 years old and Whit, about 16 years, to Francis Roulhac Ely to secure the payment of a $554.14 note made by "J. J. Finley, payable to said Ely on order dated the 10th July 1847, and due on the first day of January 1850, to bear interest at the rate of 8 per cent per annum, which interest is to be paid annually – and it is also understood that the mortgage is intended to secure the payment to said Ely of any future advances or credits which he may give the said J. J. Finley until the mortgages shall be fully and wholly satisfied."[34]

By 1850, Francis R. Ely, 38, was living in his Marianna home with his wife Frances, 36; his four children, Virginia, 14; John Randolph, 12; Anna S., 10; and Fanny R., five; and clerks John F. Hughes, 25 and Anthony Armistead, 16. He owned real estate valued at $14,156.[35] He was one of the largest slave owners in Jackson County. The 84 Africans Francis Roulhac Ely enslaved cultivated 650 acres of his 1,550-acre plantation.[36]

1850 Slave Schedule, District 4, Jackson County, FL[37]

Chapter 1

Francis R Ely	Age	Sex	Race
	46	F	B
	20	F	B
	18	M	B
	14	M	B
	8	F	B
	3	F	B
	1	F	B
	46	F	B
	15	M	B
	12	F	B
	9	F	B
	8	F	M
	3	F	M
	30	F	B
	9	M	M
	9	M	B
	7	F	B
	4	F	B
	25	F	B
	10	F	B
	4	M	B
	2	M	B
	35	F	B
	19	F	B
	21	M	B
	9	F	B
	13	F	B
	8	F	B
	2	F	B
	6/12	M	B
	25	F	B

Psalmet Gregoire Roulhac and his Descendants

Francis R Ely	Age	Sex	Race
	12	F	B
	5	M	B
	2	M	B
	1	F	B
	25	F	B
	8	F	M
	6	F	B
	3	F	M
	4/12	M	B
	25	F	B
	12	M	B
	6	M	B
	3	M	B
	2	F	B
	13	F	B
	16	F	B
	55	F	B
	6	M	M
	4	F	B
	26	M	B
	50	M	B
	30	M	B
	40	M	B
	19	M	B
	30	M	B
	22	M	B
	22	F	B
	17	M	B
	60	M	B
	36	M	B
	15	M	B

Chapter 1

Francis R Ely	Age	Sex	Race
	8	M	B
	55	F	B
	80	F	B
	30	F	B
	27	F	B
	7	F	B
	7	F	B
	16	F	B
	40	M	B
	16	M	B
	35	M	B
	23	M	B
	16	M	B
	14	M	B
	12	M	B
	11	M	B
	11	M	B
	13	M	B
	20	F	B
	5	F	M
	3	F	M
	6/12	M	B
Total	84		

In his October 1, 1855 Last Will, Francis Ely only mentions one of his African slaves by name, but he made clear his desire for his heirs to continue creating wealth from the labor of his enslaved Africans:

> Sixth. I will and desire that my land on the Chattahoochee and on the Chipola Rivers (the former having been recently purchased from Wm. Grantland of

the State of Georgia), and my Negro slaves, and all my stock of every kind and all my farming utensils, shall be kept together, and used and worked under the direction of my executors and that the produce of my two plantations shall be sold, and after deducting provisions sufficient for my family each year, and also sufficient for paying the yearly expenses of my wife during her widowhood, and for the yearly support, maintenance, and education of my children. Then the remainder, if any, shall be invested in the manner hereinafter to be pointed out.

Ninth. I will and desire that my executors take the proceeds of the sale or sales of my merchandise herein before directed, together with any money on hand at the time of my death, and also all money arising from bonds, bills, notes, accounts and other evidences of debt ... at the time of my death or which may come into the possession of my executors from the sale of my merchandise of otherwise after my death; and invest the same in the purchase of suitable Negroes to stock my Chattahoochee plantation until a sufficient number for the purpose shall have been purchased to work both the said Chattahoochee and also my Chipola plantations as they should be, my said executors to judge and determine as to when it is best to make such purchases; and if anything shall be remaining after making said purchases and fully stocking said plantations with all needful labor, I wish it invested in sound American stocks, bearing not less than six per cent interest per annum...

Eleventh. It is my desire that no overseer or overseers shall be employed and kept upon my plantations, but such as are competent, sober, and humane men, and the overseers employed on my Chipola place ... and have proper care for the young Negroes and women, and raise hogs and stock of all kinds usual and needful.

Twelfth. I wish the Negroes I inherited from my deceased mother's estate (and now in possession of my father, Horace Ely, under an agreement to pay the full value of their hire to my sister, Anna L Harrell during the time he keeps them) at my said father's death, or whenever he shall refuse to pay the reasonable hire of said Negroes to my two sisters Mary Jane Daffin, now of Alabama, and my said sister Ann L. Harrell, to whom I hereby give the said hire, to be taken into possession by my executors and worked with my other Negroes and whatever my said executors may think a reasonable hire for them shall be paid yearly by my said executors to my said two sisters, deducting expense, taxes and doctors bills, i.e. - said hires to be paid to my said sisters or their survivors during their lives, and after their death to go to my children, share and share alike.

Fifteenth. If my executors shall at any time find the working of my plantations and Negroes unprofitable and deem it advisable to do so, they may, in their discretion and with the consent of my wife, hire the Negroes or any portion of them and rent my plantations or a portions of them, or sell said plantations and also my stock and farming utensils, and appropriate the proceeds of such hiring, rent and sale so far as may be necessary to the support of my family and the education of my children...

Sixteenth. Many years since, I purchased of one O. S. Morse, a Negro man named Henry, for a certain term of time, which is now elapsed as will more fully appear by reference to the Bill of Sale from said Morse to myself. Now, I do hereby solemnly acknowledge that said Henry was entitled to his freedom, and has enjoyed it, from the expirations of the time for which I purchased his services, and I exercise no control over him save as his legally appointed guardian.

Francis R. Ely died in January 1858. His Last Will and Testament was presented in the Jackson County Probate Court February 9, 1858. Testamentary letters were issued to John F. Hughes, one of the administrators named in the will. Thomas M. White, William Nickels and W.W. Compton were appointed appraisers. A week later, John G. Roulhac transferred the land and slaves he held pursuant to the 1834 marriage contract between Francis Roulhac Ely and Frances Randolph to Francis R. Ely's estate. It provided:

> This indenture made and entered into on this the (16) sixteenth day of February A.D., 1858, between John G. Roulhac as Trustee and Frances A. C. Ely, both of the State and County aforesaid of the first part, and Frances A. C. Ely, Executrix and John F. Hughes and John R. Ely Executors of the last will and testament of Francis R. Ely, late of the State and County aforesaid.
>
> Witnesseth, that whereas by virtue of a deed made and entered into on the 9th day of April A.D., 1835, between Francis R. Ely, Frances A. C. Randolph and Richard Williams all of the State of North Carolina, I, Frances A. C. Ely, then Frances A. C. Randolph, did give, grant, bargain, sell ... unto the said Richard Williams and is heirs all the lands ... and also all the Negro slaves which with the said land which I the said Frances A. C, derived title to ... from the estate of my father Samuel Randolph, unto the said Richard Williams, his

heirs and assigns, to be held by him for and upon certain uses and trusts and with full power to convey all of the property described in said deed of the 9th day of April A.D., 1835, when thereunto requested in writing by the said Francis R. Ely, and I the said Frances A.C.; and

Whereas on the 19th day of January 1837, I the said Frances A.C., and the said Francis R. Ely, did in writing request the said Richard Williams by deed to bargain, sell and convey all of the property described in the said deed of the 9th day of April A.D., 1835, thereupon, I, the said Frances A. C. Ely and my late husband the said Francis R. Ely and Richard Williams the trustee by the stipulations and powers conferred by the said deed on the 9th day April A.D., 1835, did make, seal, sign and deliver unto John G. Roulhac, as trustee; he the said John G. Roulhac joining in the same, a deed of the 19th day of January A.D. 1837, bargaining, selling, conveying…him the said John G. Roulhac and his heirs all the lands…described in said deed of the 9th day of April A.D., 1835, also the following slaves: Cesar, Wiley, Broomfield, Davy, Roger, Grace and Charlotte & her children Sabry, Adeline, Alfred, Abram, Edmond, and Cintha and her child Dave, fifteen in number, were by said deed of the said Francis R. Ely & Frances A.C. Ely and Richard Williams, dated January 19th A.D. 1837, conveyed to the said John G. Roulhac, and his heirs to be held by him for and upon certain uses and trusts designated by the terms of said deed and to be by him conveyed whenever, the said John G. Roulhac or when the said Francis R. Ely and his wife, the said Frances A.C. Ely, in writing should request him the same John G. Roulhac to convey the said property.

Indenture[38]

And the said Francis R. Ely one of the above named parties to said deeds of the 9th day of April A.D. 1855, and January 19th A.D. 1837, on the first day of October A.D. 1855, made and published his last will and testament and made therein an ample and satisfactory provision for me, the said Francis A.C. Ely, another of the parties to said deeds, and for whose use and benefits, the same were made.

And whereas the said Francis R. Ely, by his said last will and testament requests and desires that I shall upon accepting the provision of his said last will and testament in my behalf, as the same is agreeable to me, and fully meets with my approbation, that I convey all my interest and property under said deed or marriage settlement of the 9th day of April A.D., 1835, unto his executors in trust for his estate to be used and disposed of in the manner provided in his said will in regard to his own property,

And whereas, I the said John G. Roulhac ... upon the written request of Frances A.C. Ely one of the parties to the deed of January the 19th 1837, and by the power therein stated, me moving, do desire to effectuate the intention of the said Francis R. Ely and Frances A.C. Ely, who are the beneficiaries under and by virtue of said deed.

Therefore, know ye that in consideration of the premises, that we Frances A.C. Ely and John G. Roulhac, both of the State of Florida and County of Jackson, do hereby bargain, sell, convey and deliver unto Frances A. C. Ely, executrix and John F. Hughes and John R. Ely, executors of the last will and testament of Francis E. Ely, deceased, all of the right, title and interest acquired by either of us in and any and all the property, both real and personal, described in the deeds made April the 9th, A.D. 1835, by Frances A.C. Randolph, Frances A.C. Ely, Richard Williams and John G. Roulhac, together with the increase of the female slaves and increase, rents and profits of everything remaining in-kind of every nature and description conveyed by said deeds, to have and to hold the same unto them, the said Frances A.C. Ely as executrix and John F. Hughes and John R. Ely, as executrix of the last will and testament of the said Francis R. Ely, deceased, in trust for the estate of the said Francis R. Ely, deceased and to held, used and disposed of by said executors in the manner provided in the said last will and testament of said Francis R. Ely in regard to his own property and no other whatever…

Fanny A.C. Ely
J. G. Roulhac

In the presence of us
J.J. Finley, W. W. Compton

The August 9th 1858 appraisement of enslaved persons in Francis Roulhac Ely's estate at his Chattahoochee and Chipola Plantations and in the town of Marianna is set forth below:[39]

Appraisement of Francis R. Ely's Estate

Name	Remarks	Age	Value
Caesar & Family		38	$1,000
Rosetta		38	450
Sarahann	Unlikely	14	550
Polina		10	500
Joshua	Boy	8	500
Alexandria		6	400
Hardy		3	250
Gracie & Family		40	650
William		10	400
Nathan		6	400
Calvin		4	300
Delia		3	200
Willis		19	1,000
Jonas		12	600
Alfred	Diseased	26	500
Harriett		27	900
Henry & family		55	450
Charlotte		50	350
Adeline		34	750
Edmond		30	1,000
Martha		17	900
Annette		12	550
Minerva		9	500
Eliza & Children		20	900
Julia		3	200
Ella		1	150
Jane & Children	Diseased	25	650
Angelina		1	150
Moses & wife	Crippled	40	500
Gatsy		50	350

Chapter 1

Name	Remarks	Age	Value
Clara		15	850
Florida		11	600
Emily		16	900
Mahala		40	600
Chance	Crippled	25	300
Joshua		14	750
Luke		10	650
Mary		7	500
William		3	250
Edna		1	150
Delphia & Children		18	800
Lewis		1	150
Allen		28	1200
Rachael		38	400
John		16	800
Jim		14	800
Eliza	Likely	14	700
Martha		13	650
Quamley & Family		49	900
Alcy		38	500
Pheoby		17	750
Robert		12	700
Allen		9	550
Peter		5	300
Aggy		4	200
John		1	150
Mary	Unhealthy	45	400
Amos		25	900
Wallis		22	500
Laura		16	750
Amelia		10	550

Name	Remarks	Age	Value
Israel		8	400
Sarah		4	250
Lizzy & Child		24	1,000
Warren		7	500
Amy & Child		20	850
Mary		1	150
Melvina		18	900
Ephraim		1	100
Daniel		56	550
Alice		50	350
Silvester		12	700
Ben		11	500
Clara		9	450
Noah			300
Wiley		44	700
Mathew		40	700
Riah		25	950
Dawson & Family		60	300
Cynthia		50	500
Windsor		17	1,000
David		24	1,200
Elbert		11	550
Mahala		8	450
Catherine	Diseased	13	300
Molly	Sound	14	700
Sarah	Diseased	40	300
Patty		70	100
Barbary		38	650
Edy		13	750
Simon		58	350
Caesar		75	100

Chapter 1

Name	Remarks	Age	Value
Pheoby		65	200
David		45	800
Abram & Family		23	1,000
Hannah		30	700
Preston		10	550
Francis		11	750
Ned & Wife		27	900
Edy		20	650
Reysen		36	500
Virgil & Wife		70	100
Chaney		60	100
Sandy		55	500
Dandridge		58	500
Pompey		20	1,000
Wiley		26	950
Turner		18	1,000
Washington		22	900
Amanda		25	750
Filphia & Family		40	600
Penny		13	600
Fife		8	450
Susannah		5	250
Nanny		60	100
Georgann		20	700
Betsy		16	650
Mary		15	600
Vina		15	600
	Total	120	$68,100

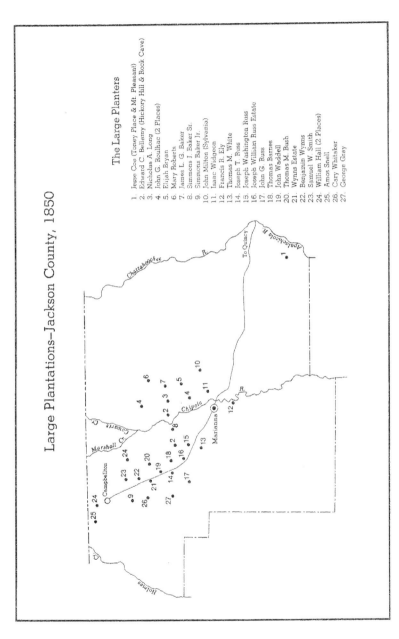

"Large Plantations – Jackson County, 1850," Paisley, Clifton, *THE RED HILLS OF FLORIDA, 1528-1865*, page 21. Reprinted with permission of the University of Alabama Press.

Francis Roulhac Ely's estate had not been settled by 1860. According to the 1860 Slave Schedules for Jackson County, his estate owned 215 slaves. His wife, 43-year-old Frances Randolph Ely, owned real estate valued at $21,000 and $61,000 in personal property.

According to the 1860 Jackson County, Florida Agricultural Census, the Estate of F.R. Ely owned 1,000 acres of improved land, 1,500 acres of unimproved land, $15,000 cash, $300 worth of farm implements and life stock valued at $4,200.

***13.3 Mary Jane**, (49), b. Sept. 20, 1816; m. when quite young Benjamin Finley, of Va., who d. in a few months after they were married. They had one child. She afterwards moved to Marianna, Fla., where she m. June 30, 1840, William R. Daffin, of Eufaula, Ala. He was descended from the French Huguenots of the Eastern shore of Maryland. He d. Nov. 21, 1865. She m. again in 1869 Mr. Tillinghast, who d. soon after. She d. Mar. 30, 1882.*

Slave History: Mary Jane Ely Finley, Benjamin Finley and William R. Daffin

In 1840, Mary Jane Ely and her husband William R. Daffin lived in Calhoun, St. Joseph, in the Florida territory. Mary Jane Ely and family were living in Barbour, County, Alabama, and had acquired six slaves.[40]

On September 7, 1852, fourteen years after slaves Quam, Penny, Lucy and Joe were conveyed, in trust, to Mary Jane's father Francis Roulhac Ely for her benefit, her husband William R. Daffin was designated as substitute trustee and the slaves were conveyed to him.

Substitution of Trustee

Whereas by the deed hereto annexed and dated the 30th day of November A.D., 1838, Joseph B.G. Roulhac of Windsor in the State of North Carolina did convey unto me the following to wit: Quam, Penny, Lucy and Joe for the uses and trusts expressed in said deed, and which provided in said deed that I reserved for myself and my representatives, the right, power and authority to substitute another trustee who shall take an absolute estate in said slaves, subject to trusts in said deed declared; - now in pursuance of said power of substitution contained and give in said deed, I do hereby name and substitute William R. Daffin the present husband of the said Mary J. Finley, as trustee in my place and stead; and accordingly I do hereby convey to said William R. Daffin, his executors and administrators the said slaves...

I William R Daffin do hereby accept the trust ...

Fourth Generation: Issue of Ann J. Blount (46) and Rev. Thomas Bog Slade

16.1 Janet Elizabeth, (58) born May 5, 1825 at Clinton, Ga.; m. July 15, 1863, at Columbus, Ga., Wm. Robert Gignilliant, b. Dec. 10, 1814, at Ardoc, McIntosh Co., Ga., son of Gilbert Gignilliant, (a descendant of the French Huguenots, who came to S.C.) and Mary McDonald, (whose ancestors came to McIntosh Co. under the auspices of Oglethorpe). He was left an orphan at an early age; was educated at the University of GA. While there he united with the Baptist Church and was ever afterwards an earnest, conscientious Christian. His was a life of good deeds, serving his Master with great simplicity, free from self-righteousness, his left hand not knowing what his right hand did. During the civil war he was on a special committee to look after the poor and needy, the widows and orphans. He also supplied to the army certain amounts of money and provisions. Being a successful planter, besides owning an interest in a cotton factory, he was enabled to supply thread and cloth to many destitute families. He never felt that he had done enough, and after the confederacy was lost, he would often rebuke himself, saying he feared the Lord took away everything because he had not used it for his glory. He d. at Marietta, Ga., Jan. 19, 1882.

Slave History: Janet Elizabeth Slade and William R. Gignilliant

When Janet Elizabeth Slade married William R. Gignilliant in 1863, he was very wealthy. According to the 1850 and 1860 Slave Schedules, he enslaved 80 and 139 persons, respectively.

In 1865, William R. Gignilliat filed a Confederate Application for Presidential Pardon pursuant to a May 29, 1865, amnesty proclamation issued by President Johnson. Pursuant to the amnesty proclamation, former confederates could apply for amnesty if they had voluntarily participated in the rebellion and had property valued at more than $20,000. Applicants were required to take an oath to defend the constitution and the Union, and to obey all Federal laws and proclamations regarding slavery made during the rebellion. In 1860, Gignilliat valued his property at $99,000, of which slaves and other personal property accounted for $59,000.[41] Gignilliat, 47 years old when the Civil War began, served in Captain Guerard's Battery, Georgia Light Artillery as a Second Lieutenant. He was a First Lieutenant when he mustered out.[42]

18.3 *Anne Louisa*, *b. Aug. 21, 1829, at Clinton, Ga., m. July 2, 1857, Roswall Ellis, b. April 8, 1822, in Putnam Co., Ga., son of Dr. Iddo Ellis and Lucy Phelps. She d. Feb. 16, 1858. In 1846 Ellis entered service in the Mexican War as 1st Sgt., Columbus Guards, Co. G 1st Reg. Ga Vol., commanded by Col. Henry R. Jackson; was promoted to 2nd Lieut.; served twelve months and was the siege of Vera Cruz. He entered the C.S.A. [Confederate States of America] as a Capt. Of Columbus Guards, Co. D, 2nd Reg. Ga. Vol., Col. Paul J. Semmes. After Col. Semme's promotion to Brig. Gen., he was appointed Asst. Adjt. Gen. and served with him. He was severely wounded at Knoxville, Tenn., in the assault at Fort Saunders. After recovery he was assigned to Maj. Gen. Field's staff as Asst. Adjt. and Inspector Gen. He was in the battles* *of Fredericksburg, Chancellorsville and Gettysburg. Lives in Oakland, Meriwether Co., Ga.*

19.4 *James Jeremiah*, *(60) b. April 28, 1831, at Clinton, Ga.; m. July 19, 1855, Annie Gertrude Graham, dau. of Dr. Wm. P. Graham and Margaret Graves, of Covington, Ga., and natives of N.C. She d. Apr. 30, 1856, leaving an infant dau., Annie Graham, one month old, who d. July 1856. He m. again Jan. 12, 1859, Leila Birchett Bonner, dau. of Col. Seymour R. Bonner, (b. in 1809 in Hancock Co., Ga.; d. in Columbus, Ga., (1856) and Marion A. Huguenin (b. in Beaufort, S.C.; d. in San Francisco, Cal., Feb. 6, 1891). He entered the C.S.A. as Capt. La. Vols. [Volunteers] which Co. disbanded, because Gov. Moore would not receive it, saying that the C.S. had troops enough, July 1861 – just after battle of Bull Run. He then joined 10th Ga. Vol as private; was promoted Lieut. day after battle of Seven Pines; was at battle of Frazer's Farm, White Oak Swamp and Malvern Hill, acting as aide to Gen. Paul Semmes; commanded Co. A 10th Ga. on the march into Md.; at the battle of Crampton Gap and capture of Harper's Ferry; commissioned in 1863, Adjt. Rank of Capt., in Gen. Semmes' Brigade. Afterwards, being pronounced unfit for field service was detailed in Quarter Master's department in the West. He is now Mayor of Columbus, Ga.*

Slave History: James J. Slade & Leila Bonner Slade

By 1860, twenty-nine-year-old attorney and planter, James J. Slade enslaved ten Africans and had personal property valued at $11,200 and real estate valued at $6,000, in Ward 7, Parish of Carroll, Louisiana.[43]

20.5 *Emma Jacqueline*, *(73), b. Jan. 10, 1833, at Clinton, Ga.; m. Oct. 19, 1854, at Columbus, Ga.; m. Alfred Prescott, of Fort Gaines, Clay Co., Ga, born Apr. 2, 1826, son of Geo. Prescott and Ann Carpenter Bacon. He enlisted in the C.S.A. in the spring of 1862, as a private in the Terrell Artillery, Capt. Edgar Dawson. They were ordered to Savannah where he remained three months. Afterwards he was to duty as Adjt. at*

Camp Randolph, the Camp of Instruction for Conscripts for Northern GA, located near Decatur, Ga. This Camp was abandoned in July 1864, when Sherman entered Atlanta, and he was transferred to the Conscript department at Savannah, where he remained until the evacuation. Then he was sent into the counties of Southeast Ga., where his life was constantly threatened by deserters and bushwhackers until the close of the war. Soon after this he moved his family to Columbus, and in 1880 to Atlanta, Ga., where they still live.

Slave History: Emma Jacqueline Slade & Alfred Prescott

In 1860, before the Civil War started, Alfred Prescott, a bank agent with $9,500 in real estate and $14,000 in personal property enslaved five persons, three females 15, 17 and 18 years old and two males, one one-year old and one 34.[44]

21.6 *Thomas Bog, Jr.*, (83) *b. Dec. 16, 1834, at Clinton, Ga.; m. Dec. 21, 1871, at Columbus, Ga., Almarine Cowdery, b. Jan. 23, 1848, daughter of Lester Leander Cowdery, (b. at Hartland, Conn., July 11, 1806), and Evilene Giddings, (b. in Union District, S.C., Sept. 25, 1825). They live in Carrollton, Ga. He entered the C.S.A. as a private in the Artillery in the fall of 1861. They served for a while in Virginia, were then sent to Savannah for coast defense, where he remained until the evacuation. While there he was transferred to Guerrard's Battery, and was with it at the battle of Olustee in Fla., also at the surrender at Greensboro, NC.*

22.7 *Martha Bog*, (89) *b. Dec. 3, 1837, at Clinton, Ga., m. Aug. 2, 1859, at Columbus, Ga., Grigsby Eskridge Thomas, b. Dec. 30, 1832; son of Samuel Butler Thomas and Ann Askew of Hancock County, Ga. He entered the C.S.A. as Lieutenant in Co. G, 54*[th] *Georgia Regiment; had command of the company in all the battles on James and Morris Islands, near Charleston, S.C. Then the regiment joined Johnson's army in North Ga., and he was actively engaged in all the fighting from Dalton down to Atlanta. In the battle of July 22, 1864 on Peachtree, before Atlanta, he was wounded and sent home, where he was ill about two months, then* *reported for duty, and served in many skirmishes up to the last battle of the war at Bentonville, NC, April 16, 1865. Here the General Commanding promoted him instantly on the field of battle for bravery and daring in leading his command into the fight.*

Slave History: Martha Bog and Grigsby E. Thomas

In 1860, Martha Bog and Grigsby E. Thomas were living in Columbus, Muscogee County, GA. According to the 1860 Slave Schedule, Grigsby E. Thomas owned 42 slaves.[45]

23.8 *Stella Bog*, *b. born July 19, 1839, at Macon, Ga.; married July 16, 1861, at Columbus, GA, Hockley Cloyd McKee, b. at Columbus, Ga., December 6, 1839, son of Hockley Cloyd McKee (b. in Chester Co. PA, 1810) and Elizabeth B. Atkinson (b. in New Jersey, 1812). They live in Columbus, Ga., on the site of the old "Sladeville" home. He joined the C.S.A. and served through the war as a private in Terrell Light Artillery [Brooks' Company, Georgia Light Artillery], army of S.C., GA and Fla; not attached to any Battalion or Regiment; was at the evacuation of Savannah, Dec. 1864, and surrendered to W. T. Sherman, at Greensboro, N.C., April 26, 1865.*

24.9 *Helen Roulhac*, *(99) b. Feb. 15, 1841 at Penfield, Ga.; m. April 23, 1863, at Columbus, GA, John Bright Lindsay, b. March 9, 1840, near Columbus, son of Sherwood Connor Lindsay and Elizabeth Bright Cooper, natives of N. C. He enlisted in the C.S.A. as a private in the Columbus Guards [17 Regt. Ga. Inf.]. Was wounded in his first fight at Yorktown; after that he went through many battles in Va. Tenn., and Ga., and was never touched, though his clothes were often torn by bullets. His servant that he took into the army said he always went on the battle field as soon as he could after a fight, "to look for Mas John," sometimes thinking he had been captured or killed, he would almost give up, knowing "he never would stop fighting till they pulled him off." After the battle of the Wilderness, when the boy got to him with a canteen of water, his clothes were literally shot off of him, and he exclaimed he had "been through hell* and come out with only a pair of blankets." He was a brave and fearless soldier, and generous to a fault. For gallantry at Chickamauga, he received a furlough signed by the immortal Lee, and during this furlough he was shot and killed by a Home Guard at Columbus, Ga., Feb. 18, 1865. The indignation was so great that the Commander of the Post narrowly escaped being mobbed by the citizens. His widow lives in Columbus with her only child, Mrs. Tigner.

Slave History: Sherwood C. Lindsay

On August 19, 1865, the provisional governor of Georgia, satisfied that applicant Sherwood C. Lindsay would "prove a loyal and useful citizen" recommended pardon and amnesty for his service in the Confederate army.[46]

25.10 John Henry, *b. Jan. 11, 1843, at Columbus, GA. At the age of 18, he entered the C.S.A. as a member of the Columbus Guards, 2nd Ga. Regt. He exhibited before Richmond and at the first and second battles of Manassas, the highest order of patriotism and fell in the battle of Sharpsburg, Sept. 17, 1862, while defending the pass of the bridge; esteemed by his comrades in arms and deeply mourned by all who knew him. But it was not only on the tented field, amid the strife of hostile armies, that his excellences were known, forever obedient and affectionate to his parents, kind and unselfish in his intercourse with brothers and sisters, he was conspicuous for his high moral character, irreproachable life, and unwavering discharge of Christian duty.*

Issue of Lavinia E. Blount (8) and Simri Rose

32.6. Helen Randolph, *(110) b. July 7, 1838, at Macon, Ga., m. June 5, 1872, in St. Luke's Church, Baltimore, Md., Vincent Boisaubin King, b. Apr. 9, 1834, in Morristown, N.J., son of Jacob Morrell King, (b. Nov. 21, 1781, in Morristown, N.J. – of the fifth generation from John King, of Devonshire, England, b. 1605, came to America, and settled in Mass., 1650), and Frances Holt Parson, b. Sept. 27, 1799, at Redhook, Duchess*

Co., N.Y., dau. of Jasper Parson, who was b. in England, and m. Tabitha Guichard, Sept. 16, 1770, in the Island of St. Christopher, West Indies, where he had plantations. Mr. and Mrs. King live in Morristown, N.J.

Issue of Thomas H. Blount (10) and Sarah R. Clarke

***36.1 James Roulhac**, (123) b. Jan. 31, 1840, at Macon, Ga.; m. Feb. 22, 1868, Ida May Graves, dau. of M. L. Graves, (a native of N. C.) and Anna Sandifef. She d. May 17, 1875, at Macon, Ga. He m. 2nd, at Eustis, Fla., Mar. 13, 1882, Susanna Elizabeth Key, b. Dec. 12, 1848, at Halbeach, Lincolnshire, England, dau. of Edward Key and Emma Basset, (m. Feb. 27, 1839, at St. Marks, Kensington, England). They live at Clear Water Harbor, Fla. He enlisted in the C. S. A. as a member of the First Ga. Regulars, and served through the entire war.*

***37.2 John William**, b. Oct. 15, 1840, at Macon, Ga.; m. Oct. 15, 1884, Lula Martha Johnson. She d. July 1, 1890, at Macon, Ga., where he now resides. He served in the C. S. A., throughout the war, as secretary of the Eighth Ga. Regt., under Col. L. M. Lamar.*

***39.4 George Norman**, b. Apr. 6, 1847, at Macon, Ga.; entered the C. S. A. when quite young, and d. at the age of seventeen, in the hospital at Petersburg, Virginia., in 1864.*

Issue of Francis Roulhac Ely (11) and Frances A. Randolph

***41.2 John Randolph**, (128), b. Sept. 8, 1838, in Plymouth, N.C., m. Feb. 18, 1864, in St. Luke's church, Marianna, Fla., Susan Evans Baker, daughter of Mr. and Mrs. James Baker of Greenwood, Jackson County, FL. (The Baker family is one of the most ancient and honorable in the South, of English descent from the House of Stuarts). She d. June 29, 1868, leaving two children. He entered the C.S.A. and served throughout the war as Assistant Adjutant General of Finley's Brigade of Florida Troops.*

Chapter 1

Reconstruction Violence: John Randolph Ely

John R. Ely was a suspect in the April 1871 murder of Republican John Q. Dickinson, a former Freedmen's Bureau agent, Jackson County clerk of court and the last Reconstruction-era Republican office holder in Jackson County. His assassination was part of intense violence against African Americans and their Republican allies between 1869 and 1871. It is estimated that up to 175 Negroes and their Republican allies were killed. Daniel R. Weinfeld, in *The Jackson County War*, makes the following observations:

> Marianna blacks were convinced that John R. Ely was the murderer. Ely, born in 1838, was a confederate army veteran and attorney. His father, Francis de Roulhac Ely, was a successful merchant and planter and among the wealthiest men in the county. By 1871, however, the Ely fortune had completely dissipated as a result of the war and subsequent economic collapse. Circumstantial evidence pointed toward Ely's culpability in the murder. In a letter Dickinson sent to Governor Reed one week before his death, he mentioned Ely's pressure on Homer Bryan [the African American tax assessor] to retract the announcement of the auction of Ely family property. Dickinson added that Ely had "repeatedly threatened me for advising and aiding the collector in his business." Richard Posser [an African American constable who had been appointed to replace the murdered Calvin Rogers] testified that when Dickinson instructed him to announce the sale of Ely lands for county tax delinquency, Ely approached Dickinson and threatened that if his property were sold, he would whip or kill Dickinson. According to Prosser, Dickinson insisted that the auction go forward and declared he was willing to risk his own life to fulfill

his duties. Later, when Posser rang the bell announcing the auction, Ely threatened Posser and demanded that Dickinson meet for a duel. The auction was postponed because of Homer Bryan's absence, but Ely demanded that the auction advertisements be discontinued. Again, Dickinson refused, but Bryan succumbed to the pressure and eventually withdrew the auction.[47]

John Randolph Ely was murdered in 1893. The circumstances surrounding his murder and life after the Civil War is described in *Jackson County, Florida – A History*, as follows:

> The other [violent crime] involved the 1891 murder of John R. Ely, son of Francis Ely, one of Marianna's largest antebellum merchants, and an active member of the [St. Luke] Episcopal Church in the late 1860s. Ely had been extremely disturbed by the enfranchisement of blacks and the Republican administration which began in the late 1860s. He had participated in the violence against Republican officials and voters which disrupted Jackson County for more than two years between 1869 and 1871. Having inherited and operated his father's store for several years, he had ultimately closed it and moved away. In the early 1880s, he was working as a clerk in a store at Neal's Landing while relatives were keeping his young sons at Greenwood. Mollie Baker had high hopes for his recovery in 1893 when she wrote that he had not had a drink in months and a little later that "cousin John has entirely reformed." Whether she was correct or not and what Ely did after that is not well-known. It is clear, however, that he disappeared in 1893 with rampant rumors that he had been murdered in nearby Alabama. Sheriff Andrew Scott, who had filled that office since 1881, seemed to many Jack-

son Countians to be disinterested in investigating the case. When prominent citizens complained, Governor Francis P. Fleming appointed Hays H. Lewis as a special investigator… Lewis found Ely's body under a pile of lumber at a sawmill near the Alabama line and gathered enough evidence for a murder indictment against Buck Hall, Sebe Espy, Choice Adams and Henry Simmons… Adams and Simmons were merely charged with being present when the murder was committed. Espy was not apprehended. Hall was convicted, but the state supreme court overturned the decision.[48]

*42.3 **Anne Louisa**, (130) b. Aug. 31, 1840, in Marianna, Fla; married Dec. 5, 1866 by Rev. Wm. Saunders, Edward Winston Henry, Jr., b. at Windstone, Va., April 19, 1840, son of Edward Winston Henry, and Jane Yuille. E. Henry, Jr., being the youngest grandson of Patrick Henry, by inheritance; now resides on the large ancestral landed estate in Charlotte Co., Va., where Patrick Henry was buried.49 They have two children. He served in the C. S. A. the first two years of the war in the 14th Va. Cav., Co I, McCauslin Brig., Fitz Lee's Division; the last two years, he held a staff appoi*

43.4 Charles Horace, (132) b. Dec. 18, 1842, in Marianna, Fla.; m. 1866 in Marianna, Virginia Milton, daughter of John Milton, ex-Governor of Fla. She d. leaving one daughter. He d. March 18, 1893.

Slave History: John Milton

John Milton (April 20, 1807 – April 1, 1865), born near Louisville, Georgia, was the son of Homer Virgil Milton (1781 - 1822) and grandson of Revolutionary War hero and former Georgia Secretary of State, John Milton (1756 - 1804), was Florida's fifth governor. He married Susan Cobb about 1830. They had four children. Susan died in 1842. In 1844, John married Caroline Howze from Alabama. They had 10 children. He practiced law in Georgia and Alabama, before settling in New Orleans. He came to Florida in 1846. In 1850, he was elected to the Florida House of Representatives.

As a strong supporter of states' rights, John Milton was an early advocate for Florida's secession from the Union. In 1860, Milton owned 36 slaves.[50] He was one of Florida's delegates to the 1860 Democratic National Convention and was also a candidate for governor. A convention was called to take up the issue of secession and on January 10, 1861, the measure passed. He took the oath of office as Florida's governor on October 7, 1861. In 1865, as the war was ending and the Confederacy close to defeat, Governor Milton left Tallahassee for his Sylvania Plantation in Marianna, Florida. In his final message to the state legislature, he said, "Death would be preferable to reunion." On April 1, 1865, with a gunshot to his head, he committed suicide. John Milton is buried at Saint Luke's Episcopal Cemetery in Marianna.[51]

Issue of Mary J. Ely (13) and 2nd Husband, William Daffin

50.2. Philip Dickenson, (130) *b. Aug. 10, 1841, in Marianna, Fla.; m. July 25, 1867, Columbia BH. Hayden, b. in Fla., 1846, daughter of Nehemiah and Marybeth Hayden. They live in Savannah, Ga. He entered the C.S.A. and served throughout the war; enlisted in Dunham's Battery of Artillery at Apalachicola, Fla.; served one year in East Fla., and was transferred to Abel's Battery. He was one of thirty-five of this Battery who escaped capture at Camp Finegan and made their way to Lake City, Fla., where they were assigned to the 1st Ga. Regulars, and were in the thick of the fight at the battle of Olustee or Ocean Pond.*

51.3 Horace Ely, (141) *b. June 30, 1843, in St. Josephs, Fla.; m. Feb. 9, 1864, Sarah Jane Dykes, b. Sept. 29, 1844, daughter of James and Jane Dykes. They live at Marianna, Fla. He entered the C.S.A. as a private in the Gulf State Guards, Capt. J. F. McLennon, 2nd Fla. Regt. Was at the battle of Seven Pines, and severely wounded on the Chickahominy River, 9 miles from Richmond, Virginia.*

Chapter 2
John Gregoire Roulhac and Descendants

*The power of the master must be absolute,
to render the submission of the slave perfect.*

First Generation: John Gregoire Roulhac[2]

***1.6 John Gregoire Roulhac**, (as called in America), was born Nov. 23, 1758, in Limoges, France. "His character was firm and courageous, and not easily daunted by difficulties. After his return from college his inclination was leading him strongly towards the army, and his ambition was to obtain a commission. His father, however, had not a favorable opinion of it, and, with difficulty, dissuaded him from his chivalrous plans, and he, at last, consented for a few years, to enter the Congregation of the Oratoire. He remained there but a few years, his independence and love of liberty suiting him badly to a life of restraint. His father dying at that time, he followed his inclination and left the Congregation in disgust. Being adventurous, and knowing that with his small means, it was nearly impossible to acquire independence in his country, he determined to go to America, and tempt his fortune there. It was certainly a leap in the dark. It was towards the end of the American Revolution, and very difficult, if not impossible to find a passage on board of merchant vessels to go to America. Having obtained from our eldest brother a small part of his patrimony, which he employed in an assortment for a venture, with difficulty he obtained a free passage as a supernumerary mid-shipman on board of*

---

2   The italicized text in this chapter represents unedited portions of the *Genealogical Memoirs of the Roulhac Family* as published in 1894 by Helen Prescott. The unitalicized portions are my annotations.

Chapter 2

a French frigate, the Medusa (or Danac ?) of 44 guns. She sailed from Rochfort on the 8th of Nov. 1782. She had on board a large sum of money for the payment of the French army then on the Continent, and besides the amount of a loan made by the French government to Congress.

The passage was short and happy till she came into the Delaware Bay, where she grounded not far from Wilmington. There she was obliged to cut her masts and throw away some of her guns, land her money and make her escape up the river, so that she should not fall into the hands of the British, who had a strong squadron in the bay and were in pursuit of her. My brother was early ordered in those difficulties, with a party of marines and sailors, to land the money. Taking also with him his clothes and venture, when he saw his charge safely delivered to a detachment of Continentals, he did not return to the frigate, but walked on to Philadelphia, where, in a few days, he disposed of his goods with advantage. Having done so he started for North Carolina to find his brother. Their meeting was not a little singular. Psalmet had not the most distant idea that his brother was in the Continent. Some months before he had been plundered by the Tories and he looked with suspicion on all strangers, who came about the house. In the dusk of the evening, seeing a young man in the garb of a sailor, approaching his house, he ran for his gun and met him so at the door. They had not met each other for several years and did not know each other, and it was some time before they came to the truth. John soon found out that his brother was very far from that ease in which he had hoped to find him, and on the contrary was reduced to great want and distress.

Thus finding himself in a foreign land, the language of which he could hardly understand and could use most imperfectly, almost destitute, he determined to become a charge to his brother as little while as possible, and applying himself to the study of the English language, in a few months, by the help of his brother, he was able to speak it with ease. This done, much against his brother's desire he resolved to go to sea, and for a short time was on board of a vessel to take a trip to the West Indies. He had entered as a common sailor, not doubting that a short practice would enable him, with *the education he had and the help of some theoretical books on navigation, to become a good sea captain. This plan however, he soon abandoned, after getting acquainted with Mr. Martin, a Frenchman at Newbern, a gentleman of talents and education. He was the first who edited and printed a newspaper in the state of N. C.; then studied law and was distinguished as a lawyer; he afterwards went to New Orleans, became one of the supreme Judges in that state, and died very rich, at an advanced age.*

The success of Mr. Martin impressed my brother with the idea that even being a foreigner could not be an unsurmountable obstacle in the profession of the law. It was the most honorable in the country, might be more lucrative to a well qualified man, and certainly was not subject to such dangers. Determined to study law, he put himself under the guidance of James Iredell, an Irishman then at the head of the bar in N. C, who became an Associate Judge on the bench of the Supreme Court of the United States, after the election of Gen. Washington to the Presidency. After obtaining a license, John began the practice of law in all the Courts of the Counties within his reach. His talents as a lawyer were solid, but not shining. He had no claim to great oratory and as a speaker he stood inferior to many others, but this was compensated by clearness of ideas, strength of judgment, a considerable law knowledge and the greatest integrity and honesty, qualities not always adorning the profession of the law. His rectitude in private life and as an attorney was so well acknowledged that he had the honorable nick-name, wherever he was known, of "The Honest Lawyer." In a few years, having obtained independence and competency, he purchased a plantation in Martin Co. and married his first wife, Jamina Maule, on Sept. 28, 1788. She was a younger sister of Psalmet's wife and very handsome; died Aug. 15, 1793, leaving one son, William.

John m. again Sept. 28, 1794, Frances Gray,52 dau. of Wm. Gray and Frances Lee, of Bertie Co., N. C. She was a woman of remarkably strong character and good sense, after the death of her husband, managing her estate, and educating her children to be ornaments to society, as well as useful citizens. "He was endowed by nature with a strong body and excellent constitution, but owing to the unhealthiness of the climate in which he lived and his traveling in all kinds of weather to his courts, his health became impaired at an early age, and in the fall of the year 1810 he had a stroke of Palsy, from which he died Nov. 4, at 51 years of age." His widow died Oct. 11, 1825.

Slave History: John Gregoire Roulhac and Jamina Maule

In 1788, when John Gregoire Roulhac married Jamina Maule, she owned more than 220 acres of land in Beaufort County, 220 acres in Pitt County and six Negro slaves - Pegg, Tony, Little Ben, Little Hannah, Rose and Kate – whom she inherited from her father John Maule when he died in 1774.

In May 1793, John Gregoire Roulhac, of Martin County, North Carolina, entered into a contract in Bertie County to buy two slaves, Titus and Simon.

Bill of Sale

North Carolina
Bertie County

Know all men by these presents that I Whitmell Hill of the County & State aforesaid for and in consideration of the sum of one hundred and forty pounds legal currency to me in hand paid by John Roulhac of Martin County & State aforesaid have this day bargained & sold in open marked delivered unto the said John Roulhac two Negro boys, viz, Titus and Simon ... In witness whereof I have hereunto set my hand and seal this 2nd day of May 1793...

Showing how slavery improves the condition of the female sex.

Selling a Mother from her Child.

Selling a Mother From Her Child, includes the following text: " 'Do you often buy the wife without the husband?' 'Yes, very often; and frequently, too, they sell me the mother while they keep her children. I have often known them take away the infant from its mother's breast, and keep it, while they sold her.' Prof. Andrews, late of University of N.C. in his recent work on *Slavery and the Slave Trade*, p. 47, relates the foregoing conservation with a slave-trader on the Potomac." Circa 1840, Library of Congress, Courtesy Dale Rich Collection.

John Gregoire Roulhac's marriage to Jamina Maule lasted less than five year. On August 19, 1793, six weeks before John's brother Francis migrated to North Carolina, Jamina Maule Roulhac drowned her infant child and herself.

Slave History: John Gregoire Roulhac and second wife Frances Gray

John Gregoire Roulhac's second wife Frances Gray, like his first, descended from a wealthy family of slave owners. Her father William

Gray, Sr., was a founder of Windsor, Bertie County, North Carolina and a Bertie County justice of the peace.[53] According to the 1790 U.S. Census for Bertie County, NC, he owned 53 slaves. The father of 12 children, he distributed his property as follows:[54]

> I give and bequest to my loving wife the following Negroes to wit: Adam, Eve, Charles, Polison and Sam. A black mare called Poll and a chestnut sorrel mare called Len, three horses, small horse, Indian and sparrow, six cows and calves, one yoke of oxen, four steers, thirty head of hogs, four sows and pigs, all my sheep, all my kitchen furniture, three feather beds and furniture, half a dozen maple chairs, all my tables, one mahogany desk and book case, all my knives and forks, plates spoons, and table linen to her and her heirs and assigns forever and the use of any one of my plantations during her natural life.
>
> To my son, Steven Gray - one Negro man named Ned which he has had in his possession some years past, small piece of land and one feather bed and furniture.
>
> To my daughter, Ann Blount - one Negro girl called Silvia which she has had in her possession.
>
> To my daughter, Elizabeth Bryan - one Negro woman named Ester which she has had in her possession.
>
> To my son, John Gray - plantation and land called Rosefield.
>
> To my daughter, Frances - one Negro girl named Grace, one feather bed and furniture, one mare called Panthy and a lot in the Town of Windsor.

To my daughter, Jannet - one Negro boy named Jack and a lot in Windsor

To my daughter, Eleanor - one Negro girl named Jude, a lot in the Town of Windsor, mare called Hiller and feather bed and furniture.

To my son, George - plantation and land called the Mill field, Negro boy named Dick, one mare called Venus, feather bed and furniture, and two sows and pigs.

To my daughter, Margaret - Negro girl named Chloe, one Negro boy named Tom, one chestnut filly called Jenny Dismal, one feather bed and furniture.

To my son, William - plantation and land where I am living now, Negro boy named Freeman, feather bed and furniture.

To my daughter, Penelope - one Negro girl named Hannah, one Negro boy named Peter, bed and furniture.

To my daughter, Polly - one Negro boy named John, one Negro girl named Rachel, feather bed and furniture.

The will was probated August 1801.

By 1800, eighteen years after arriving in America, John Gregoire Roulhac was living in Martin County, North Carolina with 22 slaves. His wife, Frances Gray Roulhac died October 11, 1825. She specified in her March 1822 last will and testament her "wish that should it be necessary to sell my land and Negroes, that my children should be the purchasers. As my Negro woman Vainey has been a faithful servant, I wish her and her children to remain in the family until she should prefer to live with some other person; in that case I wish her to her choice."

2nd Generation: Issue of John Gregoire Roulhac and Jamina Maule Roulhac

2.1 William Maule, *b. July 23, 1789, in Martin County, N.C. He settled on a plantation in Ga., but went back to N.C. on a visit where he d. May 17, 1819, aged 26 [Sic].*

Slave History: William Maule Roulhac

In 1810, according to the U. S. Federal Census for Martin County, North Carolina, 21-year-old William Maule Roulhac owned 39 slaves. In 1814, he inherited two additional Negroes, Dempsey and Adam, from his first cousin John Maule Roulhac who died that year of a self-inflicted gunshot wound to his head.

Five years later, as reported in the Edenton Gazette, William Maule Roulhac also committed suicide.

Edenton Gazette, *June 15, 1819*

> SUICIDE -- It is seldom we have to record a more cruel and premeditated murder than that which it is our painful task this day to lay before our readers in the death of MR. WILLIAM ROULHAC, a native of Martin County.
>
> MR. ROULHAC, on the morning of Thursday last, rode out of the town of Plymouth, where he had been for two or three days on a visit, and returning soon after, turned his horse loose in the street, and then, as it is supposed, walked a short distance out of town, where he committed the horrid act of putting a period to his existence by stabbing and shooting

himself in the most barbarous and shocking manner. Being missed, and fearing some accident had befallen him, diligent search was made, but without success. On the Tuesday morning following, however, he was found by means of a number of buzzards flying over the spot where the unfortunate victim lay. He was shot through the heart, his right jaw shot nearly off, several stabs in his left side, and his throat entirely cut across. He presented to beholders an awful spectacle indeed! What led to this rash, unpardonable act, his friends are at a loss to conjecture, MR. ROULHAC, who was in the prime of his life, was of very respectable connections and much esteemed as a pleasing and sociable companion.

Edenton Gazette, June 21, 1819

WILLIAM ROULHAC was the eldest son of JOHN ROULHAC, ESQ., deceased, of Martin County. He was educated at Chapel Hill; served as a Captain in the detachment of troops from North Carolina in the late war [War of 1812] at Norfolk; and at the last session of the Legislature represented his native county in the House of Commons. Since his arrival at the age of maturity, his attention has been devoted partly to merchandizing but principally to agricultural pursuits and to his fishery. In all his transactions in society, he has ever been esteemed as a gentleman of the strictest integrity and honor. He was an affectionate son and brother. But unfortunately, he was of a temperament of mind, which, while it gave him the highest relish for the enjoyment of prosperity, it totally incapacitated him for sustaining, with composure or fortitude, the slightest shock or real or imaginary adversity.

On the morning of Thursday, the 27th ult., he arrived in Plymouth from Fairfield's, the family residence, about three miles from town, and stopped, as usual, at the house of his relative, MR. HORACE ELY. No servant being at hand, he stripped his horse and turned it loose. He entered the house, apparently very uneasy and distressed. Declining a chair he observed that he would "take a walk." It is probable that, very shortly afterwards, he walked out of town, and took a path into the woods; which, pursued a few hundred yards led him to a large pine in a very secluded situation, where he completed the dreadful work of self-destruction.[55]

Issue of John Gregoire Roulhac and 2nd Wife, Frances Lee Gray Roulhac

3.2. Joseph Blount Gregoire*, (7) b. Aug. 12, 1795, at "Fairfields," Martin Co., N. C. After graduating at Chapel Hill in 1811, at the early age of 16, he studied law, but never practiced it. Being a man of very active, practical character, he turned his attention to mercantile life and with slight intermission followed it till his death. He was m. Nov. 24, 1836, by Rev. Samuel Johnston to Catherine Ruffin, eldest daughter of Chief Justice Thomas Ruffin and Annie M. Kirkland. She was b. Nov. 12, 1810, at "Ayrmount," near Hillsboro, N. C. "She was an honor to her husband, beloved by all who knew her, and her children rose up to call her blessed." "He was a man of strong, vigorous and common-sense intellect. He was fond of books, had stored his mind with varied knowledge, and there were few subjects in which he did not converse with fluency. He was remarkable for his sound judgment and keen appreciation of character, and as a business man he was a model for young men to study. His house was the home of hospitality and domestic comfort. He was ever forward in schemes of public improvement, and enterprise, and never withheld his contribution for the relief of human suffering. In 1835 he was elected one of the delegates from his County to revise the State Constitution. He was* *strongly attached to the Episcopal Church, but entirely free from sectarian bitterness and intolerance, an ideal Christian gentle man." He d. in Raleigh, N. C, Jan. 23, 1856, at the age of 60. His widow d. at Hillsboro, April 30, 1881.*

Slave History: Chief Justice ThomThomas Ruffin, Joseph B.G. Roulhac's father-in-law, was a North Carolina. Supreme Court Justice from 1829 to 1852, Chief Justice from 1833 to 1852 and Justice again from 1858 to 1859. In 1829, in his first year on the Supreme Court, he wrote the decision *State v Mann*.[56] The decision became one of the most-studied and notorious in the history of slave law. The defendant, John Mann, for a minor offense, whipped Lydia, a slave he had been renting. While Lydia was attempting to escape, Mann shot and gravely wounded her. Mann was convicted of assault and battery. On appeal, he claimed the assault on a slave by her master could not be indictable since a slave was the master's property. In rejecting the slave's right to seek judicial relief, Justice Ruffin wrote that a slave was to "labor upon a principle of natural duty," and disregard "his own personal happiness," because the legal system was designed to convince each slave that he had,

> no will of his own [and the he must surrender] his will in implicit obedience to that of another. Such obedience is the consequence only of uncontrolled authority over the body. There is nothing else that we can operate to produce the effect. The power of the master must be absolute to render the submission of the slave perfect.[57]

By 1850, Justice Thomas Ruffin was one of Alamance County's largest slave owners. Between 1850 and 1860, the number of persons he enslaved increased from 59 to 69.[58] A statue honoring Judge Ruffin stands in the foyer of the North Carolina State Court of Appeals, his portrait hangs on the walls of the law school at the University of North Carolina and a dormitory bears his name.[59]

Slave History: Joseph B. G. Roulhac and Catherine Ruffin

In 1820, in addition to owing eight slaves, Joseph B.G. Roulhac's household included a free Negro.[60] On November 14, 1831, at a sheriff's sale, Joseph B. G. Roulhac bought a number of Negro slaves - Milly, Ned, Nelly, ____, Bick, Penny, Joe, Cato, Quammie, Gabe, ____ & Dinah - owned by Horace Ely subject to a trust created by a marriage contract between Horace Ely and his wife, Mary Jane Roulhac Ely.[61]

By 1850, Joseph B.G. Roulhac was living in Raleigh, Wake County, North Carolina, and owned 15 slaves.[62] Eighty-seven years later, while providing a first-person account of slavery, 84-year-old former Wake County slave Sam T. Stewart remembered Joseph B.G. Roulhac as a slave speculator in the following narrative:

> "My name is Sam T. Stewart. I was born in Wake County, North Carolina Dec. 11, 1853. My father was a slave, A. H. Stewart, belonging to James Arch Stewart, a slave owner, whose plantation was in Wake County near what is now the Harnett County line of Southern Wake. Teresa was my mother's name. James Arch Stewart, a preacher, raised my father, but my mother was raised by Lorenzo Franks, a Quaker in Wake County. When I was two-years-old James Arch Stewart sold my father to speculators, and he was shipped to Mississippi. I was too young to know my father.
>
> "The names of the speculators were - Carter Harrison, and - a man named Roulhac. I never saw my father again, but I heard from him the second year of the surrender, through his brother and my aunt. My father died in Mississippi.
>
> "The speculators bought up Negroes as a drover [a person who drives animals] would buy up mules. They

would get them together by 'Negro drivers', as the white men employed by the speculators were called. Their names were - Jim Harris of Raleigh, and - yes, Dred Thomas, who lived near Holly Springs in Wake County. Wagon trains carried the rations on the trip to Mississippi. The drivers would not start until they had a large drove. Then the slaves were fastened together with chains. The chain was run between them, when they had been lined up like soldiers in double file. A small chain was attached to a Negro on the left and one to the Negro on the right and fastened to the main chain in the center. Ailly Askew was another speculator. He lived on the corner of Salisbury and Carbarrus Street in Raleigh. Sometimes as many as thirty slaves were carried in a drove. They walked to Mississippi."[63]

In the 1850 U.S. Census for Hind County, Mississippi, Carter Harrison, a North Carolina native, is listed as a 33-year-old planter, with real estate valued at $10,000 living with John Moore, a 25-year-old overseer.

Joseph B. G. Roulhac died in Raleigh, Wake County, North Carolina, on January 23, 1856. By 1860, his widow, Catherine Ruffin Roulhac, had relocated to her hometown, Hillsboro, Orange County, NC.[64]

Chapter 2

UNITED STATES SLAVE TRADE.
1830

Internal U.S. Slave Trade, Ca. 1830. James K. Pauling, the Secretary of the Navy, in Letters From the South, says he heard a slave trader say: "Many is the time I have separated wives from husbands, and husbands from wives, and parents from children; but then I made amends by marrying them again as soon as I had the chance; that is to say, I made them call each other man and wife, and sleep together, which is quite enough for Negroes." Courtesy Library of Congress.

In 1865, after the Civil War and freedom, the status of many former slaves was little changed. Uneducated, many remained on the same plantation and entered into labor contracts. On November 1, 1865, Catherine Roulhac and Caesar Mills, pictured on this book's cover, executed the following contract:

> Articles of agreement made this 1st day of Nov 1865 between Catherine Roulhac of the one part and Caesar Mills on the other part –
>
> Caesar Mills on his part agrees to serve said Catherine Roulhac from Jan 1st 1866 to Jan 1st 1867 and to make himself as useful and serviceable as possible in that capacity. He agrees to cultivate land for use of the family, to cultivate the gardens & the adjourning field and to keep the front yard with its flowers & borders and to attend to the cows and pigs and to do all other

duties which would naturally devolve in a servant in his position. He agrees to furnish his own clothing & medicines & medical attention when sick & to forfeit his wages during periods of sickness.

Catherine Roulhac on her part agrees to pay to said Caesar wages at rate of four dollars per month, and one half of all the produce he may raise in the garden and in the adjourning field, to give him half of the value of cows & pigs and to supply him with rations consisting of meat & vegetable from her own table. It is further agreed that she is to pay only one half of the monthly wage at the end of each month – and on January 1st 1867 to pay the whole balance that may then be due.

By 1870, five years after slavery ended, the value of Catherine's Roulhac's property had decreased substantially. Two servants, Elsey and Lizzie Cameron, lived with her in Hillsboro.[65]

*4.3 **John Gray**, (14), b. Jan. 28, 1797, at the "Fairfields," Martin Co., N.C.; graduated at the University of N. C., Chapel Hill, at the age of 14. He was not endowed with brilliant gifts, but was possessed of a clear head and well-balanced judgment. He had learning, industry, patience and remarkable equanimity, and to these qualities he added spotless integrity, set off by the graces of urbanity and high-toned courtesy; had slaves and farmed successfully in N. C. and Fla., where he moved in 1846. He m. Martha Rascoe, the daughter of Peter and Ann Rascoe, b. Aug. 5, 1800, in Bertie, N.C. She d. Oct 22, 1855, near Marianna, Fla. He d. June 16, 1858.*

Slave History: John Gray Roulhac and Martha Rascoe

Peter Rascoe, John Gray Roulhac's father-in-law, owned 30 slaves in Bertie County, North Carolina in 1810.[66] In 1820, John Gray Roulhac, 23 years old, owned 23 slaves in Bertie County, North Carolina.

[67] He is enumerated in the 1840 Federal Censuses in Bertie County, where he owned seven slaves,[68] and in territorial Jackson County, Florida.[69]

John G. Roulhac voted in Florida's first statewide election in 1845. By 1850, ten years after arriving in Jackson County, he had become the County's fifth largest slave owner.[70] He owned a 1,750-acre plantation with 87 slaves, supervised by two overseers, cultivating 850 acres.[71] The slaves were almost evenly divided between males and females – 41 males and 47 females. Only 11 were over 40 years old – six men and five women. Seventeen females were between 12 and 30. Eighteen males were between 16 and 34, including a 30 year-old mulatto. Seven boys and 23 girls were under 12 years old.

Between September 1852 and July 1857, John G. Roulhac was granted an interest in eight Jackson County land patents consisting of 720 acres.[72] When John Gray died June 16, 1858, he owned 37 slaves. In his last will, he loaned three-fourth of his estate to his children Joseph B, Clara and Frances Roulhac during their lives and upon their deaths to their children. The remaining one-fourth was loaned to his executors to benefit Peter, his oldest son, John Gray Roulhac, Jr.'s, child. In his January 14, 1858 last will, he bequeathed his slaves to his daughters Clara and Frances Roulhac, his son Joseph B. Roulhac and his grandson Peter Roulhac. John G. Roulhac's last will also provided:

> Fifth: It is my will that if there be at the time of my death any Negroes in the possession of any of my children which I may have loaned them during my life that the said Negroes then be allotted to them in the division of my Negroes and that as I have not yet loaned any to my daughter Clara there be allotted to her my Negro woman commonly called Cora and her children, the Negroes mentioned in this clause to be held as provided for in the forgoing clause of this will.

On July 9, 1858, John Gray Roulhac estate was appraised. His slaves accounted for $24,323.38 of his $28,976.30 estate. John Gray Roulhac's estate included the only antebellum record of my paternal great-great grandparents, Nero and Nelly Roulhac, and 10-year-old Fayton, my paternal great-grand father.

Appraisement of the Estate of John Gray Roul

Name	Age	Value
Will	36	850.00
Haywood	20	1116
Ned	58	383.00
George	18	1000.00
Charlotte	26	1000.00
Milley	38	633.00
Bill	20	1100.00
Julia/son Ben	21/9 mos.	1000.00
Edy	58	433.33
Nero	52	700.00
Nelly	46	700.00
Fayton	10	600.00
Peter	9	550.00
Robert	7	458.33
Angelina	12	583.33
Chatty/son Isom	19/2 mos.	1116.66
Teresa	30	66.66
Eliza	11	600.00
Maria/dau. Carolina	18/18 mos.	1033.00
Harriett	22	850.00
Cora/son Henry	30/18 mos.	1116.66
Bob	83	166.00
Ann	17	850.00

Name	Age	Value
Isabel	65	500.00
Maria	13	591.66
Beck	7	383.33
Francis	8	425.00
Edney	15	741.66
Moses	15	683.33
Tibby	10	575.00
Daniel	4	300.00
Guss??	12	491.66
Wrighten	35	950.00
Lien?	8	366.66
Total	37	**$24,323.38**

5.4. Frances Lee, b. April 16, 1799; never m.; was educated at St. Mary's, Raleigh, where she always received the highest encomiums for scholarship and deportment. After her youth, her life was spent in doing good, often at the bed of the sick, and ministering to them. She was her mother's chief attendant and nurse in her latter days. It was said by her friends that "she belonged to her **Negroes**." One of her nieces has written — "I feel if there was no one else of the name to be proud of, I should be grateful for being so nearly related to one, who so constantly and entirely acted from Christian principles — a noble heritage to any family." She d. Jan. 14, 1880.

Slave History: Frances Lee Roulhac

In 1860, Frances Lee Roulhac, 61 years old, also known as Fannie, was living in Edenton, Chowan County, North Carolina.[74] She enslaved 48 Negroes in Bertie County, North Carolina.[75]

Several slaves owned by Fannie Roulhac escaped and joined the U.S. Colored Troops. Brothers, 23-year-old David Rolack and

25-year-old Joseph Rolacke joined the 2nd North Carolina Colored Volunteers (later designated as the 36th U.S Colored Troops) at Plymouth, North Carolina on July 13, 1863. In a pension application to receive benefits based on David's service in the Union Army, their mother, Mary Roulhac stated that in 1863, they did not know they had been freed. She reported that their mistress, Fanny Roulhac, hired David out to work for John Phelps and she continued receiving his earnings. Lewis Rolack, who joined the 3rd North Carolina Colored Volunteers (later designated as the 37th U.S. Colored Troops), stated in his pension application that Fannie Roulhac had enslaved him. It is likely that Fannie Roulhac enslaved all nine Roulhacs who were living in North Carolina when they enlisted in the Civil War. She was the only Roulhac slave owner in Northeastern North Carolina in the 1860s.

Jane Roulhac, David and Joseph Rolacke's sister, who was also enslaved by Fannie Roulhac, immigrated to Liberia with her children – 10-year-old Henrietta and four-year-old Nero – in 1869.

Third Generation: Issue of Joseph B. G. Roulhac and Catherine Ruffin

8.2 Frances Gray, (1) b. Aug. 5, 1839, at the residence of NC Supreme Court Justice Thomas Ruffin, Orange Co., North Carolina, m. Dec. 8 1859 in Hillsboro, N.C., Daniel Heyward Hamilton, the eldest son of Daniel Heyward Hamilton and Rebecca Mob Middleton, b. in Charleston S. C. March 10, 1838. They live in Hillsboro, N. C. He entered the C.S.A. in May 1861, a Major of the 3rd Regt. of N.C. Volunteers; served afterwards upon the staff of Gen'l R. S. Ripley and while Adjt. of 1st S.C. Regt., was wounded in the foot and disabled, but served in a post position until the war ended.

11.5 Thomas Ruffin, (22) b. Nov. 8, 1846, in Raleigh, N.C. When the civil war began he was taken from the military school in Hillsboro and although only 14-years-old, was given a commission as drillmaster of the

N.C. troops, and assigned to the famous 6th Fisher's Reg; after that to 7th, and the 29th R. B. Vances' Reg. With the latter, he remained in East Tenn. till the spring of 1862, when his mother insisted upon his returning to school where he remained about nine months, then entered the service as a private the Ramseuer's Artillery. With that battery, under Capt. Basil S. Manly, he participated in the battles of Chancellorsville, Union Church, Winchester, Gettysburg and the subsequent battles of that year 1863. In Oct. 1863, he was appointed Sergeant Major of the 29th, Ramseur's old Regt. After also serving as Adjt. of the Regt. he was made 1st Lieut, of Co. D., participating in the battles of Drewry's Bluff, Bermuda Hundreds, Plymouth and Newborne, N. C. in the siege of Petersburg and on the Weldon, R. R. Aug. 16, 1864, was slightly wounded; made Capt. in front of Richmond, and commanded the sharp-shooters of M. W. Ramseur's Brigade at Fort Steadman, (or Hares Hill) Dinwiddie Court House, and at Five Forks was captured and taken to Johnson's Island, from where he was released after the close of the war. He m. Dec. 29, 1870, in Greensboro, Ala., Julia Erwin Jones, daughter of Allen Cadwallader and Kate Erwin Jones, b. June 2, 1846, in Greensboro, Ala. They now live in Sheffield, Alabama.

Slave History: Thomas Ruffin Roulhac

In Randall C. Jimerson's 1994 book, "*The Private Civil War: Popular Thought During the Sectional Conflict,*" is the following account of Thomas Ruffin Roulhac's recollection of his unit's slaughter of black troops during the spring 1863 Battle of Suffolk, Virginia:

> "We took Suffolk a few days ago & got into a fight with a Negro Regiment, several of them were killed, several taken prisoner & afterwards eight bayoneted or burnt, he reported; "the men were perfectly exasperated at the idea of Negroes opposed to them & rushed at them like so many devils." Despite his testimony that his comrades had fought more fiercely than usual, Roulhac concluded that "the Negroes could not stand the music of bullets & their presence in the army would prove more of an incumbrance than otherwise."[76]

THE FORT PILLOW MASSACRE
April 12, 1864

The April 30, 1864, issue of Harper Weekly, the most widely circulated magazine during the Civil War, reported on the April 12, 1864 Fort Pillow Massacre at Jackson, Tennessee as follows: "Out of a garrison of six hundred, only two hundred remained alive. Three hundred of those massacred were Negroes; five were burned alive." Library of Congress, Courtesy Dale Rich.

In 1870, Thomas Roulhac moved to Greensboro, Alabama to practice law and in 1899, relocated to Sheffield, Alabama as attorney for Sheffield Land Company. He served as state circuit judge from 1894-1898. In 1902, Republican President Theodore Roosevelt appointed Thomas Roulhac United States Attorney for the Northern District of Alabama. The appointment was opposed by Booker T. Washington, the president of Tuskegee Institute and a chief advisor to President Roosevelt in making appointments to federal offices in Southern states. Although Washington viewed Thomas Roulhac's appointment as a "slap to lily white elements in Alabama," he maintained there was no evidence of Thomas Roulhac's racial liberalism to strengthen the claims that his appointment would improve federal service in the South. Washington Booker T. Washington also opposed Thomas Roulhac's subsequent appointment as federal district judge for the middle district of Alabama. In an October 1,

1901, letter to Attorney General Philander Chase Knox, Washington wrote:

> From the best information I can get, Thomas R. Roulack [sic] is a Gold Standard Democrat. He is a man of high standing in his community and is well respected in the state. He lives outside of district where vacancy exists. Governor [Thomas Goode] Jones is much better known throughout the state and has stood up bravely for education of all people and against lynch laws and justice to the Negro. It is my opinion that Jones has better qualifications than Roulack. Jones lives in Middle District where vacancy exists.

The next day, Booker T. Washington sent a letter to President Roosevelt supporting Governor Jones' appointment.[77]

Issue of John Gray Roulhac (4) and Martha Rascoe

14.1 John Gray, Jr., (31) b. in N.C., Jan. 26 1823; m. Feb. 28, 1849, Ann E. Robinson, b. May 7, 1829, dau. of Jacob and Jane Robinson. They lived in Marianna, Fla., where he d. Oct. 21, 1857. She m. afterwards Dr. Wilson.

Slave History: John Gray Roulhac, Jr. and Ann E. Robinson

In 1850, John G. Roulhac, Jr., owned two slaves, a 30-year-old male and a six-year-old female, in Jackson County, Florida.[78] On December 30, 1857, two months after he died, the slaves in his estate were appraised as follows: woman Crafty and boy John, $1,000; woman Margaret, $700; girl Laura, $600; man Thomas, $1,200; woman Maria and children Jina and Fanny, $1,400; Flora and child, $1,150; Ann and child, $1,150 and boy Billy, $950.[79]

On December 31, 1857, Attorney John Milton filed a petition in the Jackson County Circuit Court on behalf of Ann E. Roulhac to divide proceeds from sale of the following slaves: John; Margaret; Laura; Thomas; Maria and children, Jina and Fanny; Flora and child; Ann and child, Frances, Jim, Henry and Billy.[80] The same day, the Court issued the following order:[81]

> In conformance with a decree of judge of probate of Jackson County made this day upon petition of Anne E. Roulhac, widow of John G. Roulhac, Jr., you are commanded and requested to summons "five" discreet free holders of your county as commissioners connected with the parties neither by affinity nor consanguinity and entirely disinterested who upon oath (which you are authorized to make) shall allot and set off half according to quantity and quality of the following described property as follows: nine hundred and two dollars & sixty-five cents. It being the amount of sales of personal property as sold by the administrators of said John G. Roulhac, Jr. and is in lieu thereof. Also the following slaves, Crafty, John, Margaret, Laura, Thomas, Maria & Children, Jim and Fanny, Flora & children, Ann & Child, Frances, Jim, Henry & Billy.

Four months later, the five commissioners - R. L. Smith, William Powers, William Nickels, Eli P. Moore and Thomas M. White - filed the following report:[82]

> We the undersigned commissioners summoned and sworn to a lot and set-off to Mrs. Ann E. Roulhac, her dower: Negroes Crafty, John, Margaret, Laura and Ann & Child Edy and the amount of two hundred dollars.

15.2 Joseph Blount Gregoire, *(32) b. in N. C. March 13, 1825; was m. July 31, 1850, in Talbot Co., Ga., by Rev. Thomas B. Slade, to Martha Hines Dixon, b. Feb. 3, 1833, daughter of Robert E. Dixon and Martha Marshall. They lived in Marianna, Fla., where he practiced law, and at* one time represented his Co. in the State Legislature. He enlisted in the C. S. A. at the beginning of the war, and served one year at Apalachicola, then was made lst Lieut, of "Marianna Dragoons," Capt. R. L. Smith; was at home on sick furlough, when the battle of Marianna occurred, Sept. 27, 1864; was captured with many other citizens, and after being imprisoned in several wayside prisons, was placed in Elmira, N. Y., where he was so poorly fed that he died from emaciation a few weeks after reaching home, on June 5, 1865. His widow m. Dec. 3, 1869, Col. J. F. McClellan.

Slave History: Joseph Blount Gregoire Roulhac and Martha Hines Dixon

Joseph B.G. Roulhac and Martha Hines Dixon marriage brought together two large slave owning families. As noted above, in 1850, John Gray Roulhac, Joseph's father, owned 87 slaves, making him the fifth largest slave trader in Jackson County. In Talbot County, Georgia, Martha's father, Robert Dixon owned 111 slaves[83] and real estate valued at $16,000.[84] Joseph owned 54 slaves in Jackson County, Florida, in 1850.[85]

16.3. Frances Lee Gray, (37), b. in N.C. Nov. 18, 1828; m. Dec 8, 1849, William E. Anderson, of Pulaski, Tenn., son of Samuel and Margaret Anderson. He was a fine lawyer and d. in the prime of life, leaving a widow and three children. She d. Feb. 16, 1860. They lived in Marianna, Fla.

Slave History: Frances Lee Gray Roulhac and William E. Anderson

In 1850, Frances Gray Anderson, age 20, and her new husband, lawyer William E. Anderson, age 30, were living with Horace Ely in his hotel. On August 3, 1860, when the 1860 Federal census was taken, William E. Anderson, a widower, was living with his three children – Ida, six, Warren, four and Clara, two and his deceased wife's sister, Clara Roulhac Holden and her husband, Dr. Julius Thomas Holden. Anderson estimated that he owned real estate and personal property valued at $6,000 and $26,500, respectively.[86] According to the 1860 Slave Schedule for Jackson County, Florida, William Anderson owned 20 slaves - 15 females and five males, living in four slave houses.[87]

At age 41, William E. Anderson was a brigadier general in the Florida Militia. He led the First Brigade during the little-known Calhoun County Abolition War of September-October 1860. During the battle, 27 citizens were taken prisoner. Captured during the Battle of Marianna, William E. Anderson identified himself as a "brigadier general" and was imprisoned with other officers at New Orleans, Fort Lafayette and Fort Warren. He was released June 26, 1865, after signing an affidavit denying that he was ever a brigadier general in the Confederate State of America.[88]

In 1870, William E. Anderson was living in Jackson County, Florida, with his wife Rachael, age 46, and five children – Ida, 16; Warren, 13; Clara, 11; Patton seven and Decatur, four. With the end of the Civil War and the freedom of those he had enslaved, his wealth was substantially reduced. He owned $1,000 in real estate and only $3,000 in personal property, $23,500 less than in 1860.[89]

17.4 Clara Winnefred Rascoe, (40) b. in N.C. April 13, 1835; m. Sept. 22, 1859, in Marianna, Fla., Dr. Julius Thomas Holden, b. Feb. 23, 1834, son of Thos. L. and C.A. Holden. He entered the C.S.A. and served throughout the war as Brigade Surgeon of Finley's Brigade of Florida Troops. They live in Marianna, Florida.

Slave History: Clara Winnefred Rascoe Roulhac and Dr. Julius Thomas Holden

In 1860, Clara W. Holden and her husband, Dr. J. Thomas Holden, a North Carolina native, were living with her brother-in-law, William E. Anderson, a widower, and his three children. Dr. Holden owned personal property valued at $6,000 and real estate valued at

$23,000.[90] He also owned 18 slaves.[91] The home, now known as the Holden House, was built in about 1850. It is located on Lafayette Street, across the street from St. Luke Episcopal Church where the heaviest fighting took place during the September 27, 1864 Battle of Marianna. A closet door inside the home still bears marks inflicted by the sword of a Union soldier during the battle.

4th Generation: Issue of Frances G. Roulhac (8) and D. H. Hamilton

21.4 Joseph Gregoire Roulhac, *b. Aug. 6, 1878.*

History: Joseph Gregoire Roulhac Hamilton

In 1906, Joseph Gregoire Roulhac Hamilton was appointed associate professor of history at the University of North Carolina. He became head of the History Department in 1908. He resigned in 1930 to devote his attention to the Southern Historical Collection, of which he became founder and director. With its wide-ranging holding, the Collection, located at the University of North Carolina at Chapel Hill, is noted for documenting the culture and history of the American South. According to George Stevenson, a Private Manuscripts Archivist at the North Carolina State Archives, with whom I corresponded in February 1993, Joseph Gregoire de Roulhac Hamilton, "was one of the greatest collectors of private manuscripts in the south – so much so that he is, in the "trade" of the archival world, nicknamed "Ransack" Hamilton." The Roulhac-Ruffin papers are located in the Southern Historical Collection.

Issue of Joseph B.G. Roulhac (15) and Martha . Dixon

33.2. Jeanne Marguerite, (45) b. Aug. 14, 1854, in Marianna, Fla.; m. Dec. 14, 1876, at Marianna, Beverly Baker, son of Simmons Jones Baker and Lizzie Hawkins. He was b. near Marianna, Fla., March 7, 1842. They live in Itasca, Tex. He entered the C. S. A. when a student as a Sergeant in 1st Fla. Regt. Vol., March 1861. His time expiring, he joined the Marianna Dragoons, which Co. served one year in Mobile as bodyguard to Gen'l S. B. Buckner, then went into the 15th Con. Cav. He was wounded on Santa Rosa Island, Oct. 1, 1861, and captured near Mt. Pleasant, on Ala. River April 9, 1865.

Slave History: Jeanne Marguerite Roulhac and Beverly Baker

In 1860, Beverly Baker was an 18-year-old student living with his parents in Calhoun County, Florida. His father, Simmons J. Baker, a North Carolina native owned 53 slaves.[92] His real estate was valued at $17,000 and other personal property valued at $30,000.[93]

***36.5. Frances Lee**, (56) b. Oct. 30, 1861, at Marianna, Fla.; m. Aug. 27, 1889, Gen. Stephen A. Moreno,[94] of Pensacola, Fla., b. April 15, 1839, son of Francisco Moreno and Margarita E. Lopez, both b. in Pensacola. They now live in Pensacola, Fla. He went to the U. S. Military Academy, at West Point, in 1858, but on the secession of Fla. he resigned his cadetship, and entered the C. S. A. as a 2nd Lieut, being assigned to duty as Instructor of Artillery at Ft. Barrancas. During 1861 he was on the staffs of Brig. Genl. W. H. T. Walker, Ruggles, and A. H. Gladden, taking part in the bombardments of the Forts at Pensacola Harbor, and receiving honorable mention in Genl. Gladden's report of the fight. In Feb. 1862 he accompanied Brig. Genl. John K. Jackson to Corinth, Miss., and on his staff took part in the battle of Shiloh. In the fight at Farmington, he acted under Genl. Bragg's order, as Major of the 17th Ala. Infantry, and during that fight commanded the Regt. On Jackson's staff he was in Bragg's Ky. Campaign, at the battle of Murfreesboro, the siege of Chattanooga, the battle of Chickamauga, Lookout Mountain, Missionary Ridge, the retreat to Dalton and Johnson's campaign, down as far as the New Smyrna Church line, between Marietta and Atlanta. He was promoted at Murfreesboro to Capt. and Asst. Adjt. Genl. of Jackson's Brigade. From the new Smyrna Line he was ordered with Jackson to Lake City, Fla., and with him was at the siege of Savannah. Being transferred as Asst. Adjt. Genl. to Col. G R Harrison's Brigade, he was at the surrender at Greensboro, N. C., April 1865.*

Chapter 3
Francis Leonard Gregoire de Roulhac

*Bond servants ought to be treated with kindness and humanity
as they are not brutes, but fellow creatures.*

First Generation: Francis Leonard Gregoire de Roulhac

Francis Leonard Gregoire de Roulhac, the author of the *Genealogical Memoir of the Roulhac Family in America*, was born in 1767 in Limoges, France. In 1887, with an advance on his inheritance, Francis left France for St. Domingo (Haiti) on the Island of Hispanola where he invested and became an overseer of a coffee plantation for a fellow Frenchman, from Limoges. Francis described his arrival in St. Domingo and his first contact with Africans:

> *I fount that M. Guybert was living as a place called Salines, fifteen or twenty miles by water from St. Marks. I hasten to forward to him the letters of his brother, which I had with me. The next day he [M. Guybert] dispatched a large boat with five Negro men, to bring me to his house. I must confess, that finding myself alone with five stout Negro men, half naked, who were rowing me out to sea, was not pleasing. Their features unusual to me, their color contrasted with their white teeth, their laughs, everything was disagreeably new to me, as well as their Creole jargon. The steersman, who, besides the rudder held in his hand a long whip, to make the four others pull better, was not a pleasing*

sight to a man, who had hardly seen a Negro before. If one touched me, the contact gave me an unconscious feeling.

Initially, Francis Roulhac was in charge of about 20 slaves who were making salt when they were not making bricks and tiles to cover houses. Other slaves were clearing a coffee plantation in the mountains, 40 miles from St. Marks. By the end of the first year, Francis' $250 salary was doubled. Francis relates:

I was at the head of 100 slaves, having under me two or three drivers to keep them at work, although the drivers made a great noise, with their long whips and their continual cry of "go on, keep on," they seldom used them on their miserable companions. Full time was given them to cook and eat, and they never having known any better, seemed satisfied, and were merry.

Most enslaved Africans were first enslaved in the West Indies where they were "seasoned" before being sold to slave traders in the United States.

Within a year the plantation was productive, producing 100 to 200 thousand pounds of coffee that sold for as much as 20 cents per pound. Francis Roulhac envisioned become moving up from overseer to manager of larger estates for Guybert and others who planned to return to France. Francis anticipated that in 10 or 12 years he would become independent and also return to France and *But the French Revolution came. The trumpet, which in Europe had sounded so loud, had reverberated in the French Colonies, and there unfortunately it turned all mad [sic] with the rights of men, as it had done in France. In one night, the extensive plain of Cape Francois, now Cape Haiti in high cultivation* of sugar-cane was set on fire, and the unsuspecting which inhabitants without distinction of age or sex, were by savage slave Africans brutally slaughtered or burned in their houses. In a few days the third and richest part of the Colony was in ashes and ruins. What was to be done for those who had families, but to put them in places of safety in the towns. So M. Guybert carried his wife and children to St. Marks, while he went to join the whites in the North, who vainly endeavored to subdue the revolted slaves. For about six weeks, when I was left alone, with two or three overseers, my next neighbors, we slept in the woods with our guns by us; then we were carried down into a small village, called Veretta, where were our head-quarters, ten miles from our plantation, to secure the inhabitants of that part of the plain, where there were many more slaves than in our mountains. At that place, as sentinel, for some nights, I performed all the military service I have ever seen in my life. When released from this, we were permitted to return home, and see to our own safety, as well as we could. About this time I had a falling out with my head driver, who was a square made, bowlegged, ill-looking surly Ibo African. Our hands were in the fields, when coming towards him, I saw him armed, besides his whip, with a large cutlass. I asked him what he wanted to do with it there? He answered impertinently and I jumped upon him, not considering that, had he wished to resist, I was no match for his strength. However, I seized his cutlass and used it, by its flat parts, on his head and back and finding by me some large rocks, with crevices, I took the blade and broke it in several pieces, which I threw away. The next day I heard a great noise at the Negro quarters, and one of the blacks, running to me told me that Azoo, the dread driver, would kill his wife beating her. Seeing me, he ran, but I had him caught and unmercifully flogged by the other drivers, who did not spare him and cut his back in such manner that he was laid up for a fort-night. I have always reproached myself for this act of cruelty, but the circumstances, by which I was surrounded, seemed to demand that he should be made an example of. M. Guybert returned at last, but the insurrection was gaining ground rapidly. What could half a dozen men, surrounded by as many thousand slaves panting for liberty, do, but fly in time somewhere else for safety. We took our passage on board of a large ship, loaded with produce *of the island and fugitives like ourselves. Among them were some pretty young ladies of the first classes in the island. How the tossing in the Atlantic, in a few days, spoiled their roses and lilies!*

Francis Roulhac arrived in Harve de Grace, France just as the French Revolution was beginning and by June 1791, had made his way to Paris. There he found four of his eight brothers – Martin, Joseph, Peter and Charles. Charles was near death from malignant congestive fever. Francis left Paris for Limoges on August 9, 1792, the day before Louis XVI (August 23, 1754 – January 21, 1793), a Bourbon monarch who ruled as the King of France and Navarre until 1791, and King of France from 1791- 1792, fell victim to the insurrection and was arrested and suspended. A month later, the constitutional monarch was abolished and a republic declared, ending more than a 1,000 years of continuous French monarchy. Louis XVI was executed by guillotine January 21, 1793.

The political climate generated by the French Revolution shortened Francis L. G. Roulhac's stay in France. His family was publically known as enemies of the Revolution. Some of Francis' relatives had emigrated to Germany and were serving in the army of the Prince of Conde. His mother and his oldest brother's family were eventually placed under house arrest in Limoges. With no option but to join the army and fight, Francis obtained a forged passport to return to the West Indies to take his chances fighting there rather than in France.

War had just been declared between England and France. I had no other way, than by taking passage of board of a American vessel for the United States and from there to St. Domingo, and in that way, I might visit my brothers, who had been settled in the United States for many years. To get a passport, eight different citizens, of good repute, were to testify to my civilism. Had I applied to decent people, I could never have obtained it. I presented myself to the

> *municipality, accompanied by eight apparent or real "Sans Culotes" who swore I was a good citizen, an inhabitant of St. Domingo, who wanted to return to that Island after a short visit to relations at Limoges. By the by, those good citizens who certified to my patriotism knew nothing of me, except two, one an old servant in the family and my brother's barber. Such were not very dear to purchase.*

When Francis arrived in Paris to obtain passage to America, he found his brother Martin in the St. Pelagie prison where many inmates died at the guillotine. When the ship arrived in Philadelphia after a 96-day voyage, the yellow fever was raging. The ports were filled with French ships that had escaped from St. Domingo after the burning of the Cape, the general insurrection and emancipation of the Africans by the National Convention. Abandoning plans to return to Haiti, Francis found his way to North Carolina where he joined his brothers – Psalmet and John - and studied law. After three years of studying and practicing, Francis recognized that it was easier to obtain a license than to make money. Dissatisfied, Francis abandoned the legal profession studied medicine and established an office in St. Marys, Camden County, Georgia. After curing a Spaniard of dropsy in nearby Florida, he extended his practice there. With the ability of obtain as much land as he wanted with little expense and to support himself, Francis considered becoming a Florida resident.

In 1804, Francis returned to Bertie County, where he married Margaret Gray, Psalmet's sister-in-law and a first cousin of William Blount, Tennessee's territorial governor.

> I was past thirty-seven and my wife was twenty-nine. I had about $1,000 by me. My wife had four Negroes, with a few hundred dollars in money. We must look for a home. To my wife it appeared hard to part with all her friends to go to Florida, which certainly offered the best prospects to us beginners, as we were obliged to

leave North Carolina, she was pleased to have the prospect of accompanying her sister, Mrs. Butler, to Tennessee, where Dr. Butler had promised to give her one hundred acres of land. For her sake I willingly agreed to it, and we left Windsor, May 1, 1805, for the far West, traveling 700 miles in a gig - our black people following in wagons.

By the next spring, Francis' slaves had cleared 15 acres of land in Paradise Ridge and all the houses necessary for his "new establishment." A year or two later, he rented his Robertson County plantation and moved to Montgomery County, Tennessee. He purchased 150 acres of land for 33 cents per acre and a few years later added 200 adjoining acres for $1.00 per acre. He named his plantation Mt. Airy. By 1834, with his wife in bad health, Francis left his Rutherford County plantation to his son George and moved to Lebanon, Wilson County, Tennessee to live with his son-in-law John Hill.

Francis' wife Margaret died in 1846, a few months after they returned to Rutherford County. Francis Gregoire Roulhac died August 23, 1852 at age 85.[95]

Slave History: Dr. Francis L. G. Roulhac (1) and Margaret Gray

In 1820, according to the United States Federal Census for Montgomery County, Tennessee, Francis L. G. Roulhac owned 11 slaves.[96] By 1850, Francis, 83 years old, was living with his daughter Margaret Hill in Rutherford County, Tennessee.

In his will, Francis noted that years before his death in 1852, he had transferred of his interest in a plantation in Montgomery County, TN, to his oldest son George G. Roulhac, who ultimately predeceased him, and two tracts of land in Simpson County, KY to his son Joseph B.G. Roulhac. He bequeathed his plantation in Rutherford County to his son William G. Roulhac (121 acres), daughter Margaret

Roulhac Hill (120 acres), and 134 acres of land to his son-in-law John Hill. Francis bequeathed his personal estate, which included his slaves, in equal shares to his three surviving children and to his deceased son George's children.

Francis did not mention any of those he enslaved by name in his last will. However, with the expectation that sufficient money would not be available when he died to make a charitable donation to the Catholic Hospital, he left the following directions regarding the treatment of his slaves:

> ...servants should be hired out in the vicinity, either privately or publically for one year to raise the amount of said charitable donation so that husband and wife should not be parted, or any sale should be in reach of each other – and my last request to my children is, that they should never forget that bond servants ought to be treated with kindness and humanity as they are not brutes, but fellow creatures.

Second Generation: Issue of Francis L.G. Roulhac and Margaret Gray

4.3. Joseph Psalmet Gregoire, (23) b. Jan. 29, 1810, at "Mont Airy." Montgomery Co., Tenn. He was not fond of school, and at an early age left home for the Western district, where he spent some time working as a rough carpenter. Coming of age and being heartily tired of hard work, he returned home to acquire a profession by which he might live more at ease. After studying medicine he settled in Dresden and opened a drug store. While there, he m. Oct. 14, 1836, Jane Jouette, daughter of Mathias and Martha Flemming Jouette, of Overton Co., Tenn., b. in 1806, her father being of French descent. "She had little property in Negroes or money, but she was everything that a poor man ought to desire, being extremely industrious and a good manager in her family." He moved to Caledonia and, being a well-informed physician, had a good practice, till the death of his wife, May 5, 1847, leaving five children. He then went to reside in Shelby Co. He m. 2nd, Miss Lucy Hawkins, (nee Vaughn) in 1852, by whom he had one child, Lucy, who died in infancy. This wife only lived about two years and he m. again March 10, 1857, Mildred Dupree, of Va. He d. Sept. 8, 1857. His widow was living near Memphis in 1881.

Slave History: Joseph P. G. Roulhac and Jane Jouette

In 1840, Joseph P. G. Roulhac was living in Weakly County, Tennessee. In addition to Joseph, his household included one white female 30-39 years old and two white females, less than five years old. Joseph P. G. Roulhac enslaved three persons - one male less than ten years old, a male 10 to 23 and a female, 10 to 23 years old.

*5.4 **William Gray Gregoire**, (28) b. Sept. 21, 1811, at "Mont Airy," Montgomery Co., Tenn. He fell in love quite early and m. April 10, 1832, Elizabeth L. Hill, who was only sixteen, and a daughter of the local Methodist preacher, John Hill. "However she was careful and industrious, and made him a good wife." They settled on a farm adjoining his father. He interested himself warmly in the politics of the day, and was not very successful as a farmer, but possessed of a clear head and excellent memory, by reading he had acquired a varied knowledge, and could express his ideas with fluency and eloquence. Finally, joining the Christian church, he became a minister of the Gospel and a faithful follower of Christ, devoting the last 25 years of his life to His service. A man of many friends and no enemies, yet of positive character; having the courage of his convictions, which he always presented in such a spirit of love and respect for those who differed with him, that he won the affection of all, and enmity of none, he ranked high among the ministers of his church in the West. About 1845 he moved to West Tenn., and thence to Hickman, Ky., where he d. Feb. 4, 1860, and a few days after, Feb. 9, his beloved wife followed him to the grave.*

Chapter 3

Slave History: William Gray Roulhac and Elizabeth Hill

Elizabeth Hill was one of nine children of John Hill, a former resident of Hillsville, Tennessee. In 1852, several of John Hill's children, including Elizabeth, and her husband William Gray Roulhac, filed a petition in the Haywood County, Tennessee court to divide and sell to the highest bidder slaves owned by John Hill before he died. Judge John Read, issued the following order on November 5, 1852:

> Be it remembered on this 5TH DAY OF NOVEMBER 1852, Before the Honorable JOHN READ, Judge, causes came on for further hearing on the petition of petitioner - pro confesso exhibit on the same and the report of the Clerk - master and it appearing to the Court that JOHN HILL late of Haywood County, deceased, and possessed of the several lands in the petition and exhibits specified and also the following slaves viz, Jordan, Savory, Mosey, Ben, Ira, Rufus, William, Reilly, Fanny, Agia 65 years and Fanny age 18 years & girl child about 18 months old and Sonia, it all appearing that by written agreement duly proved and registered that NANCY HILL, the widow of said JOHN HILL has renounced and conveyed to the Heirs of said JOHN HILL her interest in the said property and particularly in the Negroes Jordan and Savory ... it further appearing that said slaves cannot be equally divided between the several heirs without a sale of the same.
>
> It is therefore ordered, adjudged and decreed by the Court that WILLIAM G. ROULHAC ... sell said Land and slaves ... to the highest bidder and credit of one and two years and that he take with at least two good securities and reserve a lien - purchaser money

- and that he also sell said slaves to the highest bidder on a credit of four months taking with good Security a lien on the slaves for the purchase money...

3rd Generation: Issue of George G. G. Roulhac (2) and Agatha A. Hardeman

10.2. Constant Hardeman, *b. Oct. 29, 1832. He received at Drennan Springs, Ky., a military education, and being a civil engineer by profession, he went into the C. S. A. with the engineering corps under Gen. Joe Johnson in Va.; then he attached himself to Forrest's Cavalry and was in all his raids, fights and skirmishes until he fell by the bullet of a "Home Guard" at midnight, March 24, 1864, near Mayfield, Ky., where his body lies under the shade of an immense oak tree, the place marked by a slab, put there by the loving hands of his surviving comrades. He was wounded twice, once at Baton Rouge, the last time, the day before his death. He was Adjt. of the 7th Ky. Regt., Col. Ed. Crossland, at the time, and a general favorite with all who knew him.*

Slave History: Constant Hardeman Roulhac

In 1860, Constant Hardeman Roulhac, a 28-year-old civil engineer, is listed in the U.S. Federal Census for Hickman, Fulton County, Kentucky, living with his sister and her husband, Margaret and John Lauderdale. According to the 1860 Slave Schedule for Hickman County, Constant Roulhac owned a 23-year-old male slave.

The *History of the Third, Seventh, Eighth and Twelfth Kentucky Regiment of the C.S.A.* includes the following description of their engagement at Union City and Paducah:

> From the middle to the close of the war, portions of Kentucky and Tennessee were infested with gangs of robbers and murderers calling themselves "Home

Guards," most of whom had some sort of affiliation with the Federal armies, and if they did not act under orders from the Federal commanders they certainly made no effort to restrain them. In the vicinity of Mayfield there was a gang of these cut-throats led by a man name Gregory. This gang was a terror to the whole community. It was said that they boasted of the fact that they never took a prisoner – if a Confederate fell into their hands he was murdered; and they were guilty of as brutal conduct as any gang of cut-throats who roamed those sections during the time mentioned.

...Colonel Edward Crossland, of the Seventh Kentucky, was painfully wounded in the leg at Paducah, and on the evening of the next day after the battle a portion of the Colonel's staff and a few other Confederates stopped at Mr. William Pryor's, about four miles south of Mayfield, to spend the night; and during the night they were raided by this Gregory gang. ...Hon. Samuel H. Crossland, son of Colonel Ed Crossland, writes the details of the horrible incident:

To Hon. Henry George, I herewith give you the following statement:

The citizens were held in terror by the Yankees, and especially by Gregory's company, after the battle of Paducah, in which my father, Colonel Ed. Crossland, was wounded. He came to Mayfield and was invited by his old friend and law student, Stokley W. Slayden, to go to his father's house and stay all night. Adjutant [Constant Hardeman] Roulhac informed Colonel Crossland that the father of Mr. S. W. Slayden had expressed fears that the Yankees would burn him out when the rebels left the country if he entertained him at his house and he declined to go there and started that evening at his step-mother's in Hickman County, a distance of about twenty miles from Mayfield. On the road about four miles from Mayfield, he met Bill Pryor, who told him that the weather was so cold that he would freeze before he got to his destination, and insisted upon his staying all night with him. Being told by Crossland that he was afraid that the Yankees would burn him out if he stayed with him, Pryor still insisted, saying "let them burn," and he stopped with him. About 11 o'clock that night Crossland was aroused by someone cursing at his window, whom he supposed was somebody drunk and told them to go away, and a shot was fired through the window by him at Crossland. Roulhac and Wilborn were sleeping on a pallet in the room, and were awakened by the shot. Asking what that meant, Crossland told them that he supposed it was a crazy man, and that he shot at him.

By this time the door was burst open and Gregory gave the command to kill the last damn one of them. They asked Roulhac, who by this time was near the door, who he was and he replied that he was a rebel, and he was shot through the breast, and fell dead. Wilborn, who was not observed, crawled under the bed. This command was then addressed to Crossland: "you damn son-of-a-bitch in that bed, surrender." Crossland replied: "I am wounded and helpless, and of course I surrender." Then he was fired at, the bullet cutting through his armpit and lodging in the pillow. Crossland said: "I am killed," and fell back in the bed and lay there quietly. Gregory's cut-throats then went to the room adjoining, beat upon the door and burst it in, cursed, kicked and beat, shot and cut with their sabers, a detail of Faulkner's regiment, composed of Lieutenant Oliver, Privates Burns, Front and Hatler. If there were others their names are not remembered.

Finally Oliver and Hatler surrendered to them, and they were carried into the yard and were told to kneel. Oliver answered that he only knelt to his God. They shot and killed him at once. When the order to kneel was given, Halter, understanding what they meant, broke away and ran. He was fired upon by a fusillade from Gregory's gang, about twenty-five or thirty in number, and as he ran by the guard he fired upon him, but he was not struck in the legs, and kept running and escaped. On the next morning he was brought to Mayfield and was found to be riddled with bullets; the surgeons cut twenty-eight bullets out of his body. After Oliver was killed, Gregory's men went to the stable, and Crossland, having been wounded in the leg at Paducah, was unable to walk. He crawled out of his bed and room, into the shed-room and to the back door, where he was halted by a guard; he crawled back into the shed-room and discovered Burns, who had been pierced and chopped with sabers; also Front, who had been shot in the melee by Gregory's men; and they by this time had found some pistols and gave Crossland one, and they determined to sell their lives if again attaFinding things had become quiet, Crossland, fearing the return of the Yankees, undertook to escape. He crawled out of the house and into a chicken house coop, and covered with a wagon sheet to keep from freezing; but becoming apprehensive that they would return and burn the house, and that he would be discovered by the light, and killed, he crawled until he came to a stake-and-ridered fence, when he was unable to get over or pull down on account of his wounded and freezing condition, being in his night clothes. While there, Polk Wilborn having escaped, came to him and took him on his back and carried him to the woods, where he left him and returned to the house to get some bedclothes to cover him with. When Wilborn went into the house he found a chunk of fire had been placed in the bed where Crossland had laid, but the bed was wet from bathing Crossland's wound and the fire did not catch. After Crossland had gotten away, the Gregory gang of cut-throats returned to the room where Roulhac had been killed, and one of them caught hold of Roulhac's whiskers, pulled them and said, "Ah, yes, old Eddie, we've got you this time," mistaking Roulhac for Crossland; but Gregory looked at Roulhac and told them it was not Crossland, that he had got away.

Crossland and Wilborn remained in the woods until the next morning, when a regiment of cavalry came out from Mayfield and carried them back to Mayfield. The soldiers who were at Pryor's with Crossland, believing that there were no enemies in the country nearer than Paducah, had carelessly left the most of arms with their saddles and horses at the stables, and, being surprised, were unable to make any defense. It was learned afterward that an old Negro, name Mose Saxon, had learned that the rebels were at Pryor's and carried information to that effect to Gregory and his men, a few miles away.[97]

12.4. *Margaret Eleanor Gray*, *(37) b. Jan. 10, 1840; m. Jan. 1, 1859, John A. Lauderdale, a lawyer of Hickman, KY. He entered the C.S.A. in 1861 as a Captain in the 5th Tenn. Regt. His first severe fight being at Shiloh, his last at Murfreesboro. After that he served on Genl.*

Stewart's staff in the army of Tenn., and surrendered at Greensboro, N.C. They had two children, who both d. in infancy. Mayor Lauderdale d. in New Orleans, Feb. 17, 1872. She married 2nd Capt. William Marr, Oct. 7, 1874, who also served in the Southern Army. They live at Mont Eagle, Tenn.

Slave History: Margaret Eleanor Gray Roulhac and John A. Lauderdale

The 1860 U.S. Federal Census and Slave Schedule for Hickman, Fulton County, Kentucky, indicates John Lauderdale, a lawyer, and his wife Margaret had real estate valued at $9,000 and $6,000 in personal property, including two slaves, a 21-year-old female and an 11-year-old male.[98]

Issue of Margaret Eleanor Gray Roulhac (3) and John Hill

15.3 John Roulhac, (38) b. Sept. 24, 1837; entered the C. S. A. as a private in Co. B. 20th Tenn. Regt., the first company that left Rutherford Co.; was afterwards transferred, with the rank of Capt. to the Quartermaster's department, where he remained till the close of the war. He m. Feb. 9, 1865, Christine Caroline Townsend, at Winona, Miss., near which place she was b. Aug. 4, 1840. They live at Jonestown, Coahoma Co., Miss. Her parents were both natives of N. C; her father, Alexander McConkie Townsend, being a son of Thomas Townsend and Fannie Gaddee; her mother, Christien Herring, dau. of Wm. Herring and Penelope Williams.

17.5 Thomas Roulhac, (42), b. Jan. 21, 1841; entered the C.S.A in the summer of 1862, Carter's Company, Douglas' Battalion. In the fall of the same year Gen. Wheeler took this company for scouts, in which service T.R. Hill remained until the close of the war. He m. Dec. 8 1871, Margaret Roulhac Anderson (26), [his first cousin], dau. of J. P. G. Roulhac and Jane Jouelle. They live at LaVergne, Tenn.

Issue of William Gray Gregoire Roulhac (5) and Elizabeth L. Hill

28.1 Joseph Hill, *(78) b. Oct. 15, 1833; m. Dec. 31, 1856, near Dyersburg, Tenn., Sallie A. Lauderdale, the oldest dau. of Samuel and Mary Lauderdale. In 1855 he settled in Hickman, Ky., where he was a successful lawyer for many years. He entered the C. S. A. in April 1861, at Harper's Ferry as a commissioned officer of the "Alexander Guards," named for an old soldier of the Mexican war. This company was one of the 1st Ky. Regt. in the army of Va. where they served until the summer of 1862. Then time of enlistment expiring, they immediately re-entered the service in the Western army, most of them joining Forrest's Cavalry, but J. H. Roulhac went to Joe Johnson's army, near Dalton, Ga., and was with Genl. Stuart, who commanded one of Johnson's Corps de army until the close of the war. After surrendering at Greensboro, N. C, he returned to Hickman, Ky., and resumed the practice of law. His wife d. there June 20, 1870. He m. 2nd Mrs. Sallie P. Barfield, Feb. I, 1875, at Franklin, Tenn. She was the widow of Dr. Barfield of Franklin, and daughter of Wm. and Sallie Chappell of Maury Co., Tenn. In 1873, a desire to be more useful to his fellowmen induced him to abandon the law and become a minister of the Christian church, since which time he has devoted his life to preaching the Gospel of Christ. He lives at Union City, Ky.*

PART II
The March To Freedom

The March to Freedom
Courtesy Shirlana Roulhac, a sixth-generation descendant
of Quamley and Elsie Roulhac

Chapter 4
Civil War Pension Records of African Descended Roulhacs

When he was examined, he was weak-looking and debilitated; yet he is erect.

Enslaved Roulhacs, like the millions of others living under the oppression of slavery, were not content with their station in life. They longed for the same freedom Europeans sought during the American Revolution and that Africans had achieved under the leadership of Toussaint L'Ouverture on the island of Hispaniola in 1791. A national religious movement, the Second Great Awakening which, espoused egalitarianism, evangelical Protestantism and support of black churches enhanced their desire for freedom. As early as 1798, residents Bertie County, North Carolina, where blacks outnumbered whites, were consumed by fear. That year, three slaves were arrested for suspicion of heading a conspiracy of 150 men armed with guns, swords and knives. They each received 39 lashes and had their ears cropped. In 1802, with reports of the successful revolt in Haiti, the Gabriel Prosser revolt in Richmond and the discovery of a letter in a Bertie County slave hut containing the names of leaders of a revolt, panic increased in eastern North Carolina. Roulhac's Cesar and Ephraim, two of 41 slaves owned by Psalmet and/or John Roulhac in Beaufort and Martin County, North Carolina, were implicated in what is often referred to as the Great 1802 Bertie County Slave Conspiracy and testified during the trail.

The Bertie County court executed 11 slaves, deported six and whipped and cropped the ears of 18 others. In describing the trials, an Edenton County lawyer wrote to a friend in Martin County: "Were I permitted to give an opinion of the subject, much more ought to be apprehended from the rank unparalleled conduct of the whites than from an insurrection of the Negroes. Their trial in many cases was but persecution under the mask of justice – the judges and juries were under the popular persuasion that it was better ninety-nine innocent be punished than one guilty escape. I cannot believe the alarm was kept alive by wicked and dangerous men…"[99]

Roulhacs also fought in the Civil War. Their role, like other black soldiers who volunteered for service in the Civil War, is often overlooked. An estimated 186,000 volunteers of African descent served in the U.S. Army and Navy: 93,000 from states that seceded from the Union and formed the Confederate State of America; 40,000 from the border slave states and 53,000 from the free states.[100] On January 1, 1863, when President Abraham Lincoln issued the Emancipation Proclamation, the only enslaved persons freed were those in states that had seceded from the Union--Alabama, Arkansas, Florida, Georgia, parts of Louisiana, Mississippi, North Carolina, South Carolina, Texas and Virginia (except for certain counties and the 48 counties designated as West Virginia). Persons enslaved in the loyal slave states--Delaware, Kentucky, Maryland, Tennessee and other areas in West Virginia--were not affected by the Proclamation. However, since the slave states had withdrawn from the Union and were engaged in war against it, for all practical purposes, the Proclamation's provisions freeing the enslaved could not be enforced and many remained enslaved until after the Civil War ended in 1865.

Of major significance is the Emancipation Proclamation's declaration that all enslaved persons in the rebel states "of suitable condition will be received into the armed service of the United States to garrison forts, positions, stations, and other places, and to man vessels of all sorts in said service."[101] Ten former enslaved Roulhacs escaped from plantations to join the Union forces. Nine were born in Bertie or Washington County, North Carolina. The other was born in Rutherford County, Tennessee, where Francis L. G. Roulhac migrated in 1805. According to the pension records of Privates David Rolack, Joseph Rolacke and Lewis Rolack, Fanny Roulhac of Bertie County, North Carolina enslaved them.[102] David and Joseph Rolack were brothers.[103] They enlisted in the same regiment on the same day, July 13 1863. They were among more than 5,000 North Carolina slaves who escaped from their white owners to serve in the Union army during the Civil War in a quest for manhood and freedom.[104]

All except two Roulhac soldiers served in an infantry regiment of the United States Colored Troops (USCT). Henry and Washington Roulhac served in the Navy aboard the *USS Miami* and the *USS Southfield*, respectively. None could read nor write and as was the custom during slavery, those enslaved had no official surnames prior to their enlistment. Their military enlistment records, therefore, show various phonetic spellings - "Rolack," "Rolacke," "Rollack," "Rollax" and "Rolac"- of the Roulhac surname.

The Roulhacs' Pension Records

Civil War pension records are important sources of genealogical information. The records are filled with vital statistics such as dates of births, deaths and marriages, which generally were not officially recorded. Pension and military records also contain valuable information regarding medical histories, social relationships, property ownership, migration patterns, and genealogical information about other persons--African Americans and European Americans alike--named in the soldiers' records. Because the Roulhac Civil War pension records contain information about persons other than the applicants, the summaries that follow are rather detailed. The names of persons who completed supporting affidavits or who served as witnesses have been included. They may provide valuable leads to further records or may assist other researchers who have an interest in the areas where the Roulhac pension applicants lived.

Private Joseph Rolacke, aka Roulhac White
Co A, 2d Reg't U.S. Colored Inf.

Joseph Rolacke was the first of 10 Roulhacs to volunteer for service in the Civil War. On June 23, 1863 Captain Cogswell mustered Joseph Rolacke into the 2nd Regiment, USCT (formerly Captain Wild's African Brigade Colored Infantry as a private for a three-year term at Craney Island, Virginia.[105]

Joseph Rolacke is described in the Company Descriptive Book as 25-years-old, 6 feet, 5/8 inch, brown complexion and dark hair and eyes. Joseph's record indicated he was born in Bertie County, North Carolina. His occupation is listed as "servant" and as having fought in the Battle of the Natural Bridge in Florida on March 6, 1865.[106] In August 1865, Joseph was detailed to slaughterhouse. In September 1865, he was noted to be absent – ditched service at slaughter pen Tallahassee, since August 2, 1865. In October 1865, Joseph was again detailed to the slaughterhouse. Joseph was honorably discharged on January 5, 1866.[107] He died May 25, 1890 at Windsor, Bertie County, North Carolina.

On July 28, 1890, Mary E. White, age 38, of Bertie County, filed a declaration for a widow's pension (#532558) under the Act of June 27, 1890.[108] R. A. Myers and Kader White witnessed Mary's declaration. Mary stated she was married under the "name of Mary E. Taylor to said Roulhac White on November 8, 1884, by Rev. G. E. Freeman ... Said Roulhac White was formerly married to Harriet Winborn, now dead."[109] Mary said her living children under 16 years of age were: Elise White, born April 4, 1876; Sallie A. White, born May 10, 1878; Limas R. White, born June 7, 1890, two weeks after his father died. However, before her application could be processed, Mary died. Her October 26, 1890 death was just over four months after her youngest son, Limas, was born.

On January 4, 1898, Kitty Shaw, also known as Dorsey Shaw, age 24, of Hertford County, filed a declaration for pension (#668779) on behalf of seven-year-old Limas R. Rolack. Harrison Jenkins, Powellsville, North Carolina and Elizabeth Goodman, Bethlehem, North Carolina witnessed kitty's declaration. Kitty stated that Limas R. Rolack was the legitimate child of Joseph Rolacke, who enlisted under the name of Joseph Roulhac, alias Rolacke White. In response to the Bureau of Pensions' request for a personal description, the War Department noted that Joseph Rolacke, also known as Joseph Rolack, had been enrolled.

In an affidavit dated February 24,1898, Lewis N. Naughton, age 58, of Harrellville, Hertford County, North Carolina, stated he was personally acquainted with Harriet White, Rolack White's first wife, and he was living within 500 yards of her house when she died. He related that she left six living children but he could not give the ages of the two oldest, one of whom was dead. He provided the names of Molly White, born August 1874; Elias White, born March 4, 1878; and Sally White, born in 1879. He said Harriett White died March 26, 1883. On February 25, 1898, Dr. A. H. Askew sent the Pension Bureau an affidavit stating that Roulhac White had died from consumption and not from vicious habits.

On March 9, 1898, the Hertford County Court granted Dorsey [Kitty] Shaw guardianship over Limas Roulhac White. Moriah Taylor, age 62, of Askewsville, Bertie County, North Carolina, and the mid-wife during Limas' birth, explained in an August 15, 1898 affidavit how she remembered Limas' date of birth. She related that 7 June 1890 was the Saturday before the second Sunday in June and she was anxious to attend Piney Woods Chapel's quarterly meeting but was called away to deliver Limas. Both Moriah Taylor and Jane Shaw, age

25, of Harrellville, stated in a September 13, 1898 affidavit that they knew Limas' mother, Eliza, was dead because they were present when she died, saw her corpse shrouded, put in a coffin and buried the next day, October 27, 1890. In a September 13, 1898 affidavit, Jane Shaw stated that she was also present when Eliza died. Lizzie Sessons and J.C. Adkins witnessed her mark.

On April 27, 1899, fourteen months after Dr. Askew verified Roulhac White's death, the Pension Bureau directed the Harrellville, North Carolina, postmaster to advise of Dr. Askew's veracity and truthfulness. Not only did the postmaster, A. Booth, state in a May 3, 1898 affidavit that "you can depend on anything that Dr. A. H. Askew says," but he was joined by A. H. Simons and A. B. Adkins who had been justices of the peace in Hertford County since 1896 and 1893, respectively. Kitty Shaw's pension application on behalf of Limas was never approved. The last pension record entry is a January 26, 1900 Bureau of Pensions' request to attorney Joseph Hunter for additional information regarding Roulhac White's identity.

Private David Rolack
Co A, 36 Reg't U.S. Colored Inf.

David k enlisted for a three-year term at Plymouth, North Carolina, on 13 July 1863, as a private in Company A, 2d Regiment N.C. Colored Volunteers (subsequently designated as Company A, 36th Regiment U.S. Colored Infantry), one of four units of North Carolina Colored Volunteers (NCCV) raised in North Carolina (the 35th, 36, and 37th USCT and the 14th U.S. Colored Heavy Artillery).[110] The Company Descriptive Book described David, of Bertie County, North Carolina, as a 20-year-old farmer. During May and June 1864, he was reported to be sick in the regiment's hospital. David died on June 30, 1864 at Point Lookout, Maryland.[111]

This memorial is dedicated to the 2nd USCT who battled Confederates of the 1st Battalion, Florida Special Cavalry during a cannon duel during the February 20, 1865 defense of Fort Myers, FL. The 2nd USCT freed and enlisted over 1,000 slaves during the Civil War. Photo courtesy Julio Bateau, Ft. Myers, FL.

On May 4, 1888, Mary Roulhac, age 79, also of Bertie County, filed a declaration for an original pension of a mother (#372638). In her declaration, Mary stated that sometime in June 1864 at Point Lookout, Maryland, David "was brought [to the] hospital senseless from fatigue from an engagement or some other cause therein created and instantly died." Mary Roulhac declared that she had been partially dependent on David for her support; that her husband Limas Clary, age 50, died in 1850; and when David died he had a brother, Limas Roulhac, born January 1, 1851, who was under 16 years old.

In her July 9, 1888 affidavit, Mary Roulhac stated when David enlisted in the Army she had the following children: John Roulhac, age 36; Thomas Roulhac, age 31; Joseph Roulhac, age 27; Jane Roulhac, age 22; Rachel Roulhac, age 14; Maria Roulhac, age 33; Celia

Roulhac, age 28; Pricilla Roulhac, age 24; Frances Roulhac, age 20 and Limas Roulhac, age 13. Mary said "no one has been legally bound to support her since the soldier died except her children who were under 21 years of age and only from them until they arrived at the age of 21 years."

The Bertie County Superior Court Clerk's July 10, 1888 affidavit indicated Mary Roulhac owned 25 acres of land valued at $100 for the last 10 years. On August 2, 1888 the War Department, in response to the Bureau of Pension's request, noted the name "David Roulhac" was not on the rolls of Company A, 36th U.S.C.T., but verified a "David Rollack's" enlistment and personal description. The War Department reported that the final statement showed David died June 30, 1864 from an unknown cause at Carney Island, Virginia. The company descriptive book indicates David died of "pulmonary consumption."

Between August and December 1888, Mary Roulhac's neighbors, Logan Webb and Nathan Ward, both age 69, Roscoe Singleton, age 66, and George Spivey, age 77, filed supporting affidavits stating Mary received letters containing money from her son David, while he was in the Army, and her land was unimproved and provided no income. According to Webb and Ward, Mary's husband died in 1850. Singleton and Spivey said they believed Mary was 80 years old and, from their own knowledge, her family record showed she was born in 1809. In a September 27, 1888 affidavit Mary said David's letters to her were thrown away, lost or destroyed when her house burned completely in 1866. Thomas J. Harrell and Limas Roulhac witnessed her affidavit.

On July 10, 1890, Mary and her material witnesses were directed to appear in Windsor, North Carolina, for special examination. Her son Limas testified he was 38 or 39 years old, a teacher, Mary's youngest child, his father died the year he was born and he had siblings:

John, Maria, Thomas, Celia, Joseph, Priscilla, Jane, Francis, David and Rachel, all of whom lived to be grown, but some were dead. He stated that prior to David's enlistment, at eighteen or nineteen-years-old, his mistress Fanny Roulhac had hired him out to John A. Phelps. Limas related his brother Joseph[112] was also in the army and he and others wrote home saying David had died in June 1864 at the hospital at Point Lookout, Maryland. Limas said they had not been seen or heard from since the war and they did not know if he were dead or alive. Limas said after David died he kept working and managed to get a place, and his mother had since lived with him. According to Limas, in 1867 or 1868, the Army sent his mother some $300 as David's back pay and bounty with which she bought 25 acres of very poor land at $1 per acre from Mr. George Miller and some stock. According to Limas, David sent his mother $5 or $10 from Plymouth, North Carolina, and at least $30 from some place in Mary

In her deposition Mary Roulhac restated her life history more specifically. She explained:

> I am about 81 yrs ... I was a slave of Mrs. Fanny Roulhac of Bertie Co, N.C. near Windsor. She is dead. My husband was Limas Clary. He belonged to Major Clary of Windsor, NC. Major Clary has been dead for years. Limas Clary & myself were married as slaves with the consent of our owners in 1825 or 1826. I can't say which. We were both single people, had never been married. About one year after we took to each other our first child came & we call him John - dead (1827); Maria - dead (1830); Thomas (1835); Joseph (1836); Priscilla (1839); Jane - dead (1841); Francis (1843); David - dead (1846); Rachel dead - (1849); Limas (1851). These ages were all placed in my Bible by Mrs. Fanny Roulhac, my old mistress. She died only a few years ago here in Windsor, N.C.

Chapter 4

Pages from Mary Roulhac's Bible, entered as an exhibit during her deposition, included names of her grandchildren: Celia's (Priscilla) children: James Edward Roulhac (1850); Rasht?? Roulhac (1859); Mary Jane Roulhac (1865); Emily Roulhac (September 1869). Jane Roulhac's children: Henrietta Roulhac (1859); Nero Roulhac (1865).[113]

Mary said her husband died in 1851 in Windsor a week after their son Limas, named after his father, was born, and that she has never remarried. Mary retold how she learned of David's death and of her receipt of his back pay and bounty. She gave David's physical description and age – 18 - when he enlisted, said he worked for John A. Phelps who hired him from Fanny Roulhac, and she, Mary, depended on him for support. Mary testified that in 1863 they did not know they were free and their mistress, Fanny Roulhac, continued to get the money David earned working for John Phelps. Mary related she did not have a cent and had hardly any clothing in 1863; she used David's back pay and bounty to buy 25 acres of swampy land she tried to work; her cow died and she was forced to sell a horse. She never had any hogs and at the time did not own any livestock, not even a chicken. Mary explained she did not ask for a pension sooner because she didn't understand how until her agent, Mr. Hunter, sent the papers.

Moses Corvine, age 81, Roscoe Singleton, age 68, and Nathan Ward, age 73, Mary's neighbors, corroborated her testimony. David Phelps's son, W. S. Phelps, age 39, was also deposed. He testified that David "was a strong able-bodied field hand when he left us to go into the CS Army ... He and myself were play boys when we had no work [and] we worked together, he was about my age."

On February 12, 1890, the special examiner noted Mary Roulhac's case had been deemed "Special" by the Commissioner of Pensions, he believed her case was meritorious and recommended its approval. Mary Roulhac was granted a pension July 21, 1890. She received $12 per month, retroactive to May 14, 1888, until her death on 4 November 1898. Her son, Thomas Roulhac, was reimbursed $26 dollars for expenses associated with Mary's last illness and death.

Private Joseph k, aka Joseph Rollax
Co C, 36 U.S. Colored Inf.

Joseph k enlisted July 13, 1863 at Portsmouth, Virginia, as a private in the 2nd Regiment N.C. Colored Infantry (subsequently designated as Company C, 36th Regiment N.C. Colored Infantry) for a three-year term. The Company Descriptive Book indicates he was born in Plymouth, Washington County, North Carolina; 25 years old; 5 feet 6 inches; black complexion, hair and eyes and a farmer. When he was mustered out on July 13, 1866 in Brazos Santiago, Texas, his pay included six months of retroactive pay to account for the $3 per month difference in pay between white and black soldiers. Joseph was a private during his entire term.

On July 22, 1890 Joseph, then living in Oldenburg, Avoyelles Parish, Louisiana used the name Joseph Rollax to file a declaration for an invalid pension (#897486) under the Act of July 27, 1890. He claimed permanent disability because of rheumatism. Joseph signed his name with an "x". R. L. Lee and Sidney Berryman were witnesses. The War Department noted "Joseph Rollax" was not found on the rolls of Company C, 36th Regiment U.S.C.I., but medical records showed that a "J. Rolack," a private in Company C, had been treated for diarrhea in October 1865, and for debility from November 1-10, 1865.

In February 1896 William Fletcher & Co., of Washington, D.C., replaced William Wright as Joseph's pension attorney. At his 12 February 1896 medical examination, Joseph, 5 feet 7 inches, 160 pounds and "seventy-plus years," complained of rheumatism that caused pain in his back and right knee for five years.

In his March 28, 1896 affidavit, Joseph indicated his belief that he had enlisted about July 13, 1863 but did not remember when he was discharged at Brazos, Texas. He said he was 60 years old. Sidney Berryman, 51 years old, and Branch Hayes, 27, said they had known Joseph for 23 and 10 years, respectively, were Joseph's neighbors and he suffered from rheumatism for eight years. Joseph's 1890 application was rejected.

Ten months later, on January 11, 1897, Joseph reapplied, listing his age as 60. This time he claimed he was unable to perform manual labor because of rheumatism, heart disease and a crippled hand. J. M. Rabalain and Sidney Berryman were witnesses. In a March 25, 1897 affidavit, Dr. Gordon Morgan of Woodside, Louisiana, said he had been acquainted with Joseph for 20 years, first treated him in 1888 for chronic auricular rheumatism and he undoubtedly had a permanent affliction, which incapacitated him from manual labor about one-half of his time.

In a Bureau of Pensions questionnaire dated May 30, 1898, Joseph responded that he was a widower who was married to Indy Phillips in 1869 at Bayou Current, Louisiana, by missionary Elder Green and their eight living children were: Jimmy Rollax (1873), Ann Rollax (1875), Dave Rollax (1880), Alford Rollax (1885), Henry Rollax (1886), Jesse Rollax (1889), Magdalean Rollax (1892), and Virginia Rollax (1895).

At Joseph's July 3, 1900 medical examination in Natchez, Mississippi, he was 5 feet 7 1/2 inches, 149 pounds, 62 years old and a farm laborer. He was found to have a 4/18 disability for rheumatism, 2/18 for a crippled hand and 2/18 for gradual and senile debility. The following November 17, 1900 he filed a general affidavit, witnessed by S. Berryman and Branch Hayes, noting he cut his right forefinger in 1877 while filing a plow and had been disabled since 1892.

On March 4, 1901, Joseph completed another questionnaire. He explained he was born and lived near Plymouth, North Carolina, and prior to his enlistment he worked as a farmer.[114] He said he was a slave "owned by the Rollaxs ... belonged to Fannie R[oulhac]" when he enlisted. He noted since his discharge from the army he had lived in New Orleans for five months; East Feliciana Parish Louisiana one year and thereafter in Odenburg. F. L. Cason and R. O. Hudson witnessed Joseph's questionnaire.

Sidney Berryman, age 57, and Dan Douglas, age 38, filed general affidavits on June 19 and July 31, 1902, supporting Joseph's application, indicating they had known him for 25 years and his disability was not from vicious habits. On April 24, 1903, 13 years after Joseph's initial application, he was awarded $6 per month for rheumatism and right hand injury, retroactive to January 14, 1897.

The next year, on March 19, 1904, Joseph filed an application to determine his right to $12 per month, the full rate allowed under the Act of 27 June 1890, as amended by Act of May 9, 1900, because of rheumatism, disease of heart and debility from age. Joseph's said he was 70 years old. Dave Rollax, Joseph's son, and Matt Williams were witnesses. A May 25, 1904 physical examination in Opelousas, Louisiana, found Joseph suffering with the debility of a person four or five years older. Joseph's pension was increased to $10 per month beginning May 25, 1904 (pension #1058031). His attorney was paid $2.

On February 8, 1906, 71 year old Joseph Rollax applied to increase his pension to $12 per month. Although his prior medical records indicated that he was born in Plymouth, North Carolina, his October 17, 1906 surgeon's certificate indicated that he was born in New York. Joseph's pension was increased to $12 per month, effective, October 17, 1906, for rheumatism, heart disease, injury and senile debility.

On March 5, 1907, Joseph applied for a pension under the Act of February 6, 1907 that granted pensions to Mexican and Civil War veterans who had reached 70 years of age. In his declaration, Joseph stated he was 72 years old and was born "about 1835." In a December

15, 1908 letter to his attorney, Joseph said he was "not able to tell the day of my birth. My mistress had my age in the Bible and she did not tell me my age. I am unable to send you a family record. My mother give me my age before I was listed in the war and she is dead and I cannot tell anymore than that in my days I am unable to go back and tell you the day of my birth."[115]

Joseph's application was rejected January 8, 1909. He re-applied October 23, 1911. This time he did not use a pension attorney. Joseph's file contains his July 11, 1911 answers to special claims examiner's questions relating he was born in Bertie County, North Carolina; was 25 years old when he enlisted; his company officers were Capt. Wild, Lt. Edmond Gaski and Sgt. Jeremiah Gray; his wife Juda had been dead 10 or 12 years; his comrades in the army were James Harrell, Ivory Bickton and James Rollax;[116] he was 5 feet 6 inches; had black complexion and eyes and white hair. Joseph's application was approved for $15 per month, retroactive to October 28, 1911.

In July 1912, pursuant to the Act of May 11, Joseph filed another declaration to increase his pension. A notation on the form granting Joseph's request for an increase indicated his birth date was July 13, 1838. When his application was approved on May 8, 1913, he had moved to Melville, St. Landry Parish, Louisiana, to live with his daughter Anna (Rollax) Armstrong. He received $25 per month, starting July 5, 1912, and $30 per month beginning July 13, 1913.

Joseph Rollax died August 19, 1916 of paralysis caused by arteriosclerosis in Melville. On September 21, 1916, his daughter Anna Armstrong sought reimbursement for $72.20 to cover costs associated with Joseph's last illness. Anna stated that Joseph had been married to Indie Rollax, who died April 8, 1896. Her application was never approved. Anna did not provide bills for undertaking, livery and cemetery charges nor testimony regarding Joseph's remarriage.

Corporal Samuel Rolack, aka Samuel Rollack
Co D, 57th Reg't U.S. Colored Inf.

Samuel Rolack enlisted as a private in Captain Payne's Independent Company, Liberia Guards, September 3,1863 at Cairo, Illinois. The Company Descriptive Book describes him as 22 years old laborer; 5 feet 10 1/2 inches; black complexion, eyes, and hair and born in Rutherford County, Tennessee. Captain Payne's Company was re-designated as Company D, 4th Regiment Arkansas Infantry of African Descent, and later as Company D, 57th Regiment U.S. Colored Infantry. Remarks on company muster rolls for July 1864 - February 1865 indicate that Samuel Rolack "rec'd seven dollars per month for Jan and Feb 1864."[117] He was appointed corporal on June 30, 1864. Samuel was mustered out at Fort Union, New Mexico, October 18, 1866. He retained a Springfield rifle and accouterments.

On April 18, 1894, Samuel Rollack, then about 70 years old, a resident of St. Louis, Missouri, filed a declaration for invalid pension (#1157536) because of rheumatism, heart disease, frostbitten hands and feet, kidney disease and a broken left arm. The War Department could not locate a record for Samuel Rollack but verified "Samuel Rollack's" personal description and enlistment.

Samuel was ordered to take a physical examination in St. Louis within three months of May 15, 1894. However, in November 1894, his attorneys, H. D. and R.S. O'Brien, advised the Bureau of Pensions that Samuel could not be located; he was no longer at 303 N. Levee, St. Louis; and mail sent to the city hospital was returned. The following January, Samuel, who resided at St. Louis' Poor House, indicated his readiness to be examined. During his May 5, 1895 examination, Samuel told the physician he contracted rheumatism (left knee and ankle) and heart disease in the Army; his hand and feet were frostbitten three years ago and he broke his arm two years ago. He was 5 feet 9 1/2 inches and weighed 155 pounds. He said he was 70 years old and used a cane to ambulate. The medical board did not provide a disability rating although the examination showed that Samuel had a broken left arm; frostbitten feet; the great-toe of his left foot was partly destroyed and the stump turned under; he had problems with his right hand and that rheumatic deposits allowed only one-third rotation of his left knee and ankle.

On August 19, 1895, George Naylor, about 50 years old, of 303 N. Levee Street, and Benjamin Carter, age 39 of 1318 N. 8th Street, in separate affidavits obviously written for them by the same person and containing similar language, said they had known Samuel for over 20 years and he had complained of his illnesses to them. In his February 12, 1896 affidavit Samuel, about 70 years, indicated he had suffered from rheumatism and heart disease for 13 years from an unknown cause; six years ago he was frostbitten while working on the levee at St. Louis and broke his left arm five years ago after leaning against a railing on top of a shed. He did not know how he had acquired kidney disease but said his disabilities were not from vicious habits.

The following May, the Bureau of Pensions directed a special examiner to establish George Naylor and Benjamin Carter's veracity and credibility. During his examination, Carter, age 42, said he had known Samuel since 1876; Samuel complained of rheumatism in his hips, knees and shoulders; kidney trouble and around 1886 Samuel fell while they were working in the glass house. Carter described Samuel as a man of good habit who did not drink to excess. He indicated that Samuel was unable to perform manual labor and had been in the Poor House from 1888 until his release last fall.

Naylor said he had known and worked with Samuel from 1873 until he became disabled about two years earlier because of trouble in his arm and legs and he could no longer walk. Naylor said while they were sleeping in the same house he helped Samuel dress, carried him to the hospital and from there to the poor house. According to Naylor, after Samuel was released from the hospital shortly before he filed for his pension, he had been unable to work at anything except going around picking up rags. The examiner certified that when he questioned Carter and Naylor on June 5, 1896, their replies manifested full knowledge as stated on their original affidavits. Carter's credibility was rated "good" and Naylor's "fair."

Based on the medical referee's recommendation, Samuel's application was rejected July 14, 1896 because he was "not ratably disabled under Act of June 27, 1890." Four days later, Samuel's pension attorney filed another declaration for him. The word "dead" is circled on the Bureau's September 1, 1896 order directing Samuel to report for a physical examination.

Corporal James k
Co C, 36th U.S. Colored Inf.

James k enlisted for three years in Company C, 2d Regiment N.C. Colored Infantry (subsequently designated 36th Regiment U.S. Colored Infantry) on September 22, 1863 at Portsmouth, Virginia. He indicated that he was twenty-five-years-old, born in Plymouth, [Washington County], North Carolina; 5 feet 6 inches; dark complexion; black hair; dark eyes and worked as a farmer.

James Rollack's military file is uneventful except that in November-December 1864 he was marked present as "James Black" and on the March-April 1865 company muster roll he had been marked "absent sick since April 20, 1865." The May-June 1866 muster roll noted that James Rolack was promoted to Corporal on May 24, 1866 and he was "due soldier difference between $7 and $13 per month from Sept 22, '63 to Jan 1 '64."

On September 22, 1866, Cpl. James Rolack was discharged at Brazos Santiago, Texas. He owed the "U.S. $19.80 amount over paid by Maj. Underwood on rolls of June 30, 1866…" No pension record has been found.

Private John Rolac
Co C, 85th New York Inf.

John Rolac enlisted for a three-year term November 12, 1863 at Plymouth [Washington County], North Carolina, as a private in Company C, 85th Regiment N. Y. Infantry. Private John Rolac was one of small number of black soldiers who enlisted in white regiments. When John enrolled, three white regiments were in Plymouth: the 103rd Pennsylvania Volunteers, the 24th New York Battery and the 85th New York Infantry.[118] John Rolac was described as 21 years old; 5 feet 6 inches; once a slave; born in Plymouth, North Carolina; hazel eyes, brown hair and light complexion. During his service, he was an "under cook of African descent."

John Rolac was captured by the Confederate Army April 20, 1864, during the Battle of Plymouth and confined at Andersonville, Georgia. He was hospitalized on September 20, 1864 and died September 22, 1864, of scorbutus, also known as scurvy, a deficiency disorder caused by a lack of vitamin C. John is the only known runaway slave buried at Andersonville Prison. He either passed himself off as white or was mistaken as white. Captured slaves were generally returned to their owners or put to work as manual laborers.[119] No pension record has been located for John Rolac.

Washington Roulhac, Navy

On July 19, 1893, at Norfolk, Virginia, Albinar (Roulhac) Hardy, age 35, of Avoca, Bertie County, North Carolina, filed a declaration for pension for widows and sisters (#13740) on behalf of her brother, Washington Roulhac. She claimed that Washington had enlisted during the summer of 1863 as a "1st Class Boy" aboard the *USS Southfield* and drowned with the crew April 19, 1864, during the Battle of Plymouth. She said he left neither widow, minor child, mother (who died November 1876), nor father (who died January 1880). Albinar indicated that her brother Washington was survived by their brother,

James Blount, born 1839, the child of Hannibal Roulhac and Rebecca Roulhac. Albinar states that she was born October 25, 1858, and her parents were married as Hannibal Roulhac and Rebecca Roulhac.

In a September 25, 1893 affidavit, Dr. H. V. Dunston of Windsor, North Carolina, wrote that he knew Hannibal Johnson (alias Roulhac) and Rebecca Johnson (alias Roulhac), his wife, during their lives and was their attending physician during their last illnesses. He did not know when they died but stated that Rebecca died of dropsy four years before her husband. He said they were charity patients and no records were left. Dr. Dunston said the discrepancy in their names was "due to former owners of these slaves."

In September 1893, the Treasury and the Navy Department in response to a request from the Bureau of Pension, wrote that the name Washington Roulhac was not on the Southfield's rolls from October 1862 to April 1964, when she was lost nor on the *Southfield's* muster roll."[120]

On December 29, 1893, Albinar was notified that her claim was rejected because she was more than 16 years old when her parents died and no records were found to show that Washington Roulhac was in naval service aboard the *USS Southfield*. On May 17, 1905, Albinar Hardy, then of Edenton, North Carolina, informed the Commissioner of Pensions "Washington Roulhac was killed or drowned on board *USS Southfield* … while engaged with the Confederate Ram *Albemarle*. His duty on board ship was powder monkey…" The Commissioner told Albinar her claim had been denied and was no longer pending.[121]

Private Lewis Rolack, aka Lewis Roulhac
Co B, 37th U.S. Colored Inf.

Lewis Rolack enlisted for a three-year term January 30, 1864, in the 37th Regiment N.C. Colored Infantry (subsequently re-designated as Company B, 37th Regiment U.S. Colored Infantry). He is described in the Company Descriptive Book as 18 years old, 5 feet 6 inches, with black complexion, dark hazel eyes and black hair. He said he was born in Bertie County, North Carolina, and his occupation was "farmer." Lewis Rolack was mustered in by Capt. J. R. Gould at Norfolk, Virginia. He was a private on January 31, 1867, when he was mustered out at Raleigh, North CarolOn March 3, 1894, Lewis Roulhac applied for a pension under the name Lewis Roulhac. In his own meticulous hand-written declaration for invalid pension (#11569) under the Act of June 27, 1890, he stated he was 47 years old, a resident of Windsor, North Carolina, (P.O. Box 103), and was partially unable to support himself because of chronic bowel dyspepsia, kidney disease and impaired mind. He requested to be examined by the Board of Surgeons at Elizabeth City, North Carolina. Marcus R. Butler and Andrew J. Cherry witnessed his declaration. Pension attorney L. Wood & Co., of Washington, D.C., represented Lewis.

In a March 24, 1894 general affidavit, Marcus R. Butler, age 48, and Samuel Hoggard, age 36, stated they had known Lewis for 35 and 27 years, respectively. Marcus indicated that he had lived within a half-mile of Lewis for 15 years and saw him at least once or twice per week. Samuel said he had lived in the same town with Lewis and saw him nearly every day.

The War Department's Record and Pensions Division verified Lewis's personal description and noted the name "Lewis Roulhac" was not on the rolls of Company B, Regiment U.S. Colored Infantry, but a "Lewis Rolack" was enrolled and was treated February 11, 1865, for diarrhea. When Lewis was examined June 6, 1894, he was 5 feet 6 1/2 inches and weighed 146 pounds. No disability was found to exist.

In December 1894, Laura A. White, age 30, and Augustus Robbins, 55 years old, signed general affidavits supporting Lewis's application. Laura stated she had known Lewis for 25 years; lived across the street from him for seven years; he was totally unable to perform manual labor to support himself and about five weeks earlier she saw over a gallon of water taken from him by Dr. H. V. Dunston. She noted that Lewis had an unhealthy wife and two children, ages 10 and six months, respectively. Laura related that Lewis was forced to mortgage his household and kitchen furniture to R. C. Bazemore, the debt was due in 30 days and he had been forced to live on what he could borrow from friends and neighbors. Augustus Robbins had known Lewis for 27 years and lived within three or 400 yards of him.

Lewis's application was rejected on December 3, 1894. On January 31, 1895, almost two months later, Lewis, age 47, filed another declaration for an invalid pension. This time he claimed he was totally disabled from earning support by manual labor. In addition to the impairments set forth in his original application, Lewis complained of chronic rheumatism in the small part of his back, left hip and legs, an impaired mind and general disability. He requested to be examined by the Board of Surgeons at Windsor. Elisha Speller and R. T. Mitchell supported his Declaration. During his February 5, 1896, examination by the Board Surgeons' agent, Dr. H. V. Dunston, no evidence of rheumatism was found. However, Dunston, who had been Lewis's family physician for sixteen years, noted that Lewis had disability rating caused by chronic gastrointestinal disease. Dr. Dunston also wrote that his "impaired mind" was hypochondriasis. This man has been a school teacher and has led a very sedentary life."

In August 1896 affidavits, Henry Pugh, age 47, and Lewis T. Bond, age 26, wrote they had known Lewis for 17 years; lived within one-half mile of him; he had complained to them about his bowel condition for about five years and Lewis had not been able to work since 21 February 1895. In his affidavit of August 15, 1896, Lewis explained he was unable to furnish an affidavit from his family physician, Dr. Dunston, because he was now the U.S. medical examiner and refused to make any affidavit touching upon his bowel disease, which he had treated since its inception. Lewis in addition to medicine prescribed by Dr. Dunston, had been taking the following patent medicines: seven barks and august flower bought from Dr. E. W. Pugh of Windsor, North Carolina; medicine from Dr. J. A. Deane of Kingston, New York and Dr. Reed's and Dr. Carmick's protamuclien tablets, tissue builders and protomuclien special, among others.

Apparently questioning Lewis' ability to write, the Bureau of Pensions directed the War Department to furnish "a tracing of this soldier's signature." The Auditor of the War Department responded that the records showed the soldier signed by mark. Lewis's application was rejected on October 31, 1896. However, less than a month later, on November 24, 1896, he filed another declaration for an invalid pension. He claimed he was two-thirds unable to earn support by manual labor because of chronic bowel dyspepsia; disease of kidneys, small of back, left hip, foot and leg. This time he requested to be examined by the Board of Surgeons' examiners at Elizabeth City, North Carolina. Samuel Hoggard and William P. Mitchell who stated they had known Lewis for 26 and 27 years, respectively, witnessed his declaration. Lewis was examined June 2, 1897. Lewis was found to have a 4/18 disability for a weak leg.

Chaney Pugh, age 61, in a July 20 1897, supporting affidavit indicated he had known Lewis since 1867. Because he was unable to sign his name, W. P, Sanderlin and D.C. Williams witnessed his affidavit. In a further effort to establish his disability, Lewis, in a July 30, 1867 affidavit, again underscored Dr. Dunston's refusal to furnish an affidavit relating to his bowel condition. He noted that he "had used a hundred or more dif[f]erent kinds of patent medicines and home remedies, including "paskola, soda mint, Egyptian tea, august flower, seven barks, golden medical discovery, common soda, mustard and a number of different kinds of medicines both patent and prescription ..."

On April 1, 1898, Lewis was required to complete two questionnaires, one stated that the "information was requested for future use, and it may be of great value to your family." In one, Lewis stated he had lived in Windsor since his discharge from the military; had worked "shingling to 1869, farming to 1870, school teaching to 1894, nothing now." In the other questionnaire, Lewis related that he married "Lizzie L. Roulhac, maiden name, Watson ... March 28, 1881, at Windsor, N.C., by Rev. Luke Pierce, ... at the Courthouse in Windsor, Bertie County, North Carolina;" was never married before and his living children were Arthur B. Roulhac, born March 12, 1883, and Fanny L. Roulhac, born May 23, 1894. Lewis' November 1896 application was rejected April 13, 1898.

Five years later, on September 26, 1903, Lewis submitted another declaration for invalid pension. This time, instead of hiring a pension attorney, Lewis he represented himself. Lewis, age 56, alleged that he was "disqualified from earning a support by manual labor because of dyspepsia, general debility and weak back." Eli Jones and Daniel P. Mitchell witnessed his application. In response to an October 29, 1903 questionnaire, Lewis answered that prior to volunteering for the army he "was a slave. My owner was named, Fanny Roulhac"[122] and his present occupation was "local pension agent." He described himself as 5 feet, 5 5/8 inches, dark skin with a permanent mark or scar on his left leg and knee. George McDonald and D. L. Pierce witnessed the questionnaire.

Although Lewis's December 30, 1903 medical examination revealed "the aggregate permanent disability for earning a support by manual labor is due to rheumatism - not to vicious habits and warrants a rating of $6." His application was rejected February 5, 1904, because "a notable degree of disability is not shown under Act of June 27, 1890."

Lewis was undeterred, on October 1, 1904, Lewis, then age 57, reapplied. He said he was born April 8, 1847, and was partially disabled because of "indigestion or dyspepsia, disease of liver, rheumatism and general debility." John Buckingham and Guy Hyman witnessed his application. Because John Buckingham used a "mark" to sign his name, A. B. Roulhac and Mattie Jennett also signed the declaration. On November 7, 1904, Dr. Dunston submitted a letter to the Bureau of Pensions indicating that he examined Lewis and found he was "suffering with diabetes mellitus with a general neurasthenia [symptoms include weakness, dizziness and fainting] neither of which are disabling in an aggravated form." A month later, December 14, 1904, when the Bureau of Surgeons examined Lewis, he indicated he was a schoolteacher. The examiners found Lewis' "aggregate permanent disability ... is due to dyspepsia... and warrants a rating of ten dollars. No other disability found."

Eleven years after his first application, Lewis was finally granted a pension for partial disability. He received $6 per month, effective October 5, 1904. Lewis made two unsuccessful attempts to have his pension increased to $12, the full rate allowed under the Act of June 27, 1890, as amended by the Act of May 9, 1900. His August 1905, application, witnessed by John S. Drew and John Duers, and his May 1906 application, witnessed by Turner Bond and Joseph Allen, were both denied. In his August 4, 1905 application he complained that he was "compelled to live on milk and bread by reason of the nature of his disease, indigestion and weak stomach." When he was examined on June 6, 1906, the examiners noted Lewis Roulhac was "weak-looking and debilitated, yet he is erect. ... "

On April 18, 1907, for a third time Lewis applied for an increase because of total disability due to diabetes, rheumatism, and general debility. William M. Sanderlin and John R. Smallwood witnessed his application. In a letter accompanying his application, Lewis wrote that he had not been able to do a half-day of labor since November

24, 1906. He added, "I have no strength, because I can eat nothing but a little corn bread and hominy - I can eat an egg boiled half done once every day. I can eat nothing that contains sugar, starch, hog meat or lard - no milk, flour or oat meal - no fish of any kind unless it is fresh, and then I can eat none of that more than once in one and two weeks time - I can eat no fruit, if I do, it like the other things I have mentioned increases the flow of my urine and destroys my memory."

In the meantime, on February 7, 1908, Lewis applied for pension under the Act of February 6, 1907, which granted $12 a month pensions to Civil War veterans who had attained the age of 62. Lewis noted in his declaration that although all applications on file stated that he was born April 7, 1847, they were in error because his War Department records showed he was 18 years old when he enlisted January 8, 1864. Therefore, Lewis stated he was born April 8, 1845, and was 62 years old. Sol Cherry and A. C. Mitchell, ages 25 and 20 years, respectively, witnessed his application.

When Lewis was examined March 4, 1908, his weight had dropped to 105 pounds, down from the 146 pounds he weighed when he first applied for a pension in 1894. He was described as "very feeble and emaciated." The examiners found him permanently disabled from performing manual labor because of age and diabetes and warranted a rating of $12. Lewis' application was approved April 4, 1908, and his pension was increased to $12 per month, effective March 27, 1908. Lewis died on October 25, 1909, 18 months after he was declared permanently disabled.

On November 4, 1909, less than a month after Lewis died, his widow, Lizzie L. Roulhac, age 48, filed a declaration for widow's pension (#694629). Cato Mountain and Augustus Robbins, both 69 years old, were witnesses and filed supporting affidavits. Turner Bond, age 43, and Joseph Allen, age 45, filed affidavits stating that Fanny Lewis Roulhac (Lizzie and Lewis's daughter) was living with Lizzie and depended upon her for support. Lizzie, unable to present a birth or baptismal record of Fanny's birth, presented a Bible that indicated Fanny was born on May 23, 1894. Since Lizzie was unable to present a death record or a physician's statement proving Lewis's death, Joseph Allen and Fletcher Speller, age 44 years, submitted a sworn statement stating that Lewis was a close neighbor, they saw him after he died and Speller assisted in preparing the body for burial. Lizzie's application was approved on January 5, 1909. She received $12 per month for herself and $2 per month for Fanny.

By 1931, Lizzie was receiving $30 per month. However, on February 28, 1931, pursuant to the Act of June 9, 1930 providing $40 per month for 70-year-old widows, Lizzie informed the Bureau of Pensions her correct birth date was July 6, 1858. The Pension Bureau responded that she must have been born in 1861 rather than 1858 because her November 9, 1909 pension claim indicated that she was 48 years old. Therefore, the Bureau directed Lizzie to provide proof of her date of birth.

In a June 16, 1931 letter, Bertie County Circuit Judge Francis D. Winston explained the "discrepancy in the dates given of her birth are not surprising to those of us who know our colored friends of the pre-war days of 1861-65. They had no records and under the law of that day were not taught to read and write." In his affidavit, filled with genealogical information, Judge Winston said:

> ... I am approaching the age of seventy four years, having been born on the 2nd day of October 1857; that I have personally and intimately known the applicant herein, Lizzie L. Roulhac, from her early youth and from the year 1860; that she is a daughter of Aunt Cynthia Watson and a granddaughter of Aunt Dicey Watson, both slaves of my mother's Watson kin; that I have always understood that I was not quite a-year-

older than applicant; that for a number of years she was a nurse and servant in the family of my brother and father at Windsor; that on March 28, 1881, I was Clerk of the Superior Court of Bertie County and saw the Register of Deeds of said County on that date issue a license for the marriage of said applicant and Lewis Roulhac; that I have this day June 14, 1931, examined said application and the license issued there under and in both of said records the age of said Lizzie L. Watson now Roulhac is placed at 22 years; that I know said applicant to be a woman of truth and of high character and I accept the family tradition of her birth as having occurred on the 6th day of July 1858 ....

Lizzie's pension was increased to $40 per month, effective July 4, 1930. Less than a year later, on June 9, 1932, Lizzie died. Her daughter, Fannie L. Roulhac, age 29, was unsuccessful in her attempt to be reimbursed for expenses incurred during her mother's last illness and death. In her June 15 1932 application, Fannie claimed $15 for Dr. J. E. Smith; $30 for nurse Mary Winnie Speller; $150 for undertaker, W. H Carter; $5 for flowers; and $5 for gravedigger Hubert King for a total of $202.[123] Congressman John W. Kerr interceded on Fannie's behalf by telephoning the Pension Bureau and sending a June 15, 1932, letter of inquiry. On October 29, 1932, the Pension Bureau rejected Fannie's claim because Lizzie left assets - $525 - sufficient to meet the expenses of her last sickness and burial.

Private Rolack Winn
36th US Colored Troops

Very little is known about Private Rolack Winn's service in the USCT. His military and pension records have not been reviewed. He is described in the Company Descriptive Book for the 36th USCT as 18 years old; 5 feet 8inches; complexion, black; eyes black; hair black;

Chapter 4

born in Bertie County, North Carolina and that he enlisted at Plymouth, North Carolina, August 3, 1863.[124]

Henry Rolack, Navy
USS Miami

Henry Rolack served in United States Navy. When he enlisted at Plymouth, North Carolina, on October 29, 1863, he was described as a 27-year-old colored laborer, 5 feet 5 inches from Bertie County, North Carolina. He served aboard the *USS Miami*, a side-wheel, double-ender wooden gunboat, until January 13, 1864, when he was transferred to the hospital at New Bern, North Carolina. He was mustered out March 31, 1864.

Photo # NH 60873 Crewmembers of USS Miami

Sailor Henry Rolack, formerly enslaved in Bertie County, NC, served aboard the USS Miami. The USS Miami and the USS Southfield, while lashed together with chains, engaged the CSS Albemarle during the April 17-20, 1864, Battle of Plymouth. Several black USS Miami sailors are seen sewing and relaxing. Integrated crews were not uncommon in the Union Navy.

As the Roulhac pension records illustrate, it was not easy for African American Civil War veterans and their families to receive a pension. Proving one's entitlement could take years. The challenge in securing a pension was probably equal to that of serving in the War itself. However, it appears the applicants were not deterred by the maze of bureaucracy they encountered. As the cases of Privates Joseph Rollax and Lewis Roulhac illustrate, persistence made it possible for their descendants to continue to receive pensions for years after they died.

It is only fitting and proper that African American Civil War soldiers finally have their contributions recognized at the African American Civil War Memorial, 10th and U Streets, N.W., Washington, D.C. Private Joseph Rolacke, Private David Rolack, Private Joseph Rolack, Corporal Samuel Rolack, Corporal James Rolack, Private John Rolac, Private Rolack Winn and Private Lewis Rolack fought to free themselves and to insure the freedom of others who labored without compensation to create wealth for others. The day will come when Washington Roulhac and Henry Rolack will be included on a memorial honoring blacks sailors for their service during the Civil War.

Chapter 5
Back to Africa: Roulhacs in Liberia

After the Civil War, many freed slaves viewed their circumstances no more favorably than before their emancipation. Their lives were little changed. Despite major efforts by the Freedmen's Bureau agents and African American churches to assist the newly emancipated to organize and achieve political, economic and civil rights, many were threatened with serious setbacks as the promise of Reconstruction and "40 acres and a mule" never materialized. Although free, many saw themselves as Americans only in name. T. Thomas Fortune, a former slave born in Jackson County, Florida, who coined the term "Afro-American," recalled:

> "Nobody had his bearings. The freed people had no homes and no names except such as they inherited from their owners. They were in such a frame of mind as not to know whether to rejoice because they were free or to be cast down at their new condition of freedom, responsibility and homelessness."[125]

Some, therefore, turned to the American Colonization Society (ACS). The ACS was organized in 1816 to promote the colonization of free blacks in Africa. Its founders included wealthy and influential southern slave owners, including, Judge Bushrod Washington, President George Washington's nephew, Congressman Henry Clay of Kentucky and Francis Scott Key, the author of the Star Spangled Banner. Their interest in colonization was initially directed at the 200,000 free people of color who were characterized as an "ignorant, criminal and degraded" and the main source of slave insurrections. Rev. Robert Finley, a New Jersey Presbyterian minister, the main impetus for the Society's formation, believed Negroes were capable of improvement and self-government, but equality was impossible as long as they remained among whites; they were sons of Africa by color, temperament and fortune and God had destined them to dwell in Africa. Only in Africa, he advocated, could they find true freedom and equality and a better situation. Africa, would in turn, he reasoned, receive partially civilized and Christianized settlers. The Society's colonization efforts came under attack by leading abolitionists of the day; chief among them was William Lloyd Garrison.

The Society's interest in colonization was not a new idea. As early as 1777, Thomas Jefferson proposed a plan to the Virginia legislature for colonizing the free colored population. He observed that "among the Romans emancipation required but one effort. The slave when made free might mix without staining the blood of his master. But with us a second step is necessary, unknown to history. When freed he is to be removed beyond the reach of mixture." Jefferson proposed an emancipation plan that called for freeing all slaves after they reach maturity and the colonization of emancipated slaves in a far away place, selected "as the circumstances of time should render most proper".[12]

Several other colonization schemes followed. In 1785, William Thornton, a Quaker physician who designed the U.S. Capitol, after an unexpected inheritance of a number of West Indian slaves devised a plan to settle them in the West Indies. When the West Indies officials objected to having free Negroes living near their plantations, Thornton looked to Sierra Leone on the west coast of Africa.[127] In 1790, Ferdinando Fairfax of Virginia, who also believed that the two races could never live side by side in harmony and equality, proposed that Congress acquire a colony in Africa, the Negroes "native climate" far enough away to preclude rivalries and antagonism between the races and the free Negroes could carry Christian teachings to Africa's "rude race of men". St. George Tucker, in 1796 espoused that even if sponsored by the U.S. government, an attempt to colonize 300,000 Negroes would prove too expensive. Rather, he favored voluntary emigration in small numbers. He observed that "we have in history but one picture of a similar enterprise, and there it was necessary not only to open the sea by a miracle for them to pass, but more necessary to close it again, in order to prevent their return." Tucker recommended an experiment in lower Louisiana where the climate was more favorable and slave states would be induced to relax rigid laws against manumission.

Paul Cuffe, born in Massachusetts in 1759 to a Native American mother and an African father who purchased his freedom, believed that blacks in America would never have the full benefits of citizenship. He proposed settling them in Sierra Leone to evangelize the Africans, establish business enterprises and work to stop the slave trade at its source. In December 1815, Cuffe sailed to Freeport, Sierra Leone with 38 blacks –18 adults and 20 children – seven years before the ACS settled the first freed slaves in Liberia. By 1870, the ACS had colonized 14,574 ex-slaves and freeborn blacks and 5,722 recaptured Africans in Liberia. Of this number, 2,588 had been colonized during the five-year period since the end of the Civil War in 1865. In 1866, the ACS purchased the *Golconda*, a 1,016-ton refurbished ship that could accommodate 600 passengers. In one year, from May 1867 to May 1868, it carried 1,068 emigrants in three trips. Families were promised 25 acres of land, free transportation and six months support.

On November 11, 1869, one hundred sixty ex-slaves embarked from Hampton Roads, Virginia, on the *Golconda* for Liberia. The majority, 123 were from North Carolina – 79 from Bertie County and 44 from Martin County. Twelve Roulhacs, all women except 43-year-old Alexander Roulhac and four-year-old Nero, were among the 79 from Bertie County. They were the first settlers of Arthington, 25 miles up the St. Paul River from Monrovia, Liberia's capital.[128] The departure and arrival of the emigrants was described in a "Good News From Africa" report in *The African Repository* as follows:

> Last November, at Portsmouth, Va., it was my privilege to meet a company of freedmen, who had assembled there from different States, for the purpose of taking passage in the "*Golconda*," a large ship belonging to the American Colonization Society, as emigrants to the Republic of Liberia. They had come from Texas, Tennessee, North Carolina and Pennsylvania, all animated by one common purpose, a desire to return to the land of their forefathers, there to become citizens in the prosperous African Republic, and at the same time to promote the extension of civilization and Christianity in Africa. A very large proportion of the adults were the followers of Jesus, and among them there were many members of Baptist churches. I saw their happy faces. I heard their songs of praise and their fervent prayers. Some were skilled mechanics, and had with them their blacksmith and carpenters' tools. Others were accustomed to the hardy pursuits of agriculture and were provided with hoes, axes, saws and other implements.
>
> A large number from Bertie County, North Carolina, 79 in all, were known as the "Arthington Company." A generous philanthropist in England, Robert Arthington, had sent £1,000, which yielded, by premium on gold and interest, more than $7,000. His gift was sent, one-half to William Coppinger, Esq., and one-half to Rev. Thomas S. Malcolm, "to be laid out in sending persons to Liberia, in whom it is unmistakably evident, that they have the highest

welfare of Africa at heart, that they long to see thousands, and yet thousands more, till the heart is filled with joy unspeakable, of natives of Africa, gathered now henceforth from African soil, to the name and love of Christ, of Jesus! That dear name on whom the hope of heaven depends, that name on which all nations shall yet dwell with sweetest song." The generous donor stated that he appropriated the money to send those "whose hearts and souls are bent on Africa's regeneration, who will pray without ceasing, 'Thy kingdom come,' and labor thereunto according to their several ability."

We believe that God, by His special providence, designated the proper persons to go. The leader of the Arthington Company is Alonzo Hoggard, a deacon of a Baptist church in North Carolina. At a farewell meeting, held in the meeting house of the Zion colored church in Portsmouth, Va., Rev. E. G. Corprew, pastor, it was stated by Alonzo Hoggard that he "was not moved by the love of money or the desire for honor, but was prompted by the love of Christ to go to Africa." He added, "I thank God that my ancestors were ever brought to America; for if it had not been for slavery, they would probably have remained heathen. But here they gained the knowledge of Christ, and now we can go back with the religion of Jesus, and with the white man's trades. As God has permitted the white man to conquer and occupy all parts of the earth, except Africa, I think that he has reserved Africa for the black man. I think that it is the duty of all persons to care first for the welfare of their own kindred, and therefore, as a black man, I feel it to be my duty to promote the welfare of the people of Africa."

The "*Golconda*" … reached Monrovia, on December 19ᵗʰ, in 35 days.¹²⁹ On November 5, 1870, the *Golconda* made its fifth and last voyage to Liberia. It sailed from Hampton Roads, Virginia, with 194 emigrants. John B. Roulhac was the leader of the 111 Bertie County passengers. Eight Roulhacs from Plymouth, Washington County, North Carolina were also on the voyage.¹³⁰

In *The Price of Liberty* Claude Andrew Legg observes that not all emigrants were satisfied with conditions in Arthington. He writes:
¹³¹

> In 1871, several single women were reported "to get along badly" for lack of husbands and land, a common theme of Liberian life. Immigrants such as John B. Roulhac and Peter Mountain, both of Bertie County, craved meat, still a luxury item in Liberia. Roulhac even claimed that some individuals were actually "suffering from lack of meat" and requested that Coppinger send dogs to Liberia for the hunting of deer. As in the past, the struggle against the environment was the major preoccupation of Arthington residents. While malarial mortality there did not approach the epidemic proportions that it had in earlier years, tales of chills, sores, and other ailments were regularly chronicled in correspondence. Unfortunately, the heavy rains of the early 1870s could only have increased the sickliness of the people in the region.

Charles R. Branch, the grandson of Alonzo Hoggard, the leader of the 1869 Bertie County emigrants, was seven years old when he boarded the *Golconda*. By 1905, he had become president of the College of West Africa in Monrovia. He published the following 35-year account of the Arthington:¹³²

How to Reach Arthington and a List of the First Immigrants[133]

Leaving the city of Monrovia by a steam launch, making eight miles an hour, you will arrive at the settlement of Millsburg, the head of the navigation on the St. Paul's River, within three hours. A one hour's [walk] through this settlement will take you into the settlement of Arthington – beautifully dotted with hills, shaded with coffee and other fruit trees, with nearly each house situated on each one of those hills.

The settlement of Arthington was founded under the auspices of the American Colonization Society in the year 1869, and named in honor of Robert Arthington, of Leeds, England, who contributed largely towards the opening of that settlement. Arthington's first immigrants sailed from North Carolina, U.S.A., Nov. 10, 1869, by the ship *Golconda*, under the leadership of the illustrious and much lamented Alonzo Hoggard. These immigrants arrived at Monrovia in the month of December ensuing, just a few days before Christmas.

A site for the settlement in the rear of Millsburg was soon chosen, their lands were surveyed, and they soon left the city and went to work, to make a living for themselves on their farms, the Society allowing them rations for six months.

In1870, another colony sailed from North Carolina in the same ship, for Arthington, and arrived in Monrovia in the month of December, headed by John Roulhac. During the following year, another larger colony sailed in the *Edith Rose*, under three divisions, viz: The first, from Valdosta Georgia, headed by Jefferson Bracewell, Sr.; the second, from Ellaville, Florida, headed by Brister Wright; and the third from York County, South Carolina, led by Elias Hill.[134]

In the year 1872 or 1873, another company was sent out being led by Aaron Miller. Long before this time, the former immigrants had ceased to draw rations from the Society, and being "new-comers," (as they were commonly called by the settlers of the country) and with no money, they now began to face "hard times."

Some had built comfortable log houses, while others lived in thatch huts. They cleared up their lands the best they could and planted cassadas, potatoes, eddoes, corn and such other vegetables that the country afforded; going many a day with only one meal a day, and some days with none at all. Unfortunately for them, when they got ready for planting, in the majority of cases, they had to buy cassada-sticks and potato-vines, etc., with whatever they could painfully part with, out of the household supplies. And many a time, when the poor "new-comers" could find something to buy these vegetable scions with, the sellers would throw them away in the woods on his way home, before he would give them away; and the "new-comers" would sometimes find them.

As their cassadas, etc., grew to the size of your great toe, they were compelled to eat them. Being thus immature, a great quantity would be consumed within a very short time. This of course, suggested many ways of cooking – the good old American cook, with her sagacious eye, would cook cassada-soup one day, potato-soup the next and eddo-soup the next, and so on; the only seasoning being salt and salt-brine, when these could be had, cayenne-pepper and sweet-brier leaf. But among all soups that I have ever tasted, the cassada-soup is the most unpalatable.

The hard times caused many of the people to wish, as it were, for the "flesh pots of Egypt." But their bounds were fixed – they must live or die in Liberia. Consequently, some began to seek employment in the neighboring settlements and at Muhlenburg Mission on the St. Paul's River, to get a little flour, palm-oil, salt-meat and fish; leaving home on Monday morning and returning Saturday night, with just enough to last until the next Monday morning when they would be off again in the same pursuit.

Others would saw plank and get shingles, exposing their health to inclement weather, finding a market for these at Muhlenburg Mission and the settlements on the river, as well as at Monrovia. It was a common thing to see grown women – married and unmarried, and grown girls (as well as men and boys) - carrying large bundles of shingles as well as plank on their heads for their husbands and their fathers through the streets of Arthington and Millsburg, wading through creeks and mud to obtain food and clothing. I have met one of our leading farmer's wife many a day barefooted, on her way to Millsburg with an unmerciful bundle of shingles on her head. I should think she now enjoys the sweet remembrances of those days.

Advice of Alonzo Hoggard

Alonzo Hoggard, seeing that this mode of living would always cause the people to be from hand-to-mouth, to a poverty stricken condition, put forth every effort to dissuade them from pursuing such a course. He would often say to men in these works: "Stay at home and work and you will make yourselves a comfortable living bye and bye [sic]." He, in the meantime setting the example, caused the people to desist from leaving the settlement to seek employment, and to turn their attention to farming, being contented with such comforts as their farms afforded.

About this time many were suffering from various troubles; chief among which were ulcers on their feet and legs. John M. Mills was one of these great sufferers of whom we will say more hereafter. The people, now being constantly encouraged by the good counsels of Alonzo Hoggard, Jefferson Bracewell, Sr., Solomon Hill, June Moore, J.C. Taylor, Brister Wright, Aaron Miller and others, were inspired to go to work, raising coffee, ginger and other marketable products; as the heavy forests began to fall before them more extensively, better and more comfortable houses were built and Arthington was soon called by visitors a thriving settlement.

Union Among the People and Their Trials in Going to and From Monrovia

In that early period of the settlement there was greater love and union existing among the people than may be felt now-a-days. If a man had a large quantity of ginger to be scraped in order to dry it, (for it was never dried then, without being scraped as it is now) he would order what was called "a ginger scraping;" and, in the beautiful moonlight, out on a large, clean yard, a large gathering of people would scrape for him a thousand or more pounds of ginger within a short while and then go home feeling happy. If you were pressed for hands to gather in your coffee crop, it could be done in a similar manner. In the same way could a man that was building, have his timber carried and put on the spot and the carpentry done to a great extent.

As there was no mercantile business carried on in the settlement at that time, you had to go to Monrovia whenever you were fortunate enough to have the means to buy what you needed that could not be had on the river. The city of Monrovia then seemed to the people here, to be farther from Arthington than it really is. As there were no steamers running on the St Paul's River, the canoe was the only conveyance; and in the high-water months, you might manage to make the round trip within three days. The majority of the people of Arthington that visited Monrovia on business at that time, slept under old dilapidated sheds and in cargo boats. There was a very remarkable incident in this connection respecting Henry Taylor, one of the primitive school teachers of Arthington, who taught a school supported by the American Colonization Society. He, being able to draw a quantity of provision, cloth and tobacco, (but not much money) at the end of the quarter, was looked upon as "the big man" in Arthington, and consequently, could hire more young men of the settlement than he needed as "canoe boys" to take him to Monrovia. On reaching the city, when night came on, the thought of being a school teacher and having to make his bed with his "canoe boys," under an old shed or in a cargo board, greatly embarrassed him – so much so that the "boys" discovered it; and would say to him. "Henry, where are you going to sleep tonight?" He would answer, "Never mind, I've got a place." And the morning told the secret; for having over-slept himself he was seen by his "boys" crawling out of an empty flour barrel in the neighborhood of a shed under which they had slept. And such a hearty laugh they had. A certain man bears a mark now over his eye, received from a piece of timber in a falling shed under which he was sleeping.

The Settlement Finds a Friend in the Muhlenburg Mission

The Muhlenburg Mission, situated about three quarters of a mile from Arthington, has been, and is now a great help to the settlement. The much lamented Rev. and Mrs. Day might have been easily called the citizens of Arthington, for they were here in the early growth of the settlement and shared in our sorrows and our struggles. They rendered great assistance to many a poor widow and orphan child, in taking their vegetables, etc., for medicines and many other necessaries which they could not get for them elsewhere. And oftentimes, when they had nothing to carry, they were never turned away empty handed. Their baskets were frequently seen going to the sick, laded with dainties from their table. For many years, David A. Day served the settlement as a doctor – responding to any call at any hour of the day or night, and never asking a penny. The death of these two distinguished American citizens Arthington has lost two great friends.

Trouble with the Barveer Chief

The town of Barveer lies about three miles east of Arthington, and is of ancient date. It constitutes a part of the township. T. J. Bracewell had a large ox which he asked Nungburwool, king of the town to keep a while for him in order to avoid annoying his neighbors. The king consented and the ox was sent out to the town. Sometime afterwards, or in the year 1875, Bracewell sent to the king for his ox. But he refused to send him. He sent several times again, and he still refused to give him up, but threatened to bring war upon the settlement. The citizens became so much alarmed at this that guards were stationed and everybody was on the lookout.

The circumstances were laid before His Excellency James S. Payne, then President of the Republic, who ordered the militia of Arthington to bring this hostile chief to terms. The company assembled a day or so after receiving the command at the residence of June Moore between 4 and 5 o'clock p.m., and marched to the residence of Aaron Miller with about 40 soldiers. They left Miller's place the early part of that night and reached the large creek called Weagkbar, which is about 50 or 60 feet wide at the place of crossing, about 9 o'clock. It was in the month of September, the high-water month. Here comes the first obstacle – they found no bridge over the creek.

Some of the men suggested that they should not attempt to proceed any further, but return home. Others suggested that a tree be cut down across the creek on which they might cross over. Considerable time was taken up in trying to decide upon one of these suggestions; meanwhile, quite a number of them, being already faint-hearted, pictured themselves on the other side of this great creek, should they be defeated, like "Israel of old" – "A sea before, a host behind, and rocks on either hand," returned home leaving only the brave and true-hearted soldiers to "stand by the flag." The tree was cut down, but its top did not quite reach the opposite shore. However, they found that the water between the top of the tree and the shore was about waist deep. The Bracewells being the tallest men in the company, Littleton was detailed to take the men over from the log by wading. This duty he readily performed. When he came to Joshua Brigant, Sr., a good-old Methodist class leader, in taking him up in his arms, the muscles of which resembled those of the "old village blacksmith," in his usual jovial way (for which the Bracewells were much noted) he exclaimed, "I baptize thee" – and plunged the old man under the stream with as much earnestness as though he were authorized to do so. The old man's modesty being so shocked, when he thought of being baptized against his will, and then by an imposter, he rose fighting and scratching "Lit." [sic] all over the head and face.

All now being over, they moved onward under the heavy rain that was falling, through the dark woods, making very slow speed; it taking them the remainder of the night to reach the town which was barricaded. At 6 o'clock in the morning, the natives discovered them through the gate. One man picked up the war horn and began to blow it. He was shot. A crowd ran to close the gate facing the main road. They were driven back. One Civey Varngay, the head warrior was seen loading a double-barrel shotgun. He was shot in the arm, and of course, dropped it. This seemed to have weakened them and they fled out of the town, leaving the ox, which the company brought home.

The affair was reported in a very unfavorable manner to the Grand Jury, at the following session of the Court of Quarter Sessions and Common Pleas of the County, and might have given the settlement great trouble, had not President Payne set matters aright by stating to the Grand Jury, that it was done by his orders, and that they had not done all that he told them to do. Our enemies then, with shame began to disappear one by one. Not many months after this, the Cape Palmas war began. Soldiers were called for from Arthington and other settlements. The majority of the Arthington soldiers willingly met in Monrovia, preparatory to moving off with the Regiment; while others that feared to offer their lives as a sacrifice for their country, refused to go with their fellows; and when sent for, hid themselves in the woods, suffering to be hunted as a deer or some other wild animal.

Before the troops left for Cape Palmas, the late Rev. S.J. Campbell, of Millsburg, knowing that rumor was still extant that Nungburwool would likely attack Arthington, made it his business to go down and say before the President and his Cabinet the serious condition in which the settlement was placed. Whether he did this because he feared that Arthington, which served as a strong wall in the rear of his settlement might be broken down, thus exposing Millsburg to the enemy, or whether it was from a purely philanthropic turn of mind, it is hard to decide; for he was a man that was not easily understood. However, he succeeded in favorably impressing the Executive Government, being a man *nulli secundus* as an orator. The company was discharged and all returned home except James Delyon and James Robinson, who were determined to go.

Solomon Hill and Others' Adventure with a Wild Bull, Early in the Eighties

Solomon Hill having discovered a path, which was regularly used by wild cattle, set a gun for them. The report of the gun was heard the following night, and the next morning Hill, with five other men, went to see what was the result. On reaching the spot they found blood; by continuing the same until about 9 o'clock, it brought them in sight of a huge wild bull lying down in a creek. At the sight of them, he arose and started out of the creek; and it appeared from the noise he made, as though there were about a dozen of them going through the water. Following him for the space of an hour or more, Hill passed into a thicket; and without the least notice, found himself between the horns of this frightful animal which was tossing him in the air. He had already seized both horns with his hands, holding his gun by the breech in one hand at the same time. He paid no attention to the tossing but stuck to the horns. Meanwhile, David Moore, seeing his uncle in such a dangerous position, ran up and fired on the bull over his uncle's shoulder, the ball striking his little finger, cutting the breech of his gun in two, breaking his thumb, striking the side of the horn and glancing off. Hill managed to get away from him by some means, and as the bull's horns lay in a horizontal manner, he was not able to gore him. The other men continued to fire at him as opportunity afforded itself, and this shooting called to the battle ground nearly half of the settlement. One man said he was going to carry his ax and kill him with it. Another said he was going to walk up to him and tie him with a rope and cut his throat. But poor fellows! They did not know the folly of their speech. As this fierce animal plunged at them, the men with the ax and rope were seen falling in different directions. He would knock down a half a dozen of them at a time. One man climbed a slender tree, and another followed him. Their weight consequently made the young tree bend in the direction of the bull which was standing waiting for another attack; and much quarrelling with each other, was worth hearing.

The battle continued until about 5 'o clock that afternoon, when they succeeded in killing the bull. Fortunately for them, nobody was killed and they had plenty of fresh beef.

Our Bondor Trouble

This affair grew out of the action of certain marauders styled the Sofah war, from the far interior that had been influenced by Dowee Zwai, who was fighting to establish himself upon the throne of his deceased father.

They plundered all of the native towns near the settlement, growing so bold that they came into the settlement and killed a man at Sherman Miller's farm, taking his wife and children and carrying them away. Their headquarters were at Bondor, a native town about five miles from the heart of the settlement.

This was very provoking to the citizens; therefore, they laid their grievances before His Excellency, the President. But he, having repeatedly received contradictory statements by certain evil-hearted men respecting the same, was puzzled to know what to do. As things went on, the people considered themselves in a perilous state when their cries did not claim the attention of the executive government in a favorable way. Finally, they concluded that they might as well die one way as another. A company was formed which left the settlement about 10 o'clock one night, reached the town the next morning at sun-rising and showed those natives that they should not commit such infamous crimes against the people. Certain men who were supposed to have been in the company, were called in question before the law; but the grand jury failed to find a true bill, and therefore, they were acquitted of the charge. It cost the settlement something over $75.00. Arthington had a good many friends in this trying time who rendered great assistance of her in this matter.

Politics in Arthington

No political strife was known to exist in the settlement for many years. The "True Whig Party" was chosen as the party for the people and the Fathers taught them to stand by that Party – never dividing, for their union would be their strength.

Attempts were made at several times by shrewd politicians to sever this union, saying, it was an unheard of thing that every man in a place should vote the same way. But this union was planted deeply into the hearts and sealed at the time with fervent prayer. The people stood together, observing the instructions of the Fathers; and during campaign times, there was no fear about Arthington. Rum and gin were unknown things in the time of election. The citizens came and voted for their national leaders in a quiet manner and returned home to their work. Whatever these men said, whom God had made leaders, the people followed.

But when their Fathers were gathered home, many of them "went a whoring after other gods, and bowed themselves unto them: they turned quickly out of the way which their Fathers walked in, obeying the commandments of the Lord; but they did not so." (Judge 2, 17) Therefore, the wolf came in and scattered them; and all have not yet come back. In this age men are seen going to the polls armed with guns, razors, revolvers and clubs, I supposed, to slay their fellows.

While I do not condemn men for having different opinions to a certain extent, yet this great difference sometimes breeds too many leaders; and too many so-called leaders are detrimental to any party.

The Baptist and Methodist Churches in Arthington

Johnson Taylor, of Birtee [sic] County, North Carolina, U.S.A., sent Alonzo Hoggard one green back dollar as the first step towards building a chapel for the Baptist Church in this settlement. The settlement was perhaps three years old when the Baptist began to build their first chapel. Devotional exercises were held in a small log cabin, about 16 x 12 built for a school house on the south corner of the West road, where the late S.R. Hoggard's shop now stands.

The first church edifice was erected on one acre of land donated for that purpose by Alonzo Hoggard, behind which he and his beloved wife Nancy were buried, at their decease. The size of the building was about 16 x 25 – all framework. There was no ordained minister in the church then, therefore, they had to ask a minister of another settlement when he was needed to execute the functions of that office.

Peter Mountain held the clerkship of the Church for perhaps two years; and at one conference meeting, because things did not work to suit his fancy, he threw down the books and walked out of the Church. Then and there, Deacon John Roulhac called his stepson, William Righten Roulhac to the table, who was elected to fill the vacancy, and he served the Church faithfully, from the year 1873 until his death in the year 1902, twenty-nine consecutive years.

In those days, the Church was very strict with its members. They were not allowed to deal in alcoholic liquors directly nor indirectly. But now-a-days the Church discipline seems to have become very tame; men will do daring deeds and then challenge the Church. There was more love among the brethren – envy and strife were foreign terms with the brotherhood. "They had all things common." When you entered their service, you would surely be inspired by their melodious voices. Scott Mason was one of the choristers for the Church; and when he opened his mouth to sing, his voice was the very expression of sweet music, and would simply charm you.

The first chapel now fast decaying, the Church set about building another. At the expiration of a few more years, the second building was erected, being about 20 x 36, and a fine bell was purchased at a cost of $100. After this building had been used for a good many years and had also become dilapidated, as all of the people had moved out of town on their farms, the Church proposed building another larger and more substantial edifice, - not on the same grounds, but nearer to the center of the inhabitants. Therefore, the third Baptist Church was built 30 x 40 feet, shut in and covered with galvanized corrugated iron and painted. The building, together with a schoolhouse built on the same grounds, is worth about $4,500.

This church was organized in the settlement about the year 1873. The late Hon. B Dennis, of Monrovia, gave $100 towards building the first chapel and appropriated 10 acres of land for the same. June Moore took the job of furnishing the lumber and Solomon Hill, Sr., that of the building. The Church then began to move along nicely. A short time after this, one Flaigler arrived in the country from the United States of America and organized in Arthington the African Methodist Episcopal Church. The members of the Methodist Episcopal Church then revolted and connected themselves with the A.M.E. Church, which resulted in practically breaking up the M.E. Church; and it has never regained its foothold.

Peter Watson having deeded the land occupied by the Church in his name, the chapel was abandoned by the Church and used as a school house. The first chapel of the A.M.E. Church was built on a half acre of land obtained from Mrs. Abigail Mason; but in the course of time, it was found to be owned by Hill and Moore; consequently, it had to be removed. Clement Irons being one of the first men of the church and a devoted Christian, bought of Hill and Moore a five-acre block of land near the center of the settlement upon which the second chapel was erected, being larger and of better material. The A.M.E. Church deserves much praise for having raised up two young men in the ministry who are among the leaders of the church.

John M. Mills

John M. Mills immigrated to Arthington in the year 1870, from North Carolina, U.S.A. He was taken down the following year with a large ulcer on his right foot, which was a companion of his for 18 years. With a wife and two small children to care for, one of which died not many months after his arrival here, he began to sail as it were, through seas of trouble. But being of that class of men with an indomitable will, he was determined to succeed in Liberia. He commenced farming in the year 1876, on his 25 acre allotment. He would hobble out in the farm in much pain and sit upon a stool which his wife carried for him, with tears almost in her eyes to see her husband work with such a large ulcer and dig the holes and plant his coffee.

At last he succeeded in planting out the whole of the 25 acres with the exception of about three acres, which were left for timber. He ate some days next to nothing; and what he ate many a day, were it told here, it would shock the modesty of the present generation. By toiling on, in a few years he was able to reap a few pounds of coffee from his farm, and as soon as opportunity presented itself, he began to ship it. Being a man that never lived beyond his income, he kept out of debt and waited for the arrival of his goods. His wife was one of those women whose heart was more within than was without; she contented herself with such things as their income allowed them to provide. In the course of a few years, Mills began to reap his thousands of coffee, and could look the whole world in its face, for he owed not any man.

Having had this ulcer so long, he decided in his mind that a cure would never be effected. With renewed vigor, he opened another farm in 1890 and planted out 88 acres in coffee; and when this farm began to bear fully, he gathered from both farms, from 25 to 30,000 pounds. He owns a fine brick building on Broad Street in the city of Monrovia. The same is on rent, bringing perhaps three to $400 annually. Mills is a model for any man coming to Liberia with a view to making it his home.

Solomon Hill, Sr.

Solomon Hill came to Liberia in the immigration of 1871, with his wife, five children and a host of other relatives. Being a blacksmith by trade, he found himself busy after he had acclimated. Notwithstanding this, he saw that farming was the most profitable thing then for him to do. Therefore, instead of exacting money from the people, (which they did not have) for his labor, he would take in payment, their labor on his farm; and in a few years, he had opened a large coffee farm.

He continued working at his trade until his farm demanded so much of his attention that he was compelled to suspend blacksmithing and give his whole attention to farming. Today, he has out about 275 acres in coffee, realizing nearly 50,000 pounds yearly. He, with his brother-in-law, the late Rev. June Moore, established themselves in a business in the year 1889 and carried on the same extensively in the County until the death of Rev. Moore.

Hill owns a fine brick building on Ashmun Street, and a large business place on Water St., in the city of Monrovia; also a large zinc store in the settlement of Millsburg. He also conducts a fine business in Arthington.

Much credit is due him, (as well as other men in the settlement who have done the same) for having succeeded in making good citizens of nine native boys that were brought from the interior and raised up in his family. Some of them have married Americo-Liberian families and are farming in a most successful manner.

About the year 1901 seeing the great use of a steam boat on the St. Paul's river for the safe conveyance of the people and their produce, he ordered from Germany, a motor launch – "the *Laura-Ann*," at the cost of nearly $3,000 and placed the same at the service of the people, which boat has been a means of saving both life and property. After running this boat a few years, it was found that she was not adequate to the amount of traffic, and consequently, another large and more commodious motor launch – the "*Jessena Hill*," was purchased by Hill and Senator R. Jackson, of Louisiana, on the St. Paul's River, at a cost of $6,000 and placed at the pleasure of the people.

Brister Wright

He came to Liberia, with Solomon Hill and Jefferson Bracewell. Being a strong advocate of home industry, he made a loom and proceeded to show the people that they could manufacture their own cloth in Liberia - that one step would bring about another, on independent lines. Eight pieces of cloth were nicely woven and made into garments and worn. But, not being able to induce the people to patronize his work, and having no capital, he was forced to abandon it and take up farming, at which has been successful.

Small-Pox in the Settlement in the Year 1889

During the month of August 1889, small-pox broke out in the settlement in the family of Mrs. Amanda

Thomas with her son and daughter and one native boy. A committee consisting of Rev. June Moore and J.C. Taylor, Sr., (who had had the disease before they came to the country) was appointed by the township to visit the family and find out the certainty of it. They accordingly did so, and reported as follows: We visited the patients with small-pox on the 31st of August and made a close examination of the same. We decided that Caroline, the daughter, has it. It accordance with the request of the town meeting, we communicated the following to Doctor Hubler, of Muhlenburg Mission:

Dr. E.M. Hubler,

As information has already reached you that small-pox is in our settlement, we write to inform you that we have visited the family, and have never seen anything just like it but small-pox. This is the 9th day since they began to postulate and now, the pustules are much inflamed, causing the face to swell. The patient's face looks like one entire blister. The pustules seem to be filled with pus. We have had some experience with small-pox and we think it not a mild form, but a violent case. The pustules have come out in the palms of her hands – not much fever now. We shall visit her every day; and if you have no objection we will let you know the condition from time to time, as we have no doctor near us to decide what the complaint is. The pills you gave us for the patient did her much good. May our heavenly Father bless you for your kindness. With kindest regards,

Yours truly,
J.C Taylor, June Moore, Committee

Chapter 5

The committee received the following:

Dear Sirs:

From the description, I pronounce it vile small-pox.

         E.M. Hubler

Your Committee highly appreciates the wise action taken by the Township in compelling the diseased family to stay in their own house; and in turning the public road from their house. The citizens have been very generous in furnishing the sick family with food so far: [table omitted: John Roulhac contributed ½ kross eddoes and 1 bunches of greens.]

We visited the patients every day and feel grateful to say that they are all getting better. Caroline, the first case is now about well. The mother and her son are about out of danger. Theirs were only mild forms of the disease. The mother has not been confined to bed at all. We think in a few more weeks, the family will be well. The native boy has not had the small-pox, but a snake bit him and he has not been able to walk much for two days; during which time, Mr. Taylor carried water for them.

We employed a native man by the name of Dwal, to doctor the boy that was bitten by the snake. He visited the boy twice and charged $2.00 for his services, but we promised him only 50 cents, which is all the expense we have undergone up to the present.

Your committee recommends that after the family are well, all of the bedding and clothes used by the patients be well washed and boiled in lye, the floor and walls of the house scrubbed and scalded with lye – all mats in the house should be buried and the house well smoked with sulphur. We have addressed the following communication to Dr. Hubler:

Dear Sir:

How long after a person is well of the small-pox, must it be, before it would be safe for him to come in contact with other persons? What is the best method of cleansing the house? The Lord has blessed us so far in keeping the disease confined in the one family, and now, they are getting better and will soon want to come out.

Yours truly, J.C. Taylor, June Moore, Committee

The Doctor gave them the following reply:

Dear Sirs:

Keep them in and away from contact with other people until the eruptions have all thoroughly dried up and the scabs have all fallen off, leaving the skin perfectly healed under them. The clothing worn by the persons having the disease, or coming in contact with them, as bed clothing, etc., should be thoroughly buried or burned. All of the cotton or woolen goods in the room should be thoroughly washed; boiling is better. The house should be thoroughly scrubbed with lye, then burn quantities of sulphur all through the house with doors and windows closed.

Yours, etc., E.M. Hubler

We hope the Township will have these plans carried out before the patients are allowed to come in contact with other persons.

A vote of thanks was tendered the Committee for their able services and they were instructed to continue to do the needful services. A small amount of $6 was appropriated to compensate them. The amount of $15 was appropriated and placed at the disposal of the Committee to make the necessary arrangements respecting the house containing the diseased family, and 50 cents for curing the boy, bitten by the snake.

The patients now being well, the house was cleansed; only $3.85 being used of the $15 appropriated. Before the close of the year the disease settled down into other families and resulted in the death of Mrs. Mourning Obey and John Roulhac. The others were carefully attended and they recovered.

About the years 1897 and 1898, small-pox broke out in the family of T. J. Bracewell. Five of his children were victims to the disease, viz: Malissa (now Mrs. Turket), Rhoda, Artenee (now Mrs. F. Bernard), James and Spencer. Also five native boys. They were all nicely cared for by their father, and all recovered except one of the native boys.

Rev. A. Moses Roulhac, second from left, a third generation descent of John Roulhac, at the 2005 Roulhac Family Association Reunion in Chicago, Illinois, with, left to right: Judge Roy L. Roulhac, Edgar Roulhac and Judge Joseph D. Roulhac.

The Late Solomon York

Solomon York, one of the pioneers of the settlement, came to Liberia with a large family in the year 1869. At once he took up farming, as that was his occupation in the United States, and at which was successful. He believed in helping his fellowman; therefore he would always have something in the line of merchandise to sell; and would take in return shingles, plank – new or second-handed. If there were a dilapidated building for sale, he would buy in order to give assistance to someone. And people would sometimes wonder what could he get out of such seemingly useless things. In fact, he was one of the most wonderful men of his age. He was reliable in business, truthful in character, firm in purpose and sympathizing in heart – a true philanthropist.

He never held any public office in the settlement, choosing rather, to hold the high office of preaching the Gospel of Christ. Consequently, he was licensed to preach by the Baptist Church, which position he served faithfully until his death in the year 1889.

At a subsequent town meeting of the citizens of Arthington, the following resolution was offered by Rev. June Moore and adopted:

Resolved, that the citizens of Arthington deeply feel the vacancy that has occurred in our midst, in the death of Mr. Solomon York, who was one of the Fathers and founders of our settlement. He came to Liberia with the brave and patriotic Hoggard as pioneers.

Let us today ask ourselves shall we strive to retain the name that was given them for uprightness, goodness and truthfulness toward our neighbor? If union is strength, they taught us union; if love is power, they taught us love; if the diligent hands shall be made fit; they proved that as counselors. Mr. York will ever be remembered by the present generation. His fervent prayers in our midst were that the blessings of our heavenly Father would rest upon us and the rising generation. We shall ever cherish his good words in our memory.

Public and Private Schools

The first day school opened in the settlement was fostered by the Colonization Society. It was first taught by one Lillerson, who came here from the United States of America, with the first immigrants. This man was an old broken-down aristocrat – a mean fellow; nobody liked him of the account of his ways. In coming over on the "*Golconda*," he was always seen by himself, or near the cabin. He thought it *infra dignitatem* to sit and converse with his brethren. His days were not many here, and he died in the early age of the settlement. The next teacher of the school was the late Henry Jacobs, a citizen of Millsburg. He taught the school for a number of years and turned out some promising students; among them is the Hon. Henry Taylor, of this settlement. Jacobs was succeeded upon his resignation by the late Rev. T. B. Lane, who formerly lived on the St. Paul's River, but afterwards removed to the settlement of Millsburg, where he died some years ago. He was similar in disposition to Lillerson, and after teaching awhile, he left the chair which was filled by Hon. Henry Taylor for a number of years.

About the year 1874 or 1875, the Alexander High School, supported by the Presbyterian Board in the United States of America, was re-opened in the settlement of Harrisburg on the St. Paul's River with Dr. E. Blyden, one of the most distinguished men of the Negro race, at its head; and the scholar and statesmen – the late Senator Alfred B. King, tutor of that school.

Dr. Blyden, with an unbiased and race-loving heart, called in young men, women and boys from Monrovia and the different settlements on the river, to share in the benefits of that worthy school. He communicated with my grandfather, Alonzo Hoggard to know if he had any children that might be put in to swell the number. The old man's heart leaped for joy at receiving the communication, saying, "I will send Penelope and Charlie that they may be educated and return home and teach the other children of the settlement." The old man managed to learn to read and write well enough, during or after slavery in the United States of America, to read his own writing, but it would puzzle any one else to read it. It is said that he once wrote a letter to the agent of the Colonization Society at Monrovia, who was so puzzled at trying to read it, that he had to send for him to come down and read it for him.

Knowing the value of education, he at once made preparation for our leaving home for the school, in the best manner that his limited means would allow. We entered the school and were getting on nicely until a short while afterwards there came up one day, a very severe thunderstorm, in the midst of which, my Aunt Penelope was killed by lightning. I will always remember that awful day. The contents of my box, with leather hinges and hasp, were two pairs of blue-baft pantaloons, two calico shirts and two domestic jumpers, made to hang loosely on the boy in those days, something like a blouse. Shoes were not in the question. My straw hat for both Sunday and Monday, showed the ingenuity of our brother, the native man. I always wished I had on something much thicker on the days I did not have a perfect lesson; for my teacher thoroughly understood using the rod.

I remained in this school until the year 1878, when it was removed to the settlement of Clay-Ashland, probably on account of heavy expense which had to be met. Students then would get their tuition free, but they would have to board with private families. I was indeed greatly benefited by that school. But as my grandfather was not able to pay board and lodging for me at Clay-Ashland, I was shut out from further attending the school. Finally, my grandfather died in the year 1880, and I lost all hope then of ever attending another high school.

About the close of the same year, to my agreeable surprise, a message was borne to me from Dr. Blyden, that the Liberia College would be re-opened the following January, and that I should come down and enter the same. My grandmother somewhat objected to it upon the ground that she was getting old and wanted me near her with the rest of the children. Her eldest son, the late Joseph B. Hoggard, said, "No, mother, let this boy go to school. He may be of great service to us all bye and bye." She then waived her objections and sent me down, and I entered the college January 1881, remained there as a student until January 1884, when I left and came back home. I took charge of the Colonization school after Henry Taylor resigned, and occupied the chair until the Agent for the Society closed it. I was then appointed teacher of the government school and taught it six months and resigned.

During the operation of the Colonization school, another day school was opened in the settlement, being supported by an American philanthropist – the late Edward S. Morris, of the city of Philadelphia, PA. It was taught by the late Rev. June Moore and was closed sometime in the '80s. Rev. Moore came to Arthington in the 3rd immigration, with his wife and four children. He turned his attention to farming, and made a comfortable living. He was a great lover of education, although his was quite limited. He was a hard student and extensive reader and by this he made himself a strong man among strong men – possessing broad views and deep logical reasoning.

After the death of Alonzo Hoggard, the people accepted June Moore as their leader both spiritually and politically. He seemed to have been born a leader of men; always willing and ready to give counsel on any matter, which when given, none were able to set aside. His manner of arriving at things was usually hidden away in most charming and affectionate expressions. He could steal his way into your bosom and there read as it were, the depth of your soul before you could discern his meaning. In all things wherein the interest of the settlement was at stake, the people felt that in him they had a true representative. He served the settlement as Treasurer and Justice of the Peace for many years; and was also appointed in the latter part of his life one of the Commissioners to settle difficulties among the Golah tribes under President Coleman's administration.

He was ordained to the Gospel ministry and called to the pastorate of the St. Paul's Baptist Church and served the same faithfully until his death, which occurred at his home, December 17th, 1899. The Ricks Institute occupied a prominent seat in his heart, which was evinced at his death, by an annuity of five hundred dollars, devised for the same, out of his estate. In the death of this great man the settlement has been largely made poor.

Government schools were not called for by the settlement until these benevolent schools ceased to exist.

The Baptist Day School

For about seven years there was no school operating in the settlement, except the government school. There being a sufficient number of children in the settlement to attend three or four schools, the people became seriously interested in the education of their children. A parent and guardian meeting of the St. Paul's Baptist Church was called in the year 1894, and there, the necessity of opening a self-supporting day school, (but undenominational) that would be under their sole and immediate control for the advancement of their children in education was discussed. A constitution was adopted for its government; a board of trustees was elected and thus a little educational wheel on that line began its revolution in Arthington.

T. J. Bracewell, Esqr., was elected the first chairman and the writer, secretary. Tuition was set down at $3.00 a quarter for each pupil and the salary of the teacher at $75.00 a quarter. Pupils were not allowed to enter the school until their tuition was paid into the treasury; and by this means there was never any trouble in paying off the teacher at the end of the quarter. Solomon Hill, Sr., was elected treasurer. Another good rule was that all the lost days by the teacher, other than those especially granted by the chairman of the board of trustees, were deducted from his salary, thus making the teacher stick to his duty.

Henry Taylor was elected chairman of the board of trustees and served the position well until his health failed him, when Justice George Askie was elected to fill the vacancy, and he holds the same now. Rev. Joseph A. Johnson, B.D., of Monrovia, was the first teacher employed and taught the school during the year 1894. The next teacher was the late S.C. Coker, of Bensonville, who occupied the chair two quarters during 1895. Mr. R. Smith of this settlement, who had just arrived in the country from the United States of America, was put in charge of the school in the year 1895 and taught the same until 1902. The board then called the writer to the chair, who is still honored with that important trust.

The amount paid in as tuition from the year 1894 to 1905, was $2,979.76. For the year 1901, the tuition began to drop to a low standard, owing to the price of coffee going down in the market as well as the death of a number of the strong supporters of the school, among whom may be mentioned the lamented Rev. June Moore, T. Carter and S. R. Hoggard. This school has accomplished great good. A few of its students have already entered and passed through the preparatory department of Liberia College and are now pursuing a collegiate course. Others have taken their places in the humble walks of life and acting their part well. We shall put forth every effort to keep this school up.

Many Want to Preach

During the 1870s about a dozen men in the Baptist Church thought they were called to preach. There being so many of them, the Church wanted to refuse them; or, the majority of them anyhow, as they did not believe that God had called all of them. But Deacon Hoggard said, "Let them alone, brethren, if they want to preach; and if they are not called by God, they will, every one return from whence they came."

The Church allowed them a chance. But only two of them – June Moore and George B. Outlaw, counted up the cost and were able to hold out. The others fell by the wayside.

During one of the revivals in the early growth of the Church in the settlement, a certain man from a neighboring settlement was visiting the same and became happy one night in one of the meetings. He shouted so long, making so much noise – kicking over the pews that everybody got tired of him. However, certain mischievous young men, in holding the happy man, managed to get him out of doors, and with the spirit still on him, backed him against the wall and began to thump him until that feeling was forced out of him and he began to beg them to stop.

Strange to say, but the Baptist Church here has not ordained but one minister during the 35 years the settlement has been established. The Church is large and there is great need of young men preparing themselves for the ministry.

Arthington Militia

Before a captain was commissioned for the Arthington Militia, the company drilled for a while with the Millsburg Militia, under Captain Andrew Capehart. The first acting Captain was the late Henry Askie, who was a soldier in the United States Civil War. They had no music in the settlement to drill by, the sound of men's feet was the only music they had.

The Fifth Regiment had not been organized, in those days. The First Regiment drilled, alternately, at Monrovia and Caldwell. The men of the Arthington Company would leave home early on the morning of parade days, acting as their own canoe boys and row themselves down to Caldwell before the line was formed, drill all day and then leave for home about half past 5 o'clock, reaching home that night. They did not seem to dread the distance they had to go. They rather, appeared happy under it; for they would sing songs from the time they left the shores of Lower Caldwell, until they touched those of Millsburg. When the parade was at Monrovia, they would have remained there during that night and return home the next day.

The late William King was a great friend to the "Arthington boys" in Monrovia, in allowing them to quarter at his residence. He made them welcome whenever they visited his home. Regarding him as an all-round man, his characteristic was that of a true lover of his country. There was not a soldier in Arthington that did not like William Henry King.

The following named persons were commissioned Captains of the Arthington Militia from time to time: June Moore, Solomon Hill, St. James Delyon and George Askie. In the year 1893, the "Arthington Home Guards" were organized, over whom David Moore was elected Captain (now Lieut.-Colonel Moore). Later on, a company was organized under the name of "Mills Volunteers," with T. H. Tyler, Captain.

Trade

Much trade is carried on in the settlement. Almost surrounded as it is by native settlements, as well as being largely in touch with the trade of the industrious tribes inhabiting the far interior, Arthington is easily one of the best points of trades in the County. Until about eight years ago, the people were very much burdened in getting their stuffs [sic] down to the head of navigation. But now, that trouble is much avoided since quite a number of the citizens have introduced ox-carts on the roads.

The natives living in the neighborhood of the settlement have gone into extensive coffee and ginger-raising; thereby making themselves an independent living. The settlement of Arthington produces yearly an average of 800,000 pounds of coffee and 900,000 pounds of ginger.

It is impossible at this writing, to give a statement of the quantity of palm-kernels accumulated yearly; but suffice it to say, that in their season, it is simply wonderful to see the quantity daily hauled away to the waterside. In the early age of the settlement, you could buy as much native rice as you wanted at one yard of print per kroo. Now, the price has advanced to a dollar and from that to a dollar and a half per kroo and there are times when we cannot get it at these prices.

General Remarks

Arthington is divided into four sections, viz: the North Road, the main entrance to the settlement, is one of the most important. Prominent buildings on this road are Mrs. A.E. Diggs' store and residence, the Town Hall, St. Paul's Baptist Church and Day School house; residence of T. Thompson, the A.M.E. Church, E.S. Moore's shop and Solomon Hill's store.

The Birtee Road begins at the river on the East side of the settlement and runs west; and takes its name from the immigrants that came from Birtee County, North Carolina, and settled down on his road. The residences of some of the leading farmers on this road are: George Askie, Hon. Henry Taylor, Deputy Sheriff T. H. Tyler,

J. H. Roulhac, Mrs. S. E. Roulhac, J.M. Mills, J.C. Taylor, Sr., John Bracewell, D. J. Smallwood, Charles Clark, N Crawford, James Clark, M. S. Smallwood and A. Bradford.

Not much trade comes in from the native element on this road, on account of the settlement being contiguous to Millsburg and Clay-Ashland. D. J. Smallwood has a sugar-cane mill on this road and supplies the settlement with syrup as far as he is able. Smallwood is a man of strong will power and bids fair to make a mark in Liberia.

The South Carolina Road takes its name from the immigrants that arrived here from South Carolina, U.S.A. Among the residences of the leading farmers on this road are Johnson Mason, Lieut-Colonel David Moore, Mrs. A.D. Moore, Solomon Hill, Sr., Solomon Hill, Jr., E.S. Moore, Madison J. Moore, Mrs. M. E. Moore, John Moore, Thomas Hill, W. S. Miller and residence of Rev. R. B. Wicker, Pastor of St. Paul's Baptist Church. This road leads out to Sueh and the Bopora Country. A great many natives living on this road raise large quantities of coffee and ginger. This road will always be an open door to an extensive trade. Solomon Hill, Sr., has a steam coffee mill on his farm which cost him something over $1,500; without which he would not be able to manage his coffee since native laborers have become so scarce.

The Georgia Road takes its name from a like circumstance to those of the Birtee and South Carolina roads. The prominent buildings on this road are the residence of Mrs. M.A. Carter, T.J. Bracewell's residence and shop, S.B. Jackson's shop, the residences of L. Bracewell, Brister Wright, Eli Ponder, Jacob L. Miller, James Delyon, R. Smith, James Lewis, Justice Elijah Wright, James A. Wright, A.R. and J. Bracewell, Brister Wright, Eli Ponder, Moses Turket, Jacob Miller, Elijah Wright, Levi Ponder, James Delyon and James Lewis.

This road leading out to Barveer and the Pesseh Country, there flows equally as much, if not more, trade through it as the South Carolina road. This section of the settlement is bounded on the East and Southeast, by the St. Paul's River, on which, traveling is obstructed at this point by the rapids.

The Local Option Law: The Legislature of Liberia passed an Act about the year 1889, granting the citizens of any township within the Republic the privilege of allowing or refusing license for the sale of alcoholic liquors within the limits of their township. As soon as the existence of such a law came to the knowledge of the Township, it was adopted at the next annual meeting and continued until now. This move of the citizens was based upon the good counsel of the Fathers of the settlement.

We have not had an accession of immigration from America since the year 1873; and neither have we been longing for any; for we have raised up our own immigration. There are only 85 persons now living out of the four immigrations that established the settlement, and still our number stands, 141 families, consisting of 980 persons. Mr. and Mrs. Thomas Thompson are the only married couple now living of the four immigrations that were married when they came to the Country. They have been married 40 years – have never parted from each other on account of any misunderstanding, and have never had a misunderstanding among themselves that they did not settle. Their daughter, whom they brought with them, is living with them now. Mr. Thompson has been Sexton of the St. Paul's Baptist Church for about 17 years.

The first child born in the settlement was Jane Reynolds (now Mrs. Foster of Bensonville.) Her father died in the early age of the settlement when she was probably four or five years old. Her mother lived out her many years of true widowhood and was married the second time to Alexander Clark, a thorough going farmer who lived on the Birtee road of this settlement. Her mother died a few years after her second marriage and "Janie" (as she is familiarly called) then lived with her brother, Weston Reynolds until his death; after which she lived with her cousin, Mattie E. Moore, now widow of the Hon. Wallace F. Moore, until she married Mr. Foster in 1904.

On the morning she left for her new home, she was accompanied by a respectable crowd of young folks, far on the way to Millsburg, and a salute of one gun was fired from the terminus of the North road in honor of the first-born of the settlement and her marriage. She was then 35 years old...

The foregoing brief narrative is designed to give the public some information on the struggles through which the people of this settlement had to pass, in building a home for themselves and their children. They had not done all that they might have done; and they have not been all that they could have been. But under the circumstances, and with what means and strength they have had, Arthington has done well.

Americo-Liberians ruled Liberia until 1980, when a military coup led by Samuel Doe marked the beginning of decades instability and over 250,000 dead. A peace deal in 2003 ended of two successive civil wars. Today, Liberia is still recovering and remains one of Africa's poorest countries with over 85% of its citizens living below the international poverty line.

Chapter 6
We've Come This Far By Faith: The Roulhac Family Association

"Coming Full Circle" was the theme of the Roulhac Family Association's third family reunion, which took place on a hot July weekend in 1992 in eastern North Carolina, the same area where their ancestors were first enslaved in the colonial United States more than two centuries ago. The Roulhac Family Association, Inc., a national organization of descendants of enslaved Roulhacs who labored on plantations of French slave-owners, was organized in 1990, as a Michigan non-profit 501(c)(7) corporation. The idea for the association was conceived on Mother's Day 1990 at the home of Portia and Edgar Roulhac in Chicago where family members – descendants of Nelly and Nero Roulhac – from Detroit and Baltimore had assembled to break bread, share in prayer and goodwill and catch up on family news.

After dinner, the perennial question arose, "Why not have a family reunion?" Everyone agreed that family members needed to come together more frequently for the singular purpose of fellowship. This time, Edgar Roulhac, Jr., emphatically said, "let's stop talking about it and just do it." Three months later, from August 17-19, in Flint, Michigan, the hometown of Edgar, Sr.'s twin brother Edwin Roulhac, his wife Evelyn and daughter Charlotte, more than 70 persons attended the first Roulhac Family Gathering. Most were descendants of Nero and Nelly. Several descendants of Peter Warren Roulhac and Katherine Roulhac were present as well as extended family members and friends. The highlight of the business meeting was the unanimous decision to form a surname family association and hold the second reunion in Marianna, Florida, where in the 1840s many enslaved North Carolina Roulhacs were involuntarily relocated.

Although formed in 1990, the genesis of the Roulhac Family Association dates to 1968 at Cedar Point, an amusement park in Sandusky, Ohio, half way between Detroit and Cleveland. I was attending a Sigma Gamma Rho and Zeta Phi Beta regional picnic and enjoying fishing in Lake Erie, known for yellow perch and pickerel. Someone called out "Roulhac." I answered, thinking I was being summoned. Simultaneously, someone else responded. The other voice was Joseph D. Roulhac, an Akron Municipal Court judge, whose 1966 appointment made him the first African American to serve as a judge in Summit County. In 1957, he had been featured in *Jet*, a magazine that boasts a long tradition of documenting significant events in the African American community, for becoming the first black assistant prosecutor in Akron. Judge Joseph D. Roulhac and his wife Frances Phoenix Roulhac were the first persons I met with the Roulhac surname since leaving Florida in 1962. I was fortunate to meet them. They became my role models, mentors and friends.

Without hesitation, Judge Roulhac introduced me to his sister, Mary Roulhac Brown and her children – Joseph, Marilyn, Shirley and Johnella - in Detroit. Over the years, Mary became the mother that I lost in 1970. She always baked a cake with her secret lemon sauce topping for my birthday. Mary shared the story of her parents, Rev. Robert D. Roulhac, a Presbyterian minister and his wife, Minerva Rhodes Roulhac, both born in Marianna, Florida, in the 1800s, and their journey from Marianna to Selma, Alabama; Thomasville, Georgia and finally to Detroit. I was enthralled by the story of how her father, Rev. Roulhac insured that all of his eight children were college-educated. Although Rev. Roulhac was born in Marianna and was buried there in the Roulhac Cemetery in 1957, we did not learn of a family connection until many years later.

In 1981, as my interest in genealogy heightened, Judge Roulhac took me to Oviedo, Florida, to meet Vinnie Roulhac Hudson, his father's only living sibling. Her still sharp mind, at ninety-years-old, recalled the stories handed down by her ancestors about her great-grandparents Nero and Nelly Roulhac who were born into slavery in North Carolina, and their children. The family connection was crystalized after I found the January 1858 inventory of John Gray Roulhac's estate in the Jackson County, Florida courthouse. In those records I found the only antebellum record of Nelly and Nero, our common ancestors. This discovery verified the oral family history Cousin Vinnie shared with me. Two of Nero and Nelly's children, my great-grandfather Phaeton Roulhac, a ten-year-old, and his brother Robert Roulhac, Cousin Vinnie's grandfather, were brothers.

The Association's mission is to document and preserve historical and genealogical information about Roulhac surname. Association members include ten branches of surnamed Roulhacs, who, although not biologically related, consider themselves "cousins" because of the social, political and economic connections of their slave ancestors on southern plantations. The horrific conditions that surrounded the oppression of African-descended Roulhacs provide a unifying theme for members of the Roulhac diaspora. To insure their sacrifices are never forgotten, Association members recognize it is more important than ever for African Americans to organize beyond the traditional family to rediscover and celebrate their heritage.

The family histories of nine branches of African-descended RFA members are included in this chapter. As will become apparent, with freedom, our ancestors did not hesitate to avail themselves of new opportunities despite Reconstruction-era violence, Jim Crow and segregation.

Chapter 6

I. Nero and Nelly Roulhac

First Generation
Nero Roulhac (1) and Nelly Roulhac

1.1 Nero and Nelly Roulhac were born slaves in North Carolina, circa 1806 and 1812, respectively. The June 16, 1858 Appraisement of the Estate of John Gray Roulhac, contains the only antebellum record of their existence. Nero and Nelly, both valued at $700, are listed as 52 and 46 years, respectively. John Gray Roulhac gave all of his property, including slaves, to his children Joseph, Francis and Clara and grandson Peter Roulhac to be divided in equal shares. Three years after John Gray Roulhac died, the Civil War began. The War was the bloodiest battle ever fought on American soil and ended the "peculiar institution" that had oppressed and dehumanized over 4 million Africans and their descendants.

Throughout the antebellum period only free persons could marry. Although some slave owners allowed those they enslaved to "jump over the broom," no legal contract was established. According to Thomas Hall, a former North Carolina slave:

> Getting married and having a family was a joke in the days of slavery, as the main thing in allowing any form of matrimony among the slaves was to raise more slaves in the same sense and for the same purpose as stock raisers raise horses and mules, that is, for work. A woman who could produce fast was in great demand and would bring a good price on the auction block in Richmond, Virginia; Charleston, South Carolina and other places.[135]

Although Nero and Nelly lived as husband and wife during the antebellum period, it was not until January 11, 1866, when the Florida legislature enacted a law allowing freedmen who had lived together as husband and wife and wished to continue their relationship and legitimatize their children to remarry. On the same day that the law became effective, Nero and Nelly married (Jackson County Marriages, Book C, Page 343) and for the first time legally adopted a surname. They chose the Roulhac, the surname of French Roulhacs who had enslaved them in North Carolina and Florida.

The May 20, 1865, surrender of Confederate forces at Tallahassee, Florida, did not dramatically change conditions for ex-slaves in Jackson County. The ghost of U.S. Supreme Court Chief Justice Roger Taney was still present. In the court's 1857 Dred Scott decision, Taney wrote that "at the time of the Declaration of Independence, and when the Constitution of the United States was framed and adopted... [blacks] had no rights which the white man was bound to respect." Many whites were unwilling to accept blacks as equal. During Reconstruction they made every effort, including violence, to keep freemen in their "place." Jackson County developed a reputation as the place "where Satan has his seat." Between 1869 and 1871, more blacks and their Republican allies were murdered in Jackson County than in all other Florida counties combined.

Through it all, Nero and his family survived. For the next three generations my paternal ancestors lived off the land either as farmers or sharecroppers. In 1870 at 65 years old, Nero was working as a farm laborer. He is enumerated in the 1870 Jackson County census living outside Marianna with his wife Nellie, age 59; Charity Roulhac, 25; Ann Roulhac, 35; Robert Roulhac, 20; Mary W., 12; James Roulhac,10 and Edward Roulhac, eight. The children, most likely the children of Charity and/or Ann, were all classified as mulattoes. During five years of freedom, Nero managed to accumulate $100 in real estate and $100 worth of personal property. According to the Reverse Index to Deeds - Grantees - Jackson County Florida, in 1872, a deed transferring land from S. C. Harvey to Nero Roulhac is recorded in Book D, Page 670.

After Nelly died, between 1870 and 1875, Nero married Joicy Bright April 24, 1875 (Jackson County Marriages, Book D, Page 459). In the 1880 U.S. Federal Census, the first to record parents' birthplaces, Nero indicated that his parents, whose names are lost to history, were also North Carolina natives. They were likely born between 1780 and 1785. Nero, age seventy, was living alone in dwelling 474 next to his daughter Angelina Hayes, her children John Hayes, 9-years-old and Florence Hayes, 6 and sister Edny Roulhac, age 35. A short distance away in dwelling 460 lived Nero's son, Phaton Roulhac, wife Estoria Roulhac and children Jimmy, six and Addie, two. Living in dwelling 458 was Nero's son Robert Roulhac, 23, with his wife Fannie, 23 and children: Stella, seven and Faton, five. The adults were all farm laborers.

My great-great grandfather Nero was 86 when he died in 1896 after spending the first two-thirds of his life enslaved.

Second Generation
Issue of Nero Roulhac (1) and Nelly Roulhac

2.1 Rebecca "Chatty" Roulhac was born, circa 1839. She is listed in the June 16, 1858 Appraisement of the Estate of John Gray Roulhac as Chatty, 19 years old. She and her infant son, two- month-old Isom, were valued at $1,116.66.

Rebecca Roulhac is listed in the 1880 Federal Census for Jackson County, Florida, Precinct 6, page 48, as a 43-year-old housekeeper living with her 47-year-old husband Benjamin Smith [no marriage record in found in Jackson County], born circa 1833, and their seven children: Laura Smith, 17; Easter Smith, 14; Anthony Smith, 12; Alex Smith, 10; Margaret Smith, eight; Benjamin Smith, Jr., six; and 21-year-old William Smith. Rebecca and Benjamin indicated that they and their parents were born in North Carolina.

In the 1885 Florida Census for Jackson County, Benjamin and his family are enumerated on page 5, District 1 (microfilm, M845, Roll 5).

The family, with slight variations in ages are the same as in the 1880 Federal Census, except William is no longer at home and two additional children are there - Jim Smith, five and one-year-old Mary Smith.

By 1900, Rebecca Smith is shown in Friendship precinct 12 of the Jackson County, Florida Census, as Becky Smith, age 67, born May 1833 in North Carolina, living with husband Benjamin Smith, 67, born March 1833 in Florida. They were living with grandchildren Harriet Smith, 23, born August 1876; Thomas Smith, seven, born August 1892 and Wayman, one, born September 1898; and son Anthony, 34, born March 1866. Rebecca said she had given birth to nine children and eight were living.

In 1910, Rebecca Smith, age 70, was living in Marianna, north of the L & N Railroad, with her sister Annette Sims, who in the 1920 Federal Census she referred to as her "companion." Both worked as farm laborers. Rebecca died January 10, 1923.

3.2 Annette Sims was born November 1841, in Jackson County, Florida. She is enumerated in the 1870 Federal Census for Jackson County, living with her parents, as a 35-year-old farm laborer. She married a Mr. Sims. She is enumerated in the 1900 Federal Census for Jackson County, Florida, in enumeration district 53, precinct 6, page 8, as a 58-year-old widow, working as a farm laborer.

4.3 Edny Roulhac, born 1845 in North Carolina. She is shown in the 1880 census for Jackson County Florida, page 42, enumeration district 69, election precinct 6th, line 26, as a 35-year-old farm laborer living with her sister Angelina Hayes and Angelina's children John and Florence, nine and six years old, respectively. Edny Roulhac married Nelson Bell, born circa 1843 in North Carolina, November 3, 1889, in Jackson County, Florida (Book 1, Page 239).

Edny is listed in the 1900 Federal Census for Jackson County as "Ednie," age 54, living in district 53 with her family, Nelson Bell, 58, her husband of one year, and Nelson's sons Elsie, 23 and Richard, 18 years old, both born in Georgia. Edny indicated that she was born February 1846 and had given birth to one child, who was dead.

In 1910, Edna, age 56, was living in Rocky Creek, Jackson County, Florida, with her husband Nelson Bell, a farmer, age 70; Nelson's sons Elsie and Richard, 36 and 27 years old, respectively, and boarder Thomas Pittman, a 34-year-old farm laborer. By 1920, Edna, 73, and her husband Nelson Bell, 78, are living in Norristown, Montgomery County, Pennsylvania, where Nelson was working in a magnesium plant (1920 Federal Census, Montgomery County, Norristown ward, district 141).

5.4 Angelina Roulhac (4) was born, circa 1846 in Jackson County, Florida. Angelina is listed in the June 16, 1858 Appraisement of the Estate of John Gray Roulhac as a 12 year old valued at $583.33.

Angelina Roulhac's marriage to Emanuel Hays on January 5, 1870, is recorded in the Jackson County Marriage Index, 1866-1908, in Book D, Page 69. She is shown in the 1880 census for Jackson County Florida, page 42, enumeration district 69, election precinct 6th, line 21, as head of household working as a farm laborer. She was living with son John Hayes, age nine; daughter Florence Hayes, age six; and sister Edny Roulhac, age 35.

In the 1900 Census, District 53, page 14, Angelina Hayes, age fifty-two, is listed in the U.S. Census for Jackson County as a widow working as a farm laborer. She is living with her son John Hayes, 27, also a farm laborer, and his wife Mary, 22. Angelina died August 7, 1911.

6.5 Phaton Roulhac, my paternal great-grandfather, was born in 1848 in Jackson County, Florida. He is listed in the June 16, 1858, Appraisement of the Estate of John Gray Roulhac's estate, as "Fayton," age 10, with a value of $600. Phaton married Lizzie Robinson

January 16, 1870 in Jackson County, Florida, Book D, Page 75. Lizzie was born 1856 in Marianna, Jackson County, Florida.

By 1900, Phaton Roulhac, born February 1842 in Florida, was either a widower or divorcee who was living with four of his children – Addie Roulhac, born March 1878; Lucius Roulhac, born July 1885; Mitchell Roulhac, born September 1894 and Ester Roulhac, born January 1900. Phaton married Cindy Kelly, the mother of his oldest son Henderson Nelson, on April 20, 1904. Their marriage is recorded in Jackson County Marriages, Book 1, Page 329 as "Cinda Kelly" and "Eaton Roulhac."

Phaton Roulhac appears in the 1910 Census, enumeration district 49, precinct 6, north of the L & N Railroad, family 269. He was 69, living with wife Cindy Kelly, his son Nelson Henderson and stepsons Lucious Nelson, 16 and Pierce Nelson, 13 years old. All were farm laborers. Phaton was living two dwellings from his sisters Rebecca Smith, born about 1840 and Annette Sims, born about 1845. Phaton also had child Ella Roulhac, born about 1879.

Between 1910 and 1945, Phaton relocated from rural Jackson County to East Jackson Street in Marianna, where he had operated a business making headstones. His name appears on the corner stone of St. Luke Baptist Church. The church, established in August 1867, is one of the oldest African American churches in Jackson County. Phaton died in 1949.

7.6 Peter Roulhac was born circa 1849. Peter Roulhac is listed in the June 16, 1858 Appraisement of the Estate of John Gray Roulhac as a 12 year old valued at $550. Peter Roulhac married Amy Bryant January 25, 1873, in Jackson County, Florida (Book D, Page 300). In the 1880 Federal Census for Jackson County, Peter is listed in enumeration district 69, page 38, 6th precinct, line 48, as a 30-year-old farm laborer who was born in North Carolina [It is more likely that he was born in Florida. John Gray Roulhac, who enslaved his family and him, emigrated to Florida, circa 1840.], as were his mother and father. He was living with his wife Annie, a 23-year-old domestic worker, born in Florida, and his daughter, Ginnie, age five.

8.7 Robert Roulhac was born October 1849 in Jackson County, Florida. Robert is listed in the June 16, 1858, Appraisement of the Estate of John Gray Roulhac as a seven year old, valued at $483.33. His 1872 application to marry Viney Brown is recorded in Jackson County Marriages, Book D, Page 219. He was born March 1855, in Florida. Robert Roulhac is enumerated in the 1880 Census, enumeration district 68, sheet 4, precinct 6, line 18, as 28 years old, living with his wife, Viney (sometimes spelled "Vinnie" in census records) 25; daughter, Stella, seven; sons Fadin [Phaton], age five and Robert, six months old. Robert and his wife were farm laborers.

In 1900, Robert Roulhac, 50, is shown in the Jackson County Federal Census in precinct 6, enumeration district 53, sheet 4, page 222, line 33, living with Vinnie, 45, his wife of 28 years who had given birth to 12 children. Nine were still living. Five daughters were living at home: Emma Roulhac, 14; Delia, 12; Callie, seven; Lula, age five and Viney, four years old. In 1910, Robert was 60 and his wife Vinnie, 55. They are listed in the Federal Census with their daughters Emma, Delia, Callie, Lula and Vinnie. They are enumerated in precinct 6, enumeration district 49, sheet 39, line 5 in the 1910 Federal Census for Jackson County. Robert died December 8, 1934, in Marianna, Florida.

Third Generation
Issue of Rebecca Roulhac (3) and Benjamin Smith

9.1 Laura Smith was born, circa, 1863, in Jackson County, Florida. In the 1900 Jackson County Census, Friendship precinct 12, Laura is head of a household that included children Mary Smith, 15, born December 1884; Connie, seven, born July 1892; William, six, born May 1894; Placolia, one, born March 1899; and niece Mamie Smith, born September 1889. Laura indicated that her father and mother were born in Florida and North Carolina, respectively. According to Laura, who worked as a farmer, she had given birth to six children and five were living.

10.2 Easter Smith, born circa 1866, married Willie (aka Willis) Dickson, born circa 1864, May 30, 1885 (Jackson County Marriage Records, Book F, Page 210). In the 1885 Florida Census, page 8, precinct 1, Easter is listed with her husband Willis Dixon and daughter Lizzie, two years old, and her brother-in-law Frank Dixon.

In the 1900 Jackson County Federal Census Easter Smith, born May 1865, is enumerated in Friendship precinct 12, supervisor district 1, enumeration 49, with her husband Willis Dixon, born March 1865, with sons Nicolas Dixon, born December 1886; Alexander Dixon, born March 1889; Earnest Dixon, born December 1892; Eddie Dixon, born March 1894 and daughter Willie, born April 1890. In the 1920 Federal Census for Jackson County, Easter is a 51-year-old laborer, living in Friendship precinct 12, supervisor's district 3, enumeration district 77, Malone, Jackson County, Florida, with husband Willie Dixon, a 56-year-old farmer and nine children: Bessie Dixon, 20; Joshie Dixon, 19; M.C. Dixon, 14; Gussie Dixon, 14; Possie Dixon, 12; J. C. Dixon, eight; Johnny L Dixon, two and Leo Dixon, three and two-month old grandson Leroy Dixon.

11.3 Anthony Smith was born circa 1868, in Jackson County, Florida.

12.4 Alex Smith was born circa 1870, in Jackson County, Florida.

13.5 Margaret Smith was born circa, 1872, in Jackson County, Florida.

14.6 Benjamin Smith, Jr., born August 1876, married Eula Rivers, born August 1877, on March 2, 1896, in Jackson County, Florida

(Book 3, Page 41). In the1900 Jackson County, Federal Census, they were farming and living with daughters Carrie Smith, born April 1894, Lella Smith, born September 1896; Neta Smith, born March 1898 and son Early Smith, born January 1900 (Friendship precinct 12, supervisor district 134, enumeration district 48 [Malone, Florida]).

15.7 William Smith, born circa1859, married Lucy Daniels, December 30, 1886 (Book F, Page 351).

16.8 Jim Smith, was born in in 1875 in Jackson County, Florida.

17.9 Mary Smith was born in 1879 in Jackson County, Florida.

Issue of Angelina Roulhac (5) and Emanuel Hays

18.1 John Hays, born circa 1871, in Jackson County, Florida.

19.2 Florence Hays, born March 1876, in Jackson County, Florida. Florence, using the surname "Hayes" married Harrison Stephens, born 1869, on December 20, 1899 in Jackson County, Florida (Book 4, Page 70). They are enumerated in the 1900 Federal Census living in precinct 6 in Marianna, Florida.

Issue of Phaton Roulhac (6) and Lizzie Robinson

20.1 Ella Roulhac was born about 1874 in Jackson County, Florida. She married James Jackson March 17, 1894 (Book 2, Page 298). In the 1900 Federal Census for Jackson County, Florida, James Jackson, born August 1874, and his family are listed in Friendship precinct 12, enumeration district 49, page 1. James' household included wife Ella Jackson, born December 1874; daughters Roslie, born June 1895, Willie H., born August 1896, and Lizzie, born 1899; son Faton, born September 1897; father Charles Nelson, born August 1850, in Alabama; boarder James Rivers, a farm laborer, born December 1886 and nephew Charles Newton, born January 1887.

21.2 Addie Roulhac was born March 1878, in Jackson County, Florida. She is enumerated in the 1900 Federal Census for Jackson County, in precinct 6, with her father, Phaton and three siblings Lucious, Mitchel and Ester. She was employed as a farm laborer. She married Guy Bryan January 15, 1909 in Jackson County, Florida (Deed Book 7, Page 356).

22.3 Lucius Roulhac, my paternal grandfather, was born July 1885, in Jackson County, Florida. He is enumerated in the 1900 Federal Census for Jackson County, in precinct 6, with his father, Phaton and three siblings – Addie, Mitchel and Ester. He was working as a farm laborer. He married Ira (sometimes spelled "Arrie") Nelson on April 10, 1907 (Jackson County Marriages, Book 6, Page 486). In 1910, Lucius is enumerated with his family – wife Ira and three children: Margaret, four; Robert, three and seven-month-old daughter Lodee. Two dwellings away lived Lucius' oldest son, four-year-old J. Y. Baker, living with his mother, Luella Baker, 23, with her parents – Frank Baker, 45 and Eliza Baker, age 22 – and their other children: Plassie Baker, 18; Aggie Bell Baker, 16; Josephine Baker, 16; Amanda Baker, 14; Henry Baker, 10; Mary E. Baker, six; Frank Baker, Jr., four; A.B. Baker, two and daughter Beaman, one.

On January 8, 1916, my grandmother Luella Baker married Alabama-native Marshall Griffin, a farm laborer. In 1920, Luella Griffin, 37 was living in Greenwood, Florida with Marshall Griffin, 47 and J. Y. Baker, her 16-year-old son. Ten years later, grandmother Luella was living in Greenwood working as a laundress, with her husband Marshall, a farmer laborer, and children Refair, nine, and Clem, one. Luella died in March 1986, at age ninety-eight.

23.4 Mitchell Roulhac was born September 1894 in Jackson County, Florida.

24.5 Ester Roulhac was born January 1900 in Jackson County, Florida.

Issue of Peter Roulhac (7) and Annie Bryan

25.1 Ginnie Roulhac was born, circa 1875, in Jackson County, Florida. She married Mr. Holmes.

26.2 Amy Roulhac was born in Jackson County, Florida.

Issue of Robert Roulhac (8) and Viney Brown

27.1 Stella Roulhac was born in 1873 in Jackson County, Florida. She married Willie Smith, born circa 1873 in Gadsden County, Florida, November 29, 1893 (Jackson County Marriages Book 2, Page 244). Stella, 27, is enumerated in the 1900 Federal Census for Jackson County, Florida living in Carpenter precinct 9, with her husband Alabama-native William Smith, 26, a transportation laborer; daughter Susie Roulhac, age five; sons William Smith, age three and infant Robert Smith, 11 months old and 13-year-old brother-in-law Leman Smith. Stella Roulhac died in 1914.

28.2 Phaton Roulhac was born in Jackson County, Florida, circa 1875. He married Lillie Leslie August 17, 1918 (recorded in Jackson County Marriages, Book 12, Page 23 as "Fate Rhoulac"). Phaton is enumerated in the 1920 Federal Census for Jackson County, precinct 6, district 85, page 19 as "Fayton" Roulhac, with Georgia-born wife Lillie, 29; son Fayton (Phaton, Jr.), 13 and daughters Lillie, less than one month old; Castell, 11 and Cola, 10.

In 1930, Phaton, 56, is shown in the 1930 Jackson County Federal Census as "Phation" Roulhac, living in Precinct 6, Marianna, enumeration district 32-8, district 1, page 1B, with wife, Lillie Roulhac, 30. Lillie indicated that she was 28 years old when she first married and Phaton noted that he was 20. The household also included Phaton's children Castelle Roulhac, 20; Cola Roulhac, 19; Frances Roulhac, 10; son Charles Peter Roulhac, nine and stepson Ulysses Roulhac, 11 years old.

By 1945, Phaton Roulhac, is enumerated in the Florida Census as 87 years old living in Marianna with Lillie, 53 years old. Living next door is Frances Lee, 30, and first grader Joseph F Lee, age six. They were living on East Jackson Street in Marianna, Florida. Phaton Roulhac died in Jackson County in 1955.

29.3 Robert Daniel Roulhac was born in Jackson County, Florida, November 9, 1880. He married Minerva Rhodes September 19, 1906 (Jackson County, Florida Marriages Book 6, Page 359). In 1910, Robert, was a 30-year-old Presbyterian preacher, was living in Selma, Dallas County, Alabama, ward 5, district 0100, with his wife Minerva, 24, and sons Robert A. Roulhac, two years old and seven month old John Roulhac.

By 1920, Robert, 39, was still preaching in Selma. He was living with wife Minerva, 28; sons Robert Roulhac, 12; John R. Roulhac, 10; Simeon Roulhac, eight and daughters Mary, five and Ruth, 13 months old. After leaving Selma, Robert and his family moved to Columbus, Georgia and later to Tuscaloosa, Alabama, where he also served as a pastor.

By 1930, Robert had relocated to Thomasville, Thomas County, Georgia, with his wife, Minerva Roulhac, 40; Simeon Roulhac, 18; Mary Roulhac, 16; Joseph Roulhac, 13; Ruth Roulhac, 11; and twins Edgar Roulhac and Edwin Roulhac, eight-years-old (enumeration district 138-5, supervisor's district 14, page 5A). For more than twenty years, Rev. Roulhac served as minister of Second Presbyterian Church that was established in 1886, by teachers and workers who attended the predominately white First Presbyterian Church. All eight of Rev. Roulhac and Minerva's children were college-educated. Rev. Roulhac died July 29, 1957. He is buried in the Roulhac Cemetery in Marianna, Jackson County. Minerva Roulhac died in 1975 in Detroit.

30.4 Charles Peter Roulhac was born February 14, 1882, in Marianna, Jackson County, Florida. Ruth Roulhac was born January 20,

1904, from a union between Charles Peter Roulhac and Hattie Cora Davis. Charles Peter was sometimes referred to as Peter Charles Roulhac. According to October 8, 1908 correspondence from U. S. Navy Commander Shoemaker, it was noted that "Peter C. Roulhac is now serving on board the USS. Montana and letters should be addressed to him on board that vessel in care of the Postmaster, New York, N.Y. Charles Peter Roulhac is enumerated in the 1910 Federal Census for the U.S. Navy, Military and Naval force aboard the USS Montana as fireman first-class. On April 1, 1916, Charles, at 34 years old, was assigned to the USS Wisconsin in Philadelphia, Pennsylvania, as a fireman first class. During World War I, from April 16, 1916 to November 11, 1918, he served aboard the USS Charleston as oiler and first and second-class engineman. When the 1920 Federal Census was taken for the U.S. Military and Naval forces, Charles Peter Roulhac, a 37-year-old widower, was a machinist aboard the USS Black Hawk. Charles Peter Roulhac died in Jackson County, Florida, December 9, 1937, and is buried in the Roulhac Cemetery in Marianna.

31.5 Emma Roulhac was born October 25, 1885, in Jackson County, Florida. She married Archie Denard November 23, 1923, in Jackson County, Florida (Book 13, Page 398). In 1930, Emma Denard, 45, is living with husband Arch Denard fifty-five-years-old in Spring Creek, Seminole, Georgia, working as farm laborers. In 1943, she moved to Oviedo, Florida. She died November 14, 1974 and is buried in the Roulhac Cemetery in Jackson County.

32.6 Delia Roulhac, born circa 1888, in Jackson County. Delia married John Gaddis, and later George English. In the 1920 Federal Census for Bessemer, Jefferson County, Alabama, Delia, 25 years old, is living with 46-year-old husband George, who was working as an ore miner. The household included six-month-old son Charles P. [Peter] English, Delia's three-year, five-month-old nephew Joseph Roulhac and boarders Marg Jones, 25, a cook in a private home and her daughter Octavia Jones, five. By 1930, Delia was living in Logan, Logan County,

West Virginia with her husband George who was listed at 47 years old, only one year older than he was in the 1920 Census. They were living with their son Charles English, 10-years-old and daughter Delia English, eight. George English was working as a coal miner. See the 1930 Logan County, West Virginia, Federal Census, district 24, page 28A. George English died in 1939. Delia Roulhac English died in 1966.

33.7 Callie Roulhac was born about 1893, in Jackson County, Florida. She married Walter Harvey, January 9, 1914 (Jackson County Marriages, Book 10, Page 219).

34.8 Lula Roulhac was born about 1895, in Jackson County, Florida. She married Henderson Nelson, December 8, 1908 (Jackson County Marriages, Book 8, page 435).

35.9 Elviney Roulhac was born May 4, 1896, Jackson County, Florida. Elviney, listed in Jackson County Marriages as "Vina," married William Taylor November 19, 1914. Subsequently, Elviney married Mr. Hudson.

During an oral history interview with the writer on December 30, 1986, with her still sharp mind at ninety-years-old, she provided the major portion of the genealogy of her grandfather, Nero Roulhac, who died the year she was born. Affectionately known as "Hon," Elviney Roulhac Hudson was noted for a broad smile, a willingness to assist others and a strong interest in preserving the Roulhac family history. Elviney Roulhac Hudson died Thursday September 29, 1994, in Oviedo, Florida, survived by 12 nieces and nephews. She was the last of 10 siblings. She is buried at the Roulhac Cemetery in Marianna, Jackson County, Florida.

36.10 Mary Roulhac

Fourth Generation
Issue of Laura Smith (9)

37.1 Mary Smith was born December 1884 in Jackson County, Florida.

38.2 Connie Smith was born July 1892 in Jackson County, Florida.

39.3 William Smith was born May 1894 in Jackson County, Florida.

40.4 Placolia Smith was born March 1899 in Jackson County, Florida.

Issue of Easter Smith (10) and Willie [aka Willis] Dixon

41.1 Lizzie Dixon was born about 1883 in Jackson County, Florida.

43.2 Nicholas Dixon was born about 1886 in Jackson County, Florida.

44.3 Alexandra Dixon was born about 1889 in Jackson County, Florida.

45.4 Willie Dixon, a female, was born about 1890 in Jackson County, Florida.

46.5 Earnest Dixon was born about 1892 in Jackson County, Florida.

47.6 Eddie Dixon was born about 1894 in Jackson County, Florida.

48.7 Bessie Dixon was born about 1900 in Jackson County, Florida.

49.8 Joshie Dixon was born about 1901 in Jackson County, Florida.

50.9 M. C. Dixon was born about 1906 in Jackson County, Florida.

51.10 Gussie Dixon was born about 1906 in Jackson County, Florida.

52.11 Possie Dixon was born about 1908 in Jackson County, Florida.

53.12 J. C. Dixon was born about 1912 in Jackson County, Florida.

54.13 Leo Dixon was born about 1917 in Jackson County, Florida.

55.14 Johnny Dixon, a female, was born about 1918 in Jackson County, Florida.

Issue of Benjamin Smith, Jr. (14) and Eula Rivers

56.1 Carrie Smith was born in Jackson County, Florida, April 1894.

57.2 Lella Smith was born in Jackson County, Florida, September 1896. Lella Smith married Myers Smith November 13, 1913 (Jackson County Marriages, Book 8, Page 428).

58.3 Neta Smith was born in Jackson County, Florida, March 1898. Neta Smith married Alex McKay August 10, 1917 (Jackson County Marriages, Book 11, Page 284). Neta, age 37 and her husband Alex McKay are enumerated in the 1935 Florida Census living with their children A.D. McKay, Jr., age 17; Bessie McKay 15 and Robert McKay, 13.

59.4 Early Smith was born in Jackson County, Florida, in January 1900.

Issue of Benjamin Smith, Jr. (14) and second wife Homie

60.5 Essie Smith was born about 1909 in Jackson County, Florida.

61.6 Nellie Smith was born about 1912 in Jackson County, Florida.

62.7 Clyde Smith was born about 1915 in Jackson County, Florida.

63.8 Marvin Smith was born about 1915 in Jackson County, Florida. Marvin Smith married Ruby Lee May 24, 1937 (Jackson County Marriages, Book 18, Page 221).

64.9 Chester Smith was born about 1920 in Jackson County, Florida. Chester Smith married Fannie Mae Smith February 22, 1941 (Jackson County Marriages, Book 19, Page 393).

Issue of Ella Roulhac (20) and James Jackson

65.1 Litena Jackson was born in Jackson County, Florida.

66.2 Roslie Jackson was born June 1895 in Jackson County, Florida.

67.3 Willie H. Jackson was born August 1896 in Jackson County, Florida.

68.4 Faton Jackson was born September 1897 in Jackson County.

69.5 Lizzie Jackson was born in November 1899 in Jackson County, Florida. She married Ruben Gipson [Gibson] December 26, 1918 (Jackson County Marriages, Book 12, Page 88). Ruben registered for World War I, September 12, 1918, three months before his marriage. Lizzie and Ruben Gibson are enumerated in the 1935 Florida Census with children Ella Mae Gibson, 15; Carrie Gibson, 14 and R. B. Gibson, Jr., 12. Ruben Gibson, the oldest child of my maternal grandparents, Noah and Estella Gibson, died May 16, 1992. Ella Mae Gibson Hayes lives in Greenwood, Jackson County, Florida. She is my oldest living relative on the maternal side of my family and the second oldest of my paternal cousins.

70.6 Corina Jackson was born about 1901 in Jackson County, Florida.

71.7 Ossie Jackson was born about 1902 in Jackson County, Florida. She married Eddie Mobley December 11, 1944 (Jackson County Marriages, Book 21, Page 330).

72.6 Ollie Mae Jackson was born about 1903 in Jackson County, Florida. She married Alex Williams November 5, 1927 (Jackson County Marriages, Book 15, Page 26).

73.7 Macon Jackson was born about 1905 in Jackson County, Florida. He married Bertha Lee Glover September 18, 1937 (Jackson County Marriages, Book 18, Page 276).

74.8 L. K. Jackson was born in Jackson County, Florida. He married Annie Mae Smith October 21, 1950 (Jackson County Marriages, Book 22, Page 149).

75.9 Edith Jackson was born in Jackson County, Florida. She married S.L. McKay December 1, 1929 (Jackson County Marriages, Book 15, Page 351).

76.10 Lillie C. Jackson was born in Jackson County, Florida.

Issue of Lucius Roulhac (20) and Luella Baker

77.1 J. Y. Rolack, born May 6, 1906, is my father. He is listed in the 1920 federal census as J.Y. Baker, 16 years old, living in Greenwood with his 37-year-old mother and 47-year-old stepfather Marshall Griffin, who was born in Alabama.

During the next six years, my father experienced the second of several surnames changes. His October 9, 1926, marriage is recorded as J. Y. Griffin and GeHazia Gipson [GeHazel Gibson] in Jackson County, Florida Marriage, Book 14, Page 335. My mother, GeHazel Gibson, born December 5, 1905, was the sixth of 15 children of Noah Gibson and the fifth of Estella Anderson Gibson's 14 children. My grandparents were sharecroppers in the McChapel Community, in northern Jackson County.

Between 1926 and 1931 my parents changed their surname to Rolack and named their oldest son, who was born in1931, J. Y. Rolack. He lived only a few days. Four years later, my parents are enumerated in the 1935 Florida census living in Greenwood, Florida, as J. Y. Roulhac, a 24-year-old farmer working for wages, and JaHazel Roulhac, age 24. The same year, my oldest sister Willie Hazel was born, and given the Rolack surname.

Subsequently, my parents relocated to Bartow, Polk County, Florida, in search of better living conditions. My father, with a first grade education, found work at the Swift Fertilizer Co, where he remained until August 12, 1942 when he, at 37 years old, 5' 7", 134 pounds, was inducted into the US Army at Camp Blanding in Polk County. He served dutifully in a quartermaster unit in the Philippines and Okinawa. Seven months after he was drafted, I was born in Marianna. In 1945, when World War II ended, my father returned to Jackson County where he resumed work as a farm laborer in Greenwood. Two years later, my brother Sylvester Roulhac was born. Unlike the Rolack surname of my parents and sister, my parents selected "Roulhac" as the surname for my brother and me. Gehazel Rolack died April 10, 1970. J. Y. Rolack died in March 15, 1986.

J. Y. Rolack, ca., 1944. Roulhacs of African descent have honorably served in every war since the Civil War.

Chapter 6

GeHazel and Willie Hazel Rolack, ca. 1942, Bartow, FL.

Issue of Lucius Roulhac (20) and Ira Nelson

78.2 Margaret Roulhac was born in 1906, in Jackson County, Florida. No marriage record found. She had two children Sara and Mary.

79.3 Robert Roulhac was born in October 6, 1907, in Jackson County, Florida. He married Lizzie S. Milton, born December 24, 1909, to Willie and Dollie Milton, December 1, 1929 (Jackson County Marriages, Book 15, Page 352). They had five children: Robert Roulhac, Jr.; Catherine Roulhac Barkley; Dollie Mae Roulhac

Boykins; Earl Roulhac and Raymond Roulhac. Robert Roulhac died May 6, 1987 in Panama City, Bay County, Florida.

80.4 Lodee Roulhac was born about 1909, in Jackson County, Florida. On March 15, 1941, she married R. [Richard] W. White (Jackson County Marriages, Book 19, Page 241). They had no children.

81.5 Samuel Roulhac was born in Jackson County, Florida, November 15, 1915. He married Ester Mae Milton, September 22, 1937 (Jackson County Marriages, Book 18, Page 279. They had one child, Emma Lee Roulhac Sapp. Samuel died August 4, 2000, and is buried in the Pope Chapel A.M.E. Church Cemetery in Jackson, County.

82.6 Catherine Roulhac was born in Jackson County, Florida, June 16, 1912. She married George McElroy. No marriage record found. Catherine, who lives in the Pope Chapel Community, a few miles northeast of Marianna on the Blue Springs Highway, had three children – Pelt, Fred and Annie Mae. Catherine McElroy celebrated one hundred years June 16, 2012. Through her working career she worked as a maid. She is the oldest known living descendant of Nero and Nelly Roulhac.

83.7 Waymon Roulhac was born in Jackson County, Florida, about 1919. Waymon married Louise Garret, December 21, 1940 (Book 19, Page 360). They had no children. He died in 2004.

84.8 Arlena Roulhac was born in Jackson County, Florida, in about 1923. She had two children – Arrie Roulhac and Lucius Roulhac. Arlena resides in a long-term nursing facility in Blountstown, Calhoun County, Florida.

85.9 Addie Roulhac was born in Jackson County, Florida, April 9, 1922. In 1949, she married Zannie French of Greenwood, Florida and relocated to Jacksonville, Duvall County, Florida. She died in Jacksonville August 18, 2012, survived by five daughters: Betty French Thomas, Evangelist Mary French Mack, Gail French Haigler,

Deleanor French Teage and Arrie French Kirkland; 47 grandchildren, seventeen great-grandchildren; six great-great grandchildren and two sisters Catherine Roulhac McElroy and Arlena Roulhac.

87.1 Estelle Roulhac was born in Jackson County, Florida. She married Zannie Long February 3, 1942 (Jackson County Marriages, Book 20, Page 81). They had ten children: Verdell Long, David Long, Zannie Long, Jr., Frank Long, Morris Long; Shirley Long; Willie Long; Emma Long; Raymond Long and James Long.

88.11 Bertha Roulhac was born in Jackson County, Florida, about 1927. She died in 1970.

Issue of Stella Roulhac (27) and William Smith

89.1 Susie Smith was born December 21, 1894 in Jackson County, Florida.

90.2 William Smith was born October 29, 1896 in Jackson County, Florida.

91.3 Robert Smith was born June 7, 1899 in Jackson County, Florida.

92.4 Aron Smith was born June 29, 1901 in Jackson County, Florida.

93.5 Joseph Smith was born June 25, 1903 in Philadelphia, Pennsylvania.

94.6 Ethel Smith was born February 17, 1905 in Philadelphia, Pennsylvania.

95.7 Lula Leslie Smith was born February 2, 1907 in Tuskegee, Alabama.

96.8 Eliza Smith was born October 25, 1909.

97.9 Benjamin Smith was born December 25, 1911.

98.10 Mary Smith was born September 19, 1912.

Issue of Phaton Roulhac (28) and Lillie Leslie

99.1 Phaton Roulhac, Jr., was born about 1907 in Jackson County, Florida.

100.2 Castelle Roulhac was born about 1909 in Jackson County, Florida.

101.3 Cola Roulhac was born about 1910 in Jackson County, Florida. She married Willis McCoy August 28, 1930. [Note: Phaton, Jr., Castelle and Cola are Phaton's children by a prior marriage.]

102.4 Ulysses Roulhac was born about 1918 in Jackson County, Florida. He married Edna Parker. They had children Ulysses Roulhac, Jr., and Reginald. Ulysses died about 1969 in New York. Edna died in 1991 in New Jersey. [Note: Ulyssee is Phaton's stepson.]

103.5 Frances Roulhac was born December 20, 1919, in Jackson County, Florida. In the 1930s Francis relocated to Jacksonville, Florida. She died in Jacksonville, Florida in 1996. She had three children: Mary L. Roulhac Smith, Joseph Roulhac (wife Marjorie Brooks Roulhac, the daughter of Albert Lee Brooks and Phyllis Irene Bartley) and Walter Lee. Frances, Joseph and Marjorie were founding members of the Roulhac Family Association.

104.6 Lillie Roulhac was born about1920 in Jackson County, Florida.

105.7 Charles Peter Roulhac was born December 21, 1921, in Marianna, Jackson County, Florida. Charles married Carrie Mae Williams. She was born March 27, 1921. They had no children. He served in the European Theater of Operations from April 29, 1943, until November 17, 1945. He was a driver in Gen. George S. Patton's Third Army. Charles and other soldiers in a segregated quartermaster unit formed the famous "Red Ball Express."[136] For eighty-two days, with little rest or comfort, they supplied the allied armies as Paton made his armored advance across France - from the beaches of Normandy, through the Battle of the Bulge and the conquest of Germany - in 1944. They played a major role in the defeat of the Nazis by ensuring U.S. and Allied war fighters and Tuskegee Airmen had the supplies needed to sweep across France into Germany. Carrie Mae Roulhac died February 9, 1987. Later, Charles married Jacquet Ross. He was a founding member and avid support of the Roulhac Family Association. Charles died October 9, 2010.

Issue of Robert D. Roulhac (29) and Minerva Rhodes

106.1 Robert Alpheus Roulhac, the first born of Robert D. and Minerva Rhodes, was born June 29, 1907, in Selma, Alabama. He was educated in Selma, Alabama and Stillman College, Tuscaloosa, Alabama. He served in the U.S. Army and was severely injured in the Battle of the Bulge during World War II and was honorably discharged. He relocated to Macon, Georgia in 1946 and shortly thereafter married Hazel Mitchell. They had one son, Robert Wayne Roulhac. He was employed for over 20 years as assistant director of the Hutchings Funeral Home. He led an active civilian life as an undertaker in Macon, Georgia, and died September 25, 1969.

107.2 John Maynard Roulhac was born September 28, 1909, in Selma, Alabama. He drowned at the youthful age of 16 in 1925 in Marianna.

108.3 Simeon Adolphus Roulhac was born December 6, 1911, in Selma, Alabama. His early education was completed at the Sylvan Street Presbyterian School in Selma, high school at Stillman in Tuscaloosa, Alabama. In 1931, at the beginning of the Great Depression, he left home and found work in Philadelphia to help his parents finance the education of his younger siblings – Edgar, Edwin, Mary and Ruth. In 1935, he relocated to New York City where he worked as an assistant electrician at the Taft Hotel.

Simeon Roulhac was inducted into the Army at Fort Jay, Governor's Island, New York July 24, 1942 and served with distinction in the Pacific Theater during World War II. He was honorably discharged in the 1945 as a sergeant. He married Doris Green October 26, 1946. Simeon Roulhac was a founding member of the Roulhac Family Association. Simeon Roulhac died December 8, 1993.

109.4 Mary Lee Roulhac Scott Brown was born in Selma, Alabama, February 22, 1914. She married twice – first to Joseph Scott and later to John William Brown. Mary began playing the piano and organ at her father's church when she was three years old. She graduated from Knoxville College with a degree in Music. Following in the footsteps of her mother, she became an elementary school teacher until 1945 when she relocated to Detroit and became a church social worker for the Detroit Presbytery. After retiring, she served as Minister of Music at several Detroit Presbyterian churches. Mary had four children: Joyce Marilyn Scott Allen, Joseph Leroy Scott, Shirley Arnetta Brown Walls and Johnella Minerva Brown Frazier. Mary and her family were founding members of the Roulhac Family Association. Mary was the Association's first chairperson and an avid supporter. Mary died August 19, 2003.

110.5 Judge Joseph D. Roulhac, was born August 18, 1916, in Selma, Alabama. He was Rev. Roulhac and Minerva's fourth oldest son. He received his high school diploma and associate's degree from Stillman Institute in 1934 and 1936, respectively. He graduated from Lincoln University in Pennsylvania with a degree in Sociology. He taught at the University while earning a master's degree in Sociology in 1940. While stationed at Camp Lee, Virginia, Sgt. Roulhac married Frances P. Phoenix on December 21, 1942. Within months, he was promoted to master sergeant. Everything went well until he refused to enforce the

Army's segregation policies on his black subordinates. Weeks later, he was shipped to the Philippines as an unassigned master sergeant. After his honorable discharge, he used the G.I. Bill to attend the University of Pennsylvania School of Law where he earned a law degree in 1948. He was in private practice until 1957, when he was appointed as an assistant Summit County prosecutor in Akron, Ohio, becoming the first African American prosecutor in the county's history. After six years, he returned to private practice and in May 1967, Governor James Rhodes appointed him to the Akron Municipal Court. He became the first African American Judge in Summit County and served for twenty years.

Throughout his career, he received many citations and awards for his outstanding achievements. In 2003, Stillman College conferred upon Judge Roulhac an honorary doctorate degree and dedicated the Joseph D. Roulhac Hall, a 350-unit, $6.8 million dormitory in his honor. The residence hall houses 298 female students and contains two computer laboratories and a food court. In 1998, the City of Akron and the Municipal Housing Authority named a street, Roulhac Circle, and low-income housing development in recognition of Judge Roulhac's 20 years of service as Akron's first African American municipal judge. Joseph and Frances had one daughter, P. Delores Roulhac Nance. Judge Roulhac and his family were founding members of the Roulhac Family Association and consistent supporters. He died March 5, 2008.

111.6 Ruth Roulhac Best, the youngest daughter of Rev. Roulhac and Minerva, was born December 5, 1918, in Selma. She attended elementary and high school at Stillman Institute and Lincoln Norman High School in Selma. Ruth earned a college degree from Florida A & M University in Tallahassee, Florida. She married Eugene Best in 1942. They had four sons. All died in infancy. Ruth became a highly respected kindergarten and elementary school teacher in the Chicago Public Schools before retiring in 1986. Ruth was a founding member of the Roulhac Family Association and a consistent supporter. Ruth died December 26, 2010.

112.7 Edwin Elisha Roulhac, one of Rev. Roulhac and Minerva's twin sons, was born January 6, 1922 in Selma, and attended Stillman College, Fort Valley State College and Tuskegee Institute. He served in the U.S. Navy as a member of the distinguished 80th Seebees during World War II and the Korean Conflict. He married Evelyn Viola Alexander June 3, 1944. To this union, two daughters were born – Charlotte Roulhac and Ruth Olivia Roulhac, who died in infancy.

Edwin, with his electrical training and experience in the Navy, relocated to Flint to work with his Navy buddy, John Speed of Speed's Electrical Service. Later, Edwin accepted a position with the Flint Board of Education in maintenance and operations where he served for over twenty-one years. After retirement, Edwin received special joy in using his talents as custodian at Bethel United Methodist Church where he was a faithful and dependable member. Edwin and his family were founding members of the Roulhac Family Association. He died December 17, 1991, sixteen months after hosting the first Roulhac Family Association gathering.

113.8 Edgar Elijah Roulhac was born January 6, 1922 in Selma, Alabama. He was the fraternal twin of younger brother Edwin Elisha Roulhac. Edgar and Edwin began their primary education at Stillman Institute's elementary school in Tuscaloosa, Alabama and continued at the private Allen Norman School in Thomasville, Georgia. Both returned to Stillman Institute to complete high school and their collegiate freshman and sophomore years. Edgar and Edwin spent their junior and part of their senior year at the Tuskegee Institute, in Tuskegee. World War II interrupted Edgar's college studies, forcing him to withdraw and enlist as a civilian reservist and pursue special pre-radar training before entering the U.S. Army Signal Corps.

After serving in one of the few all-black military radar units that trained troops being rushed into war zones across the globe, the Signal Corps's 235th Anti-aircraft Gun Battalion was disbanded near the end of the war. Edgar was honorably discharged as a Technical Sergeant. Edgar married Portia Jean

Goodloe August 20, 1944. They lived in Chicago, Illinois until the 1990s when the relocated to suburban Matteson. Edgar completed his bachelor of science degree in Industrial Arts and became an inspiring classroom teacher in aviation electronics at the Paul Laurence Dunbar High School in the Chicago Public Schools system. He retired as assistant principal in 1985.

Edgar and Portia's union gave birth to Edgar Edwin Roulhac and Karen Michele Roulhac. Edgar, the last surviving member of Robert and Minerva Roulhac's children, celebrated his 90th birthday in Chicago in January 2012. He will forever be noted and celebrated for serving as the dedicated and faithful caregiver for his wife Portia, daughter Karen and sister Ruth Roulhac Best during their final illnesses. Edgar and his family were founding members of the Roulhac Family Association and faithful supporters.

Descendants of Nero and Nelly Roulhac, and Warren and Kate Roulhac, attend the first Roulhac Family reunion, Flint, MI, 1990. Left to right: Charles P. Roulhac, Frances Roulhac, Ruth Roulhac Brown, Edgar Roulhac, Portia Roulhac, Mary Roulhac Brown, Edwin Roulhac, Evelyn Roulhac, Judge Joseph D. Roulhac, Frances Roulhac, Simeon Roulhac, Christopher Roulhac. All except, Edgar Roulhac and Frances Roulhac, third from left, have joined the Roulhac ancestors. Photo courtesy Patricia Roulhac.

Issue of Charles Peter Roulhac (30) and Hattie Cora Davis

114.1 Ruth Roulhac was born in Chipley, Washington County, Florida January 20, 1904. She lost her mother at an early age and was raised by her paternal uncle and aunt, Rev. Robert D. Roulhac, a Presbyterian minister, and Minerva Rhodes Roulhac. They afforded her the same opportunities as their children. She was educated in the Washington County Public Schools.

Ruth relocated to Chicago and married Wesley Jackson, who preceded her in death. She worked many years in domestic service as a seamstress and cook. She was a member of the Presbyterian Church before uniting with the Seventh-day Adventists. Ruth Roulhac Jackson died January 12, 1999, eight days before her 95th birthday.

Issue of Delia Roulhac (32) and George English

115.1 Charles Peter English was born July 1, 1919 in Bessemer, Jefferson County, Alabama. Charles Peter English. On September 11, 1947, he married Vera Jean Grace, born November 19, 1930, to Irving Grace and Emma Taylor of Bessemer, Alabama. They had three children: Patricia English, Audrey English Williams, Nerissa English Phillips, Valerie Ann English Parks, Charles Peter English, Jr., and George Gregory English. Charles Peter Roulhac and his family were hosts for the 1994 Roulhac Family Association Reunion. Charles Peter English, a World War II veteran, died June 3, 2000, in Braeholm, West Virginia, where he was employed as a janitor and in the coal mines.

116.2 Leona English Holloway was born December 12, 1921, in Bessemer, Jefferson County, Alabama. She migrated to West Virginia. Leona died April 17, 1999, at Logan General Hospital, Logan, West Virginia, after a long stay in the Genesis Health Care Nursing Home.

117.3 Kathryn English was born and died in 1925.

Chapter 6

II. Mary Roulhac and Limas Clary

First Generation
Mary Roulhac (1) and Limas Clary

1.1 Mary Roulhac was born in Bertie County, North Carolina circa 1810. Frances (Fanny) Roulhac of Bertie County, North Carolina, enslaved her. Mary and her husband Limas Clary were married while enslaved in 1825 or 1826. Major Clary of Bertie County enslaved Limas Clary. Mary and Limas had ten children.

Second Generation
Issue of Mary Roulhac (1) and Limas Clary

2.1 **John Roulhac** was born in North Carolina about 1826.

3.2 **Maria Roulhac** was born about 1830 in North Carolina.

4.3 **Thomas Roulhac** was born in North Carolina about 1832.

5.4 **Celia Roulhac** was born about 1835 in North Carolina.

6.5 **Joseph Rolack**, born in 1836, escaped from Fanny Roulhac's plantation in Windsor, Bertie County, North Carolina and served in Company C, 36th Regiment, U.S. Colored Troops from July 1863 until July 13, 1866 when he was mustered out in Brazos Santiago, Texas. After the war, Joseph abandoned the "Rolack" surname and became known as Joseph "Rollax". In 1869 he married Indy [aka Indie] Phillips at Bayou Current, Louisiana. In July 1890, when he filed for an invalid pension, he was living in Odenburg, Avoyelles Parish, Louisiana. His application was approved on April 24, 1903, 13 years after he applied. Joseph was granted $6 per month retroactive to January 1897. Indy Rollax died April 8, 1896. Joseph and Indy had eight children. Joseph died in Melville, St. Landry Parish, Louisiana in 1916.

7.6 Priscilla Roulhac was born about 1839 in North Carolina.

8.7 Jane Roulhac was born 1841 in Bertie County, North Carolina. Jane, a single mother, immigrated to Liberia, West Africa, with her 10-year-old daughter Henrietta and four-year-old son Nero, and 160 former Bertie County slaves on November 11, 1869. They were among the first settlers of Arthington, Liberia, 25 miles up the St. Paul River from Monrovia.

9.8 Frances Roulhac was born about 1843 in North Carolina.

10.9 David Rolack was born in Bertie County, North Carolina in 1846. In 1864, David, like his brother Joseph Rolack, escaped enslavement from Fannie Roulhac. He joined the Company A, 36th Regiment, U.S. Colored Troops. David died June 30, 1864 at Point Lookout, Maryland. Mary Roulhac's application for David's Civil War pension was granted February 12, 1890. She received $12 per month, retroactive to May 14, 1888, until she died November 4, 1898.

11.10 Rachel Roulhac was born about 1849 in North Carolina.

12.11 Limas Roulhac was born in 1851, a week after his father, for whom he was named, died. By 1880, 28-year-old Limas Roulhac was living with his 18-year old wife Frances and their one year old son George W., in Whites, Bertie County, North Carolina. By 1900, Limas had remarried and relocated to Washington, D. C., where he was working as a laborer for the federal government. He was living with his wife Cora, 28, and sons William, six; George E. three; and five-month-old Reuben C. Roulhac. By 1910, Limas, 48, was living in Washington, D.C. with wife Cora, 38 and six children: William, 16; George E., 12; Reuben C., 10; Hattie, seven; Martin, four and four month-old James. Limas was working as a laborer doing street work. By 1930, Limas Roulhac, 78, was a retired widower, living in Washington with his 27-year-old daughter Hattie Wilson and son William, 36, a clerk employed by the federal government.

Chapter 6

Third Generation
Issue of Joseph Rolack (6) and Indy Phillips

13.1 Jimmy Rollax was born in 1873.

14.2 Ann Rollax was born in 1875. Ann married an Armstrong.

15.3 Dave Rollax was born in 1880.

16.4 Alford Rollax was born in 1885.

17.5 Hemy Rollax was born in 1886.

18.6 Jesse Rollax was born in 1889

19.7 Magdalean Rollax was born in 1892.

20.8 Virginia Rollax was born in 1895.

Issue of Jane Roulhac (8)

21.1 Henrietta Roulhac was born in about 1859 in North Carolina. She emigrated to Arthington, Liberia in 1869.

22.2 Nero Roulhac was born in about 1865 in North Carolina. He emigrated to Arthington, Liberia in 1869.

Issue of Limas Roulhac (11) and first wife France

23.1 George W. Roulhac was born about 1879 in Bertie County, North Carolina.

Issue of Limas Roulhac (11) and second wife Cora

24.1 William Roulhac was born about 1894 in Washington, D.C.

25.2 George Edward Roulhac was born about 1897 in Washington, D.C. The 1930 Federal Census for the District of Columbia shows him living with his wife Susie, 23 and children, two-year-old George and Constant, their one-year-old daughter.

26.3 Reuben C. Roulhac was born about 1900 in Washington, D.C.

27.4 Hattie Roulhac was born about 1903 in Washington, D.C.

28.5 Martin Roulhac was born about 1906 in Washington, D.C.

29.6 James Roulhac was born about 1910 in Washington, D.C.

Issue of George Edward Roulhac (25) and Susie

30.1 George Norman Roulhac was born about 1928, in Washington, D.C. He married Samantha and had two children – Dorothy Roulhac and Tracy Roulhac. In 1950, George Norman Roulhac was a rebuttal witness for the prosecution in one of the most controversial criminal trials in American History – *United States of America vs. Alger Hiss*, 185 F 2d 822 (2nd Cir. 1950). During the 1930s, Hiss worked as a diplomat for the Department of State. The trial, a precursor to the McCarthy congressional hearings of the 1950s, centered around accusations that Hiss passed government documents to the Soviet Union in an effort to prove President Franklin D. Roosevelt's New Deal had been infiltrated and compromised by Communist spies. George Norman Roulhac's testimony related to whether he saw a Woodstock typewriter, allegedly used by Hiss to prepare documents passed to the Soviets, at the home of Claudie Catlett, Hiss' maid. George, who lived with Catlett, reinforced the Government's case when he testified that he did not see a typewriter until about three months after he moved into the home – April 1938. However, according to FBI documents released pursuant to a 1975 Freedom of Information Act request, George Norman Roulhac told the FBI that he was not sure when he first saw the typewriter, a small portable that did not resemble a larger Woodstock, and that it might have been there before he moved. For more information about the trial and Roulhac's testimony see: https://files.nyu.edu/th15/public/roulhac.html

31.2 Constant Roulhac was born about 1929 in Washington, D.C.

III. John B. Roulhac and Rose Roulhac

First Generation
John B. Roulhac (1) and Rose Roulhac

1.1 John Roulhac and Rose Roulhac were born into slavery in about 1838 and 1827, respectively, in Bertie County, North Carolina. In September 15, 1870, John Roulhac and his family are enumerated in the 1870 U.S. Federal Census for Bertie County as John (Jhn) Roulhac, age 32, a farmer laborer, Rose Roulhac, 43 years old, keeping house; Writen, 19, a farm laborer; Grace Roulhac, 13, keeping house; James Roulhac, 12 and Dick (Richard), 10 years old.

On November 5, 1870, fifty days after the Census was taken, John and all members of his household enumerated in the 1870 Census, in addition to John Roulhac, age 2, were among 194 emigrants onboard the ship *Golconda* on its final voyage to Liberia. John B. Roulhac was the leader of the 111 passengers from Bertie County. Eight additional Roulhac emigrants on the 36-day voyage were from Plymouth, Washington County, North Carolina. All, apparently dissatisfied with conditions in Reconstruction-era North Carolina, were among the initial settlers of Arthington, Liberia. John B. Roulhac was one of the first deacons of the Baptist Church in Arthington and was among a number of settlers who died in 1889, when Arthington experienced an outbreak of smallpox.

Second Generation
Issue of John Roulhac (1) and Rose Roulhac (2)

2.1 William Wrighten Roulhac, John B. Roulhac's stepson, was born about 1851 in Bertie County, North Carolina. William Wrighten Roulhac was among the emigrants on the ship *Golconda* on its final voyage to Liberia in November 1870. He was elected church clerk in the first Baptist Church in Arthington and served for 29 years, from 1873 to 1902.

3.2 James Roulhac was born about 1858 in Bertie County, North Carolina.

4.3 Richard (Dick) Roulhac was born about 1860 or 1862 in Bertie County, North Carolina and was among the emigrants that on the slave ship *Golconda* on its final voyage in November 1870. He married Margaret York, one of eight children of Solomon York and Adeline Bond York, all were among the 160 ex-slaves on the Golconda when it embarked from Hampton Roads for Liberia November 11, 1869. Richard Roulhac and Margaret York Roulhac's daughter, Adeline York Roulhac married

5.4 Henry Roulhac was born about 1866 in Bertie County, North Carolina.

6.5 John Roulhac was born about 1868 in Bertie County, North Carolina.

Third Generation
Issue of Wrighten (aka known as Writen) Roulhac

7.1 George Roulhac was born in Arthington, Liberia. George had eight children: Moses, Jordan, Olivia, Jefferson, Benetta, Tempa, Alexandra and Tillah.

Issue of Richard (Dick) Roulhac and Margaret York

8.1 Adeline York Roulhac married John Wesley Clark (1884 – 1968), the second child of Ned Clark I and Dinah Clark. Adeline York Roulhac and John Wesley Clark had five children: Ned Richard Clarke II, Diana Clark, Thomas Clark, Melton Clarke, James Clark, Spencer Clarke and Charles "Charlie" Clark, who died at a young age. On April 21, 1878, Ned Clark I, born in 1855, his wife Dinah Clark, his 70-year-old father, James Clark; 60-year-old uncle Joseph Clark and brothers Alexander "Aleck" Clark, Jackson Clark and Rufus Clark left behind a life of limited freedom in Clarendon, South Carolina, aboard the Bark *Azor* to permanently resettled in

Arthington, Liberia. The Clarks were racially mixed and members of the Creeks, a Native American Tribe who resided in the Fort Sumter, South Carolina area. For more information about the Clark family see *http://clarkeextendedfamily.com/index.html*

The Bark Azor was purchased by the Liberian Exodus Joint Stock Steamship Company, an organization formed by blacks to encourage emigration to Liberia. Many blacks, dissatisfied with conditions after the 1876 political campaign and the overthrow of the Radical Republicans wanted a place where "educated black men and women could maintain a position equivalent to their attainments and talents" and avoid being "confined to subordinate and menial position in America."137 The Bark Azor left Charleston April 21, 1878, with 206 passengers for a 42-day voyage to Monrovia. Twenty-four died.138

Fourth Generation
Issue of Moses Roulhac

9.1 A. Moses Roulhac was born in Arthington, Liberia. He earned a bachelor of theology degree and a master's degree in Christian Work. Rev. Roulhac returned to Liberia at the request of then Liberian President Dr. William R. Tolbert, Jr., to participate in the country's nation building. Rev. Roulhac organized Liberia's first indigent children's home and served as its director until the bloody coup d'etat in 1980. The April 2 uprising against President Tolbert led to the murder of Tolbert and 26 supporters and the public execution of 13 cabinet members. The coup d'etat, led by U.S. Army Special Forces trained Liberian Army Master Sergeant Samuel Doe, a member of the Krahn ethnic group, ended 133 years of Liberian political control by Americo-Liberians.

The uprising did not deter Rev. Moses in his Christian mission. He pastored three of the leading Baptist Churches in Liberia: Effort Baptist Church, established in November 1875 in Paynesville, (1984-86) Zion Praise Baptist Church in Bensonville and Zion Grove Baptist Church in Brewerville. All were organized by Americo-Liberians in the 1770s. Rev. Roulhac served as vice president of the Liberian Council of Churches; was a delegate to the Liberian Conference on Peace and Reconciliation in August 2002; served the Liberian Baptist Missionary and Educational Convention, Inc.; is President Emeritus of the Liberia Baptist Theological Seminary and in 2009 was named by current Liberian President Ellen Johnson Sirleaf to the reconstituted Board of the Liberia Broadcasting System.

Coincidently, in July 2005, Rev. Roulhac was in the United States for his daughter Meribah's wedding in Illinois at the same time the Roulhac Family Association's annual reunion was being held in Chicago. After meeting RFA member Edgar Roulhac (the first U.S. born Roulhac that Rev. Roulhac would meet) at the wedding and learning of the upcoming reunion, Rev. Roulhac and his grandson Alaric made plans to attend as surprise guest.

Needless to say, their visit was memorable for all. However, for me, their attendance was also an extraordinary full-circle experience. During the summer of 1987, I made my second research trip to North Carolina and spent several days in Beaufort, Bertie and other eastern counties. Surprisingly, I met several Roulhacs. While there, I made two interesting discoveries. First, I learned Roulhacs did not willingly accept their enslavement. They were an integral part of the slavery protest movement. At least two enslaved Roulhacs, Cesar and Ephraim, were part of the 1802 Bertie County Slave Conspiracy, an outgrowth of the Gabriel Prosser uprising in nearby Virginia. Their conspiracy to free themselves occurred 29 years before the more celebrated 1831 Nat Turner Rebellion in nearby Virginia.

It was also during that 1987 visit, I learned that in 1869 and 1870, former enslaved Roulhacs had emigrated to Liberia under the auspices of the American Colonization Society. I never imagined I would have the opportunity to meet one of their descendants, especially one as distinguished as Rev. Roulhac. I became aware of him, as fate would have it, because of my affinity for the food and fellowship found at the Chic Afrique, a Liberian restaurant in Detroit. The owner assured me that Martinus Whitfield, the President of the Liberian Association (Martinus is still President), would be the person most likely to know how to contact Roulhacs living in Liberia. As predicted, Whitfield knew Rev. Moses Roulhac was pastor of Effort Baptist Church in Paynesville, Liberia. I immediately addressed a long letter to Rev. Roulhac sharing my research and expressing an interest in producing a study of the experiences of Roulhacs who returned to Africa and those who remained in the United States. However, Rev. Roulhac never received the letter. His stint as pastor of Effort Baptist Church ended in 1986, one year before the letter was sent. Eighteen years later, the circle was closed when Rev. Roulhac attended the 2005 Chicago reunion I was able to share with him and those in attendance the long ago sent but never received letter.

Rev. Roulhac returned to Liberia and the following year, in July 2006, organized a Liberian Roulhac Family Association. In addition to Rev. Moses, the board of directors includes Augustus Lawrence,

George Kannah Julay, Lucretia Roulhac, MacArthur Gerring and Ellen Gerring Varfley.

Edmond Roulhac, Rev. Moses' son recently graduated, with financial support from the U.S.-based Roulhac Family Association, from the A.M.E. Zion University College of Business with a major in public administration and minor in management. The continuing fallout from the twenty-three year Liberian Civil War has severely hampered employment opportunities in Liberia and Edmond remains unemployed.

10.2 Jordan Roulhac was born in Arthington, Liberia.

11.3 Olivia Roulhac was born in Arthington, Liberia.

12.4 Jefferson Roulhac was born in Arthington, Liberia.

13.5 Bernetta Roulhac was born in Arthington, Liberia.

14.6 Tempa Roulhac was born in Arthington, Liberia.

15.7 Alexandra Roulhac was born in Arthington, Liberia.

16.8 Tillah Roulhac was born in Arthington, Liberia.

IV. Peter Warren and Katherine Roulhac

First Generation
Peter Warren Roulhac (1) and Katherine Roulhac

1.1 Warren (aka Peter Warren) Roulhac was born circa 1851 in Florida. He is listed in the August 9, 1858, Appraisement of Francis Roulhac Ely as 7-year-old Warren valued at $500, with his 24-year-old mother Lizzy and child, appraised at $1,000. In the 1870 Federal Census for Washington County, Florida, Warren Roulhac, a farmer laborer, is living with his wife, Kate, 18. By 1880, 29-year-old Warren Roulhac and his wife Catherine Roulhac, age 26, had five children

Robert Roulhac, 10; Maggie Roulhac, eight; Thomas Roulhac; six; Roxy Ann Roulhac, four and Christopher Roulhac, 10 months. Also living in the household were niece Stella Clark, 16 and nephew Amos Roulhac, 11 years old. All family members are described as mulattos.

In the 1900 Federal Census for Davis Mill, Washington County Florida, District 0117, Page 1, [Peter] Warren Roulhac, a 57-year-old mulatto, is enumerated with wife Manerva Roulhac, 46 and children: Lawrence Roulhac, 19; Catherine Roulhac, 17; Lillian Roulhac, 15; and twins Herbert Roulhac and Hubert Roulhac, 13 years old. All worked as farm laborers, except Catherine, who was a teacher.

Warren was living in the dwelling next to his son Thomas J. Roulhac and his family; his son Herbert M. Roulhac; daughter-in-law Naomi Roulhac and their children Warren Roulhac, three; Dorothea Roulhac one; and newborn Herbert Roulhac. Living two dwellings away from Peter Warren Roulhac and Manerva Roulhac were their son Robert Roulhac, 39; his wife Elizabeth Roulhac, 36; and their 10 children: Elbert Roulhac, 19; Meredith Roulhac, 17; Minerva Roulhac, 15; Jahaza Roulhac, 13; Moses Roulhac, 11; Mamie Roulhac, nine; Roberta Roulhac, eight; Jay Roulhac, five; Larachman, four and Robert Roulhac, one year old.

Second Generation
Issue of Peter Warren Roulhac (1) and Katherine Roulhac

2.1 Robert Roulhac was born about 1870 in Washington County, Florida. He married Martha Jenkins December 14, 1990 (Washington County Marriages, Book C, Page 5).

3.2 Maggie Roulhac was born about 1872 in Washington County, Florida. She married A.D. Potter May 6, 1888 (Washington County Marriages, Book A, Page 214).

4.3 Thomas Joseph Roulhac was born December 24, 1872, in the Orange Hill Community of Washington County, Florida. He married Patience Goode April 11, 1897, in Washington County, Florida (Washington County Marriages, Book E, page 14).

According to oral family history, Thomas J. Roulhac was taught to read and write by his Aunt Stella. He later earned a first grade teacher's certificate and in July 1913, he was contracted to supervise Washington County's Negro schools. He earned $40 per month from the Anna T. Jeans Fund, which was managed by Dr. J. H. Dillard of New Orleans and $60 from the Washington County Board of Public Instruction. Because there were no high schools for blacks in Washington County and they were not allowed to attend the all-white Chipley High School, with financial assistance from Washington County, Thomas J. Roulhac was able to send his children to Tallahassee, over 100 miles away, to continue their education. To remedy this inequality, Thomas vowed to work until black students could attend a high school in Washington County.

In 1928, a high school was established in Washington County and Thomas J. Roulhac became its first principal. The school was housed in an African Methodist Episcopal Church until 1941 when its own building was constructed and named Roulhac High School. The first class graduated in 1942 with 16 students. The last class graduated in 1968, when the schools in Washington County were finally integrated. Roulhac High School students were transferred to formerly all-white Chipley High School. Middle school students transferred to what later became Roulhac Middle School so named to continue to honor the legacy of Thomas Joseph Roulhac whose career in education spanned 49 years.

Thomas J. Roulhac and Patience Roulhac had 10 children between 1898 and 1915. According to the 1910 Federal Census for Davis Mill, Washington County, Florida (District 0117, page 1), Thomas J. Roulhac, 36 and wife Patience Roulhac, 33, were teachers. They were living with their children Claudia C. Roulhac, 12; Jessie P. Roulhac, age 10;

Oswald B. Roulhac, nine; Alma C. Roulhac, seven; Kate V. Roulhac, two; and Grace A. Roulhac, nine. Thomas and his family were living next to his father Warren Roulhac, his wife Minerva Roulhac and their family.

By 1920, Thomas Roulhac and Patience Roulhac had added three daughters to their family - Bernice, eight, Annie, six and Maude five. Each of Joseph and Patience Roulhac's 10 children and many of their 80 grandchildren became educators or education advocates. Others had successful careers in business, religion and medicine.

5.4 Roxy Ann Roulhac was born about 1876 in Washington County, Florida.

6.5 Christopher Roulhac was ten months old when the 1880 U.S. Federal Census was taken. He was Peter Warren and Catherine Roulhac's youngest child. He was born in Chipley, Washington County, Florida. After completing Florida A & M College and Atlanta University, he attended Howard University Medical School in Washington, D.C. and graduated in 1910. There he met his wife, Isabelle Roden Wood, who was a teacher in the D.C. school system. After medical school, they relocated to Memphis, Tennessee.

He began his private practice in 1914 and continued for over 50 years. He taught at the University of Tennessee Medical School and was a surgeon at old Mercy Hospital. He was past president of the Bluff City Medical Association, a board member of the Union Protective Live Insurance Company and the Abe Scharff YMCA. He served as medical examiner for the Universal and Atlanta Life Insurance companies and athletic physician at St. Augustine Catholic School, Booker T. Washington High School and Lemoyne College. He was a trustee of Owen College and St. Augustine Catholic Church and was involved in many social organizations including, Alpha Phi Alpha fraternity and the Delta Boule of Sigma Phi Pi fraternity.

The Roulhac family home, a two-story stone house with huge columns and a porch that extends across the front of the house was placed on the National Register of Historic Places in 2004. It now serves as The Roulhac Mansion, a bed and breakfast named in Dr. Roulhac's honor.

Dr. Christopher and Isabelle Roulhac had two children: Alma Roulhac Booth and Christopher M. Roulhac, Jr. Dr. Christopher M. Booth, Sr., died December 1965.

Issue of Peter Warren Roulhac (1) and Minerva

7.6 Catherine Roulhac was born about 1883 in Florida. She married Keith Williams September 3, 1939 (Washington County Marriages, Book L, Page 113). By 1900, Catherine Roulhac was a teacher.

8.7 Lillian Roulhac was born about 1885 in Florida. She married V. Stiller November 14, 1928 (Washington County Marriages, Book J, Page 191).

9.8 Herbert Roulhac was born about 1887 in Florida. He married Naomi Wilson June 18, 1916.

10.9 Hubert Roulhac was born about 1887 in Florida.

Third Generation
Issue of Thomas Joseph Roulhac (4) and Patience Goode

11.1 Claudia C. Roulhac was born about 1898 in Washington County, Florida. She married Oscar N. Harmon August 21, 1921 (Washington County Marriages, Book H, Page 409). They had eight children: Louise, Virena Harmon, Baline Joseph Harmon, Oscar Harmon; Goode Harmon, Claudia Harmon, Eva Mae Harmon and Grace Harmon.

12.2 Essie P. Roulhac was born about 1900 in Washington County, Florida. She married James Garfield Conoly. They had children: Vivian Conoly, Sylvia Jewel Conoly; Maudelyn Conoly; James Garfield Conoly, Jr., and Althea E. Conoly

13.3 Oswald Bennett Roulhac was born about 1901 in Washington County, Florida. He married Isabelle. He died in 1940 in Leon County, Florida.

14.4 Alma Katurah Roulhac was born about 1903 in Washington County, Florida. She married Asa Jenkins March 7, 1929 (Washington County Marriages, Book J, Page 118). They had children: Eliza Jenkins, Elizabeth Jenkins, Frank Jenkins, Alvin Jenkins and Lawrence Jenkins.

15.5 Eliza Roulhac was born in Washington County, Florida. She married Mr. Davis and had children Gladys Pauline Davis and Vyrle Davis. Vyrle, a retired area school superintendent in St. Petersburg, Florida, is the recipient of many awards, including the Liberty Bell, the Suncoast Chamber Outstanding Educator of the Year Award. The Vyrle Davis Commons Room at Academy Prep, a school that serves at-risk boy and girls in grades five through eight, was named in his honor by a $65,000 grant from the Rotary Club.

16.5 Kate V. Roulhac was born about 1907 in Washington County, Florida. She married M. D. Bethea March 24, 1929 (Washington County Marriages, Book J, Page 122). They had children Doris Bethea, Mildred Bethea, Edwin Bethea and Joyce Bethea.

17.6 Grace A. Roulhac was born about August 1909, in Washington County, Florida. She married Howard Horn March 8, 1931 (Washington County Marriages Book J, Page 299). They had children Annie K. Horne and Howard Horne, Jr.

18.7 Bernice Roulhac was born about 1912, in Washington County, Florida. She married Mr. Gibson and had son William H. Gibson.

19.8 Annie Roulhac was born about 1914, in Washington County, Florida. She married Arnold Campbell December 25, 1940 (Washington County Marriages, Book L, Page 315). They had children Janice Campbell and Jacqueline Campbell

20.9 Maude Deborah Roulhac was born August 16, 1917, in Washington County, Florida to Thomas Joseph and Patience Goode Roulhac. She received her early education in the Washington County Public Schools. Because there were no schools beyond eighth grade for black students to attend in Washington County, her parents sent her to Florida A & M College to complete high school and college. She received a master's degree in educational administration and supervision from South Carolina State University. Maude D. Roulhac married Shelby Campbell March 24, 1940 in Washington County, Florida (Book L, Page 190). She taught at Excelsior High School, St. Augustine, Florida; in the Washington County Public Schools; Tivoli High School in Defuniak Springs, Florida and T. R. Jackson High School, Milton, Florida. She ended her career at Pensacola Junior College as a guidance counselor.

Maude was active in various A.M.E. churches providing service as church secretary, steward, deaconess, and trustee; and was president of the West Florida Conference of the Women's Missionary Society for 16 years. Maude Roulhac Jackson, a long time member and supporter of the Roulhac Family Association, wrote A Biographical Sketch of Thomas Joseph Roulhac, her father for the Fall 1992 issue of The Roulhac Quarterly, the Association's newsletter. She died December 30, 1997.

Issue of Christopher M. Roulhac (6) and Isabelle Roden Wood

20.1 Alma Burchett Roulhac Booth was born in 1914 in Memphis to Dr. Christopher Maxwell and Isabelle Roulhac. She graduated from Lemoyne High School and from 1931-33 attended Lemoyne Junior College. She graduated from Howard University in 1935 with a bachelor of arts degree in history. In 1953, she earned a master's degree in special education from Columbia University.

Alma B. Roulhac married Philip S. Booth, Jr. Alma taught elementary and high school in the Memphis School System and later served as principal of the Keel School for Handicapped Children. For two summers she taught special education and tests and measurements at Lemoyne College. She was a member and leader in many social, civic and church organizations including, Beta Epsilon Omega Chapter of Alpha Kappa Alpha, Inc., Emmanuel Episcopal Church, the Urban League, Jack and Jill, Memphis Links, the Memphis Brooks Museum of Art and the West Tennessee Historical Commission. Alma has appeared in several historical videos, *Delta Area Agency on Aging Memphis Living History Seniors, 1998, 50,000 Watts of Goodwill, The WDIA Story* [the first black formatted radio station in the country], *The Links, Inc., Memphis Chapter* and *History of Elwood Cemetery*.

At age 85, Alma chronicled her life in *Tender Memories – A Grandmother's Legacy* and has since written Part II of her memoirs. Alma and Phillip Booth have a son, Christopher Roulhac Booth, III, who is married to Delorise Joyner, stepson, Philip Sylvester Booth, III, who is married to Jean Mahadeo, six grandchildren and six great grandchildren. Alma, now 98-years-old, lives with her son and daughter-in-law in Philadelphia.

21.22 Christopher M. Roulhac, Jr. was born in 1917 in Memphis to Dr. Christopher Maxwell and Isabelle Roulhac. He was a product of the Memphis Public Schools. He earned bachelors, master's and doctorate degrees from LeMoyne College, Springfield College and the University of Sarasota, respectively. He married Nellie Gordon Roulhac, the author of several books including, Jumping Over the Moon, a biography of Olympic-gold medalist Alice Coachman.

Professionally, he was director of admissions and foreign-student advisor at Cheney State University; American Red Cross water safety and life-saving instructor at Tennessee State College; assistant freshman football coach at Springfield College; physical education instructor and football, basketball and track coach at Arkansas A.M. & N. and Corbin High School; athletic director, football and track coach at Albany State College, and YMCA director. While at Albany State, Chris coached Alice Coachman, a gold medal winner when she won the high jump by leaping 5 feet, 6½ inches at the 1948 summer Olympics in London. Coachman's gold was the first for an African American woman and the only medal awarded to an American during the 1948 games.

Christopher was a charter member of the Roulhac Family Association, a life member of Alpha Phi Alpha fraternity and the International Association of retired Directors of YMCAs; a member of Sigma Pi Phi; and a number of other civic organizations. He was quarterback for the 1939 Negro All-American Football team against the Chicago Bears. Chris attained the rank of lieutenant in the U.S. Army and earned decorations and citations while in service in North Africa and Italy. Christopher died February 21, 1997. His widow, Nellie, died August 1, 2002.

V. Quamley Roulhac and Elsie Roulhac

First Generation
Quamley Roulhac (1) and Elsie Roulhac

1.2 Quamley Roulhac and Elsie Roulhac were born in North Carolina in about 1809 and 1820, respectively. They are included in the August 9, 1858, Jackson County Probate record of Francis Roulhac Ely. They were among Ely's 120 slaves. Quamley (identified as Qluomner) was 49 years old and his wife Elsie (spelled Alcy) was 38. They were valued at $900 and $500, respectively. They had children Pheoby, 17; Robert, 12; Allen, nine; Peter, five; Aggy, four; and John, one year old. Their assigned values ranged from $750 for Pheoby to $150 for John.

Quamley (Wommer) and Elsie (Ilsy) were legally married June 5, 1866 (Book C, Page 27, as Wommer Roulhac and Ilsy Roulhac). In the 1870 Jackson County Federal census, 57 year old Quamley and his 50-year-old wife Elsie, both born in North Carolina, were living in Marianna with their Florida-born children: Peter, age 17; Aggie, 16; John, 13 and an unnamed infant son, six months old. In 1880, Quamley is listed in the Federal Census as 73 years old living in Jackson County's 6th precinct with Elsie, age 65 and children Aggie, age 23; John, 21; Isaac, 17 and a grandson William Robert, 16.

By 1900, Quamley had died. His 80-year-old widow, Elsie Roulhac, was living in Marianna with her children, Isaac Roulhac, age 39, who was designated as head of the household; Aggie, age 41; and adopted daughters Minerva Rhodes, age 15 and Emma Rhodes, 10, both born in Florida. In the 1910 Census, Elsie's age is listed as 97 years old, 17 years older than shown in 1900. Most likely, in 1910, Elsie was closer to 102 years old. According Francis Roulhac Ely's probate record, she was 50 years old in 1858.

Second Generation
Issue of Quamley Roulhac (1) and Elsie Roulhac

2.1 Pheoby Roulhac was born about 1841. The only official record of Pheoby is found in the August 9, 1858, Appraisement of the Estate of Francis Roulhac Ely as a 17 year old valued at $750.

3.2 Robert Roulhac was born about 1846 in Jackson County, Florida. The only official record of Robert is found in the August 9, 1858, Appraisement of the Estate of Francis Roulhac Ely as a five year old valued at $300.

4.3 Allen Roulhac, born about 1849 in Jackson County, Florida. He is listed in the 1858 probate record of Francis Roulhac Ely as a nine year old valued at $550. Allen Roulhac married Margaret Garner January 8, 1874. In the 1880 Jackson County Federal Census, he was living in precinct 6, with his 23-year-old wife and sons Harmony, six years old and Donny H., born April 1880.

Allen Roulhac re-married Margaret Roulhac March 15, 1897 (Jackson County Marriages, Book J, Page 299), a week before he was granted a Land Patent for 120.18 acres of land under the Homestead Act of 1862. To insure that there would be a burial place for Roulhacs, Allen designated a portion of his property to be used as the Roulhac Cemetery. The Cemetery is located on Wynn Street, south of Marianna, in the Ephraim Hill community. Allen died July 8, 1939. He was 90 years old.

5.4 Peter Roulhac was born about 1853 in Jackson County, Florida. The first official record of Peter is found in the August 9, 1858, Appraisement of the Estate of Francis Roulhac Ely as a five year old valued at $300. During Reconstruction, Jackson County was one of the most violent counties in Florida. John Q. Dickinson, a Vermouth native, who came to Marianna as a Freedmen's Bureau agent, in 1868, became a victim in 1871. After the February 1869 assassination of county clerk Dr. John L. Finlayson, Dickinson was appointed as his replacement. However, he met the same fate as his predecessor. He was murdered April 3, 1871, shortly before reaching his home near the site of the present day Davis-West House on Madison Street in Marianna. Francis Roulhac Ely's son, John Randolph Ely, and Frank Bryan, a former slave, were implicated in Dickinson murder. Peter Roulhac, who saw Dickinson after his murder, was one of the witnesses called to testify during the April 4, 1871, Coroner's Inquest. He testified as follows:

> I stayed at John Q. Dickinson's last night; been staying with him for the last three weeks. There was a colored man at Captain J.Q. Dickinson's last night. He ate supper there. I saw nothing more of him till the body of Captain D. was brought in. Major Milton told me and

him to go for General Anderson and the Doctor. His sir [sic] name was Bryan. I was lying down. Aunt Clarissa [In 1870, she was 65 years old, living next to John Q. Dickinson and worked as his servant] gave him his supper. He only set, let us go on and get the Doctor; he was sleepy. He looked like he was grown; don't know if I would know him if I was to see him again.

After the Inquest the juror concluded John Q. Dickinson death occurred by some person or persons unknown to them. The verdict was unchanged after the inquest was reconvened on April 6, 1871.

6.5 Aggie [aka Aggy] Roulhac was born about 1854 in Jackson County, Florida. The first official record of Aggie is found in the August 9, 1858, Appraisement of the Estate of Francis Roulhac Ely. She is listed as a four year old valued at $200. Aggie is enumerated in the 1870 Federal Census as a 16-year-old farm laborer living at home with her parents. However, in the 1880 census, inconsistent with the 1870 census, Aggie birthday is listed as January 1859. This is incorrect since she was four years old in the August 9, 1858 Appraisement of Francis Roulhac Ely estate. Aggie's age discrepancy continues in the 1900 and 1910 Federal Censuses.

7.6 John Roulhac was born about 1857 in Jackson County, Florida. John is listed in the August 9, 1858 Appraisement of the Estate of Francis Roulhac Ely as a one year old valued at $150. In 1880, John is shown in the census as 21 years old working as a school teacher. John is enumerated in the 1900 Federal Censuses as a 58-year-old widow, living with his children: Mary, 21 years old; Johnnie, 16; Nora, 15 and Douglas, 12.

8.7 Isaac Roulhac was born April 1861 in Jackson County, Florida. In 1880, he is described as a 17-year-old farmer laborer living with his parents, his sister Aggie and 16-year old nephew Robert Williams. Isaac L. Roulhac married Pinkey Clayton December 23,

1889 (Jackson County Marriages, Book 1, Page 255). By 1900, Isaac is living on his own farm with his siblings – Aggie, 41 and John, 38 – his 80-year-old mother Elsie and adopted daughters, Minerva and Emma, 15 and 10 years old, respectively. However, in 1910, Isaac L. Roulhac is enumerated in the Federal Census as a 47-year-old widowed head of household living with his mother Elsie, 97 years old, and sister Aggie A. Roulhac, 52. Isaac Roulhac died in 1929 (Florida Death Index, Vol. 414, No. 4029).

Third Generation
Issue of Allen Roulhac (4) and Margaret Garner

9.1 Harmony Roulhac was born about 1874 in Jackson County, Florida.

10.2 Donnie H. Roulhac was born April 1880, in Jackson County, Florida. He married Nettie Wynn, born about 1883, in Jackson County, Florida, November 1, 1904 (Jackson County Marriages, Book 5, Page 419). According to the 1920 Jackson County Census, they had a seven-year-old daughter, Inez Roulhac. He was living in Cypress, Florida, next to his father, Allen Roulhac, who was 70, and his brother Alex, 38. Living next to Alex was brother Cleve and family. Donnie H. Roulhac's daughter Inez Roulhac had a son Donnie Roulhac. Donnie and his wife Shirley Roulhac are charter members of the Roulhac Family Association. Their daughter Kesha Roulhac-Walker is the current editor of The Roulhac Quarterly, the newsletter of the Roulhac Family Association. Their daughter Shirlana Roulhac painted The March to Freedom, pictured at the beginning of Part II.

11.3 Allen Roulhac, Jr.

12.4 Alex W. Roulhac was born June 24, 1881, in Jackson County, Florida. Alex Roulhac married Lula Shavers December 18, 1907 (Jackson County Marriages, Book 7, Page 132). By 1920, Alex was a widow living in Cypress, Jackson County, Florida with three children – Maggie Roulhac, eight years old; Annie Mae Roulhac, five and Pearl Roulhac, four. Alex Roulhac married Clissie McElroy May 20, 1921 (Jackson County Marriages, Book 13, Page 55).

13.5 Cleve Roulhac was born about 1886 in Jackson County, Florida. He married Lillie Shavers January 1, 1908 (Jackson County Marriages, Book 7, Page 150). When the 1920 Federal Census was taken January 2, 1920, he was living with his wife and 4 children: Christell, 10-years-old; George, eight; Cleve, Jr., three and Johnson, 11 months old. Cleve Roulhac, 59, is enumerated in the 1945 Florida Census living in Marianna with wife Lillie, 47; James, a 21-year-old laborer; 18-year-old, Robert who was in the 10th grade; George, a 24-year-old laborer with a 6th grade education; daughter Willie Lee, a cook with a 5th grade education; Cleve, Jr., 28, a laborer with a 6th grade education; Ella, 25, a washer, completed the 8th grade; Gene, five years old; daughter Lula Williams, 21, with a 12th grade education and her son Carl, Jr., two-years-old; and Lillie Mae Roulhac and her son., less than one year old.

Cleve Roulhac was one of many African Americans who operated thriving businesses in downtown Marianna until the end of segregation during the Civil Rights era of the 1960s. Cleve's daughter, Lula Roulhac Williams, a graduate of White's Beauty School, operated a beauty salon with Claudia Gant in the Blue Front section of Marianna. Lula married Carl Edwards Williams. In addition to Carl, Jr., they had children Earnest Williams, a former St. Petersburg City Councilman; Jean Williams Jasmin; Rhonda Williams and Michael Williams.

Adopted Children of Isaac Roulhac (8)

14.1 Minerva Rhodes was born May 1885 in Jackson County, Florida. She is listed in the 1900 Federal Census for Jackson County, Florida as the 15-year-old adopted daughter of Isaac Roulhac. Minerva married Robert Daniel Roulhac, a descendant of Nelly and

Nero Roulhac, September 19, 1906 (Jackson County Marriages, Book 6, Page 359).

Minerva Roulhac, a mulatto, with keen facial features and straight hair, is the protagonist in *"Passing: The Play,"* written by her great-granddaughter Dara Frazier-Walker. *Passing* tells one aspect of the history of the Roulhacs of African descent and their quest for equal opportunity. It confronts issues of race, interracial relationships, complexion, ethnicity and class that still figures prominently in America today. Minerva, who could have easily passed for white, refused to cross the color-line and enjoyed a rich life, albeit not without complications, as a Negro. Minerva, with her European looks, and her husband Robert, with his dark skin and African features, were often the victims of overt racist remarks and treatment as they travelled throughout the South. The play has been successfully staged off-Broadway in New York, in Detroit, in several other mid-western cities and during the 2011 Roulhac Family Association Reunion, at the Chipola College Theater in Marianna, Florida.

15.2 Emma Rhodes was born about 1890 in Jackson County, Florida. She is listed in the 1900 Federal Census for Jackson County, Florida as the 10-year-old adopted daughter of Isaac Roulhac

VI. Sampson Roulhac and Clara Roulhac

The following information is adopted, with some additions, from an article submitted to *The Roulhac Quarterly* by Edward T. Roulhac, the great-grandson of Sampson Roulhac and Clara Roulhac.

> As of the 1880 census, Bertie County, Merry Hill Township, North Carolina, Sampson age 35, and his wife Clara, age 39, had five children: Agnes, 18; Annie, nine; Samuel, six; Ida, five and Isom, three. Sampson operated a farm on Merry Hill Road near Avoca Farm

Chapter 6

Road and Peterson Chapel Road. Clara worked as a washer woman.

Twenty years later, Sampson and his family are enumerated in the 1900 census for Bertie County, merry Hill district. Sampson, 56, and his wife Clara, 58 had the following children in the household: Isom, 23; William, 19; Ned, 17 and a grandson, Simon or Simeon Douglas, age seven. Clara was recorded as being the mother of nine children with five living as of the 1900 Federal Census. William Roulhac is Edward T. Roulhac's paternal grandfather.

As was common in those days in the South, neither Sampson nor Clara had any schooling. Both were listed as being unable to read, write or speak English. However, Ned, listed as a farm laborer could read, write and speak English. Sampson was born June 1844 and Clara, March 1842. The 1900 census indicated they had been married 30 years. Strangely, however, they were both listed as being single.

By 1900, Samuel, 26, whose last name is spelled "Rolack," was married to Laura, and had a son William, born December 1898. Samuel worked as a log hauler and Laura as a day laborer. Both could read, write and speak English. Sampson's son, William, married Lizzie P. Holley (1889-), one of Mary Holley's three children.

In 1920, Sampson Roulhac, age 70, is a widower, living with his daughter Ida, 44; granddaughter Hattie King, 21, and her husband Joe King, 44 and their children: William King, 2 1/2 and Melvin King, one year old. Also living in the household were grandchildren: Alice Roulhac, 16; Isom Roulhac, 14 and Eugenia Roulhac, 10. Living next door to Sampson were Sampson's son Samuel and his wife Laura Roulhac and their son James, age 19.

James Clinton Roulhac married Sophia Watson. In 1942, when James Roulhac, age 41, registered for the World War II draft, he was living in Tyrell County and employed by the Tyrell Lumber Company in Columbia. He was living with his wife Sophia Roulhac.

Sampson Roulhac died July 13, 1922, in Merry Hill, Bertie County, North Carolina. According to his death certificate, recorded in the Ancestry.com on-line database of North Carolina Death Certificates, 1909-1975, Sampson's father's name was Jack Roulhac. In the 1880 census for Bertie County, North Carolina, page 25, line 41, Jack Roulhac, age 69, was living with his wife Peggy Roulhac, 68 and five-year-old granddaughter Rose Roulhac.

Long time Roulhac Family Association members Della Roulhac Bowser, Mary Roulhac White; Virginia L. Roulhac Watford, Cordelia Roulhac Davis and Doris Bonner and their families are Sampson Roulhac's descendants.

VII. Eliza Roulhac

First Generation
Eliza Roulhac

1.1 Eliza Roulhac was born about 1853 in Jackson County, Florida. According to oral family history, Eliza was 12 years old when she was freed from the Bellamy Plantation in Jackson County, Florida. In 1910, Eliza Roulhac, age 53 was living with her son Eddie Roulhac, 40; his wife Jennie, 38 and eight grandchildren – Edmond, 16; Flozell, 14; Julius 12; Phillip, eight; Albert, seven; Roland, six; Annie, three and Lucretia, two years old. Eliza indicated that she had given birth to five children and three were still living. No marriage record or other census records have been found for Eliza.

Second Generation
Issue of Eliza Roulhac

2.1 Eddie Roulhac was born about 1870 in Jackson County, Florida. He married Jennie Harvey, April 3, 1889 (Jackson County Marriages, Book 1, Page 199). In 1910, 40 year old Eddie Roulhac, was a farmer on his own farm is living with his wife Jennie, 38, and eight children – Edmond, 16; Flozell, 14; Julius 12; Phillip, eight; Albert, seven; Roland, six; Annie, three; Lucretia, two years old and his 53-year-old mother Eliza Roulhac. By 1920, Eddie, a widower, is working as a farm laborer and living with children Julius, 22; Phillip, 20; Albert, 18; Roland, 16; Annie, 14, Lucretia, 12 and Fannie, nine.

2.2 Robert Roulhac was born about in Jackson County, Florida. He married Ethel Guyton September 16, 1924 (Jackson County Marriages, Book 11, Page 84). Ethel, maiden name Bowers, had married Joshua Guyton on August 23, 1905 (Jackson County Marriages, Book 6, Page 130). In the 1910 Jackson County Census, Ethel Guyton, a 25-year-old cook, is living with husband Joshua, 28; Robert Bowers, 17; and Mary Bowers, 10. Robert and Mary Bowers are identified in the 1910 Census as Joshua's brother and sister, but they are more likely Ethel's siblings. Robert Roulhac and Ethel Roulhac adopted Orabelle Roulhac.

3.3 Missie Roulhac married Edward R. Williams October 24, 1921 (Jackson County Marriages, Book 7, Page 497).

Third Generation
Issue of Eddie Roulhac (2) and Jennie Harvey

4.1 Edmond Roulhac was born about 1884 in Jackson County, Florida. He married Lucy Wynn, December 27, 1913 (Jackson

County Marriages, Book 8, Page 472). In 1935, Edmond and his wife are living at 612 East End, Panama City, Bay County, Florida. Edmond was working at South Kraft Co. Edmond and Lucy Roulhac had seven children, five boys and two girls.

5.6 Flozell Roulhac was born about 1886 in Jackson County, Florida. Flozell Roulhac married Frank Bryant May 7, 1913 (Jackson County Marriages, Book 8, Page 319). In 1935, Frank and Flozell Bryant were renting a home at 658 Massalina Avenue, Panama City, Bay County, Florida (Ohio and Florida, City Directories, 1902-1960, p. 56).

6.7. Julius Roulhac was born about 1888 in Jackson County, Florida. In 1920, Julius, age 22, was living at home with his father. He was working as a woodcutter. Julius Roulhac married Lizzie Kelly January 25, 1921. They had two children – Julius Roulhac, Jr., and James B. Roulhac.

7.8 Phillip Roulhac was born about 1902 in Jackson County, Florida. Phillip Roulhac married Leola McDaniel August 27, 1934 (Bay County Florida Marriages, Vol. 4, Page 421. They had two sons, Phillip, Jr., and a son whose name is unknown.

8.9 Albert Roulhac was born about 1903 in Jackson County, Florida.

9.10 Roland Roulhac was born about 1906 in Jackson County, Florida. He married Bert Samuel Jackson, February 21, 1935 (Jackson County Marriages, Book 17, Page 265). They had one daughter, Lucretia Roulhac.

10.11 Annie Roulhac was born about 1907 in Jackson County, Florida. In 1935, she was living in Panama City, Florida working as a maid at the Bay Hotel. She had daughter Louise.

11.12 Lucretia Roulhac was born about 1908 in Jackson County, Florida. Lucretia Rolack married Amos Barkley June 14, 1925 (Jackson County Marriages, Book 14, Page 39).

12.13 Fannie Roulhac was born about 1909 in Jackson County, Florida. She had a daughter, Gwendolyn.

Issue of Robert Roulhac (2) and Ethel Bowers Guyton

13.14 Orabelle Roulhac, adopted daughter, married Doby Cornelius March 28, 1943 (Bay County Florida Marriages, Vol. 7, Page 306). She died while giving birth to son Robert Cornelius.

Fourth Generation

Issue of Edmond Roulhac (4) and Lucy Wynn

14.1 Henderson Roulhac married Bedie Bell April 25, 1938 (Bay County Marriages, Vol. 5, Page 320). He later married Bernell Campbell, September 13, 1949 (Bay County Marriages, Vol. 10, Page 115).

14.2 Edgar Roulhac married Marie Steel March 12, 1938 (Bay County Florida Marriages, Vol. 5, Page 320.

15.3 Jenny Roulhac

16.4 Irvy Roulhac was born about 1929 in Jackson County, Florida. He married Earnestine ___.

17.5 Hosea Roulhac

18.6 Nathaniel Roulhac

19.7 Alexander Roulhac, and his brother Nathaniel were charter members of the Roulhac Family Association and hosted the 1995 Reunion in Marianna, Jacksonville, Florida. The family will host the Association's 2013 Reunion from July 18-21.

VIII. Abraham Rhoulhac

First Generation

1.1 Abraham Rhoulhac was born about 1898 in Florida. He married Stella ___, born about 1901. In 1921, they moved to Daytona Beach, Volusia, Florida. According to the 1930 U.S. Federal Census, 32-year-old Robert and wife Stella Rhoulhac were living in Daytona with sons Robert, nine years old, and Sam, eight. They were paying $16 per month for their rented home.

Second Generation
Issue of Abraham Rhoulhac

2.1 Robert Charles Rhoulhac was born June 3, 1919, in Quincy, Gadsden County, Florida. He was educated at the Campbell Street School. In 1947, his first daughter, Sharon Cato was born and in 1952, son Robert C. Rhoulhac, Jr., was born. Robert Charles Roulhac married Yeasier Robinson Roper. Yeasier, born to Willie and Annie Mae Robinson, February 22, 1926, in Houston, Florida, was first married to James Roper and had daughter Frankie Roper. Robert and Yeasier had three daughters: Karen Yvette, Michelle Renee and Sheryl Monique. In 1970, Robert Rhoulhac, a laborer, and his wife Yeasier Rhoulhac, the manager of the Paradise Inn, were living at 2281 N. W. 10th Street, Pompano Beach, Florida.

Robert died January 28, 1978. Yeasier Rhoulhac died April 27, 2000. Yeasier daughters – Vivian Bryant, Karen and Monique Rhoulhac, and Michelle Renee Francois - hosted the July 2000 Roulhac Family Association Reunion in Fort Lauderdale, Florida.

3.2 Samuel T. Rhoulhac was born about 1920.

IX. Abraham Roulhac

First Generation

1.1 Abraham Roulhac married Lizzy Roulhac, October 15, 1882, according to the Jackson County Marriage Records, Book E, Page 491. By 1910, Lizzie Roulhac, 45 years old, was a widow farming her own land in Campbellton with her four children – Isaiah, 22; Malissa, 22; Willie 16 and Henry nine. She reported to the census taker that she had given birth to four children, all of whom were alive.

Second Generation
Issue of Abraham Roulhac

2.1 Isaiah Roulhac was born July 17, 1886, Jackson County, Florida. The Jackson County Marriage Records, Book 8, Page 38, notes that an application to marry was filed by Isaac Roulhac and Callarada Wynn. Isaiah died April 26, 1961, in Jacob, Jackson County, Florida.

3.2 Malissa Roulhac, aka as "Melissa" was born January 2, 1888, in Jackson County, Florida. She married Abram Brantley April 30, 1904 (Jackson County Marriages, Book 5, Page 332). She died May 19, 1991.

4.3 Henry Roulhac was born about 1901in Jackson County, Florida. He married Quintiney Russ, October 28, 1929.

5.4 King David Roulhac was born in Jackson County, Florida. He married Ida Gray November 16, 1931. See Jackson County Marriages, Book 16, Page 182.

6.5 Willie Roulhac was born in Jackson County, Florida.

7.6. Ciller Roulhac Was born in Jackson County, Florida.

Third Generation
Issue of Isaiah Roulhac (2) and Lucy Wynn

8.1 Willie Roulhac was born in Jackson County, Florida, February 26, 1907. She married Elijah Pittman April 14, 1928. See Jackson County Marriages, Book 15, Page 103.

9.2 Carrie Roulhac was born April 21, 1915. She married Crawford Bailey December 5, 1932. See Jackson County Marriages, Book 16, Page 333.

10.3 Pecola Roulhac was born November 16, 1919. She married a Mr. Smiley.

11.4 Hemor Henderson Roulhac was born February 14, 1925.

12.5 Charlie Roulhac was born December 11, 1926. He Married a Miss Mary. The had children Charlie Roulhac, Jr., Michael Roulhac, Derick Roulhac Ali, Shelton Roulhac, Jeffery Roulhac, Jerome Roulhac, Earl Roulhac and Eric Roulhac.

13.6 Doll Baby Roulhac died at two years old in Jacob, Florida.

14.7 Isaac Roulhac died at two week old in Jacob, Florida.

15.8 Abraham Roulhac died at two years old in Jacob, Florida.

Issue of Malissa Roulhac(3) and Abram Brantley

16.1 Minnie Lee Brantley

17.2 Lizzie Mae Brantley was born February 16, 1916. She died October 13, 1984, in Jackson County, Florida.

The Negro National Anthem

(Lift Every Voice and Sing, Excerpt)
by James Weldon Johnson

GOD of our weary years, GOD of our silent tears
Thou Who has brought us thus far on the way
Thou Who hast by Thy might, led us into the light
Keep us forever in the path we pray.

Chapter 6

Roulhac Family Association members attend the 2005 reunion is Chicago, IL. Photo courtesy Edgar Roulhac, Jr.

Roulhac Family Association Reunion, St. James A.M.E. Church, Marianna, Florida, July 1991. Photo courtesy Edgar Roulhac, Jr.

Appendix 1
Memoir of the Gregoire de Roulhacs in France

"These sheets are by the author [Francis Leonard Gregoire de Roulhac – 1849] *written to leave behind him to his children, a memorial of the variegated events of his life, and to make them acquainted with their ancestors and the individuals of the numerous members of the family to which he belongs. It is very natural for all men to feel an interest, I say, even pride in the history of our own country, then why should we not feel the same in hearing of those who are so nearly related to us, and have preceded us on the scenes of this world? If they had virtue, talents, etc., even in a humble walk of life, it ought to be an incitement to follow them in these. We have, all of us, a conscious pride in the glory of our native land; be it in war, in peace, in sciences, in arts or in laws and civilization and why? It is because we identify ourselves with it. Can it be then wrong to feel a noble pride, if it can be called so, to know of the virtues, talents and consideration which belonged to our progenitors in time past, and to value ourselves for belonging to such family? My children know that I was born and raised in France, and consequently I must have brought, at 26 or 27 years of age many ideas, (prejudices you may call them), natural to a Frenchman raised and educated under a different government, different laws, customs and manners, from those which exist in this country. Our ideas of propriety and rights are generally formed from what we see and hear in early life, and in fact depend mostly on education. The French Revolution threw me here, not an Englishman or Anglo-American, but a mere Frenchman with his native prejudices or prepossessions. This will account for the value I have always put on the advantage which really exist in belonging to a*

respectable family, although my reason and common sense teach me that as we receive nothing from our ancestors but life, and sometimes property, consequently the pride or vanity of being well born, as it is called, is absurd and ridiculous when to the virtues of our forefather, which are foreign to use, we join meanness and vices, which are our own. I confess that I am not so far divested of family prejudices not to find great pressure in reflecting that my forefathers for several generations enjoyed the esteem and consideration of their contemporaries. This being premised, I come to my subject, wishing that those of my children or grandchildren who may peruse this writing, should remember, that as they bear a respectable name, they should never deviate from the virtues which have made it so."

Account in General of the Roulhac Family

"The family of de Roulhac was for a long time known in the Province of Limosin now known by the name of Department of Haute Vienne, where several of its branches resided and now reside generally as landed proprietors. The head of one of them originally at least, belonged to the order of the nobility. The coat of arms preserved in each branch, is a proof that they were all of the same stock.

My grandfather, Guillaume Gregoire de Roulhac, I believe, added to his name Dethias from a landed property which belonged to that branch of the family, and which in fact his son, my father, sold out many years before I was born and which he had inherited from one of his paternal aunts. Now as I understand, the grandfather of my grandfather, being either a younger brother or being reduced in worldly affairs, put his sword by and turned merchant. He was associated with a man of capital by the name of Gregoire. I am not informed what kind of trade it was, or of what nature and extent. However, that step was not relished by his family and relations, who all prided themselves on their noble blood, and then, in France, a noble degraded himself in following trade in his own country. According to the prejudices then existing, it was natural for his relations, who thought he had brought disgrace, not only on himself but also on his whole family, to become cool.

So it came to pass, in the course of time that the relationship between his descendants and those of the older branches, were not any more claimed. His partner, Gregoire, dying without children, left to my progenitor, the whole of his property, which was considerable, with the condition that himself and posterity, should add forever the name of Gregoire to the family name of Roulhac, and also, he should form a new coat of arms, one-half to be half of the coat of arms of the Roulhac; the other half of that of the Gregoire family. That of the Roulhac is that on the left, and on the right is that of the Gregoire, as may be seen in an engraving on a form and spoon which I have given to one of my children. This will explain why the name of Gregoire is added to our name. Probably here in America the branches of our family will drop if off, though as may be a bare possibility that they might inherit from France for generations past by the descendants of the old gentleman I speak of. The elder branches of the Roulhacs, in my day, were divided into two branches – Roulhac, Marquis of Rasay and Roulhac de Roulhac. The branch of the other Roulhacs, who had the Gregoire prefixed to our family name, was divided into many sub-divisions, such as Faugeras, Dethias, Du Clasang, Du Ronvaix and Dupuisfaucher, such names were given, besides the proper name for country estates, to distinguish families all coming from the same stock. Christian names were seldom used in those days.

My grandfather lived on an estate called Boisseul, five or six miles from Limoges. He was married to a lady of the name of Maldant, a family which prided itself on its noble descent and which was rich and influential. He purchased from the government an office, whose duties were only nominal, but which gave dignity and respectability to the purpose invested with it, and which became the property of the incumbent, who could keep or sell it. The traditions of the family represent my grandfather as an upright, virtuous, honest and religious man. After his death my paternal grandmother lived and died with her son, my father. My grandfather left three sons and a daughter. The son's Christian names were Joseph, Francis Leonard and Peter Paul, commonly called as customary in France, le Chevalier.

As the right of primogeniture was then in force, the portions of my uncles and aunts were probably not very large. My father, as the eldest, inherited the half of the property and, divided in equal shares, the other half among his brother and sisters."

Joseph Gregoire de Roulhac Dethias

"He was the second son; his elder brother, who had been destined to the order of the clergy, died before he entered Holy orders and so left my father the eldest of his family. He was born in 1721. He gave early proof of a strong mind capacity, with diligence and application to study. At fifteen or sixteen he was sent to Paris to the College of Louis le Grand, kept by the Jesuits, one of those which belonged to the University of Paris, where he distinguished himself by his talents and proficiency in all his studies. His collegiate education being ended, he was prevailed upon to enter the Congregation of Oratoire, whose members were a body of public teachers, who had the direction and management of a great many colleges in France. My father spent a few years in that congregation, where he was professor of Belles Lettres and Eloquence.

At twenty-four years of age he went to Paris to study law, and having, in due time, obtained a license to practice, settled himself in his native city as an advocate, and in a short time rose to the head of his profession, in his province, where his application and strict honesty enabled him to begin to build the foundation of a well-earned fortune and reputation. At about the age of thirty, he became acquainted with a young widow lady, about twenty-four, whose maiden name was Dumas, a respectable family in the province.

They were united about 1750, and for thirty years have one of those few but happy examples of conjugal union and love. They gave being to thirteen children, all of whom came to years of maturity – nine sons and four daughters. For these, my father kept at home a well-informed tutor, who constantly remained with us and prepared us to enter college at a certain time, he was well convinced that a good and solid education would, in a great degree, make up for the small property that he could, at his death, *leave to his younger children. His hopes were not in vain, for in the sequel of times, the French Revolution came and upset their prospects in life, bringing some nearly to beggary, but the solid education they had received enabled them to overcome the effect of his unforeseen and unavoidable event. At the death of my grandfather, my father purchased an office in the Court of the Treasures of France. This was only kept because like many offices in Frances, it had become a kind of property, and besides, if possessed by three generations in a family, it ennobled their posterity. A few years after he left the bar, he purchased also an office of Associate Judge in the first tribunal of justice in his province. The head judge or president, held one of the first ranks among his fellow citizens, not only from his office, but from the income attached to it. The president of that court lived in the greatest intimacy with my father, and dying of consumption, directed that if my father desired the office it should be given up to him at a sum equal to about $12,000, although worth much more. In this office my father remained until his death, sixteen years later, in 1781. To my father as regulator of the police, and for many years mayor of the City, Limoges was indebted for several improvements and embellishments.*

Some time before his death, my father sold his office of the Treasures of France, and purchased another, known as Secretary of the King. This was only a high sounding name. The functions attached to it were fulfilled by deputies not near the King, but near some of the parliaments or high courts of appeal, of which there were several in the kingdom; but the beauty of it and what made the office desirable was that the incumbent was "ipse facto," ennobled himself and his posterity forever, so that in fact it was nothing more than purchasing nobility. It may appear that such a step was grounded in vanity, but it was not entirely so, in a county where nobility enjoyed many privileges, and, another consideration, his ancestors were noble, the old branches of the family were, and some of the Gregoire Roulhacs, by purchase of offices which ennobled, had got again in that order. It was then very natural in his rank and station for my father to procure to his children the advantages attached to nobility. To bestow on us the best education that his circumstances could afford, he procured the assistance and care of a certain Heritte, which good luck had thrown in his way, and who had received his education at the College of Vendome, one of the first educating establishments in France. He came into our family very early and became the preceptor or tutor of all of us, males and females, from the oldest to the youngest.

He even imparted to some of my sisters a sufficient knowledge of the Latin tongue to perfectly understand the public service and prayers used in the Catholic churches. He was treated as a friend and son and remained in our house even after the death of my father. From the age of four or five until twelve or fourteen we were put under the care of this excellent man. Although raised in a town, we were never permitted to ramble about the streets and mix with other children.

A not very spacious court and garden were the only places we were allowed to frequent and play in, so that we should not make any noise to disturb my father or the rest of the family. If we were permitted to take a walk, either in town or country, it was always in the company of our preceptor. Even when we went to visit relations, where there were children, they were generally kept as strictly as ourselves, so that neither at home nor abroad was there any quarreling or fighting. Our hours of study and play were regulated and rigidly enforced, and this without severity, for I do not remember, though at that age I was a perfect blockhead, that I was ever flogged by that good man.

It was in this manner that we were raised. Under our tutor we received, according to our capacity, the principle of religion, the first rudiments of the Latin language, and of some other useful knowledge. Kept by ourselves under his eyes, not suffered to mix with improper company, we were raised with as much innocence, and, contracting from example, as few vices and bad habits as can be well conceived. With our parents there was only union and love; no discord or jarring. Their interesting and instructive discourses could only tend to our improvement. At about twelve or fourteen we were sent to college, at a great distance from home, not to return until our collegiate education was ended. It was the same with our sisters – at a certain age they were sent to some nunnery of repute for the education of young girls. When all this was ended, the young men and young ladies were given, at home, several masters of more modern improvements, such as drawing, music, dancing, embroidering, fencing, etc., to finish their education.

My father was attacked, in the fall of 1781, with a malignant fever, which, on Oct. 3, deprived my mother of the best of husbands and his children of a most valuable father, and the public of an upright and learned magistrate, at the age of sixty or sixty-one. A modest epitaph in Latin, written by M. Heritte and some of my brothers, was put near his tomb on a plate of brass, at his parish church, where he was buried. He was tall, being nearly six feet, French measure, but illy-shaped, with remarkably lean and slender legs, but his countenance made up for those corporeal defects. It depicted intense thought; it was grave and severe; his eyes were black, small and penetrating and full of fire. He had a Roman nose and a handsome mouth. His goodness of heart was not always depicted on his high and noble forehead; it was only with a few friends or in his family that the severity of his countenanced disappeared."

Francis Leonard Gregoire de Roulhac

"My uncle Francis, early entered the Church and became a Canon of the Abbottal and Collegial Church of St. Martiel at Limoges. Those collegial churches in Catholic countries had been monasteries in the Middle Ages, their head, called the Abbot, and with his monks, who themselves kept the only schools known in those ages and who cultivated and preserved all the learning which then existed. Each Canon had a house and a certain income, which made them independent and live at their ease if not in affluence. My uncle was a very charitable man. He was till his death an administrator of the general hospital of the city, which contained from 800 to 1200 inmates who were either sick, poor, destitute children or decrepit old men and women. His brother, le Chevalier, was in moderate circumstances, and two of his sons, by the joint means of my father and uncle, the Canon, were sent to the same college where he received an education. He took also to his *house, his sister, who in her young days belonged to a nunnery which had been suppressed for I know not what reason. They went by the name of Sisters of Providence. She became housekeeper to her brother and survived him. Another inmate of his house was a rich old aunt of the name of Maldant and sister to my grandmother. This old lady never married, and was, when I knew her, very old, very deaf, and confined for years before to her bed by rheumatism or gout. My uncle and herself were my Godfather and mother and gave me my Christian name Francis Leonard. The management of her estate during her life made my uncle much more affluent, and by her death he became very rich as she left him her universal legatee, except a sum which she willed to my father. When my uncle himself died, he made large provision to his brother and sister, now grown old and infirm, and to all of us a sum about equal to $400, double that sum to me, his Godson and three times that amount to one of my sister, his Goddaughter. The bulk of his property, yet very considerable, he devised to my eldest brother.*

Peter Gregoire de Roulhac Dupuisfancher

My uncle, le Chevalier, got his surname of Dupuisfaucher from some landed property, where he generally resided. He was poor and had no pretention to any great endowment but one, it was courage, for he was as brave as his sword. He had been in the army bearing the commission of Lieutenant and served in Germany where he distinguished himself by his bravery. His circumstances, by the death of his brother, became much easier in his old age. He left four sons. The eldest entered the church St. Martiel. The French Revolution came soon after and he, as many thousand of the clergy refusing to take the oath to maintain the new Constitution was arrested and imprisoned, then in irons sent to Rochefort and there with many other clergymen, put on board of an old vessel, to be transported to the island of Rhi on the coast. On the passage they were all shot, by a detachment of soldiers on board, by order of the captain. His brother studied medicine at Montpelier; he married and dying, left an only daughter, who is now a worthy little woman at Limoges. The two younger sons went into the army and never returned.

Issue of Joseph Gregoire de Roulhac and Marie Jeanne Dumas

1. Baron Guillaume Gregoire de Roulhac de La Borie *was born at Limoges, May 7, 1751. "By law of primogeniture, he became heir to my father, so that we younger children although our father might be considered rich in that part of the country where there were few overgrown fortunes, had but a small share, say to each about $3,000, while the property of our brother amounted to over $40,000. By our father's will, though, he was to be at the expense of our education, if it was not ended, and we had a right to remain in his house till we should come of age at twenty-five. By marrying a rich lady, his cousin, the only heiress of the branch of the Roulhac de Faugeras, and inheriting other property from our uncle, the Canon, he became one of the richest men in town. This so intoxicated him for a time that he seemed to forget the ties of nature. My mother was entitled by law to live in the Mansion House, which was large and spacious, but the expensive life, which she saw my brother was going to take after his marriage that a daughter-in-law will seldom agree with a mother-in-law, she consented without difficulty to the arrangements he made for her to go live with one of her married daughters. This step was severely censured by all of us who considered it not respectful or dutiful to our mother. In place of the frugality and economy which had been observed in my father's lifetime, everything was changed. His modest post-chaise was replaced by a gay and handsome chariot sent from Paris. The servants who had grown gray in the family were replaced by laquais and filles de chamber; everything went on in great style; grand dinners and suppers were given to the elite of the city; in this manner he went on in expending his income and probably going over it. I must, however, say that he never neglected his official duties, and that he maintained the reputation of integrity and talents which our father enjoyed in his life. It was in this manner that he lived when the French Revolution began its destructive career. Having succeeded his father as President of the Court at Limoges, to this office, he owed the distinction of being called to the two "Assemblies of Notables," convened by the King, which preceded the Revolution. Soon after he was chosen by his fellow citizen a member of the "Constituent Assembly," and* *although a strenuous Royalist, he became unwillingly one of those who overthrew the French throne. However, he could not so dissemble, but that the Jacobin party continually had an eye on him and he became an object of distrust.*

Forced loans to the government and a thousand vexations from those in power, in a little while reduced him more than half his fortune. At the raising of the Constituent Assembly, he retired to private life and opened an office as advocate and counselor at law. This lasted but a short time as the days of Robespierre were at hand, when all the men who had been known as friends of monarchy, had belonged to the first classes, or who had any property above their fellows, were marked by the tyrant and his satellites for their victims. Prisons were not numerous enough to contain all the suspected, but they were confined in their own houses with all those who belonged to them. Thus it was, my respected and venerable mother was received again into the house where she had passed the greatest part of her life. A few days before, for the crime of assisting at a mass celebrated by a non-assermented clergymen [sic], she was pursued by a mob, who covered her in mud. It was then that the Revolutionary Tribunal in Paris sent its hundreds of victims to be guillotined. When the tyrant fell, no less than 300,000 individuals were in the state of arrest which I have described, ready to be sent to Paris for execution. My brother being an eminent lawyer, in a short time, repaired in great measure the shock the Revolution had give his fortunes. To our mother, he showed new regard and attention and prevailed on her to make his house her home. She did so and never repented it to the last day of the existence. She lived but a few years more, for on March 9, 1790, she died of pneumonia at the age of eighty-two. Her soft and virtuous bosom never knew real sorrow till her old age. She was separated from all her children except her daughters. Three of her sons were in America. She survived the death of her youngest who died in the army; she saw the rack which all of them had experienced in their property, and she had often trembled for their safety and their lives. Surely, there is a place of rest and happiness for the virtuous. The rulers of the day, desiring to heal the public wounds, endeavored to put in office men of talent and standing. My brother was then called to one of the most important offices in his province. He kept his property with the government of Bonaparte and even with Louis XVIII, but during the hundred days of Bonaparte, after his return, having shown that he was rather more a friend of the Emperor than of Louis, he lost his office, with, however, the grant of a pension for life. Before the fall of Bonaparte he had received a patent of Baron, which was to be hereditary in his family. A few months before his death, which took place in his seventy-sixth year, October 7, 1824, he seemed to be heart-broken, not only for the loss of power, but also the death of an only son on the eve of being married to a very rich lady. He left two daughters, who both married rich."

(1) Josephene married M. Lamy de la Chapelle. (An ancestor of M. Lamy, was a grand patriarch of Jerusalem). She had six daughters and six sons, and died 1879. Her eldest daughter, Angelina b. in 1809, m. Paul de Lavergne, an officer in the French army. Madame Lavergne had three children, Emma, William and Bertha. Another daughter was Madame Le Gorce.

(2) The youngest daughter m. Dumont Saint Priest, President of the Court of Limoges, succeeding his father-in-law to the office. She had two daughters, one of whom m. M. Romanet, and one son, who succeed his father to the Court.

2. Psalmet Gregoire de Roulhac Dethias, b. Oct. 30, 1752. *(Came to America, and his life will be found at the beginning of Part I, Chapter 1).*

3. Antoinette Gregoire de Roulhac Des Crousils "*from infancy had a weak constitution and not naturally handsome or pretty, the smallpox left early on her face deep marks of its ravages, but her mind and education redeemed those bodily blemishes. She possessed all the goodness and virtue, which adorns the female sex. After returning from the convent where she was educated, she remained under the paternal roof till our father's death, she went with my mother to live at M. Guybert's who had married one of her sisters." With the exception of several months, during the Reign of Terror, when she was imprisoned with the family at the elder brothers, she spent the rest of her life in this family, educating the young children. She died August 15, 1804, at the age of fifty years.

4. Leonarde Gregoire de Roulhac De La Beauserie. "She at an early period was remarkable for vivacity and liveliness, and when she grew up was very handsome. She was educated at a nunnery in the city of Portiers and a few years after married to M. Georges Guybert, a rich draper of Limoges. This match was made by her father and an old lady and was consummated in less than two weeks after the parties met, but my sister never repented of the hasty manner in which she was married. He died rich and left considerable property to his seven children. She survived him many years, become very corpulent in her old age, and died April, 1828." Her eldest daughter married M. Fraisseix and had sixteen children, another married M. Desvorch; and the youngest was Madame Laforest. The oldest son, Alfred, was a physician, (d. 1888); the other sons, Louis and Victor, were a long time in the army, were at the battle of Waterloo, and afterwards settled in the country.

5. Marie Jeanne Gregoire de Roulhac Des Saignes. "She had a strong mind and firmness of character, was of a dark complexion, with animated dark eyes, and, although she could not be called handsome, she was rather comely than otherwise. Educated with her sisters at Portiers, after a few years at home she desired to return there to become a nun. To this her parents objected, but finally consented, and she became a novice for something more than a year; but as she could not take the veil until a certain age, she came home, and finally married M. Henry de Cledat, of Uzerche, a small town about forty-five miles from Limoges. He belonged to a good and respectable family and had a good property. She died from over fatigue in nursing a number of sick prisoners of war, at the age of fifty-two, leaving three daughters. They all married; one to M. Lacoste, of very noble family but poor, who left two daughters and two sons; another married M. Fouilloeux, a doctor, and had an only daughter married to a captain in the French army, serving in Algeria; the other married M. de la Bachelerie and left one son.

6. Jean Baptiste Ignace Gregoire de Roulhac, b. Nov. 24, 1758. *(Came to America and his life will be found at Part I, Chapter 2).*

7. *Joseph Gregoire de Roulhac Des Crousils*, *became a teacher in a college and before the French Revolution was president of the College of [a commune in Burgundy in eastern France, that was founded during the reign of Roman emperor Augustus (23 BC-14 AD), and was famous for having schools of rhetoric.], a city in France: "Having secured orders, he was then a clergyman of the Roman Catholic Church, but the persecution against the clergy, which was conducted with the greatest inveteracy, induced him to pass over to England, where he supported himself, first by becoming a teacher of the French language in some academy. Afterwards he was employed as a chaplain to a wealthy family of Catholics in the north of England. He remained there for nearly, if not quite, thirty years, and only returned to his native land when the Bourbons were restored to the throne by the last fall of Bonaparte. His small patrimony had increased by his long exile, as it was impossible to transport to him, in England, his funds during the long and protracted war between England and France. Through his correspondence with his brothers in America, he was indebted for family news, which he could not obtain for some time by any other means. On his return to France, after spending two or three years in re-establishing an old college, he went to live at his eldest brother's home, where, also, lived his brother Charles. There, in peace and quietness, after a life of virtue and piety, he died in his seventy-fourth year, May 1, 1833. He left the principal part of his property to the poor of the asylum and hospital at Limoges. With the rest he insured an income to his brother Charles, which, at his death, should be vested in the hospital. He also left a sum of one hundred guineas each to two nieces and myself."*

8. Guillaume Gregoire de Roulhac Dupereix, "Junior," *as he might be denominated, was the fifth son. It was the custom that the day after the birth of a child, he was carried to the parish church of his parents to receive baptism, accompanied by a God-father, and God-mother. A rich relative, but not an inhabitant of the town, had been selected to be the God-father, and was to give his own name to the child. As the gentleman was not in town, my eldest brother was deputized to replace him, with the injunction to give to the child the name of his real God-father. He was himself ten or twelve years old, and thinking that his name sounded much better than the one he was ordered to give, when asked by the priest what name the child should receive he answered Guillaume. This being done and registered, there was no remedy, and two brothers had the same name. However, the elder was handsomely chastised for not obeying orders. After his collegiate education was ended, my father had some trouble to induce him to enter the Congregation of the Oratoire, where his two elder brothers, Jean and Joseph, then were, and to which Psalmet had belonged and had not left to go to America. With ill grace he consented, but our father dying, he left there in a few years to take up an occupation more suited to his taste, civil engineering. He received the appointment of sub-engineer at Billom, in the province of Auvergne, where he remained many years. After suffering many reverses by the Revolution, he married a widow of some property and by the influence of his elder brother, obtained the commission of engineer-in-chief, and took up his residence at Bourges, a large city in the heart of France. That office brought him an affluent income, and by economy he became very rich. Owing to age, he lost his commission, the government giving him a pension during the rest of his life. He died at the age of eighty-two, Dec. 7, 1841, a day only after his brother Charles." He had an only son, Guillaume Hospice Gregoire de Roulhac, president of the Court Chamber of Bourges, (born at Billom, May 22, 1802, died Feb. 20, 1881), who married Josephine Brunet, and they had two sons, Joseph and Silvain.*

9. Charles Martial Gregoire de Roulhac De Mouthele, *born 1762, "after completing his education, entered the Congregation of the Oratoire,* *and when the Revolution came on was professor of Eloquence and Rhetoric at the College of Autun, of which his brother was President. Losing everything to bankruptcy he became in a great measure, dependent on his friends, and lived for a while with his sister Guybert to educate her two sons. Then his eldest brother having considerable landed estates, employed him for many years to manage them, which enabled him to accumulate a sufficiency for his old age, when he came to live at the old home in Limoges. Here he was made a Director of the General Hospital, and spent most of his time ministering to the unfortunate inmates, until his death, Dec. 6, 1841, having reached his four-score."*

10. Martin Gregoire de Roulhac Du Maupas, *named by M. Heritte, who became his god-father, and bestowed great care upon his education. His forward mind made him able to complete his collegiate education earlier than any of us had ever done, and he entered the Congregation of the Oratoire, where he remained 7 or 8 years, to the great advantage of his literary improvements. When he left it he was profession of Dead Languages at the college of Lions, the second city in France. He went to Paris to study law, and there his inflexibility of character, that nothing could turn him when he thought he was right, brought his twice to the brink of the scaffold during the Revolution which soon followed. He beheld it with all the enthusiasm natural to a benevolent mind, and was even one of those who attacked the famous Bastile. Through the influence of his elder brother, who was then in the Constituent Assembly, he obtained a clerkship in a board established for the liquidation of the National debt, where he remained about two years. By this time he had lost much of his admiration for the new order of things. All those who were employed by the Government were obligated to take an oath to support the new constitution lately made, and this oath my brother, although now a lukewarm friend of it, had taken as prescribed by law. But this first Constitution, which he had sworn to support was abolished. Another Revolution had taken place, and the King, the head of that first Constitution had been dragged by factious and furious mobs to the scaffold. The Reign of Terror had begun, and the Jacobin Club was supreme. Some spies of the police had heard Martin deploring the hard* *lot of the clergy, who were now pursued like wild beast, for no other crime than of refusing from conscientious motives, to take an oath of submission to the law called the Constitution of the Clergy." Those spies denounced him and he was ordered to appear before the section and to take the oath of submission and support the ecclesiastical constitution, which, by the by, was only enacted for clergymen. This he refused to do, with sternness, persuaded in his conscience that the law as striking at the fundamental principles of his religion. In doing so he knew he was not only exposing himself to eminent danger, but also might bring to destruction all that was dear to him in life. He was arrested and thrown in prison. The next morning the Minister of the Board of Liquidation was denounced at the bar of the convention, as one to be suspected, since he kept, as one of his principal clerks an enemy of the Revolution, namely, Martin Francis Roulhac, belonging to an aristocratic family. (In fact the unfortunate chief of the bureau lost his head a few months after for this unheard of crime.) His imprisonment at St. Pelagie, where several hundred had been massacred a few months before, was, we thought, to seal his doom. It was in that gloomy and bloody abode that I saw him for the last time, in the end of March, 1793, a short time before I took my passage to America, after doing all I could in his behalf. His friends in the convention shrank in the days of his danger; none dared to step forth to snatch him from apparent destruction. There was only one, and that a middle-aged woman, not in affluent circumstances, but sincerely religious, who became enthusiastic in his cause, I believe for no other reason than his refusal to take the oath demanded from him. After I left, this comparable friend was not idle. She found out that the member of the committee of Public Safety, who was to examine his case, had a mistress, whom she went to and bribed with a round sum, which his friends and relations furnished, and he was liberated without being sent to the Revolutionary Tribunal. He had been detained six months at St. Pelagie. After his release he led a very private and obscure life, until that blood-thirsty Robespierre was himself brought to that block where he had sent so many. Then he re-appeared and endeavored to maintain himself by the law. But his misfortunes were not yet ended, for under Bonaparte he was accused of having something to do with a conspiracy against the Government, and* he was arrested and detained as a State prisoner for two years. It was only the interference of our elder brother, then in the legislature, that he was at last released, when he returned to Limoges and remained a kind of exile till the storm had blown over. Better times came to him, when the Bourbons re-ascended the throne. Then at the age of fifty-six he married a young lady of twenty-four, the daughter of one of the attending physicians of the King. To him he owed the appointment of General Director of the Asylum of Charenton, a few short miles from Paris. He retained this office about sixteen years, accumulating a comfortable fortune, and when he retired, a handsome pension for life was granted to him. He ended his days at about seventy-four years of age, on an estate which he had purchased in the old province of Champagne. His wife died of cholera in Paris 1849. They left a son Joseph Du Maupas, a lawyer in Paris, and a daughter, Madame de Givery, who had two daughters, Marie and Louise.

11. Therese Gregoire de Roulhac Moutheley. From ill-heath, she was the only one of my sisters who was not sent to a convent for her education. In fact, her sisters so much older than herself were well calculated, the eyes of her parents, to raise her well. After her father's death she went with her mother to M. Guybert's, where she devoted herself to the improvement of her nieces. This was gratuitous, as they were boarders. She was imprisoned, under the Robespierre's reign with her mother and sister, at her eldest brothers. After this she went to live with her other married sister in Uzerche, making herself useful in instructing her daughters, until her death, at about forty years.

12. Francis Leonard Gregoire deRoulhac de Laverge, b. at Limoges, March 15, 1767, (came to America, and his life will be found at the beginning of Part I, Chapter 3).

13. Peter Paul Gregoire de Roulhac Du Gallant. He was five years younger than myself and the last of us all. With a great aptitude to learn, he early ended his education, and went to Paris to study medicine. The Revolution coming, the youth of France were compelled to enter the *army, and he received a commission as Assistant Surgeon in it. He was first employed in the Vendee, where a most cruel civil war was raging, and thence transferred to the army of Italy, a year or so before Bonaparte became its commander, where, by his talents and dexterity in his profession, he was promoted and would have obtained the highest rank had not death stopped his career. He was wounded near Piedmont, and carried to Nice, where he died at the age of twenty-four in 1796. So untimely ended my poor brother, the first, though the youngest, to pay the tribute we all owe to nature.*

Appendix 2
Memoir of Francis Leonard Gregoire Roulhac

1.*12*. *Francis Leonard Gregoire Roulhac* was born Mar. 15, 1767, at Limoges, France. He says in his memoirs: "At an early period I learned to read, under the tuition of that good man, M. Heritte, who immediately put in my hands the rudiments of the Latin tongue. I had neither desire nor aptitude for it, and my preceptor, who was then studying law, did nothing to make me love my books except to tell me often that I was a fool, which I consciously believed. Instead of studying, I would read Robinson Crusoe or Don Quixote, two books which began to make of me a passionate reader much sooner than it generally happens to other people. At about eleven or twelve years old, I and my younger brother, were sent to college Notre Dame de Grace, where all our brothers had been educated and where three of them yet remained. It was 250 miles from our native place, on a mountain at the foot of which extended a large plain dotted with villages, and through which flowed the River Loire. It was certainly the most beautiful landscape I ever saw. Here I spent several years to no very great profit, with the exception of one, when I had a master of talent, good taste and literature. During the whole time however, I had the advantage of a good library and being fond of reading, even in that pleasing task many advantages accrued imperceptibly to me. I also got in the habit to write down the small occurrences of our college, tearing in ridicule my class-mates and fellow collegians. In this I was encouraged by my brother William who had seen some of those precious bits of my genius. So I went on with what I called my miscellanies, lashing, with all the asperity I was able, all my contemporaries whom I disliked. Possessed of the vanity *so often found in authors, I was easily persuaded by my brother to intrust him, when he went away, with those writings, which he showed to my father and the rest of the family. I was then about twelve years old and my ludicrous sketches not a little diverted my father, who laughed heartily at some of them. He wrote to me, however, a long lecture, blaming in strong terms the spirit of misanthropy and satire he discovered in them. Had a proper bias been given to the natural turn of mind which I then did show, it is probable I should have received more advantage from it, than to follow reluctantly and with disgust the study of a dead language which I hated.*

A year or two later the discipline of the college got so relaxed that we did pretty near what we pleased, and I saw plainly that to end my collegiate education it was necessary to go somewhere else, and I wrote to my eldest brother, who was left my guardian after the death of my father, how business was carried on. I was then above sixteen years of age and began to think as I ought. He sent his secretary with a led horse to bring me home. Now it must be known that in France, in those days at any rate, we did not go to college to wear fine clothes, but to study if we would. Seven brothers before me had been at the college and left behind much clothing to be worn by juniors. French common cloth lasted for centuries— it may be judged how fashionable and well fitting might be the clothing I wore, which had been worn by my predecessors twenty years before. In the indescribable or small clothes I was most unfortunate, either in length or amplitude, so that for some time, I went by the name of "culotte," or breeches. When I complained that all my clothes were too large I was told that I would out grow them or that they were not worth refitting for me, so that on the whole I made no shining appearance. So elegantly accoutred we started for home. I had never in my life been on horseback and dreaded it terribly. It took one or two days before I could be sure that I would not fall at every step, although the horse took it very easily in a slow walk or trot. My hat, I do not know how many generations it had lasted, was not one of the best and I was ashamed of it, so that coming into a little town, where we were to pass the night, I wisely folded it and put it under my arm. My horse tak-

ing to some of his high trots I seized the mane and came triumphantly into town. It was not surprising that I attracted a parcel of little rag-muffins who began to shout and run behind me. Arrived at home I stayed but a few days, and being refitted in some better clothes and a more decent hat, I was shipped to Agen. My conveyance was by a carriage, and for the first time in my life I was left to my own discretion, money more than enough to pay my traveling expenses in my pocket. I thought myself nearly a man. I was far from it, for I believe an American boy of eight years old is better informed of the ways of the world than I was at double his age. We took our own time and were about a week to travel 100 miles. We put up, on the way at a small town called Berjerac, famous for its delicate white wines; in the morning, for my breakfast I was served with a good quantity of oysters and a bottle of the most delicious wine I had ever tasted. Wine is a common beverage in France, but I had never been permitted to drink it, either at home or at college, except well watered. The raw oysters were so palatable, the wine in his genuine nature so enticing that I took an overdose and I believe emptied my quart bottle. Without being absolutely drunk, I became very merry. My host easily perceived it, and when I went to settle with him, he charged about four times more than he ought to have done, but the consciousness that I had done wrong prevented my disputing the bill.

I arrived at last at Agen, where I found my brother Joseph, who was one of the masters. Here I found myself at the head of a very numerous class and at the end of the year was rewarded by various prizes. Next year I was in the lst class and employed chiefly in works of composition, oratory, poetry, etc. At the end of this year, out of seven prizes, five were adjudged to me. The following year I attended lectures in philosphy, morals, metaphysics, etc. I will confess that I could find no charm in logical argumentation, and at hours of study I employed my time to write prose and verses in the French language. My work was to be divided into four or five cantos, but never was completed, as it would have taken me a long time to perfect it. It was discovered by my brother Joseph, who delivered to the flame my precious effusions and advised me to quit poetry, a poor occupation indeed, although he had been amused with some of them.

That long year ended, I was free and at home again with my mother and friends, having passed eight years at college, to study principally a dead language, Latin. Of what advantage it has been to me through life, I am yet to learn. Like all my brothers, after they returned from college I received at home lessons in writing, music, dancing, fencing, etc. But I remained bashful and wanted confidence in myself, was irresolute and undecided in mind as to the mode of life I should follow for the future to acquire a descent support or independence. Some of my friends advised me to enter the Congregation of the Oratoire, as many of my brothers had done before, but I had no inclination that way, neither to the church, law, or medicine. My inclination led me to a mercantile life, and at last made me bold enough to ask my brother's consent. This did not suit him. Not to offend his personal vanity, I was willing to go to any mercantile city. It was not long after this that an opening was offered me to go to the West Indies. My eldest brother advanced a few hundred dollars, to be laid out in goods proper to be disposed of advantageously in the West Indies, and money sufficient to carry me there.

I left his house in the Spring of 1787 for Hispaniola, well furnished with letters of introduction, to some of his friends in the Parliament of Bordeaux, and was received with the greatest politeness and attention. There I took passage to St. Marks, a thriving town in Hispaniola near the residence of M. Guybert. The name of the vessel on which I sailed was the Alligator, formerly belonging to the British Navy, which had been taken by the French during the Revolutionary war of America. She had been sold by the government and had become, from a sloop of war, a merchant vessel. With superior wine and an excellent cook we lived sumptiously for exactly a month that it took us from Bordeaux to St. Marks, at an expense of less than $50. On board I found, belonging to the captain, a well assorted collection of bad books. He offered me their perusal, and there I was taught many things I ought never to have known, for in them there were not a few books of infidelity. Let those who read this, fly from such temptation as they would fly from drinking a potion of poison. It had certainly a bad effect upon me and I must thank my God that under the excellent religious education I had received I was not entirely corrupted by their perusal. With the letters of introduction I had I was received with all possible hospitality by those to whom they were directed, for no country in the world possessed that virtue in a more eminent manner than St. Domingo. Anyone with the appearance and manners of a gentleman could travel from one end of the island to another without expending a cent. Carriages, horses, and servants were offered to him from place to place, only by expressing his desire to proceed.

I found that M. Guybert was living at a place called Salines, fifteen or twenty miles by water from St. Marks. I hastened to forward to him the letters of his brother, which I had with me. The next day he dispatched a large boat with five Negro men, to bring me to his house. I must confess, that finding myself alone with five stout Negro men, half naked, who were rowing me out to sea, was not pleasing. Their features unusual to me, their color contrasted with their white teeth, their laughs, everything was disagreeably new to me, as well as their Creole jargon. The steersman, who, besides the rudder held in his hand a long whip, to make the four others pull better, was not a pleasing sight to a man, who had hardly seen a Negro before. If one touched me, the contact gave me an unconscious feeling. I was received by M. Guybert and his lady with cordiality and kindness, their real property consisted in their establishment at the Salines, where with about twenty slaves, they made salt, when not engaged in making bricks and tiles to cover houses. The rest of their slaves were under an overseer in the mountains, beginning the clearing of a coffee plantation, forty miles from St. Marks. I remained at the Salines but a few months, disposing of my little venture to excellent advantage and the proceeds I loaned to M. Guybert. Our next step was to move to the mountains; arrived at the summit, you found yourself in the region of perpetual Spring. The landscape possessed great beauties on every side, the view extending from 20 to 60 miles. In that delightful abode, I lived nearly five years, till the French Revolution came to annihilate my hopes of obtaining more than independence.

In a short time after my arrival, I was made manager of the plantation, with a salary of about $250, being found besides, with board, *washing, lodging, etc., as a member of the family. At the end of that year, my salary was doubled. I was at the head of 100 slaves, having under me two or three drivers to keep them at work, although the drivers made a great noise, with their long whips and their continual cry of "go on, keep on," they seldom used them on their miserable companions. Full time was given them to cook and eat, and they never having known any better, seemed satisfied, and were merry. The treatment I received from M. Guybert, deserved my gratitude; knowing he was in an embarrassed situation, until his plantation should be made more productive, I loaned him what funds I had in France, in the hands of my oldest brother. In a short time the plantation began to be productive, and in a year or so, with the blessing of providence should have made 100 to 200 thousand pounds of coffee, which was selling at 20c. per pound. So that I saw the time approaching, when from being an overseer I should be manager of large estates for Mr. Guybert, and others, who also were determined to return to France. Those head managers were generally well paid. I had more than doubled my small patrimony, so I was not too sanguine, to hope, that in ten or twelve years, I could obtain easily more than independence and return to my native land and settle for life.*

But the French Revolution came. The trumpet, which in Europe had sounded so loud, had reverberated in the French Colonies, and there unfortunately it turned all mad with the rights of men, as it had done in France. In one night the extensive plain of Cape Francois, now Cape Haity, in high cultivation of sugar-cane was set on fire, and the unsuspecting white inhabitants without distinction of age or sex, were by the savage slave Africans brutally slaughtered or burned in their houses. In a few days the third and richest part of the Colony was in ashes and ruins. What was to be done for those who had families, but to put them in places of safety in the towns. So M. Guybert carried his wife and children to St. Marks, while he went to join the whites in the North, who vainly endeavored to subdue the revolted slaves. For about six weeks, when I was left alone, with two or three overseers, my next neighbors, we slept in the woods with our guns by us; then we were carried down into a small village, called Veretta, where were our head-quarters, ten miles from our plantation, to secure the inhabitants of that part of the plain, where there were many more slaves than in our mountains. At that place, as sentinel, for some nights, I performed all the military service I have ever seen in my life. When released from this, we were permitted to return home, and see to our own safety, as well as we could. About this time I had a falling out with my head driver, who was a square made, bowlegged, ill-looking surly Ibo African. Our hands were in the fields, when coming towards him, I saw him armed, besides his whip, with a large cutlass. I asked him what he wanted to do with it there? He answered impertinently and I jumped upon him, not considering that, had he wished to resist, I was no match for his strength. However, I seized his cutlass and used it, by its flat parts, on his head and back and finding by me some large rocks, with crevices, I took the blade and broke it in several pieces, which I threw away. The next day I heard a great noise at the Negro quarters, and one of the blacks, running to me told me that Azoo, the dread driver, would kill his wife beating her. Seeing me, he ran, but I had him caught and unmercifully flogged by the other drivers, who did not spare him and cut his back in such manner that he was laid up for a fort-night. I have always reproached myself for this act of cruelty, but the circumstances, by which I was surrounded, seemed to demand that he should be made an example of. M. Guybert returned at last, but the insurrection was gaining ground rapidly. What could half a dozen men, surrounded by as many thousand slaves panting for liberty, do, but fly in time somewhere else for safety.

We took our passage on board of a large ship, loaded with produce of the island and fugitives like ourselves. Among them were some pretty young ladies of the first classes in the island. How the tossing in the Atlantic, in a few days, spoiled their roses' and lilies! We arrived in the British channel, just when the war of the French Revolution had begun. As there was not yet any war between England and France we arrived safely at Havre de Grace. A few months after we should have been captured. It was true I was out of danger from the blacks but had hardly enough in my pocket to carry me to my native place, distant 400 or 500 miles. Communicating with my *friends, I received remittances by mail, from my mother and my brother William, Jr. From my oldest brother, who had now begun to experience his share of the misfortunes brought on by the Revolution, I received proofs of real affection, sending me pressing invitations to come and take shelter under his roof. We all started by stage, through the beautiful valley of the Seine and arrived safe in Paris in the month of June, 1792.*

Our stage stopped in a large square, the general Post-Office, and I was just getting down when I was seized by the hand, by a gentleman whom I did not recollect. It was my brother Martin, or Dumapas, whom I had not seen for five years. Besides Dumapas I found there Joseph, Charles, and Peter, but Charles was at the point of death from malignant or congestive fever, which left him but few lucid intervals, though under the care of most eminent physicians. We for several weeks despaired of his recovery and he was barely convalescent when I left the city. While there, in one of my rambles, I witnessed the fitting of the Legislature Assembly and their tumultuous debates. The impression that I received was that they were a parcel of cut-throats. The only apparent gentlemen were the door-keepers and servants of the Assembly. The members threatened each other from their seats. The bell of the President or Speaker continually ringing and a mad man in the Tribune haranguing against Monarchy and Aristocracy, when the galleries, filled up with rabble, continually echoed their applause or hisses. Even in the Jacobin Club, at which I was once present, there was more decorum. There you saw but red caps on their heads, for then if you had none on your head you had one in your pocket to show your civilism, and men and women harangued in the Tribune, belching their imprecations against the King and the ministers, but yet as they all agreed in their plots against the government, there was decency if you compared it to the pandemonium of the legislature.

The storm which had been rising for three years, burst at last on the head of the unfortunate Louis XVI, on Aug. 10 1792. The day before I had taken my departure for Limoges, so I was not in Paris on that memorable day and subsequently regretted, that had I known what was to happen the day after, I had not remained to die like many did in defense of my King and Monarchy. In my native place I was received with friendship and sympathy by all my relatives. The reception of none flattered me more than that of my eldest brother. Cold, reserved and haughty in the days of his prosperity, his own losses had taught him to sympathize with the misfortunes of others. Then it was with rapture that I found him friendly and compassionate to me. When I left Hispaniola, no other consideration had influenced me so much as to save my life, which I considered in the greatest danger, hoping that if I were to lose my all, some way could be found to support myself in France, but I was undeceived. I had no pecuniary means left and I began to see that probably M. Guybert would never be able to pay me what he owed me. In reality nothing could I see but go in the army, but I never found myself much of a fighting man as a common soldier, and had I to fight as such, it would not have been in the armies of the sans culotes, that I detested. Besides this the whole of my family was publicly known as enemies to the Revolution. None of my brothers, indeed, had emigrated, but many of my name and relatives had, and were then in the army of the Prince of Conde in Germany. I must have had something aristocratic in my countenance for once riding with my brother Peter, we met a battalion of volunteers on their march to the frontiers. They were a rabble without arms or uniform — my brother saluted them by huzzahs and "long live the nation," when we passed their colors. I tried to imitate him, but it was so badly done, that I heard some of them remark, that the small one, meaning my brother, was a good patriot, but for the other, he must be an aristocrat and ought to be dismounted to help some of their over fatigued companions.

Forced levies succeeded one another rapidly, and to avoid one of them for raising 300 men, in our town, I started afoot, to go to Uzerche, forty-five miles for fear of being drafted. A little after dusk in sight of the town, I was stopped by an old mendicant, who, I thought asked for charity at an improper time. I had a large sum of money in paper, which one of my friends had requested me, to deliver to someone there. So I answered the request with a volley of curses and passed on my way, looking behind me *and hearing him grumbling at my refusal. At my sisters, recounting this, I heard that two nights before a robbery and murder had been perpetrated at the bridge just where I had been stopped. Seeing plainly that I must fight and lead the life of a soldier, I thought I had best do it in the West Indies, so I requested M. Guybert to have a settlement. After giving him credit for the little I had ever received from him, as well as my expenses from the West Indies to France, and paying me down $1000, he gave me his note for $4000. Next I was to consider how I was to reach the West Indies. War had just been declared, between England and France. I had no other way, than by taking passage on board of an American vessel for the United States and from there to St. Domingo, and in that way, I might visit my brothers, who had been settled in the United States for many years. To get a passport, eight different citizens, of good repute, were to testify to my civism. Had I applied to decent people, I could never have obtained it. I presented myself to the municipality, accompanied by eight apparent or real "Sans Culotes" who swore I was a good citizen, an inhabitant of St. Domingo, who wanted to return to that Island, after a short visit to relations, at Limoges. By the by, those good citizens, who certified to my patriotism knew nothing of me, except two, one an old servant in the family and my brother's barber. Such were not very dear to purchase.*

I immediately proceeded to Paris, on my way, to Havre de Grace, expecting to find an American vessel there for the United States. In Paris, I found Martin incarcerated in St. Pelagic. I went to the committee of Public safety, to solicit favor for him, from one of his constituents, who himself was a member of that committee. There, I found in the anti-chamber, a man more than six feet high, in the uniform of a Hussar, in a little while, the moustached citizen soldier addressed himself to me, pacing the anti-chamber and dragging on the pavement a monstrous broad-sword hanging to his belt, he asked my name and my business there, I told him I wanted to speak to citizen Mignet, a member, about a brother of mine incarcerated at St. Pelagic. On hearing my name, he repeated it with an oath, and "Is he not," said he, "the same man who was in the constituent Assembly, and a damned Aristocrat. Oh! they will all have their dues."

Having been told that I could not see M. Mignet, I took my departure, and immediately wrote to my oldest brother the circumstances; it was then with a broken heart, that I left Martin to his fate.

At Havre, it was found that my passport was not a lawful one, and such as I needed, could only be granted at the foreign office. However, through the agency of a friend, I obtained the permit of the Custom House. This was in the beginning of May, 1793, just when the Gironde faction was crushed by the monster Robespierre and party. At the time of embarkation, the deck of our vessel was filled with Custom House officials and agents of the police, to see that no aristocrat should escape, and looking at the papers, as Providence ordered, I was not noticed, as certainly my papers were not legal, and on them I should have been arrested and declared suspected, which in those days was enough to send one to the Guillotine. I then left France with more pleasure than even I did when I left St. Domingo. Our vessel, "Salomah," was a large brig, commanded by a good natured Yankee, named Watson, but she was a miserable sailer. When about Madeira, we were met by an English Privateer, who after examining our papers and finding no doubt there were on board French goods and property, in spite of the reclamation of our American Captain, put a prize-master on board and six men and ordered us to Liverpool, and we passengers, the men at least, were shut down below, and placed under guard. We had sailed in company with our captor for three days when we met two French Privateers from Nantz, and much superior to the Englishman, to which they gave chase, but being the best sailor, it was soon out of sight, and consequently we remained in the power of the Frenchman. Our noisy countrymen were soon on board. They made prisoners of the six Englishmen, but as the Prize- Master had been kind to the American Captain, he persuaded them to let him pass as one of his sailors and work his passage to Philadelphia. Our captors were inclined to carry us to Nantz, saying if we were a good prize to the British, we must be to themselves, but some of us Royalists, would have preferred to go rather to Liverpool than to Nantz, as some flaws might be found in our passports and be sent to the Guillotine as attempting to emigrate, so we then unanimously joined with our American Captain, who claimed the neutrality of the flag of his country and that it was an unlawful act for the British Privateer to have detained us, and would be so in them to send us to Nantz. We should probably have failed, had it not been for Mrs. Menton, a virago, of the Sans Culotes, whom we had on board. Were she compelled to go to France, she would denounce the officers of the two Privateers at the tribunal of the Jacobin Club." Her eloquence and earnestness intimidated our captors, who after keeping us under their guns for about 12 hours, reluctantly permitted us to proceed on our voyage.

On account of these delays, and contrary winds when we were about half way, our provisions were nearly exhausted and we were put on short rations — one pint of water, one-half pint of bad wine, a slice of pork or beef — and this would have been reduced, and we must have starved had we not spoken to two vessels, which furnished us a few barrels of worm-eaten biscuits and some casks of water. After a passage of 96 days we arrived in Philadelphia, and there I found that my intended return to St. Domingo, was to be abandoned, as all the ports of the United States were crowded with French vessels, which, under convoy of some men-of war, had escaped from the island, after the burning of the Cape and the general insurrection, and emancipating of the blacks by the National convention. To add to my distress, the yellow-fever was raging, and though all who could had left, the mortality was such that hundreds every day were carried off by it, and nothing was seen on the streets but hearses going to different graveyards. It may be supposed I was anxious to quit the city, for my finances were low and could not last much longer. I could indeed read English and nearly understood what I saw printed, but could not speak a single word when spoken to. I ran from wharf to wharf to find a N. C. vessel. At last I found a Va. small sloop for Norfolk. I knew that Edenton, where my brothers were known, was not very far from Norfolk, and once there I might reach them even on foot. I immediately came aboard with my trunks, and next morning we started, after having been two weeks in Philadelphia in the midst of pestilence and death.

In four days we arrived at Norfolk and were coming to the wharf, when a Custom House officer stepped on board with a proclamation from the Governor of Va., forbidding us to land, and ordering us to Crany Island, where we should perform a quarantine of 20 days. Knowing that a letter directed to my brother John in Plymouth, N. C, could reach him in a few days, I wrote him my situation. I received no answer, but the day before the last of our quarantine, standing at the gangway of the vessel, I saw a boat coming from town and making for our vessel, in it, a gentleman in black whom I took for a health officer. The boat reached us, and standing under our stern he asked in English, if there was any one on board by the name of Roulhac? Extremely surprised, I, by signs, answered the question, when the gentleman speaking in French, told me he was my brother, and that knowing from my letter that our quarantine was ending he had come to carry me home. Tears of joy and gratitude sprang to my eyes. The next day we started for his house about 100 miles off. On our way we stopped at Edenton, where we received the greatest hospitality, principally from a Mr. Charles Johnston, a Scotchman by birth. We were invited to his house with a large party of gentlemen. I could not speak or understand a word of English, but easily perceived that they were all great admirers of the French Revolution, and made me sing the Marselaise Hymn, which I had heard so long repeated in my ears. Patriotic indeed and poetical, but full of sentiments of blood and cruelty.

The next day John brought me to his house. He was then living by himself, his wife having, about six weeks before drowned herself with her little child, so that his style of living was little calculated to please a Frenchman just from France, used to much better. I remained there but a few days, as I was very anxious to see my brother Psalmet, whom I did not remember ever to have seen. My first impressions of him and his family were not pleasing. He was laboring under bad health, gifted with a gay, contented, philosophical mind, his temper seemed the reverse. His wife was cold and reserved and had no animation, taking no command of her children, who appeared uncouth and not much better than cubs. They appeared to me like wild Indians, with their feet and legs bare, clothes coarse, dirty and ragged or badly fitted to their bodies. I took such a distaste to the country that I took no pains to learn the language. My two brothers treated me with all the delicacy and affection I could desire, but they could not drive away my gloom or despondency. John, himself of a gloomy turn of mind, was often alone. I was much better pleased when at Psalmet's. He, in course of time, had recovered his health. He was open and gay, and the perfect gentleman.

The first year I passed in the United States was the most miserable of my life, for I did nothing for myself or for anybody else, if I except teaching to Betty Roulhac, afterwards Blount, her A. B. C's and to spell; also, grubbing an old field of persimmon bushes, grafting and planting some apple trees for my brother Psalmet. It was about a year after my arrival that John was married to his last wife. Being invited I became acquainted with the Gray family and was well pleased. Here I found open, easy manners, something like what I had been used to in France. Besides my brother's wife there were four younger sisters. One of them, Miss Margaret, who afterwards became my wife, accompanied my sister-in-law to her new home, and inspired me this early with those feelings which were to make the happiness of my future life, sentiments which were never known to anyone, even to herself, for many years. I was then sorry I could not speak English, and in her company, as well as with my new sister, I made more progress in a month than I had done in a year. My brother Psalmet losing his wife, who died at the birth of her son John, made it necessary for me to live with him. My hopes of returning to, or getting anything from the West Indies, having vanished, John advised me to study law. Being a Frenchman could not be an objection to this, and to encourage me, he gave not only himself for an example, but the success of Mr. Martin in Newbern and Duponceaux in Philadelphia, who both, though Frenchmen, had made a fortune at the bar. So three years was devoted to the study and practice of law, but in good conscience I could do nothing at it. To obtain a license was much easier than to make money by it, and I found my extreme diffidence was a "bar I could never surmount and on which I was shipwrecked. At this time my brother Psalmet advised me to abandon an unprofitable business and try medicine. I was then thirty-four and it was late to prepare myself for a new profession, but I gathered all the books in French or English and applied myself as assiduously to my new studies, as I had previously to the law. Meanwhile I received from France a remittance of my share of my mother's estate, after her death, and which I employed in getting an assortment of books and medicine. I selected Ga. as the field of my future operations and went to St. Mary's, where I found one physician, a New Yorker, who by his supercilious manners displeased the people and who by high charges, had lost his practice. This and my introductory letters put me in immediate practice in the town and its vicinity. Having the good fortune to cure of the dropsy a Spanish gentleman, by the name of Fernandes, in Fla., my practice extended itself there — what I saw of the country, the facility to obtain, as much land as I wished, with hardly any expense made me think, that I might, one day, become an inhabitant of that region. Seeing that my practice would support me, my desire to be united with one that I loved and esteemed, was uppermost in my heart.

I then left St. Mary's, after collecting the greatest part of what was owing to me. I took passage by a coaster to Charleston where I met many of my countrymen, prisoners of war to the British, some of the remnant of an army, of 25,000 men, sent to St Domingo by Bonaparte to reconquer that Island, under his brother-in-law, Gen. Le Clerc. They were a set of well looking officers, as demoralized as could be, who filled up all the gambling houses of that city. For the first time since I had left France I was present at the celebration of Mass, by a French priest. I found a sloop, going to Washington, N. C. loaded with Irish potatoes. The Yankee Captain was as ignorant a navigator as could be found; he and two other sailors were the crew. On the third day, the Capt. said that we were in the latitude of Ocracoke bar and steered for the land, which came in sight, but I could not recognize the coast, as I had been there before. There was no light house in sight and we begun to see breakers ahead, when we saw a small vessel coming from the land and I prevailed on the captain to speak to her. By her we learned we were about sixty miles south of Ocracoke bar and should we follow our course we would immediately fall into Beaufort breakers and be lost. Changing our course we were soon out of danger, but that same night *we found ourselves in another one; for we were overtaken by a storm such as I had never seen or experienced before. My captain, who, if he was a bad navigator, was, however, a good sailor, and soon had the helm latched and we were at the mercy of the sea and storm, and bare poles. After calling me on deck to look at the top of the mast at a St. Elm fire, he coolly laid down and went to sleep. We were tossed about at such a rate that I was in continual fear, for nearly twenty-four hours, and took the firm purpose, if ever I could be safely on land, never more to put my foot on a vessel. The hurricane passed and we were driving before the wind at the rate of twelve knots the hour, passing two capsized vessels, with nobody on board that we could see. How far we were blown to south-east I could not say, but it took us more than a week to gain Ocracoke bar.*

We landed in some hours in Washington, which was only eighteen miles from my brother Psalmet's. He desired me to settle in that part of the country, and his wife had a cousin there by the name of Barrow, whom she thought would suit me. She was really a very handsome lady, between twenty and twenty-five, so that in her person and also in property, she was superior to the one to whom I had been so long attached. I had, however, something like an afterthought, which was, to court Miss Barrow, in case I should not succeed with Miss Gray. Not a word had ever escaped me to show the latter my feelings, as, previous to my going to St. Mary's, I had thought a union with her was absolutely impossible, as we were both poor. I had even thought to marry a rich wife to put me at ease in my worldly affairs. The next neighbor to my brother, John, happened to die; he was very well off, leaving a young, clever and handsome widow. This was exactly the thing for me, and I was seriously thinking of it, as my sister-in-law gave me several hints on the subject, when we heard that, the night before, she had been married, not more than a month after the death of her first husband. I, good soul, had thought that decency required to let two or three months pass before I should address her, and so I learned that procrastination in courtship is bad policy. My second notion on that score, for it was but a notion, was towards a certain Miss Fanny Blount. She was the daughter, by a first wife, of the same gentleman, (Col. Edmund

Blount,) who had deprived me of the pleasure of courting Mrs. Ward, whom he had married in the handsome style I have just mentioned. She had nothing pleasing in my eyes, either in mind or body, rather something wild, self-willed and bold, but it was reported and believed that her father would give her a certain plantation of his, by the name "Tarover," so that she went by that nickname. She was often at my sisters who was fond of company, giving, from time to time, small parties or dances to the young people. I started once to break the ice and paid her a visit of three days. They were living five or six miles from us. I tried vainly to spur me up to the point. I could not come it, when in mind, I compared her to the one I really loved. So I asked for my horse and gave up Miss Fanny.

But let this pass, in due time I obtained the consent of the one I had so long loved, and on Dec. 26, 1804 we were made happy in each other. I was past thirty-seven and my wife was twenty-nine. I had about $1,000 by me. My wife had four Negroes, with a few hundred dollars in money. We must look for a home. To my wife it appeared hard to part with all her friends to go to Florida, which certainly offered the best prospects to us beginners, and as we were obliged to leave North Carolina, she was pleased to have the prospect of accompanying her sister, Mrs. Butler, to Tennessee, where Dr. Butler had promised to give her one hundred acres of land. For her sake I willingly agreed to it, and we left Windsor, May 1, 1805, for the far West, traveling 700 miles in a gig, our black people following in wagons. In about six weeks we arrived at our destination in Robertson Co., and by the next spring I had about fifteen acres of land cleared and all the houses necessary for our new establishment. My practice, as a physician, helped me but little, as the neighborhood was healthy, and the people poor, but it procured us some comforts that would have been out of reach without it.

A year or two later, by the death of a sister and her brother George, my wife received some legacies from North Carolina, which would enable us to move into a better neighborhood. Going with Mr. West, a relative of my wife's, to look at some land, we called at Major Baker's, and there his son-in-law, afterwards Gov. Willie Blount, induced me to purchase the place I afterwards called "Mt. Airy." My wife was delighted with the prospect to live in a neighborhood where she could associate with old friends and relatives, and to quit Paradise Ridge, of which we were both tired, so she willingly moved to Montgomery County. My first purchase was 150 acres for $3 1/3 per acre, and a few years after I added 200 acres adjoining it for $1 per acre. I rented out my other place.

A few weeks after we moved, I started on business to Dr. Butler's house, thirty miles off, when my horse ran away and threw me. Not only my arm was broken but my body miserably bruised all black and blue, so that I was confined to my bed several weeks at his house. On my return home I found many things going wrong on my farm and my prospects were not pleasing or flattering. It is true my practice, as a physician, was much better than in Robertson County, but I desired to live without it and at ease on my farm. So that I saw, with very little concern, the arrival in my vicinity of another Doctor, and I recommended him to my acquaintances, declaring that I wished to have done with pill making. My pecuniary circumstances at this time were much ameliorated, having received from France and North Carolina remittances proceeding from the death of relatives in both places. The greater part of these amounts were loaned out to insure a life of more ease on the interest and produce of my farm, for I was determined not to use the principal, and be content according to my income.

Fifteen years after my removal to Tennessee, Mrs. Butler, desiring to go on her own land and keep house with Tom Butler, the nephew of her late husband, in order to induce us to accompany her, offered to make me a deed of one half of her land. This I declined, until telling me that, at her death she intended to leave the best part of her property to my wife. I no longer refused the friendly and generous offer. Having lived with us since the death of her husband, she was generally good company for my wife and a great help in raising our children. Her benevolence and generosity was as great as could be conceived. For many years, as executor to the will of her husband, and afterwards as her agent, I was involved in numerous lawsuits about land, in which he was a large speculator. So, against my inclination, I left my old home in Montgomery county. In going to Rutherford, I was to begin the world, I might say, again, but as my wife was ready to make the sacrifice, for the welfare of our children, we determined to go. The first year I lived there I began preparations for a better dwelling, and was having some planks put upon a scaffold to season, when a storm came up and we took shelter underneath. A violent puff of wind coming on, the whole castle went over on us, breaking my thigh bone. I was extended on my back for six weeks in a small low cabin, in the sultry month of August. After two months I was able to walk with crutches, which I carried for several months. This accident has been the most serious one I have met in my long life.

In December, 1834, as my wife was in bad health, and we were both advancing in years, we left our farm in the hands of our son, George, and went to Lebanon, Tenn., to live with Mr. Hill, our son-in-law, and we were afterwards joined by Mrs. Butler who also boarded with Mr. Hill and my daughter. At the time we were living at Lebanon, a happy event took place. Meeting with a Catholic Priest, I was induced to the practice of those duties which my religion required, and determined from that moment to be a Catholic, not only in name, but in all sincerity. My beloved wife, being enlightened by conversation with Mr. McGuire, the Priest, some Catholic ladies and the books she perused, was entirely converted to the conviction of the truth that there was no surety of salvation but in the bosom of the Catholic Church. She asked eagerly to be admitted into it. To my great joy, it was done, so that we were joined in a better manner than we had been before, being one in affection, in faith, in hope of eternal life. These events took place in 1843-4. About the year 1845, Mr. Hill, having the misfortune to lose heavily by the burning of a large factory, and the failure of his partner in business, we returned to Rutherford county, where Mr. Hill took charge of my farm and Negroes, Mrs. Butler having died May 20, of the same year.

I come now to record the death of the dear companion, who, for forty years, had sweetened my existence. This took place in February, 1846, a *little more than three months after returning to Rutherford county. It was, even to her, a consoling reflection, when we left Lebanon, to think when she should die, her remains would rest near those of our beloved son, George. All the attention which could be expected, from the few friends who were around, was bestowed on her, and principally by her daughter-in-law, Betsy Roulhac, whose attention and tenderness was not surpassed by any of us.*

Having nearly completed my eighty-second year, it is time to finish this long narrative. Being separated by death or the uncontrollable circumstances from all I held most dear, can it be surprising that, at my advanced age, I should look for comfort in that religion in which it has been my happiness to be raised, the principles of which, though dormant the greater part of my life, have never been eradicated. In His mercy, God touched my heart, and with all my mind I endeavored to return to Him by faith, hope and love. But not only we must possess the true faith, which shall be granted to us, if we sincerely seek it, but also we must obey His commandments before we can call ourselves Christians, or His followers. Oh, how much we will be deceived in our expectations, if, on the last day, instead of being found in the divinely appointed Church, we are found to belong to the synagogue of Satan! Oh, may this, the greatest of all evils, never be the lot of those of mine, who will chance to peruse these sheets! Amen. Feb. 28, 1849. Francis Gregoire Roulhac d. Aug. 23, 1852, aged 85.

Appendix 3
Jackson County FL Marriage (Roulhac Grooms, 1866 – 1910) [139]

Brides	Grooms	Date	Book	Page
Fate Rhoulac	Lillie Leslie	8/17/1918	12	23
Joe Rhoulac	Dafney Baker	1/4/1910	9	55
Rhoulock, Sam	Mamie Lee Brew	1/6/1910	9	61
Daniel Rolack	Agnes Bellamy	1/16/1873	D	286
Peter Rolack	Annie Bryant	1/26/1873	D	300
Nero Roulhac	Nelly Roulhac	1/11/1866	C	343
Wommer Roulhac	Isley Roulhac	6/5/1866	C	27
Hilton Roulhac	Grady Roulhac	8/5/1866	C	48
Alfred Roulhac	Matilda Roulhac	8/5/1866	C	74
William Roulhac	Sally Dixon	8/5/1866	C	76
Daniel Roulhac	Adeline Myrick	1/20/1867	C	203
Haywood Roulhac	Amanda Russ	1/6/1870	D	70
Phaton Roulhac	Lizzie Robinson	1/16/1870	D	76
Robert Roulhac	Viney Bryan	App Only	D	219
Daniel W. Roulhac	Henrietta Hughes	12/18/1872	D	288
Daniel Roulhac	Agnes Bellamy	1/16/1873	D	296
Peter Roulhac	Annie Bryant	1/25/1873	D	300
Allen Roulhac	Margaret Garner	1/8/1874	D	269
Nero Roulhac	Joicy Bright	4/24/1875	D	459
Shadrick Roulhac	Louvenia Chambliss	1/18/1877	D	593
Samuel Roulhac	Sarah Jordan	1/30/1879	E	179

Appendix 3

Brides	Grooms	Date	Book	Page
Faton Roulhac	Estelle Vick	1/22/1880	E	272
George Roulhac	Martha Hunter	1/27/1882	E	276
Daniel Roulhac	Lucy Baker	1/26/1880	E	487
Abraham Roulhac	Lizzie Brantley	10/15/1882	E	491
Benjamin Roulhac	Ann Eliza Summerville	12/12/1882	E	515
Alfred Roulhac	Daisy Ann Blackshear	12/20/1885	F	251
Warren Roulhac	Minerva Bryan	12/13/1886	F	331
Alfred Roulhac	Sarah Dudley	7/10/1887	1	3
Peter Roulhac	Maria Anderson	2/2/1889	1	179
Eddy Roulhac	Jennie Harvey	4/3/1889		1
Isaac L. Roulhac	Pinkey Clayton	12/23/1889	1	256
Nero Roulhac	Brittia Ann Wynn	11/6/1890	1	
Peter F. Roulhac	Hannah McIntosh	1/10/1894	2	271
Alfred L. Roulhac	Mary Lee Lewis	2/29/1895	2	417
Sandy Roulhac	Fanny White	1/25/1897	3	164
Allen Roulhac	Margaret Roulhac	3/15/1897	3	179
Joseph Roulhac	Molly Johnson	10/21/1897	3	242
Dempsey Roulhac	Mary Debolee	8/20/1899	4	22
P. H. R. Roulhac	Annie Grant	11/2/1899	4	45
Robert Roulhac	Addie Lee Montgomery	11/1/1900	4	205
William Roulhac	Amy Milton	12/7/1900	4	224
A. L. Roulhac	Cora Pittman	5/10/1902	4	483
Shade Roulhac	Mahala Buie	12/3/1903	5	235
Abraham Roulhac	Penny Long	2/10/1904	5	297
Faton Roulhac	Cinda Kelly	4/20/1904	5	329
Johnie Roulhac	Lizzie Wynn	9/8/1904	5	391
Donnie Roulhac	Neta Wynn	11/1/1904	5	419
Nero Roulhac	Emma Robins	2/15/1905	5	45

Brides	Grooms	Date	Book	Page
Perry Roulhac	Nora Barnes	7/10/1906	6	104
Isakiah Roulhac	Polina Jones	12/25/1905	6	206
Douglass Roulhac	Stella McRoy	5/8/1906	6	302
Robert Roulhac	Minerva Rhodes	9/19/1906	6	359
Lucius Roulhac	Ira Nelson	4/10/1907	6	486
Alex Roulhac	Lula Shavers	12/18/1907	7	132
C. R. Roulhac	Lillie Shavers	1/1/1908	7	150
Durrah Roulac	Hattie Miller	9/9/1908	7	268

Appendix 4
Jackson County, FL Marriages (Roulhac Brides) 1848 - 1925[140]

Brides		Date	Grooms		Bk	Pg
Rolack	Callie	1/9/1914	Harvey	Walter	10	219
Rolack	Cillie	1/15/1922	Pittman	Sam	13	157
Rolack	Lucrecy	1/14/1925	Barkley	Amos	14	139
Roulack	Donie	10/10/1899	Trueblood	William	4	39
Roulhac	Aggie	2/19/1897	Reagius	Hiram	3	333
Roulhac	Angeline	1/5/1870	Hays	Emanuel D	D	69
Roulhac	Ann	10/5/1859	Wilson	William S	A	264
Roulhac	Betsy	7/21/1866	Ephraim	Alexander	C	60
Roulhac	Carrie	12/14/1878	Lee	James	E	94
Roulhac	Charlotte	5/5/1876	Daniels	Daniel D	D	344
Roulhac	Clara	9/22/1859	Holden	J Thomas	A	260
Roulhac	Crady	6/5/1866	Roulhac	Riton	C	48
Roulhac	Creacy	12/8/1892	Johnson	Willie	2	119
Roulhac	Edny	11/3/1889	Bell	Nelson	1	239
Roulhac	Eliza	7/13/1894	Bellamy	Hollister	3	323
Roulhac	Eliza	8/25/1895	Hoffman	Nathaniel	2	452
Roulhac	Ella	3/17/1894	Jackson	James	2	298
Roulhac	Frances G	12/5/1849	Anderson	William E	A	11
Roulhac	Ilsy	6/5/1866	Roulhac	Wommer C	C	27
Roulhac	Jennie	App Only	Robinson	Baldwin	2	239

Appendix 4

Brides		Date	Grooms		Bk	Pg
Roulhac	Jennie M	12/12/1876	Baker	Beverly	D	574
Roulhac	Judy	8/31/1867	Sampson	William C	C	240
Roulhac	Julie Ann	6/5/1866	Sullivan	Milledge	C	25
Roulhac	Margaret	3/15/1897	Roulhac	Allen	6	179
Roulhac	Margaret	6/5/1866	McIntosh	Robert C	C	4
Roulhac	Mariah	7/21/1866	Bryan	James	C	62
Roulhac	Martha	7/5/1888	Allen	Charles	1	108
Roulhac	Martha W	9/18/1879	McClellan	Chandler Y.	E	231
Roulhac	Mary	1/28/1867	Long	Frank	C	210
Roulhac	Mary	1/9/1870	Long	Robert D	D	70
Roulhac	Matilda	8/5/1866	Roulhac	Alfred	C	74
Roulhac	Nelly	1/11/1866	Roulhac	Nero	C	334
Roulhac	Penny	3/8/1876	Bryan	Homer Jr	D	527
Roulhac	Sallie	App Only	Nickels	Frank	1	175
Roulhac	Silvia	1/9/1890	McElroy	Ed	1	268
Roulhac	Stella	11/29/1893	Smith	Willie	2	244
Roulhac	Winnie	4/29/1898	Davis	Monk	3	358

Appendix 5
Roulhacs in the 1870 US Federal Census (Partial List)

Name	Home 1870	Born Ca.	Date, Ca.	Race	Sex	Occupation
Theodore Rolack	Subdiv 3, Bibb, GA	VA	1791	B	M	Farm laborer
Mary Rolack	Subdiv 3, Bibb, GA	SC	1805	B	F	Keeping house
Thos Rolack	District 3, Shelby, TN	NC	1826	B	M	Farmer
Melinda Rolack	District 3, Shelby, TN	TN	1840	B	F	Keeping house
Charlotte Rolack	Marianna, Jackson, FL	NC	1840	M	F	laundress
Clary Rolack	Merry Hill, Bertie, NC	NC	1842	B	F	Keeping house
John Rolack*	Marianna, Jackson, FL	NC	1844	B	M	Carpenter
Sampson Rolack	Merry Hill, Bertie, NC	NC	1844	B	M	Farm Laborer
Sophia Rolack*	Marianna, Jackson, FL	FL	1850	M	F	Laundress
Edward Rolack	District 3, Shelby, TN	TN	1851	B	M	At home
Caroline Rolack	District 3, Shelby, TN	TN	1854	B	F	At home

Appendix 5

Name	Home 1870	Born Ca.	Date, Ca.	Race	Sex	Occupation
Henry Rolack	District 3, Shelby, TN	TN	1860	B	M	At home
Maggy Rolack	Merry Hill, Bertie, NC	NC	1863	B	F	At home
Gilford Rolack	District 3, Shelby, TN	TN	1864	B	M	At home
Easter Rolack	Merry Hill, Bertie, NC	NC	1867	B	F	At home
Annie Rolack	Merry Hill, Bertie, NC	NC	1869	B	F	At home
Litta Rolack	District 3, Shelby, TN	TN	1869	B	F	At home
Robert Rolax	Gadsden County, FL	FL	1842	B	M	Farm Laborer
Nancy Rolax	Gadsden County, FL	FL	1836	B	F	Keeping House
Lauvina Rolax	Gadsden County, FL	FL	1860	B	F	
James Rolax	Gadsden County, FL	FL	1862	B	M	
Mary Rolax	Gadsden County, FL	FL	1864	B	F	
Matilda Rolax	Gadsden County, FL	FL	1866	B	F	
Robert Rolax	Gadsden County, FL	FL	1869	B	M	
Rebecca Rolax	Gadsden County, FL	FL	1850	B	F	Farm Laborer
Joseph Rolax	St Landry Parish, LA	VA	1841	B	M	Farm Laborer

Roulhacs in the 1870 US Federal Census (Partial List)

Name	Home 1870	Born Ca.	Date, Ca.	Race	Sex	Occupation
John Rolax	Talbot County, GA	GA	1847	B	M	Works on Farm
Margaret Rolax	Talbot County, GA	GA	1848	B	F	Keeping House
Lucy Rolax	Talbot County, GA	GA	1853	B	F	Works on Farm
John Rolax	Talbot County, GA	GA	1855	B	M	Works on Farm
Hanna Roulhac	Windsor Bertie, NC	NC	1796	B	F	Keeping house
Luke Roulhac	Snake Bite, Bertie, NC	NC	1796	B	M	On farm
Edith Roulhac	Marianna, Jackson, FL	NC	1808	B	F	Cook
Rose Roulhac	Windsor, Bertie, NC	NC	1827	B	F	Keeping house
Jno (John) Roulhac	Windsor, Bertie, NC	NC	1827	B	F	Farmer labor
Rose Roulhac	Snake Bite, Bertie, NC	NC	1830	B	F	Keeping house
Charles Roulhac	Windsor, Bertie, NC	NC	1830	B	M	Farm laborer
Jno (John) Roulhac	Windsor, Bertie, NC	NC	1827	B	M	Farmer
Celia Roulhac	Windsor, Bertie, NC	NC	1834	B	F	Keeping house
Louisa Roulhac	Windsor, Bertie, NC	NC	1834	B	F	Keeping house
Grace Roulhac	Windsor, Bertie, NC	NC	1837	B	F	Keeping house

Appendix 5

Name	Home 1870	Born Ca.	Date, Ca.	Race	Sex	Occupation
Priscilla Roulhac	Windsor, Bertie, NC	NC	1840	B	F	At home
Harriet Roulhac	Snake Bite, Bertie, NC	NC	1851	B	F	housekeeping
Writen Roulhac	Windsor, Bertie, NC	NC	1851	B	M	Keeping house
Eliza Roulhac	Snake Bite, Bertie, NC	NC	1852	B	F	Laborer
James Roulhac	Windsor, Bertie, NC	NC	1858	B	M	At home
Limas Roulhac	Windsor, Bertie, NC	NC	1852	B	M	Farmer laborer
Alfred Roulhac	Snake Bite, Bertie, NC	NC	1854	B	M	Farm laborer
Ester Roulhac	Snake Bite, Bertie, NC	NC	1855	B	F	At home
Rance Roulhac	Windsor, Bertie, NC	NC	1860	B	M	At home
Fred Roulhac	Snake Bite, Bertie, NC	NC	1861	B	M	At home
Solomon Roulhac	Windsor, Bertie, NC	NC	1862	B	M	At home
Carey Roulhac	Snake Bite, Bertie, NC	NC	1863	B	M	At home
Margaret Roulhac	Windsor, Bertie, NC	NC	1864	B	F	At home
Caroline Roulhac	Snake Bite, Bertie, NC	NC	1864	B	F	At home
John Roulhac	Windsor, Bertie, NC	NC	1865	B	M	At home

Roulhacs in the 1870 US Federal Census (Partial List)

Name	Home 1870	Born Ca.	Date, Ca.	Race	Sex	Occupation
Joseph Roulhac	Windsor, Bertie, NC	NC	1868	B	M	At home
Luke Roulhac	Snake Bite, Bertie, NC	NC	1868	B	M	At home
Frank Roulhac	Snake Bite, Bertie, NC	NC	1869	B	M	At home
Rose Roulhac	Snake Bite, Bertie, NC	NC	1869	B	F	At home
Edward Roulhac	Windsor, Bertie, NC	NC	1856	B	M	At home
Washington Roulhac	Windsor, Bertie, NC	NC	1857	B	M	At home
Deck Roulhac	Windsor, Bertie, NC	NC	1860	B	M	At home
Henry Roulhac	Windsor, Bertie, NC	NC	1866	B	M	At home
Emily Roulhac	Windsor, Bertie, NC	NC	1869	B	F	At home
Lucretia Roulhac	Marianna, Jackson, FL	NC	1810	M	F	At home
Quamley Roulhac	Marianna, Jackson, FL	NC	1813	B	F	Farmer
Righter Roulhac	Marianna, Jackson, FL	NC	1815	M	M	Farm laborer
Ailsay Roulhac	Marianna, Jackson, FL	NC	1820	B	F	At home
John Roulhac	Marianna, Jackson, FL	NC	1842	M	M	Carpenter

Appendix 5

Name	Home 1870	Born Ca.	Date, Ca.	Race	Sex	Occupation
Allen Roulhac	Marianna, Jackson, FL	FL	1849	B	M	Farmer laborer
Sophia Roulhac	Marianna, Jackson, FL	FL	1850	M	F	Keeping house
Peter Roulhac	Marianna, Jackson, FL	FL	1853	B	M	At home
Agga Roulhac	Marianna, Jackson, FL	FL	1854	B	F	At home
John Roulhac	Marianna, Jackson, FL	FL	1857	B	M	At home
Benjamin Roulhac	Marianna, Jackson, FL	FL	1860	M	M	At home
Bell Roulhac	Marianna, Jackson, FL	FL	1860	M	F	At home
William Roulhac	Marianna, Jackson, FL	FL	1868	M	M	At home
Infant Roulhac	Marianna, Jackson, FL	FL	1869	B	M	At home

Appendix 6
List of Emigrants for Liberia by Ship Golconda, From Baltimore, November 3 and Hampton Roads November 11, 1869[141]

From East Liberty (Near Pittsburg), Pa., for St. Paul's River, Liberia

Name	Age	Occupation	Education
Robert Carroll Griffin	49	Farmer	R & W
Mary Ann Griffin	43		R & W
Elizabeth Ann Griffin	16		R & W
Sarah Melissa Griffin	14		R & W
Harriet Almira Griffin	11		Read
James Stevens	24	Farmer	Read
Rebecca Griffin Stevens	21		Read
James Dimmy	22	Farmer	Read

From Wilkes-Barre, Pa., for St. Paul River

Henry C. Theatcher	54	Blacksmith	R & W
Emma Thatcher	9		Read
Phillip A. Thatcher	6		
Lafayette Thatcher	3		

From Philadelphia, Pa., for St. Paul's River

Richard Howard	27	Farmer	R & W
Martha Howard	18		Read

Appendix 6

From Nashville, Tenn., for Monrovia

William Slatter	53	Minister	R & W
Maria Slatter	58		
Mary Ellen Slatter	24		R & W
Martha Cooper	27		Read
Nancy Cooper	10		Read
Maria Carothers	60		
Eliz Ann Carothers	15		Read
Allen Davis	31	Carpenter	Read
Willis Murphy	62	Farmer	Read

From Mason, Tipton Co., Tenn., for Monrovia

Jacob Mordecai Davis	54	Wheelwright	R & W
Caroline Davis	25		
Thomas N. Davis	3		

From Philadelphia, Tenn., For Bexley

Richard Upton	40	Blacksmith	Read
Caroline Upton	36		
Silvie Jane Upton	15		
Hersey Upton	13		
Thomas Upton	9		
Melvina Upton	6		
Burnela Ann Upton	4		
Peter Franklin Upton	1		
William Coleman	29	Farmer	
William Harvey Bacon	26	Farmer	

From Windsor, Bertie Co., N.C., for St. Paul's River

Alonzo Hoggard	47	Farmer	R & W
Nancy Hoggard	42		

List of Emigrants for Liberia by Ship Golconda

Name	Age	Occupation	
Joseph B. Hoggard	21	Farmer	Read
Penelope Jane Hoggard	17		R & W
Vander H. Hoggard	14		
Samuel R. Hoggard	7		
Henry Lee Hoggard	5		
Mattie E. Hoggard	2 mos.		
Robert Branch	26	Carpenter	
Catherine Branch	23		Read
Charles R. Branch	7		
Emma Branch	4		
Solomon York	38	Farmer	Read
Adeline Bond York	36		
Washington York	18		Read
Hannah York	16		
Affa York	12		
Esther York	9		
Margaret York	6		
Phaeton York	5		
John Bond York	4		
Mary York	1		
Henry Reynolds	35	Blacksmith	Read
Rachael Reynolds	26		
Western Reynolds	4		
York Outlaw	23	Farmer	
Thomas Outlaw	19		
George Outlaw	17		
Cato Bond	36	Farmer	
Marine Bond	29		
Patsey Bond	13		
James Bond	5		
Joseph Bond	3		
William Bond	1		

Appendix 6

Name	Age	Occupation	
Shadrach Gilliam	60	Farmer	
John Foulk	23	Farmer	
Anna Maria Foulk	25		
Daniel W. Foulk	11		
Matthew G. Lawrence	45	Farmer	
Maria Lawrence	50		
Clara Lawrence	13		
Mack Lawrence	11		
Lila Lawrence	8		
Ann Lawrence	7		
Romulus Lawrence	5		
Heriah Lawrence	4		
Mary Ellen Lawrence	2		
Armistead Lawrence	6/12		
Henry Askew	27	Farmer	Read
Anika Askew	20		
Mary Jane Askew	1		
Andrew Askey	22	Farmer	Read
Rachel Askew	17		
Daphney Roulhac	50		
Alexander Roulhac	43		
Ann Eliza Roulhac	25		
Ann Maria Roulhac	4		
Fanny Roulhac	27		
Viney Roulhac	12		
Clara Roulhac	8		
Daphney Roulhac	5		
Roxana Roulhac	3		
Jane Roulhac	27		Read
Henrietta Roulhac	10		
Nero Roulhac	4		
Peter Sutton	23	Farmer	
Easter Sutton	21		

Samuel Sutton	2		
Mary Eliza Sutton	2/12		
Dawson Jenkins	27	Farmer	
Benjamin Askew	27	Farmer	
Frederick Hoggard	40	Farmer	
Hagar Hoggard	42		
Henry Hoggard	17		
Margaret Hoggard	17		
Celia Hoggard	12		
Deborah Hoggard	5		
Hannah Ann Hoggard	20		
Lizzie Holley	19		

From Jamesville, Martin Co., N.C. for St. Paul's River

John B. Munden	45	Farmer	R & W
Emily Munden	41		
William Watson	18		Read
George Robert	1		
John Smith	50	Farmer	
Celia Smith	35		
Ella Smith	13		
Alice Smith	11		
Leah Smith	3		
George Latham	15		
Wilson Slite	27	Farmer	
Maria Slite	21		
Lula Slite	5		
David Slite	2		
Nathan Bridges	28	Farmer	
Matilda Bridges	27		
Henry Bridges	8		
Arabella Bridges	3		

Rosanna Bridges	2/12		
Cooper Bowen	35	Farmer	Read
Lucy Bowen	28		Read
Isaac Bowen	12		
Mary Bowen	9		
Jordan Wilson	52	Farmer	
Catherine Wilson	36		
Anthony Wilson	13		
Andrew Wilson	6		
Augustus Freeman	21	Farmer	
Harmon Saunders	21	Farmer	Read
Silas McClees	32	Farmer	
Joel Saunders	22	Laborer	
Mary Frances Oden	18		Read
Ferreby Rhodes	42		
Henry Clements	22	Farmer	R & W
Violet Clements	18		
Mingo Alexander	35	Farmer	
Charles Alexander	27	Farmer	
Jane Alexander	19		
Mary E. Alexander	1/12		
Gray Spate	25	Farmer	Read
Mary Jane Spate	25		
Moses Spate	1		
Jeremiah McDonald	21	Farmer	
George Moore	19		

From Galveston, Texas, for Monrovia

Henry Gomez	30	Teacher	R & W

Appendix 7
List of Emigrants For Liberia
By Ship Golconda, From Baltimore, November 1 and Hampton Roads
November 5, 1870142

From Windsor, Bertie County, N.C., for Arthington

No.	Name	Age	Occupation	Education
1	John Roulhac	37	Farmer	
2	Rose Roulhac	40		
3	Wrighten Roulhac	17		Read
4	Hannah Roulhac	70		
5	Grace Roulhac	30		
6	James Henry Roulhac	13		
7	Richard Roulhac	8		
8	John Roulhac	2		
9	Charles Roulhac	46	Farmer	
10	Edie Carter	40		
11	Mary Carter	14		
12	Grace Carter	9		
13	John Mills	27	Farmer	
14	Emily Mills	24		Read
15	Major Mills	3		
16	Deliah Mills	6/12		
17	Samuel Taylor	45	Farmer	
18	Tilda Taylor	50		
19	Mary Taylor	18		Read
20	Henry Taylor	15		Read

Appendix 7

No.	Name	Age	Occupation	Education
21	Julius C. Taylor	30	Farmer	
22	Lucy Taylor	25		
23	Amanda Taylor	8		
24	Pamalia Taylor	4		
25	Jane Taylor	3		
26	Jane Smith	16		
27	Bryan Askew	30	Farmer	Read
28	Sarah Askew	28		
29	Isaac Askew	40	Farmer	
30	Priscilla Askew	40		
31	Roxanna Askey	15		
32	Henry Askew	12		
33	Jacob Askew	8		
34	Willis Askew	4		
35	Cornelia Askew	3		
36	Charles Askew	1		
37	Nancy Askew	60		
38	Caroline Askew	28		
39	George Askew	17		
40	Cheney Askew	16		
41	Alfred Askew	14		
42	Simon Askew	8		
43	George Dana Askew	2		
44	Moning Askew	32		
45	Catharine Askew	11		
46	Benjamin Askew	9		
47	Nancy S. Askew	5		
48	Mary Askew	30		
49	Anna Askew	14		
50	Rhoda Askew	11		

List of Emigrants For Liberia

No.	Name	Age	Occupation	Education
51	Missouri Askew	2		
52	Stephen Abraham	26	Farmer	
53	Mary Abraham	20		
54	Susan Abraham	3		
55	Thaddeus Warsaw	42	Farmer	
56	Rhoda Warsaw	50		
57	Jane Warsaw	4		
58	Turner Warsaw	2		
59	Thomas Thompson	23	Farmer	
60	Vina Thompson	27		
61	David Thompson	5		
62	Robert Henry Turner	19		
63	Martin Hoggard	26	Farmer	26
64	Viney Hoggard	18		
65	Ida Hoggard	1		
66	Hastie Hoggard	55		
67	Harry Mitchell	42	Farmer	
68	Venus Mitchell	35		
69	Samuel Mitchell	14		
70	Robert Mitchell	10		
71	Eliza Mitchell	8		
72	Nancy Mitchell	6		
73	Matilda Ann Mitchell	4		
74	Frank Mitchell	2		
75	Rachel Mitchell	1/12		
76	Richard Rayner	47	Farmer	Read
77	Nancy Rayner	43		
78	Mary Rayner	16		
79	Benjamin Rayner	13		
80	Marina Rayner	11		
81	Tempa Rayner	8		

Appendix 7

No.	Name	Age	Occupation	Education
82	Charles Rayner	5		
83	Priscilla Rayner	4		
84	Margaret Rayner	2		
85	Richard Rayner	2/12		
86	Matthew Miller	40	Farmer	
87	Maria Miller	40		
88	Valden Miller	18		Read
89	Lewis Miller	16		Read
90	Reuben Miller	10		
91	Nancy Miller	8		
92	Lizzie Miller	5		
93	Sherman Miller	3		
94	Caroline Weston	35		
95	Johanna Weston	70		
96	Amanda Weston	10		
97	Harriet Weston	8		
98	Penny Outlaw	35		Read
99	Barbara Smith	50		
100	Charles King	19		
101	Mary Ann Watson	34		Read
102	Nelson Watson	17		
103	Vina Watson	15		
104	Charles Watson	13		
105	Mahala Watson	9		
106	Peter Edward Watson	5		
107	Mary L. Watson	3		
108	Amanda Cobb	35		
109	Victoria Cobb	10		
110	Henry E. Cobb	3		
111	Priscilla Douers	60		

From Plymouth, Washington County, N.C., for Arthington

112	James Roulhac	30	Farmer	Read
113	Clarissa Roulhac	25		
114	William T. Roulhac	10		
115	John T. Roulhac	8		
116	James E. Roulhac	3		
117	Mary M. Roulhac	1		
118	Peyton Roulhac	47	Farmer	
119	Keziah Roulhac	35		
120	Sarah J. Roulhac	14		
121	Martha A. Roulhac	12		
122	Edney Roulhac	5		
123	Martha Beasley	20		
124	Edgar Beasley	1		
125	Peter Warsaw	20	Farmer	

From Plymouth, Washington County, N.C., for Brewerville

126	Benjamin Newberry	40	Farmer	
127	Marinda Newberry	47		
128	Richard Newberry	21	Farmer	Read
129	Ann Eliza Newberry	25		Read
130	Laura Newberry	5		
131	Matilda Newberry	16		Read
132	Washington Newberry	15		
133	Derry Newberry	13		
134	Johnson Newberry	11		
135	Gilbert Newberry	8		
136	Anice Newberry	65		
137	Jesse Newberry	43	Farmer	
138	Amy Newberry	43		
139	Henry Newberry	14		

Appendix 7

140	Lettice Newberry	13		
141	Betsy Newberry	12		
142	Isaiah Newberry	5		
143	Maria Newberry	4/12		
144	Warren Newberry	19		
145	Aaron Lewis	48	Farmer	
146	Athey Lewis	20		
147	Mary Lewis	19		Read
148	Eliza Lewis	18		Read
149	Henry Lewis	16		
150	Isaiah Lewis	3		
151	Henderson Sherron	26	Farmer	
152	Rosetta Sherron	24		
153	William Sherron	4		
154	Caroline Sherron	6/12		
155	Warren Phelps	25	Farmer	Read
156	Polly Phelps	28		
157	Joseph Phelps	24	Farmer	
158	Eliza Phelps	21		
159	Sarah Frances Phelps	1		
160	Grandwilliam Swanner	23	Farmer	
161	Elizabeth Swanner	20		
162	Sarah A. E. Swanner	3		
163	Wm. Henry Swanner	6/12		
164	Edward Norman	50	Farmer	
165	Eliza Norman	50		
166	William Norman	18		Read
167	Mary Norman	15		
168	Cheney Norman	15		
169	Franklin Norman	14		

List of Emigrants For Liberia

170	Alice Z. Norman	12		
171	Cheney Norman	35		
172	Phoena Norman	8		
173	Thomas Standard	40	Farmer	
174	Job Chesson	41	Famer	
175	Charity Chesson	50		
176	Henry Chesson	17		
177	Frank Chesson	16		
178	Beauregard Chesson	8		
179	Elizabeth Chesson	3		
180	Gabriel Joiner	50	Carpenter	Read
181	Alice Walker	18		
182	John Anderson	20		
183	Judy Ann Anderson	19		
184	James Henry Anderson	1		
185	Washington Terry	50	Farmer	
186	Annisee S. Terry	45		
187	Daniel Spilla	19		
188	John Gatley	22	Engineer	
189	James H. Bailey	24	Farmer	
190	Martha Bailey	21		
191	Margaret E. Bailey	2		
192	Wilson Grice	17		

Appendix 8
*Roulhac World War I Draft Registrants*143

Name	Birthdate	Occupation	County/State	Nearest Rel.
Sandy Roulhac	1872		Jackson Co. FL	
Thomas Joseph Roulhac	12/24/1872	School Teacher	Washington Co. FL	Patience Roulhac
Joe Roulhac	3/18/1874	Waiter	Escambia Co. FL	Teresa Allen
Phaton Roulhac	3/18/1874		Jackson Co. FL	
Robert Roulhac	8/16/1874	Carpenter	Jackson Co. FL	Ethel Roulhac
Tomas Rolack*	12/25/1874	Laborer	Springfield MA	
Christopher M Roulhac	7/2/1876	Physician	Shelby Co. TN	Illegible
Allen Roulhac	7/4/1877	Laborer	Polk Co. FL	Illegible
Edward Roulhac	1877	Farmer - self	Bertie Co. NC	Mandy Roulhac
Henry Roulhac	2/1/1877	Farmer	Bertie Co. NC	Rosetta
George Roulhac	12/24/1879	Laborer	Bertie Co. NC	Frances (Illegible)
Robert Daniel Roulhac	11/9/1879	Pastor	Dallas Co. FL	Minerva Roulhac
Wright Roulhac	11/10/1879	Laborer	Nansemond Co. VA	Arizona Roulhac

Appendix 8

Name	Birthdate	Occupation	County/State	Nearest Rel.
Donnie Himway Roulhac	4/13/1880	Farming – Self	Jackson/FL	Neta Millie Roulhac
Ed Roulhac	10/24/1880	Laborer	Duvall/FL	Annie Roulhac
Robert Fulton Roulhac	11/8/1880	Farming	Washington/FL	Elizabeth Roulhac
Walter Smith Roulhac	10/9/1880	Farming	Bertie/NC	Eva Roulhac
William Alfred Roulhac	9/24/1880	Illegible	Bertie/NC	Lizzie Roulhac
Joe Roulhac	7/7/1881	Farming	Jackson/FL	Daffin Roulhac
Joseph Edward Roulhac	9/20/1881	Labor	Philadelphia/PA	Sara J Roulhac
Lawrence Roulhac	7/9/1881	Carpenter	Shelby/TN	Annie Roulhac
Alex Maxwell Roulhac	7/24/1882	Farmer	Jackson/FL	Maggy Jane Roulhac
Douglas Roulhac	7/5/1882	Sawmill Laborer	Bay/FL	Mary Roulhac
John Francis Roulhac	10/20/1882	Labor/ Freight Depot	Escambia/FL	Joe John Roulhac
William S Roulhac	11/30/1882	Mt Vernon NY	Office Manager	Charlotte Brook Roulhac
Arthur Brackston Roulhac	5/12/1883	Cook	Norfolk/VA	Lizzie Roulhac Windsor, NC
Dock Roulhac	9/10/1883	Farmer	Jackson/FL	Hattie Roulhac
Eugene Roulhac	12/13/1883	Boss? Dyer	Philadelphia PA	Mary Roulhac

Roulhacs in the 1870 US Federal Census (Partial List)

Name	Birthdate	Occupation	County/State	Nearest Rel.
Geo Henry Roulhac	4/17/1883	Farmer	Bertie/NC	Sarah J Roulhac
Geo Erwin Roulhac	8/16/1883	Bank cashier	Colbert, AL	Olivia D. Roulhac
Ned Roulhac	9/1883	Farmer	Bertie/NC	Lena Roulhac
Perry Roulhac	6/18/1883	Laborer	Jackson/FL	Nora Roulhac
Richard Roulhac	2/11/1833	Farming-Self	Jackson/FL	Grace Roulach
Sam Rolack	5/12/1884	Shelby Co TN	Laborer Southern RR	Luella Rolack
Cleveland Roulhac	10/15/1884	Farmer/Allen Roulhac	Jackson/FL	Lilly Roulhac
Isaiah Roulhac	7/7/1885	Jackson Co, FL		
Sidney Rees Roulhac*	1/3/1886	Washington, AR	No Employment	J. P. Roulhac
Ed Roulhac**	4/2/1881	Jackson Co, FL	Laborer	John Tillis***
Benjamin Alexander Rolack	7/22/1888	Walton Co TN	Waiter	---- Hotel
Henry Roulhac	2/14/1890	Cottondale FL		
Ed Roulhac	4/2/1891	Jackson Co, FL		
Bob Rolack**	1889	Shelby Co TN	Farming	R & W/ Ricks
John Rolack	8/17/1893	Gates Co, TN	Farming	Not given
Edmond Roulhac**	3/17/1894	Jackson Co, FL	Laborer	H. A. Baltzell***

Appendix 8

Name	Birthdate	Occupation	County/State	Nearest Rel.
George Edward Roulhac	5/26/1894	Washington, DC	Laborer navy yard	U S Government***
Joe Hargan Roulhac*	12/29/1894	Memphis, TN	Printing pressman	Hotel Gaylord??***
Ned Roulhac**	3/9/1894	Bertie, NC	Laborer	Illegible
Peter Roulhac	2/20/1894	Bertie Co, NC	Farmer	Self
William Limas Roulhac	2/15/1894	Washington, DC	Skilled laborer	Bur. Engrav US Gov
George Rolack	10/4/1895	Clark Co, KY	Laborer	Illegible
Sallie Rolack**	6/4/1895	Shelby Co TN	Farming	R. & W. Ricks**
Dave Roulhac	12/22/1895	Bertie Co, NC	Farm laborer	F P Hoggard**
James Henry Roulhac**	10/9/1895	Jackson Co, FL	Farmer	Self
John S Roulhac	11/20/1895	Memphis, TN	Student	Officer Training Corp
Abraham Roulac**	2/8/1896	Jackson Co FL	Laborer	John Milton***
Charlie Roulhac	12/25/1896	Eros, LA	Tremont Lumber	Mattie Roulhac
Large Rolack	1896	White, AR	RR ext. gang??	St L & M Railroad Co.
Fred Rolack	5/5/1897	Shelby Co, TN	Self employed	Quincy Rolack
Roger Rolack	2/18/1897	Pasquotank Co, NC		
Herbert Roulhac	3/9/1897	Washington Co, FL	Self employed	Lawrence Roulhac

Roulhacs in the 1870 US Federal Census (Partial List)

Name	Birthdate	Occupation	County/State	Nearest Rel.
Julius Roulhac	7/1898	Jackson Co, FL	Laborer	Ed Roulhac
Robert Roulhac	1898	Washington, DC	Farm laborer	John Davis
Reuben Carl Roulhac	12/9/1899	Washington, DC	Laborer	Cora Ann Roulhac
John Roulhac	4/25/1900	Bertie, NC	Farmer	Peter Roulhac
Henry Rolack	6/15/1900	Shelby Co TN		
Phillip Roulhac	9/7/1900	Jackson Co, FL	Laborer	Jennie Roulhac

*White **Indicated Race as African ***Place of Employment

Appendix 9
Roulhac World War II Enlistments144

Roulhacs were among 8.3 million men and women who enlisted in the U.S. Army during World War II. In addition to the information set forth below, the database includes: army serial number, grade, army branch, component, enlistment term, birth place, race and citizenship, height and weight, education, marital status and box and reel number of the microfilmed records.

Roulhac - World War II Army Enlistment Records, 1938-1946

Name	Birth Year	Birth State	Enlistment Date	Residence State	Enlistment State
Kenneth W. De Roulhac	1923	AZ	7/29/1944	AZ	AZ
Joseph H. De Roulhac	1926	AR	2/2/1945	AR	AR
Joseph L Roulhac	1904	NC	10/19/1942	NY	NY
Stephen Roulhac	1905	NC	7/24/1942	NY	NY
Robert Roulhac	1906	FL	10/12/1942	FL	FL
Julian T Roulhac	1907	TN	10/30/1943	MS	MS
J Y Rolack	1907	FL	8/12/1942	FL	FL
Robert A Roulhac	1907	AL	6/5/1942	FL	FL
Michael S Rolack	1908	FL	2/6/1946	PA	MD
James A Roulhac	1909	DC	5/12/1943	DC	VA
George Roulhac	1910	FL	11/30/1943	FL	FL
Hubert O Rolack	1912	IL	4/27/1942	NY	NY
Simeon A Roulhac	1911	AL	7/24/1943	NY	NY
Charles Roulhac	1916	NC	2/13/1941	MD	MD

Appendix 9

Name	Birth Year	Birth State	Enlistment Date	Residence State	Enlistment State
Peter W Roulhac	1916	FL	7/23/1943	FL	FL
Christopher M Roulhac Jr	1917	TN	5/12/1942	TN	TN
George N Roulhac Jr	1917	DC	11/121/941	DC	MD
Goodwin Roulhac	1917	NC	9/15/1942	NC	MD
T Roulhac Doctor	1917	NC	4/12/1941	NC	NC
Waymon Roulhac	1919	FL	6/9/1945	FL	FL
William D Roulhac	1919	NC	9/30/1942	NC	NC
Clarence Roulhac	1920	NC	1/30/1942	VA	VA
Charles P Roulhac	1921	FL	11/2/1942	FL	FL
Howard N Roulhac	1921	FL	11/29/1942	FL	FL
James E Roulhac	1921	NC	11/9/1945	NC	
Arthur L Roulhac	1922	FL	12/8/1942	FL	FL
Edgar E Roulhac	1922	AL	10/5/1943	GA	GA
Ivry Roulhac	1922	FL	12/6/1943	FL	FL
Alexander Roulhac Jr	1923	FL	2/2/1943	FL	FL
Alphonso T Roulhac	1923	DC	6/3/1944	DC	MD
John L Roulhac*	1923	NC	2/19/1943	NC	NC
Allen F Roulhac	1924	FL	11/20/1945	FL	AZ
Hosea Roulhac	1924	FL	12/5/1945	FL	AZ
Humor H Roulhac	1925	FL	8/5/1943	FL	FL
James B Roulhac	1925	FL	1/18/1944	FL	FL
Orlando M Roulhac Jr	1925	FL	7/17/1943	FL	FL
Plumer E Roulhac	1925	NC	4/17/1943	NC	NC
Rudolph C Roulhac	1925	DC	12/7/1943	DC	VA
Charlie C Roulhac	1926	FL	12/1/1945	FL	MO
Robert Roulhac	1927	FL	11/8/1945	FL	FL

*Included on U.S. Rosters of World War II Dead, 1939-1945, Rank PFC

Appendix 10
Roulhac Cemetery – Marianna, FL145

SURNAME	GIVEN	BORN	DIED	MILITARY/ NOTES
Avery	Henry			
Anderson	Neal	12/26/1856	5/29/1948	
Ephraim	Lille	2/14/1900	3/12/1950	
Roulhac	Ed	4/12/1888	5/7/1975	Pvt US Army WWI
Collins	Christell	5/16/1909	9/24/1991	
Collins	Sam	4/15/1905	1/19/1986	Sgt US Army WW II
Roulhac	Willie L	7/29/1904	4/7/1974	
Roulhac	George	10/27/1910	7/26/1974	Pvt US Army
Roulhac Jr	Cleve	3/8/1917	7/27/1970	
Roulhac	Robert	4/26/1927	12/14/1979	Not good but the best
Roulhac	James Wesley	11/19/1923	6/29/1968	
Roulhac	Cleve Ralph	10/18/1888	1/5/1981	Gone but not forgotten
Roulhac	Lillie S	12/21/1890	8/8/1981	
Williams	Carl	10/2/1919	8/17/1991	PFC US Army WWII
Myrick	Inez R	6/24/1909	11/18/1987	Mother
Warren	Pearl R	4/17/1915	4/11/1988	
Pittman	Maggie	6/24/1911	7/24/19?1	
Pittman	Isaiah	3/19/1908	12/19/1996	

Appendix 10

SURNAME	GIVEN	BORN	DIED	MILITARY/NOTES
McMillan	Annie	4/1914	3/1984	
Roulhac	Robert D	1880	1957	Reverend
Roulhac	John Maynard	1909	1925	
Denard	Emma	10/25/1885	11/14/1974	
Roulhac	Lula	5/4/1894	12/9/1970	
Hudson	Elviney	6/20/1895	9/29/1994	
Roulhac	Charles Peter	2/14/1882	12/9/1937	
Roulhac	Vinnie			
Roulhac	Robert	10/2/1858	1934	
Ephraim		5/1871	1934	Rev
Aver	Sophia	8/2/1869	6/16/1928	
Robinson	Willie	4/2/1875	1/16/1887	
Williams	Lula Roulhac	10/17/1922	8/20/2000	
Roulhac	Lillie Mae	1921	2012	Added June 19, 2012

Appendix II
Charter Members - Roulhac Family Association, Inc.

Allen, Joyce – Matteson, IL
Baker, Juanita – Chicago, IL
Bellamy, Freddie – Jacksonville, FL
Best, Ruth Roulhac – Chicago, IL
Bethea, Edwin A. – Tallahassee, FL
Booth, Alma R. – Memphis, TN
Boykins, Dollie Mae – Marianna, FL
Brown, Mary Roulhac – Detroit, MI
Champ, Rose E. – Cleveland, OH
Couch, Rhonda W. – Marianna, FL
Cornwell, Estella S. – Ft Meade, FL
Daniels, Lonely Lou – Riviera Bch, FL
Davis, Eliza R. – Tampa, FL
Davis, Vyrle – St Petersburg, FL
Edwards, Karen K. – Marianna, FL
English, Charles– Amherstdale, WV
English, Patricia – Amherstdale, WV
Foster, Gertrude – Chicago, IL
Frazier, Greg – Detroit, MI
Frazier, Johnella – Detroit, MI
Gibson, Bernice Roulhac– Tampa, FL
Gray, Johnny – Chicago, IL
Gray, Karen – Chicago, IL
Green, Toney A. – Miami, FL
Handley, Anthony – Summerville, SC
Hunter, Barbara Koonce – Tallahassee, FL
Jasmin, Jean Williams – Tallahassee, FL
Johnson, Maudelynn – Sierra Vista, AZ
Koonce, Vivian Conley – Marianna, FL
McElroy, Catherine – Marianna, FL
McGriff, Ronald – Saudi Arabia
McGriff, Sheryl – Fayetteville, NC
Meeks, Leon – Gainesville, FL
Meeks, Ruth P. – Gainesville, FL
Montgomery, Palmas – Palatka, FL
Morris, Willie Hazel – Opa Locka, FL
Murray, Oryntha M. – Thomasville, GA
Nance, Delores Roulhac – Detroit, MI
Nance, Elbert – Detroit, MI
Phoenix, Naomi – Philadelphia, PA
Pittman, Annie Mae – Marianna, FL
Potter, Oscar – West Palm Beach, FL
Quates, John – Detroit, MI
Reynolds, Leon II – Detroit, MI
Richardson, Andrea – Ft Washington, MD
Richardson, Elizabeth – Ft Washington, MD

Appendix 11

Richardson, Jonathan – Ft Washington, MD
Richardson, T. Carlton – Ft Washington, MD
Robinson, Josephine – Chipley, FL
Rolack, William Earl – Miami, FL
Roulhac, Arleanor – Marianna, FL
Roulhac, Alexander – Jacksonville, FL
Roulhac, Betty Jean – Jacksonville, FL
Roulhac, Charles P. – Lake City, FL
Roulhac, Charlotte E. – Flint, MI
Roulhac, Christopher, Jr. – Philadelphia, PA
Roulhac, Donnie – Marianna, FL
Roulhac, Doris – Chicago, IL
Roulhac, Edgar, Jr. – Baltimore, MD
Roulhac, Edgar – Chicago, IL
Roulhac, Edward T. – Yeadon, PA
Roulhac, Edwin – Flint, MI
Roulhac, Evelyn – Flint, MI
Roulhac, Frances E. – Jacksonville, FL
Roulhac, Frances P. – Akron, OH
Roulhac, Isaac – New York, NY
Roulhac, James S. – Landover, MD
Roulhac, Joseph D. – Akron, OH
Roulhac, Joseph F. – Jacksonville, FL
Roulhac, Lizzie – Marianna, FL
Roulhac, Marian – Jacksonville, FL
Roulhac, Marjorie – Jacksonville, FL
Roulhac, Nathaniel – Jacksonville, FL
Roulhac, Patricia J. – Baltimore, MD
Roulhac, Portia – Chicago, IL
Roulhac, Robert – Tallahassee, FL
Roulhac, Roy L. – Detroit, MI
Roulhac, Simeon – New York, NY
Roulhac, Sylvester L. – Miami, FL
Russ-Kearse, Denise – Tallahassee, FL
Walls, Shirley Brown – Detroit, MI
Williams, Audrey – Mayberry, WV
Williams, Carl – New York, NY
Williams, Earnest – St Petersburg, FL
Williams, Lula – Marianna, FL
Williams, Michael – Marianna, FL
Wimberly, Beverly – Flint, MI

INDEX

Note: **Boldtype** indicates an illustration. Identical names numbered in order of appearance in text.

Abigail (slave) 33, 36
Abigal (slave) 9
Abolitionists 148
Abram & family (slaves) 53
Abram (slave) 48
Adam (slave) 9, 34, 74
Adams, John 6, 18-19
Adams, William Barrow 18-19
Adeline (slave) 4, 39-41, 48, 50
Adkins, A.B. 122
Adkins, J.C. 121
Affrica (slave) 7
African American Civil War Memorial (Washington, D.C.) 144-145
African Methodist Episcopal Church (Liberia) 166
Agia (slave) 106
Alamance County, North Carolina 79
Alexander High School (Arthington, Liberia) 176
Alexandria (slave) 50
Alfred (slave) 48, 50
Alice (slave) 52
Allen (slave) 51
Allen, Corey **xviii**
Allen, James **xviii**
Allen, Joseph 140-141
Allen, Joyce Marilyn Scott 217
Alligator 278
Amanda (slave) 54
Amelia (slave) 52
American Colonization Society xii, xxxviii, 147,150,153,157,179, 231
Amos (slave) 52
Amy & child (slaves) 52
Anderson, William E. 92-93
Andrew (slave) 8
Angelina (slave) 51, 85, 196

Angus (slave) 7
Ann & child (slaves) 90-91
Ann (slave) 85
Annette (slave) 51
Armistead, Ann L. 25 *See also* Harrell, Ann L.
Armstrong, Anna Rollax 130
Arthington Company 150
Arthington Home Guards 183
Arthington Militia 158, 182-183
Arthington, Liberia (Africa)
   Baptist church 227, 230-231
   Charles R. Branch's account of 152-188
   coffee farms 153,156, 168, 184-185
   colonization of freed slaves 149
   conditions in 152
   employment for immigrants 155
   food availability 154-155
   health issues 155
   housing 154
   Local Option Law (ca.1889) 186
   Methodist church 164-165
   politics 163-164
   schools 176-181
   smallpox outbreak 170-174
   trade 183-184
   travel to Monrovia 156-157
   union among immigrants 152
Arthington, Robert 150
Asia (slave) 10
Askew, Ailly 81
Askew, Ann 60
Askew, Dr. A.H. 121-122
Askie, Captain Henry 182
Askie, George 183,185-186
Atkinson, Elizabeth B. 61
Azor **225**, 226

Index

Bailey, Carrie Roulhac 253
Bailey, Crawford 253
Baker, A.B. 201
Baker, Aggie Bell 201
Baker, Amanda 201
Baker, Beaman 201
Baker, Beverly 94
Baker, Eliza 201
Baker, Frank E. Jr. 201
Baker, Frank Sr. 201
Baker, Henry 199
Baker, J.Y. 201 *See also* Rolac, J.Y.
Baker, Josephine 201
Baker, Mary E. 201
Baker, Plassie 201
Baker, Susan Evans 63
Baptist church (Liberia) 165-166, 175, 179, 180-182, 184-185, 187
Barbary (slave) 53
Barfield, Sallie P. 113
Barkley, Amos 246
Barkley, Catherine Roulhac 213
Barkley, Lucretia Roulhac 250
Bartley, Phyllis Irene 215
Barveer, Liberia 186
Bazemore, R.C. 136
Beck (slave) 9, 85
Bell, Elsie 196
Bell, Nelson 196
Bell, Richard 196
Bellamy, Freddie xxi
Bellamy, James xxi
Ben (slave) 10, 15, 18, 27, 29, 31, 33, 38, 53, 72, 106
Berjerac, France 277
Bernard, Artenee (Mrs. F.) 174
Berryman, Sidney 124, 127
Bertie County Slave Conspiracy, North Carolina (1802) 117, 230-231
Bess (slave) 9
Best, Eugene 219
Best, Ruth Roulhac, 218-219, **221**, 230
Bethea, Doris 237
Bethea, Edwin 237
Bethea, Joyce 237

Bethea, Kate V. Roulhac 237
Bethea, M.D. 237
Bethea, Mildred 23
Betsy (slave) 54
Bick (slave) 25, 80
Bickton, Ivory 130
Bill (slave) 33-34, 83-84
Billy (slave) 88, 89
Bina (slave) 7
Binah (slave) 9
Black Loyalists 349
Blount, Ann 72
Blount, Ann Jacqueline 33-35, 57, 74
Blount, Edmund (L.) Sharpe 19, 33-35, 290
Blount, Elizabeth "Betty" Roulhac 15-16, 19-22, 33, 34
Blount, Fanny "Tarover" 290-291
Blount, George Norman 63
Blount, Gov. Willie 291
Blount, Ida May Graves 63
Blount, James 19-21, 33-34
Blount, James Roulhac 63
Blount, John Maule Roulhac 21
Blount, John William 63
Blount, Lavinia E. 61
Blount, Lula Martha Johnson 63
Blount, Susanna Elizabeth Key 63
Blount, Thomas Hamilton 21, 37
Blyden, Dr. D.E. 176, 178
Bob (slave) 29, 85
Boisseul (Limoges, France) 259
Bond, Lewis T. 137
Bond, Turner 140-141
Bondor, Liberia 162-163
Bonner, Doris 248
Booth, Alma Burchett Roulhac 235, 238
Booth, Christopher Roulhac III 238
Booth, Christopher M. 238
Booth, Delorise Joyner 238
Booth, Jean Mahadeo 238
Booth, Philip S. Jr. 238
Booth, Philip Sylvester III 238
Bowers, Mary 249

Bowers, Robert 249
Bowser, Della Roulhac 248
Boykins, Dollie Mae Roulhac 213
Bracewell, A.R. 186
Bracewell, J. 186
Bracewell, James 174
Bracewell, Jefferson Sr. 153, 156, 170
Bracewell, John 185
Bracewell, L. 186
Bracewell, Littleton 159
Bracewell, Rhoda 174
Bracewell, Spencer 174
Bracewell, T.J. 158, 174, 180
Bradford, A. 185
Branch, Charles R. 152-188
Brantley, Abram 243-254
Brantley, Lizzie Mae 254
Brantley, Malissa (Melissa) Roulhac 243-254
Brantley, Minnie Lee 254
Brigant, Joshua Sr. 159
Brooks, Albert Lee 215
Broomfield (slave) 48
Brown, John William 217
Brown, Mary Lee Roulhac Scott 190, 217, **221**
Bryan, Addie Roulhac 201
Bryan, Elizabeth 74
Bryan, Guy 201
Bryant, Amy 197
Bryant, Flozell Roulhac 250
Bryant, Frank 250
Bryant, Vivian 252
Buckingham, John 139
Butler, Dempsey (slave) 22, 34
Butler, Marcus R. 136
Caesar & family (slaves) 50
Caesar (slave) 53
Caesar (slave) 82
Calvin (slave) 50
Cameron, Elsey 82
Cameron, Lizzie 82
Campbell, Arnold 237
Campbell, Jacqueline 237
Campbell, Janice 237

Campbell, Rev. S.J. 161
Campbell, Shelby 238
Cap (slave) 16, 23
Cape Francios 100
Cape Haiti 100
Cape Palmas war (Liberia) 160
Caroline (slave) 39
Caroline (slave) 41
Carter, Benjamin 131, 132
Carter, Mrs. M.A. 186
Carter, T. 181
Carter, W.H. 143
Cason, F.L. 128
Cate (slave) 11
Catherine (slave) 53
Catlett, Claudie 226
Cato (slave) 31, 32
Cato (slave) 15
Cato (slave) 25
Cato (slave) 33
Cato (slave) 36
Cato (slave) 80
Cato, Sharon 252
Celia (slave) 16
Celia (slave) 22
Celia (slave) 10
Cesar (slave) 7, 9, 33, 38, 48, 117, 230
Chance (slave) 33
Chance (slave) 36, 51
Chaney (slave) 54
Charles (slave) 74
Charlotte (slave) 48
Charlotte (slave) 50
Charlotte (slave) 84
Cherry, Andrew J. 13
Cherry, Sol 141
Chloe 16, 23, 33, 36, 39, 41, 75
Cime (slave) 15
Cintha (slave) 48
Civil War (U.S.)
    amnesty proclamation 58
    Fort Pillow Massacre (1864) **88**
    pension and military records 117-145
    Roulhac slaves' involvement xxxviii, 117-145

USS Miami 119, 143, **144**
USS Southfield 119, 134
Clara (slave) 51
Clara (slave) 53
Clark, Melton 228
Clark, Adeline York Roulhac 228
Clark, Alexander 187
Clark, Alexander (Aleck) 225
Clark, Charles 185
Clark, Charles (Charlie) 228
Clark, Diana 228
Clark, Dinah 228
Clark, Jackson 228
Clark, James 185, 228
Clark, John Wesley 228
Clark, Joseph 228
Clark, Ned I 228
Clark, Ned Richard II 228
Clark, Rufus 228
Clark, Spencer 228
Clark, Stella 234
Clark, Thomas 228
Clary, Limas 123, 125, 222
Clay, Henry (Congressman) 147
Cledat, Henry de 268
Cledat, Marie Jeanne Gregoire de Roulhac Des Saignes de 268
cloth, French common 276
Coachman, Alice 235, 236
Confederate Park (Marianna, FL) **31**
Conoly, Althea E. 236
Conoly, James Garfield Jr. 236
Conoly, James Garfield Sr. 236
Conoly, Maudelyn 236
Conoly, Sylvia Jewel 236
Conoly, Vivian 236
Cooper, Elizabeth Bright 61
Cora & children (slaves) 84-85
Cornelius, Doby 251
Cornelius, Orabelle Roulhac 251
Cornelius, Robert 251
Corprew, Rev. E.G. 151
Corvine, Moses 126
Cowdery, Almarine 60
Cowdery, Lester Leander 60

Crafty (slave) 90-91
Crawford, N. 185
Crees (slave) 9
Cuffe, Paul 149
Cynthia (slave) 53
Daffin, Horace Ely 67
Daffin, Mary Jane 46 *See also* Ely, Mary Jane; Finley, Mary Jane Ely
Daffin, Philip Dickenson 67
Daffin, Ralph xxi
Daffin, William 23, 56-57. 67
Dandridge (slave) 54
Daniel (slave) 38
Daniel (slave) 52
Daniel (slave) 85
Dave (slave) 48
David (slave) 53
David (slave) 53
Davis, Cordelia Roulhac 248
Davis, Eliza Roulhac 237
Davis, Hattie Cora 204, 221
Davy (slave) 48
Dawson & family (slaves) 53
Day, Rev. David A. (& wife) 158
Deane, Dr. J.A. 137
Delia (slave) 50
Delphia & children (slaves) 51
Delyon, James 161, 186
Delyon, St. James 183
Dempsey (slave) 34, 76
Denard, Arch 204
Denard, Archie 204
Denard, Emma Roulhac 198, 204
Dennis, Hon. B. 166
Dethias 1, 2, 258, 260, 267
Deylon, St. James 183
Dick (slave) 8
Dick (slave) 75
Dickens, Ora Mae xxiv
Dickinson, John Q. 32, 63-64, 242-243
Diggs, Mrs. A.E. 184
Dinah (slave) 15
Dinah (slave) 25
Dixon, Alexander 199, 206
Dixon, Bessie 199, 206

Dixon, Earnest 199, 206
Dixon, Easter Smith 199
Dixon, Eddie 199, 206
Dixon, Frank 197
Dixon, Gussie 199, 206
Dixon, J.C. 199, 207
Dixon, Johnny L. 199, 207
Dixon, Joshie 199, 206
Dixon, Leo 199, 207
Dixon, Leon 199
Dixon, Lizzie 199, 206
Dixon, M.C. 199, 206
Dixon, Martha Hines 91, 94
Dixon, Nicholas 199, 206
Dixon, Possie 199, 206
Dixon, Robert 91
Dixon, Willie 199, 206
Dixon, Willis 199
Doe, Samuel 188
Doll (slave) 9
Donas (slave) 9
Door of No Return **vii**
Dorcas (slave) 9
Douglas, Dan 128
Douglas, Simon (Simeon) 247
Dred Scott v. Sanford 193
Drew, John S. 140
Duers, John 140
Dunston, Dr. H.V. 134, 136, 137, 139
Dupree, Mildred 105
Dupuisfancher name 264
Ede (slave) 15, 23
Ede (slave) 10
Edith Rose 153
Edmond (slave) 48
Edmond (slave) 50
Edna (slave) 51
Edney (slave) 85
Edy (slave) 53
Edy (slave) 54
Edy (slave) 84
Elbert (slave) 53
Eliza & children (slaves) 51
Eliza (slave) 52
Eliza (slave) 85

Ella (slave) 51
Elleck (slave) 8
Ellis, Iddo 58
Ellis, Martha 37
Ellis, Roswall 58
Ely, Anne Louisa 66
Ely, Cato 32
Ely, Charles Horace 66
Ely, Frances Adelaide Randolph 37, 55-56, 63, 240
Ely, Francis R. xxxvi, 25, 26, 33-34, 38-39, 40-42, 44, 46-47, 49-50, 63-65, 343
Ely, Horace xxxvi-xxxvii, 22-25, 28-31, 37 45, 67, 77, 80, 93, 232, 240-243-30
Ely, John Randolph 47, 49, 63-65, 63, 64-65, 242, 340
Ely, Mary 32
Ely, Mary Jane 25, 67 *See also* Daffin, Mary Jane; Finley, Mary Jane Ely
Ely-Criglar House (Marianna FL) 37
Emanicipation 102, 147-148
Emancipation Proclamation 118
Emily (slave) 51
English, Charles Peter Jr. 222
English, Charles Peter Sr. 222
English, Delia 205
English, Delia Roulhac Gaddis 204
English, George 204
English, George Gregory 222
English, Kathryn 222
English, Patricia 222
English, Vera Jean Grace 222
Enoch (slave) 21
Ephraim (slave) 117, 230
Ephraim (slave) 52
Ester (slave) 74
Eve (slave) 74
Fairfax, Ferdinando 148
Fanny & child (slaves) 104-105
Fanny (slave) 106
Fanny (slave) 88, 89
Farewell (slave) 7, 9

Index

Fife (slave) 54
Filphia & family (slaves) 54
Finley, Benjamin 56
Finley, J.J. 28, 40-41, 50
Finley, Mary Jane Ely 57
Finley, Rev. Robert 148
Flora & child (slaves) 90-91
Florida (slave) 51
Folk medicine 137
Fort Pillow Massacre (1864) **88**
Fortune, T. Thomas 147, 349
Foster, Jane Reynolds 187
Frances (slave) 90
Francios, Michelle Renee Roulhac 252
Francis (slave) 53
Francis (slave) 85
Frank (slave) 16, 21
Frank (slave) 22-23
Frazier, Greg xxxiv
Frazier, Johnella Minerva Brown 217
Frazier-Walker, Dara 246
Freeman (slave) 75
French Revolution 99, 101, 257, 261, 264, 265, 269, 279-281, 287, 337
French, Addie Roulhac 213
French, Zannie 213
Frinkalo (slave) 9
Gabe (slave) 25, 80
Gabe (slave) 9
Gabriel Prosser uprising 117, 231
Gaddis, John 204
Garrison, William Lloyd 148
Gatsy (slave) 51
Genealogical Memoir of the Roulhac Family in America xxxi-xxxii, xxxv
Georgann (slave) 54
George (slave) 84
GIbson, Bernice Roulhac 234, 237
Gibson, Carrie 208
Gibson, Ella Mae 208
Gibson, Estella Anderson 208
Gibson, GeHazel xviii, 209
Gibson, Lizzie Jackson 208
Gibson, Noah 209
Gibson, Ruben B. Jr. 208

Gibson, Ruben Sr. 208
Gibson, William H. 237
Giddins, Evilene 60
Gignilliant, William Robert 57-58
Golconda 149-153, 176, 227
Goree Island (Dakar, Senegal) **vii**
Grace (slave) 48
Grace (slave) 74
Gracie & family (slaves) 50
Gray, Ann Blount 74
Gray, Elizabeth 74
Gray, Frances xxxvii, 71, 73, 87
Gray, Eleanor 75
Gray, Frances Lee 74, 78
Gray, George 74
Gray, Isa 253
Gray, Jannet 74
Gray, John 74, 83
Gray, Penelope 75
Gray, Polly 75
Gray, Steven 74
Gray, WIlliam Jr. 75
Gray, WIlliam Sr. 71
Great Tom (slave) 8
Green, Toney Anthony xxi
Gregoire name origin 258-259
Griffin, Clem 201
Griffin, J.Y. 209
Griffin, Luella Baker 201
Griffin, Marshall 201, 209
Griffin, Refair 201
Guernsey (slave) 21-22
Guss (slave) 85
Guybert, Georges 268
Guybert, Leonarde Gregoire de Roulhac De La Beauserie 268
Guybert, M 97, 99-101, 278, 280-81, 283-284
Guyton, Ethel 249
Guyton, Joshua 249
Haigler, Gail French 214
Haley, Alex xvii
Hamilton, Daniel Heyward 87, 93
Hamilton, Frances Gray Roulhac 85
Hamilton, Joseph Gregoire Roulhac 93

340

Index

Hamilton, Thomas 21
Hannah (slave) 15
Hannah (slave) 20
Hannah (slave) 39, 41
Hannah (slave) 53
Hannah (slave) 7
Hannah (slave) 72
Hannah (slave) 75
Hannah (slave) 9
Hardy (slave) 50
Hardy, Albinar Roulhac 134-135
Harmon, Baline Joseph 236
Harmon, Claudia 236
Harmon, Claudia C. Roulhac 236
Harmon, Eva Mae 236
Harmon, Goode 236
Harmon, Grace 236
Harmon, Louise 236
Harmon, Oscar 236
Harmon, Virena 236
Harper Weekly **88**
Harrell, Anna 45-46
Harrell, Anne L. 45
Harrell, James 130
Harrell, Thomas J. 121
Harriett (slave) 50
Harriett (slave) 85
Harrison, Carter 80-81
Harry (slave) 33, 38
Harry (slave) 9
Harvey, Callie Roulhac 198, 205
Harvey, Jennie 249
Harvey, S. C. 193
Harvey, Walter 205
Hawkins, Lizzie 94
Hawkins, Lucy 105
Hayes, Angelina Roulhac 194-195
Hayes, Branch 127-128
Hayes, Ella Mae 208
Hayes, Florence 194, 196, 200
Hayes, John 194, 196
Hays, Emanuel 196
Haywood (slave) 84
Hector (slave) 8
Henry, Edward Winston, Jr. 66

Henry & family (slaves) 50
Henry, John 62
Henry (slave) 38
Henry (slave) 46
Henry, Edward Winston Jr. 66
Hill, Elias 153
Hill, Elizabeth 1-5, 106
Hill, John 103-106
Hill, John 102, 288
Hill, John Roulhac 112
Hill, Margaret P. G. Roulhac 104
Hill, Nancy 106
Hill, Solomon Jr. 185
Hill, Solomon Sr. 156,
    161,166,168,170, 180, 183
Hill, Thomas 185
Hill, Thomas Roulhac 112
History of the Third, Seventh, Eighth and Twelfth Kentucky Regiment of the C.S.A. 107
Hoggard, Alonzo 151-153, 155-156,
    164, 177, 179
Hoggard, Joseph B. 178
Hoggard, Samuel 136, 138
Holden House (Marianna, Florida) 93
Holden, Clara Roulhac 92
Holden, Clara Winnefred Rascoe Roulhac 93
Holden, Dr. Julius Thomas 92-93
Holley, Sharon Jordan **vii**
Holloway, Leona English 222
Horace (slave) 15
Horne, Annie K. 237
Horne, Grace A. Roulhac 234, 237
Horne, Howard Jr. 237
Horne, Howard Sr. 237
Howard (slave) 21
Hubler, Dr. E.M.170-171
Hudson, Elviney "Vinnie" Roulhac 191,
    203, 205
Hudson, R.O. 128
Hyman, Guy 139
Ira (slave) 106
Isabel (slave) 85
Israel (slave) 52

341

Jack (slave) 33, 38
Jack (slave) 74
Jackson County Courthouse (Florida) **xxxiii**
Jackson County, Florida
    map of large plantations(1850) 55
    murder case 63-66
    Reconstruction-era violence 19
Jackson County, Florida--A History 65-66
Jackson, Annie Mae Smith 207
Jackson, Bertha Lee Glover 209
Jackson, Corina 208
Jackson, Ella Roulhac 200, 208
Jackson, Faton 208
Jackson, James 200, 208
Jackson, L.K. 209
Jackson, Lillie C. 209
Jackson, Litena 208
Jackson, Macon 209
Jackson, R. (Senator) 169
Jackson, S.B. 186
Jackson, Wesley 221
Jackson, Willie H. 208
Jacob (slave) 12, 13
Jacobs, Henry 176
James (slave) 15
Jamia (slave) 23
Jane & children (slaves) 51
Jefferson, Thomas 148
Jem (slave) 9
Jenkins, Alma Katurah Roulhac 236
Jenkins, Alvin 236
Jenkins, Asa 236
Jenkins, Eliza 236
Jenkins, Elizabeth 236
Jenkins, Frank 236
Jenkins, Lawrence 236
Jennett, Mattie 139
Jim (slave) 11,18
Jim (slave) 51
Jim (slave) 90
Jimerson, Randall C. *The Private Civil War: Popular Thought During the Sectional Conflict* 88

Jina (slave) 90
Joe (slave) 25, 56-57, 80
John (slave) 51
John (slave) 75
John (slave) 90-91
Johnson, Andrew (U.S. President) 58
Johnson, Hannibal 134. *See* Roulhac, Hannibal
Johnson, Barbara **xviii**
Johnson, Rallien **xviii**
Johnson, Sharee xviii
Johnson, Rebecca 134. *See* Roulhac, Rebecca
Johnson, Robert xxiv
Jonas (slave) 50
Jones, Eli 139
Jones, Marg 205
Jones, Octavia 205
Jordan (slave) 106
Joshua (slave) 50
Joshua (slave) 51
Jouette, Jane 105
Jude (slave) 75
Julia (slave) 51
Julia (slave) 84
Jumping Over the Moon (Nellie Gordon Roulhac) 239
Kate (slave) 10
Kate (slave) 72
Kerr, John W. (Congressman) 140
Key, Edward 63
Key, Francis Scott 147
Key, Susanna Elizabeth 63
King, Alfred B. 176
King, Edward 63
King, Hattie 247
King, Hubert 143
King, Joe 247
King, Martin Luther Jr. xv, xvi, xxvi, xxvii, **xxvii**
King, Melvin 247
King, Vincent Boisaubin 62
King, William 183
King, William Henry 183
Kirkland, Arrie French 214

Kirkland, Arrie French 214
Kope (slave) 8
Lamy de la Chapelle, Josephene Roulhac 267
Lancashire (slave) 38
Lauderdale, John 107, 111-112
Lauderdale, Margaret Eleanor Gray Roulhac 112
Lauderdale, Mary 113
Lauderdale, Sallie A. 113
Laura (slave) 52
Laura (slave) 90-91
Lavergne, Angelina Lamy 267
Lavergne, Bertha 267
Lavergne, Emma 267
Lavergne, Madame 267
Lavergne, Madame Le Garce 267
Lavergne, Paul de 267
Lavergne, William 267
Lee, Frances 71, 78
Lee, Francis 203
Lee, Joseph 203
Lee, R.L. 61, 127
Lee, Ruby 208
Lee, Walter 215
Legg, Claude Andrew 152
Legislative Assembly (Paris, France, 1792) 278
Lem (slave) 15
Lewis (slave) 51
Lewis, James 186
Liberia (West Africa) xxxviii
Liberia College 178
Liberian Exodus Joint Stock Steamship Company 229, 350
Liberian Roulhac Family Association 231
Lien (slave) 85
Lincoln, Abraham (U.S. President) 118
Lindsay, John Bright 61
Lindsay, Sherwood Conner 62
Little Ben (slave) 72
Little Cato (slave) 15
Little Hannah (slave) 72
Lizzy & child (slaves) 52, 232

Local Option Law (Liberia) 186
London (slave) 7
Long, David 214
Long, Emma 214
Long, Estelle Roulhac 214
Long, Frank 214
Long, James 214
Long, Morris 214
Long, Raymond 214
Long, Shirley 214
Long, Verdell 214
Long, Willie 214
Long, Zannie Jr. 213-214
Long, Zannie Sr. 213-214
Louis XVI 101, 282
L'Ouverture, Toussaint 117
Lucy (slave) 21, 22
Lucy (slave) 56-57
Luie (slave) 12
Luke (slave) 51
Lydda (slave) 21, 22
Lydia (slave) 79
Mack, Evangelist Mary French 214
Mahala (slave) 51
Mahala (slave) 52
Maldant family 259
Mann, John 79
Margaret (slave) 90, 91
Maria (slave) 85
Maria (slave) 85
Maria (slave) 90, 91
Marina (slave) 21, 22
Marquis of Rasay 259
Martha (slave) 50
Martin, Eddie XXIV
Mary (slave) 20, 22
Mary (slave) 51
Mary (slave) 52
Mary (slave) 52
Mary (slave) 54
Mason, Abigail 167
Mason, Johnson 185
Massinpsey, William 13
Mathew (slave) 53
Maule, Ann Hare 7

Maule, Elizabeth (1) 7
Maule, Elizabeth (2) 8
Maule, Elizabeth (3) 9
Maule, John 7-11
Maule, Mary 8
Maule, Moses 5, 8, 11, 14, 20, 23, 32
Maule, Patrick 7, 9
Maule, Penelope 10, 75, 112, 177
Maule, Sarah 8
McDonald, George 139
McElroy, Annie May 213
McElroy, Catherine Roulhac 213-214
McElroy, Clissie 244
McElroy, Fred 213
McElroy, George 213
McElroy, Pelt 213
McGriff, Aaron **xviii**
McGriff, Daniel **xxvii**
McGriff, Dr. Sheryl xxiv, xxix, **xviii**
McKay, A.D. 207
McKay, Alex 207
McKay, Bessie 207
McKay, Edith Jackson 209
McKay, Neta Smith 207
McKay, Robert 207
McKay, S.L. 209
McKee, Hockley Cloyd 61
Melvina (slave) 52
Mike (slave) 21
Mill (slave) 16, 23
Miller, Aaron 153, 156-157, 159
Miller, George 125
Miller, Jacob L. 86
Miller, Sherman 163
Miller, W.S. 185
Milley (slave) 84
Mills Volunteers 183
Mills, Caesar 82
Mills, John M. 156,167-168,185
Milly (slave) 23,24,80
Milton, John 31, 66, 90
Milton, Virginia 66
Minerva (slave) 51
Mingo (slave) 15,33, 36
Mitchell (slave) 33, 36

Mitchell, A.C. 141
Mitchell, Daniel P. 139
Mitchell, Hazel 216
Mitchell, R.T. 137
Mitchell, William P. 138
Mobley, Eddie 209
Mobley, OssieJackson 209
Molly (slave) 53
Monrovia, Liberia (Africa) 147,149, 150, 153-156, 160, 166, 168, 176, 177, 180, 183, 223, 229
Moore, David 162, 183
Moore, E.S. 185
Moore, Gov. 59
Moore, Hon. Wallace F. 187
Moore, John 185
Moore, June 156, 158, 166, 167, 169,170-172,175,178,181
Moore, Madison J. 185
Moore, Mattie E. 187
Moore, Mrs. A.D. 185
Moore, Mrs. M.E. 185
Moreno, Fernando 345
Moreno, General Stephen A. 94
Morgan, Dr. Gordon128
Morse, O.S. 46
Mose (slave) 16, 23
Moses & wife (slaves) 51
Moses (slave) 33, 36
Moses (slave) 85
Mosey (slave) 106
Mountain, Cato 141
Muhlenburg Mission, Liberia 155, 157, 170
Mustapha (slave) 8
Myers, R.A. 120
Nance, P. Delores Roulhac 218
Nancy (slave) 33, 36
Nanny (slave) 54
Nat Turner Rebellion (1831) 231
Nathan (slave) 50
Naughton, Lewis N. 121
Naylor, George 131
Ned & wife (slaves) 54
Ned (slave) 25, 80

Ned (slave) 38
Ned (slave) 74
Ned (slave) 84
Nell (slave) 15
Nell (slave) 33, 36
Nell (slave) 10
Nelly (slave) 25, 80
Nelson, Charles 200
Nelson, Henderson 197, 205
Nelson, Lucious 197
Nelson, Ira 201, 212
Nelson, Lula Roulhac 206
Nelson, Pierce 197
Newton, Charles 200
Noah (slave) 53
Notre Dame de Grace (France) 275
Nungburwool (king of Barveer) 158
Obama, Barack vii
Obey, Mourning 173
Old Ben (slave) 15
Old Ben (slave) 33 38
Old Cato (slave) 33, 36
Old Negro Cinder (slave) 33
Old Pompey (slave) 16
Orrell, William Sr. 13
Outlaw, George B. 182
Parks, Valerie Ann English 222
Passing: The Play 246
Patty (slave) 53
Payne, James S. (President of Liberia) 158, 160-161
Peg (slave) 8
Pegg (slave) 10, 72
Penny (slave) 23-24, 80
Penny (slave) 54
Penny (slave) 56-57
Peter (slave) 52, 75
Phelps, John 86, 124, 126
Phelps, Lucy 58
Phelps, W.S. 126
Pheoby (slave) 52
Phillips, Nerissa English 222
Phillis (slave) 9
Pierce, D.L. 139
Pierce, Rev. Luke 138

Pittman, Elijah 253
Pittman, Thomas 196
Pittman, Willie Roulhac 243
Polina (slave) 50
Polison (slave) 74
Pompey (slave) 20-22
Pompey (slave) 54
Ponder, Eli 186
Ponder, Levi 186
Potter, A.D. 233
Potter, Maggie Roulhac 22-233
Prescott, Alfred 59-60
Prescott, Helen xxxv, 69
Prescott, George 59
Preston (slave) 53
Pugh, Chaney 138
Pugh, Dr. E.W. 137
Pugh Drug Store 348
Pugh, Henry 137
Quam (slave) 16, 23
Quam (slave) 56-57
Quamans (slave) 10

Quammie (slave) 25, 80
Rabalain, J.M. 127-128
Rachael (slave) 51
Rachel (slave) 75
Rascoe, Clara Winnefred 93
Rascoe, Martha 83
Rascoe, Peter 81
Reconstruction era politics xxxviii, 63, 193, 227, 342
Red Ball Express 216, 350
Reilly (slave) 106
Reilly (slave) 12
Reynolds, Jane 187
Reynolds, Weston 187
Reysen (slave) 54
Rhodes, Emma 241, 246
Rhodes, Gov. James 218
Rhodes, Jane 187
Rhodes, Judity 19
Rhodes, Minerva 203, 216, 245
Rhoulhac, Abraham 251
Rhoulhac, Karen Yvette 252

Rhoulhac, Michelle Renee
Rhoulhac, Robert Charles 252
Rhoulhac, Samuel T.
Rhoulhac, Sheryl Monique 252
Riah (slave) 53
Richards (slave) 7
Ricks Institute (Arthington, Liberia) 179
Rivers, Eula 207
Rivers, James 200
Robbins, Augustus 136, 141
Robin (slave) 7
Robinson, Ann E. 89, 90
Robinson, Annie Mae 252
Robinson, James 161
Robinson, Jacob 89
Robinson, Jane 89
Robinson, Lizzie 196, 200
Robinson, Willie 252
Roger (slave) 48
Rolac, John 133-134, 15
Rolack, David 84-85,117,121-124,220
Rolack, GeHazel Gibson xxi, 207-208,**209**
Rolack, J.Y. (1) xxi, 207-208,**208** *See also* Baker, J.Y. and Griffin, J.Y.
Rolack, J.Y. (2) 207
Rolack, James 128,131
Rolack, Joseph. *See* Rollax, Joseph
Rolack, Lewis. *See* Roulhac, Lewis
Rolack, Limas R. *See* White, Limas Roulhac
Rolack, Lizzie P. Holley 243
Rolack, Samuel 128-130
Rolack, William xxi
Rolack, Willie Hazel 207,**209**
Rolacke, Joseph   Civil War pension record 118-120
Rollack, Samuel. *See* Rolac, Samuel
Rollax, Alford 126,221
Rollax, Dave 126,127,221
Rollax, Henry 126,221
Rollax, Indy Phillips 126,128,219
Rollax, Jesse 126,221
Rollax, Jimmy 126,221

Rollax, Joseph 84-85,117,124-128,219,220
Rollax, Juda 127-128
Rollax, Magdalean 126,221
Rollax, Virginia 126,221
Rollick,Lewis. *See* Roulhac, Lewis
Roots (Alex Haley) xvii
Roper, Frankie 248
Rose (slave) 10,70
Rose (slave) 22
Rose, Helen Randolph 61
Rose, Lavinia Elizabeth Blount 32,34,35
Rose, Simri 36, 62
Rosetta (slave) 49
Roulac, Edgar 247
Roulhac Ali, Derick 250
Roulhac de Faugeras family 261
Roulhac de La Borie, Baron Guillaume Gregoire de 260-263
Roulhac de Laverge, Francis Leonard Gregoire de. *See* Roulhac, Francis Leonard Gregoire de
Roulhac De Maupas, Martin Gregoire de 266-268,278,280
Roulhac De Mouthele, Charles Martial Gregoire de 266,278
Roulhac Des Crousils, Antoinette Gregoire de 263
Roulhac Des Crousils, Joseph Gregoire de 264-265,273,27
Roulhac Dethias, Joseph Gregoire de 255,256-259
Roulhac Dethias, Psalmet Gregoire de. *See* Roulhac, Psalmet Gregoire
Roulhac Du Gallant, Peter Paul Gregoire de 269,278
Roulhac Dupereix, Guillaume Gregoire de (Junior) 265-266
Roulhac Dupuisfancher, Peter Gregoire de (le Chevalier) 260
Roulhac Family Association xxxix
  mission 189
  organization 187
  reunions **172**,187-188,**217**,**251**,**252**

Index

Roulhac family
  early history in France 1-2,253-269
  Gregoire branch coat of arms **1**,255
  reunions **172**,187-188,**217,251,252**
Roulhac Moutheley, Therese Gregoire
  de 268-269
Roulhac name
  country estates related to 255
  phonetic spellings 117
  pronunciation xxx-xxxi
  See also (individual names with
  variant spellings: Rolac, Rolacke,
  Rollack, Rollax, Rollick)
Roulhac, (Peter) Warren 51,228-229
Roulhac, Abraham (1) 247-248
Roulhac, Abraham (2) 248
Roulhac, Abraham (3) 250
Roulhac, Aggie (Aggy) 51,236,239,240
Roulhac, Agnes 242
Roulhac, Albert 244,245,246
Roulhac, Alex W. 240
Roulhac, Alexander 147
Roulhac, Alexander 247
Roulhac, Alexandra 224,228
Roulhac, Alice 243
Roulhac, Allen Sr. 50,236,237-238
Roulhac, Allen Jr. 240
Roulhac, Amos 229
Roulhac, Amy 195,200
Roulhac, Ann 191
Roulhac, Ann E. Robinson 88,89
Roulhac, Anne Hare Maule
  4,5,9,283,284
Roulhac, Annie (1) 196
Roulhac, Annie (2) 242
Roulhac, Annie (3) 244,245,246
Roulhac, Annie Mae 240
Roulhac, Arlena 210,211
Roulhac, Arrie 210
Roulhac, Arthur B. 136,137
Roulhac, Bedie Bell 247
Roulhac, Benetta 224,228
Roulhac, Bernell Campbell 247
Roulhac, Bert Samuel Jackson 246
Roulhac, Bertha 211

Roulhac, Callarada (Lucy) Wynn 249
Roulhac, Carrie Mae Williams 212,213
Roulhac, Castelle 200,212
Roulhac, Catherine Ruffin 76,79,80
Roulhac, Celia 121,122,123,219
Roulhac, Charity 191
Roulhac, Charles Peter (Peter Charles)
  (1) 201-202
Roulhac, Charles Peter (2)
  200,201,212-213,**217**
Roulhac, Charlie Jr. 250
Roulhac, Charlie Sr. 250
Roulhac, Charlotte 187,216
Roulhac, Christell 241
Roulhac, Christopher M. Jr. 235
Roulhac, Ciller 253
Roulhac, Cindy (Cinda) Kelly 197
Roulhac, Clara 246
Roulhac, Cleve Jr. 245
Roulhac, Cleve Sr. 245
Roulhac, Clissie McElroy 244
Roulhac, Cola 215
Roulhac, Constant 107
Roulhac, Constant Hardeman 107
Roulhac, Cora 224-225
Roulhac, Doll Baby 254
Roulhac, Donnie 244
Roulhac, Donny (Donnie) H. 241
Roulhac, Doris Green 217
Roulhac, Dorothea 233
Roulhac, Dorothy 225
Roulhac, Douglas 243
Roulhac, Dr. Christopher M. Sr. 238
Roulhac, Earl 213, 254
Roulhac, Earnestine 251
Roulhac, Eddie 248-249
Roulhac, Edgar 251
Roulhac, Edgar Edwin 220
Roulhac, Edgar Elijah 219-221, 255-
  256
Roulhac, Edgar Jr. 189
Roulhac, Edgar Sr. **172**,187, **221**, 230
Roulhac, Edmond 231-232
Roulhac, Edmond 249-250
Roulhac, Edna Parker 215

Index

Roulhac, Edny 194-195
Roulhac, Edward 193
Roulhac, Edward T. 246
Roulhac, Edwin Elisha 189, 203, 217, 219-220, **221**
Roulhac, Elbert 233
Roulhac, Eliza 237
Roulhac, Elizabeth 12, 19, 36
Roulhac, Elizabeth Barrow 18
Roulhac, Ella 197, 200, 208
Roulhac, Elsie (Alcy/Ilsy) 117, 240
Roulhac, Emily 125
Roulhac, Eric 254
Roulhac, Ester 195, 198, 199
Roulhac, Estoria 194
Roulhac, Ethel Bowers Guyton 249
Roulhac, Eugenia 247
Roulhac, Evelyn Viola Alexander 219, **221**
Roulhac, Fannie 86. 223, 250
Roulhac, Fanny 86, 119, 124, 126, 139
Roulhac, Fanny Lewis 141
Roulhac, Faton (Phaton, Fayton, Fadin) xxxiii, 84, 85, 196, 198, 200, 202, 215
Roulhac, Frances 83, 123, 202, 215, **221**, 223
Roulhac, Frances Gray 75
Roulhac, Frances Lee 75
Roulhac, Frances Phoenix 190, **221**
Roulhac, Francis xxxvi, 23-24, 26, 37-38, 41, 47, 50, 56, 63-64, 98-99, 101, 232, 241, 242, 272
Roulhac, Francis Leonard Gregoire de xxxvii, 99, 101, 157, 161, 169
Roulhac, Gene 245
Roulhac, George 228
Roulhac, George E. 224
Roulhac, George Norman 225-226
Roulhac, George W. 224-225
Roulhac, Ginnie 198, 202
Roulhac, Guillaume Gregoire de 258, 265
Roulhac Guilaume Gregoire de Duperiex, Jr. 269

Roulhac, Guillaume Hospice Gregoire de 270
Roulhac, Gwendolyn 250
Roulhac, Hannibal 134
Roulhac, Harmony 241, 244
Roulhac, Hazel Mitchel 216
Roulhac, Hemor Henderson 254
Roulhac, Henderson 251
Roulhac, Henrietta 86, 125, 223, 225
Roulhac, Henry 119, 227, 253
Roulhac, Herbert Jr. 233, 236
Roulhac, Herbert M. 233
Roulhac, Hosea 251
Roulhac, Hubert 233
Roulhac, Ida Gray 253
Roulhac, Inez 244
Roulhac, Ira (Arrie) Nelson 201, 212
Roulhac, Irvy 251
Roulhac, Isaac 241, 244, 245, 246, 253
Roulhac, Isabelle Roden Wood 235-236, 239-239
Roulhac, Isaiah 253
Roulhac, Isom 194, 246-247
Roulhac, Isom (3) 247
Roulhac, J.H. 113, 185
Roulhac, Jack 248
Roulhac, Jahaza 233
Roulhac, James 63, 224-227, 247
Roulhac, James B. 250
Roulhac, James Clinton 247
Roulhac, James Edward 125
Roulhac, Jamina Maule xxxvii, 10, 71, 72, 76
Roulhac, Jane 12, 86, 223, 225
Roulhac, Jay 233
Roulhac, Jean Baptiste Ignace Gregoire de. *See* Roulhac, John Gregoire
Roulhac, Jeanne Marguerite 94
Roulhac, Jefferson 232
Roulhac, Jeffery 254
Roulhac, Jeanne Marguerite 94
Roulhac, Jennie Harvey 248-249
Roulhac, Jenny 251
Roulhac, Jerome 254
Roulhac, Jimmy 194

Index

Roulhac, John 12, 14, 72, 77, 112, 117, 123, 153, 165, 171, 13, 174, 203, 222, 226, 228, 243
Roulhac, John B. 152
Roulhac, John Gray Sr. xxxii-xxxiv, 83-86, 192, 196, 198
Roulhac, John Gregoire xxxv-xxxvii, 67-71, 282-283
Roulhac, John Maule Gregoire 12, 17, 32, 47-48
Roulhac, John Maynard 216
Roulhac, Johnnie 243
Roulhac, Johnson 134, 245
Roulhac, Joicy Bright 193
Roulhac, Jordan 228, 232
Roulhac, Joseph 83, **84**, 101, 174, 190, 205, 218, 221, 259, 261
Roulhac, Joseph B.G. xxxvii, 24, 26, 38, 80, 94, 104
Roulhac, Joseph Blount Gregoire 78, 91
Roulhac, Joseph Du Maupas 273
Roulhac, Joseph Gregoire de 93, 260, 265, 269, 270
Roulhac, Joseph Hill 113
Roulhac, Joseph Psalmet Gregoire 104-105
Roulhac, Josephine Brunet 270
Roulhac, Judge Joseph D. **174**, 190, 217-218, **221**
Roulhac, Julius 248-249, 250
Roulhac, Katherine 189, 232
Roulhac, King David 253
Roulhac, Larachman 233
Roulhac, Laura 247
Roulhac, Lawrence 233
Roulhac, Leola McDaniel 250
Roulhac, Lewis 135-136, 140, 142, 144
Roulhac, Lillie 245
Roulhac, Lillie Leslie 202
Roulhac, Lillie Mae 245
Roulhac, Lillie Shavers 245
Roulhac, Limas 120-125, 222-224
Roulhac, Lizzie 250
Roulhac, Lizzie Kelly 246
Roulhac, Lizzie L. Watson 142

Roulhac, Lizzie Robinson 196, 200
Roulhac, Lizzie S. Milton 212-213
Roulhac, Louise 236, 250
Roulhac, Louise Garret 212
Roulhac, Lucius xix, xxiii, 7, 195, 201, 209, 214
Roulhac, Lucretia 232, 248, 250
Roulhac, Lucy Wynn 249, 250, 253
Roulhac, Lula Shavers 244
Roulhac, Maggie 232, 233, 244
Roulhac, Mamie 233
Roulhac, Manerva 233
Roulhac, Margaret 201, 212, 107
Roulhac, Margaret Anderson 112
Roulhac, Margaret Eleanor Gray 111-112
Roulhac, Margaret Garner 241
Roulhac, Margaret Gray 103-104
Roulhac, Margaret York 227-228
Roulhac, Maria 123-125, 223
Roulhac, Marie Jeanne Dumas 265
Roulhac, Marie Steel 251
Roulhac, Marjorie Brooks 215
Roulhac, Martha Hines Dixon 91
Roulhac, Martha Jenkins 233
Roulhac, Martin 101-102, 225, 271-272, 282, 284
Roulhac, Mary 8, 123-125, 190, 203, 206, 221-222, 248
Roulhac, Mary Jane 125
Roulhac, Maude Deborah 237
Roulhac, Meredith 233
Roulhac, Michael 245, 254
Roulhac, Minerva 190, 203, 216, 218, 220, 233-234, 236, 241, 243, 246
Roulhac, Mitchell 201
Roulhac, Moses 228, 230-31, 233
Roulhac, Mrs. S.E. 182
Roulhac, Naomi 233
Roulhac, Naomi Wilson 236
Roulhac, Nathaniel 251
Roulhac, Ned 247
Roulhac, Nellie 193, 240
Roulhac, Nellie Gordon 239

Index

Roulhac, Nelly xxxii-xxxiii, 5, 189, 191-193, 213, 221, 245
Roulhac, Nero xxxii, 84, 86, 125, 149, 189, 191, 193, 194, 205, 213, 221, 223, 225, 245
Roulhac, Nettie Wynn 244
Roulhac, Nora 243
Roulhac, Olivia 232
Roulhac, Oswald B. 234, 236
Roulhac, Patience Goode 233, 234, 236
Roulhac, Pearl 244
Roulhac, Peggy 248
Roulhac, Peter 84, 192, 197, 202, 242
Roulhac, Peter Warren 232, 236
Roulhac, Pheoby 241
Roulhac, Phillip 248-250
Roulhac, Pinkey Clayton 243
Roulhac, Portia Jean Goodloe 189, 220, **221**
Roulhac, Priscilla 123-124, 223
Roulhac, Psalmet Gregoire
  born in France 267
  death 6, 15
  descendants' involvement in slavery xxxvi-xxxvii
  immigration to US xxxv-xxxvi, 3-4
  last will & testament 15-17
  letter to mother 4-5
  marriage to Anne Hare Maule 4
  marriage to Elizabeth Barrow 6
  slave owner 14, 15
Roulhac, Quamley 52, 52, 240
Roulhac, Quintiney Russ 253
Roulhac, Rachel 123, 124, 224
Roulhac, Rasht 125
Roulhac, Raymond 213
Roulhac, Rebecca 134
Roulhac, Rebecca (Becky) "Chatty" 85, 193-195, 197, 198
Roulhac, Reginald 215
Roulhac, Reuben C. 224
Roulhac, Rev. A. Moses 148, 190, 22-231, **174**
Roulhac, Rev. Robert Daniel Jr. 148, 188, 190, 196, 201, 218
Roulhac, Richard (Dick) 228
Roulhac, Robert 191, 194, 198, 202, 212, 232, 234, 241, 249, 251
Roulhac, Robert Alpheus 216
Roulhac, Robert Charles 252
Roulhac, Robert D. 190, 216
Roulhac, Robert Wayne 216
Roulhac, Roberta 233
Roulhac, Roland 248-249, 250
Roulhac, Rose 226-227, 248
Roulhac, Roxy Ann 232
Roulhac, Judge Roy L.
  childhood xvii-xxiv
  childhood home **xx**
  Detroit xxviii-xxx
  family photo **xviii, xxii**
  family reunion **174**
  high school graduation xxiv, **xxv**
  Washington D.C. xxv-xxviii
Roulhac, Ruth Olivia 219
Roulhac, Samantha 225
Roulhac, Sampson 246-248
Roulhac, Samuel 252
Roulhac, Sara 212
Roulhac, Shelton 254
Roulhac, Sheryll Monique 252
Roulhac, Shirlana **116**
Roulhac, Shirley 244
Roulhac, Silvain Gregoire de 270
Roulhac, Simeon Adolphus 203, 217, **221**
Roulhac, Sophia Watson 243
Roulhac, Stella 247-248
Roulhac, Susie 202, 225
Roulhac, Sylvester **xxii**, 210
Roulhac, Tempa 228, 232
Roulhac, Thomas 87, 112, 123, 126, 223, 232, 234
Roulhac, Thomas Joseph 233-234, 236, 238
Roulhac, Thomas Ruffin 88
Roulhac, Tillah 232
Roulhac, Tracy 225
Roulhac, Ulysses 202, 215

Index

Roulhac, Viney (Vinnie) Brown 198, 202
Roulhac, Warren 232-234
Roulhac, Washington 119, 134, 145
Roulhac, Waymon 213
Roulhac, William 233, 34, 76-77, 225, 247
Roulhac, William Gray Gregoire 113
Roulhac, William Maule xxxvii
Roulhac, William Wrighten 165, 227
Roulhac, Willie 253
Roulhac, Willie Lee 245
Roulhac-Ruffin papers 92
Roulhac-Walker, Kesha 240
Ruffin, Roulhac and Hamilton Family Papers 393
Ruffin, Thomas 87-89
Ruffin, Thomas Chief Justice xxxvii, 78-79
Rufus (slave) 106
Sabry (slave) 48
Salomah 285
Sam (slave) 16
Sam (slave) 74
Sampson (slave) 20-21
Sanderlin, W.P. 138
Sanderlin, WIlliam M. 140
Sandy (slave) 54
Sandy (slave) 10
Sapp, Emma Lee Roulhac 213
Sarah (slave) 53
Sarah (slavc) 52
Sarahann (slave) 50
Savory (slave) 106
Saxon, Mose 111
Scott, Joseph 217
Scott, Joseph Leroy 217
Second Great Awakening 117
Sessons, Lizzie 121
Shaw, Dorsey (Kitty) 121
Shaw, Jane 121
Smith, Eliza 215
Smith, Essie 207
Smith, Ethel 214
Smith, Eula Rivers 199

Sherman, W. T. 61
Sid (slave) 10, 21
Sierra Leone, Africa 148-149, 349
Siloy (slave) 15
Silvester (slave) 52
Silvia (slave) 74
Simon (slave) 53, 72
Sims, Annette 195, 197
Singleton, Roscoe 124, 126
Sirleaf, Ellen Johnson (Pres. of Liberia) 230
Sisters of Providence 264
Slade, Anne Louisa 58
Slade, Emma Jacqueline 59-60
Slade, Helen Roulhac 61
Slade, James Jeremiah 59
Slade, Janet Elizabeth 57-58
Slade, John Henry 62
Slade, Martha Bog 60
Slade, Stella Bog 61
Slade, Thomas Bog Jr. (T.B.) 34, 57, 60
Slave law 79, 342
Slave trade vi, xxxii, **73, 81**, 96
Slave uprisings xxxviii, 64, 100, 117, 231
Smallpox 170-174, 227, 267
Smallwood, D.J. 185
Smallwood, John R. 140
Smallwood, M.S. 185
Smiley, Pecola Roulhac 253
Smith, Alex 194, 199
Smith, Anthony 194, 199
Smith, Aron 214
Smith, Benjamin 215
Smith, Benjamin Jr. 194, 198-199
Smith, Benjamin Sr. 194, 195
Smith, Carrie 200, 207
Smith, Chester 208
Smith, Clyde 208
Smith, Connie 198, 206
Smith, Dr. J.E. 143
Smith, Early 200, 207
Smith, Harriet 195
Smith, James Joyner **18**
Smith, Jim 195, 200
Smith, Joseph 214

Smith, Laura 194, 198, 206
Smith, Lella 200, 207
Smith, Leman 202
Smith, Lula Leslie 215
Smith, Mamie 198
Smith, Margaret 194, 199
Smith, Marvin 208
Smith, Mary 195, 198, 200, 206
Smith, Myers 207
Smith, Nellie 208
Smith, Placolia 198, 206
Smith, R. 181
Smith, Robert 202, 214
Smith, Ruby Lee 208
Smith, Stella Roulhac 194, 198, 202, 214
Smith, Susie Roulhac 202, 214
Smith, Thomas 13
Smith, Thomas 195
Smith, Wayman 193
Smith, William 19, 200, 202, 206, 214
Sofah war (Liberia) 162
Sonia (slave) 106
Sook (slave) 33, 38
Southern Historical Collection (Chapel Hill, NC) 93-94
Speller, Elisha 137
Speller, Fletcher 141
Speller, Mary Winnie 143
Spivey, George 124
St. Domingo, Hispaniola 275
St. Mark's, Hispaniola 278
Standland, Robert Earl IX
State v. Mann 79
Stephens, Florence Hayes 194, 196
Stephens, Harrison 200
Stewart, A.H. 80
Stewart, Sam T. 80
Stiller, Lillian Roulhac 236
Stiller, V. 236
Suck (slave) 22
Sue (slave) 8
Sue (slave) 12
Susannah (slave) 54

Taney, Roger Taney (Chief Justice) 193
Taylor, Henry 157, 176, 178, 180, 185
Taylor, J.C. 156, 170, 172, 185
Taylor, Moriah 121
Teage, Deleanor French 214
Tender Memories--A Grandmother's Legacy (Alma Booth) 239
The African Repository 150
The Price of Liberty (Claude Andrew Legg) 152
The Private Civil War: Popular Thought During the Sectional Conflict 88
The Roulhac Mansion (Memphis, TN) 235
Thomas (slave) 90
Thomas, Amanda 170
Thomas, Betty French 214
Thomas, Grigsby Eskridge 60, 61
Thomas, Samuel Butler 60
Thompson, Barbara Jean xxiv, **xviii**
Thompson, Thomas & wife 186, 187
Thornton, William 148
Tibby (slave) 85
Tindel, Sue ix
Tip (slave) 15
Tolbert, Dr. William R. (Pres. of Liberia) 229
Tom (slave) 7
Tom (slave) 75
Toney (slave) 12, 13
Toney (slave) 15, 33, 36
Tony (slave) 10, 72
Townsend, Christine Caroline 112
Treasa (slave) 85
Tucker, St. George 149
Turket, Malissa Bracewell 174
Turket, Moses 186
Turner (slave) 54
Tyler, Captain T.H. 183, 185
U.S. Colored Troops 86, 117-145, **120**
United States of America v. Alger Hiss 226
USS Black Hawk 204
USS Charleston 204
USS Montana 204

USS Wisconsin 204
Vainey (slave) 75
Varngay, Civey 160
Venus (slave) 9
Vina (slave) 54
Virgil & wife (slaves) 54
Wallis (slave) 52
Walls, Shirley Arnetta Brown 217
Ward, Nathan 126
Washington (slave) 54
Washington, Booker T. 89
Washington, Judge Bushrod 147
Watford, Virginia L. Roulhac 248
Watson, Aunt Cynthia 142
Watson, Aunt Dicey 142
Watson, Lizzie 138
Watson, Peter 167
Watson, Sophia 247
Webb, Logan 124
Whit (slave) 40, 41
White, Elias 121
White, Elise 121
White, Harriet Winborn 120
White, Laura A. 136
White, Limas Roulhac 121
White, Lodee Roulhac 201, 213
White, Mary E. (Eliza) Taylor 120
White, Mary Roulhac 86, 120, 123, 124, 126
White, Molly 121
White, Rolacke (Roulhac). *See* Rolacke, Joseph
White, Sallie A. 120
Whiter, Kader 120
Whitmel (slave) 21
Wicker, Rev. R.B. 185
Wiley (slave) 48
Wiley (slave) 44
Wiley (slave) 54
Will (slave) 15
Will (slave) 84
William (slave) 50
William (slave) 51
William (slave) 106
Williams, Alex 209
Williams, Audrey English 222
Williams, Carl Jr. 245
Williams, Carl Sr. 245
Williams, Catherine Roulhac 236
Williams, D.C. 138
Williams, Earnest 245
Williams, Jean 245
Williams, Keith 236
Williams, Lula Roulhac 245
Williams, Matt 129
Williams, Michael 245
Williams, Ollie Mae Jackson 209
Williams, Rhonda 245
Williams, Robert 243
Willis (slave) 50
Wilsie (slave) 16
Wilson (slave) 21
Wilson, Hattie Roulhac 224
Windsor (slave) 53
Wingood (slave) 16, 23
Winn, Rolack 143
Winston, Judge Francis D. 142
World War II 212-213, 345-346
Wright, Brister 153, 156, 170, 186
Wright, James A. 183-184
Wright, Justice Elijah 186
Wright, Kenyatta ix
Wright, William 127
Wrighten (slave) 84
Yellow fever 102, 286
Yonge, Walter S.C. 39, 41
York, Solomon 174-175, 227
Young Ben (slave) 15, 56
Young Hannah (slave) 7
Young Negro Cinder (slave) 33, 36
Young Pompey (slave) 16
Zwai, Dowee 163

Index by Janet Sue Curtiss, M.A. School of Library and Information Science, Wayne State University

Endnotes

[1] By secret ballot, the National Press Club voted 377 to 281 to admit Louis R. Lautier, fifty-six, representative of the *Atlanta Daily World* and the *National Negro Publishers*, as it's first Negro member. In March 1947, he had become one of the first blacks admitted to the Congressional Press galleries. *Jet Magazine*, February 18, 1955; March 23, 1998.

[2] For a video clip of Dr. King's July 19, 1962 speech at the National Press Club, see:
http://crdl.usg.edu/cgi/crdl?format=_video&query=id:ugabma_wsbn_36234&_cc=1&Welcome.

[3] The school was the successor to Gilmore Academy, one of two Rosenwald schools in Jackson County. Between 1916 and 1932, Booker T. Washington and Julius Rosenwald, a philanthropist and president of the Sears Roebuck, caused the construction of over 3,200 schools to address sub-standard educational opportunities for Negro children throughout the South.

[4] The *Memoir* was updated and published by Helen M. Prescott, one of Francis' great nieces.

[5] For a quick lesson on the National Assembly of 1789 and its role during the French Revolution, see: http://www.britannica.com/EBchecked/topic/219315/French-Revolution

[6] Maule Family
Patrick (?) Maule and his wife, Mary had issue –
1. Mary, m, a Mr. Bonner and lived near Washington, N. C.
2. John, m. Elizabeth Hare, of Va. He was elected to the legislature, from Beaufort Co. in 1769.
3. Elizabeth, m. a Mr. Hare, brother to Elizabeth, from Elizabeth, from Va.
John Maule (2) and Elizabeth Hare had issue –
(1) Anne Hare, b. Friday, Mar. 22, 1765, m. P.G. Roulhac
(2) Elizabeth, m. a Mr. Smith; had no children.

(3) Jamina, m. John G. Roulhac; lived in Martin Co., N.C.

(4) Penelope, m. a Mr. Bryan; lived near Newbern, N.C., left issue.

(5) Moses, never m., lived with P.G. Roulhac.

All born at Smith's Point on Pamlico River, Beaufort Co., N.C.

7 Ancestry.com. *North Carolina Wills and Inventories* [database on-line]. Provo, UT, USA: Ancestry.com Operations Inc., 2002. Original data: J. Bryan Grimes, comp. *North Carolina Wills and Inventories: Copied From Original and Recorded Wills and Inventories in the Office of the Secretary of State*. Raleigh, NC, USA: 1912.

8 According to the 1764 Beaufort County Taxables, of twelve taxables attributed to John Maule, eleven were slaves.

9 *Ibid.*

10 Ancestry.com: North Carolina Wills and Inventories Chapter: Surnames, M – N, Page: 299.

11 Ancestry.com. *1790 United States Federal Census* [database on-line]. Provo, UT, USA: Ancestry.com Operations, Inc., 2010. Images reproduced by FamilySearch.

12 Ancestry.com. *1800 United States Federal Census* [database on-line]. Provo, UT, USA: Ancestry.com Operations, Inc., 2010. Images reproduced by FamilySearch.

13 Hyde County Wills, 1764-1818, C.053.8001, Vol .1 page 432 (Recorded copy).

14 Jones County, GA Probate Court Records, Wills, pp. 221-222.

15 Ancestry.com. *1840 United States Federal Census* [database on-line]. Provo, UT, USA: Ancestry.com Operations, Inc., 2010. Images reproduced by FamilySearch.

16 Ancestry.com. *1850 United States Federal Census* [database on-line]. Provo, UT, USA: Ancestry.com Operations, Inc., 2010. Images reproduced by FamilySearch.

17 Ancestry.com. *1850 U.S. Federal Census - Slave Schedules* [database on-line]. Provo, UT, USA: Ancestry.com Operations Inc., 2004.

Endnotes

18. Ancestry.com. *1850 U.S. Federal Census – Slave Schedules* [database on-line]. Provo, UT, USA: Ancestry.com Operations Inc., 2004.
19. Shofner, *supra*, page 172.
20. Ancestry.com. *1850 U.S. Federal Census – Slave Schedules* [database on-line]. Provo, UT, USA: Ancestry.com Operations Inc., 2004.
21. *Cato, a Slave v State*, 9 Fla. 163 (1860); Denham, James M., *"A Rogue's Paradise" – Crime and Punishment in Antebellum Florida, 1821-1861*, University of Alabama Press, 1997.
22. Jackson County, FL Marriages, Book B, Page 178.
23. Ancestry.com. *1870 United States Federal Census* [database on-line]. Provo, UT, USA: Ancestry.com Operations, Inc., 2009. Images reproduced by FamilySearch.
24. *Beaufort County Orphan Book A, 1808-1828,* page 265, December Term, 1816.
25. Ancestry.com. *1850 U.S. Federal Census – Slave Schedules* [database on-line]. Provo, UT, USA: Ancestry.com Operations Inc., 2010.
26. Ancestry.com. *1860 U.S. Federal Census – Slave Schedules* [database on-line]. Provo, UT, USA: Ancestry.com Operations Inc., 2010.
27. Ancestry.com. *1860 U.S. Federal Census – Slave Schedules* [database on-line]. Provo, UT, USA: Ancestry.com Operations Inc., 2010.
28. *Civil War Soldiers & Sailors System,* on-line, blacks.itd.nps.gov/cwss.
29. 1840 Jury List, Jackson County, Florida, Chancery Order Book B, pp. 122-123-124-125.
30. Deed Book A Page 302-3, Jackson County Records.
31. *Ibid*, 303.
32. Deed Book A, page 95, Jackson County Deeds.
33. Deed Book A Page 302-3, Jackson County Records.
34. Deed Book A, page 95, Jackson County Deeds.

Endnotes

35. Ancestry.com. 1850 United States Federal Census [database on-line]. Proof, UT, USA: Ancestry.com operations, 2010. Images reproduced by Family Search.
36. Shofner, *p.* 118.
37. Ancestry.com. *1850 U.S. Federal Census - Slave Schedules* [database on-line]. Provo, UT, USA: Ancestry.com Operations Inc., 2010.
38. Jackson County Deed Book B, p. 725
39. Jackson County Records, Estate Book D, See pp. 267, 271, 272, 627.
40. *1850 U.S. Federal Census - Slave Schedules* [database on-line]. Provo, UT, USA: Ancestry.com Operations Inc., 2004.
41. *Confederate Applications for Presidential Pardons, 1865-1867* [database on-line]. Provo, UT, USA: Ancestry.com Operations Inc., 2008.
42. National Park Service. *U.S. Civil War Soldiers, 1861-1865* [database on-line]. Provo, UT, USA: Ancestry.com Operations Inc., 2007.
43. Ancestry.com. *1850 U.S. Federal Census - Slave Schedules* [database on-line]. Provo, UT, USA: Ancestry.com Operations Inc., 2004.
44. Ancestry.com. *1860 U.S. Federal Census - Slave Schedules* [database on-line]. Provo, UT, USA: Ancestry.com Operations Inc., 2010.
45. Ancestry.com. *1860 U. S. Federal Census* [database on-line]. Provo, UT, USA: Ancestry.com Operations, Inc., 2009. Images reproduced by FamilySearch.
46. Ancestry.com. *Confederate Applications for Presidential Pardons, 1865-1867.*
47. Weinfeld, Daniel, *The Jackson County War*, University of Alabama Press (2012), pp. 120-21, fn. 48 indicates: On the eve of the war, John R. Ely and his mother, Frances A.C. Ely, widow of merchant and planter Francis de Roulhac Ely, owned 2,500 acres and 101 slaves. U.S. Census, 1860, Jackson County Slave Schedule.

⁴⁸ *Id, Jackson County,* pp. 377-378.

⁴⁹ Patrick Henry (May 29, 1736 – June 6, 1799) served as the first post-colonial Governor of Virginia from 1776 to 1779. A prominent figure in the American Revolution, Henry is known and remembered for his "Give me Liberty, or give me Death!" speech, and as one of the Founding Fathers of the United States. Along with Samuel Adams and Thomas Paine, he is remembered as one of the most influential (and radical) advocates of the American Revolution and republicanism, especially in his denunciations of corruption in government officials and his defense of historic rights.

⁵⁰ *1850 U.S. Federal Census - Slave Schedules* [database on-line]. Provo, UT, USA: Ancestry.com Operations Inc., 2004.

⁵¹ From Wikipedia, the free encyclopedia.

⁵² Gray Family:

John Gray, a native of Scotland, b. in 1690, came to N. C., m. Ann Bryan, lived in Bertie Co., and there d. Oct. 11, 1756. She was b. 1698; d. Aug. 24, 1770. Both interred at Rosefield, near Windsor, N.C. They had issue—

1. Janet, b. Dec. 7, 1721; m. Kenneth McKenzie, an Episcopal Minister and had issue— Janet, Anne and William.
2. John, b. May 16, 1724; m. and had dau. Susan, who m. Thomas Hart, and had six children. One of these, Lucretia, m. the Hon. Henry Clay, of Ky.
3. Barbara, b. May 31, 1726; m. Jacob Blount and had issue— William (Ter. Gov.), Ann, John Gray, Louisa, Reading, Thomas, Jacob, Barbara and Harvey.
4. Anne, b. June 12, 1728; m. John Slade, and had issue— John, Barbara and Amelia.
5. William, b. June 17, 1730; m. Frances Lee, dau. of Stevens Lee and Elizabeth West (b. July 18, 1737; d. Nov. 9, 1786); d. June 23, 1801 and was interred at Rosefield, near Windsor, N. C They had issue— (1) Stevens Gray; (2) Anne, m. Joseph Blount; (3) Elizabeth, m. Wm. Bryan; (4) John; (5) Frances

Lee, b. Aug. 15, 1760, m. John Roulhac; (6) William; (7) Janet; (8) Barbara; (9) Eleanor, m. Bryan Butler; (10) George; (11) Margaret, m. Dr. Francis Roulhac; (12) William Lee, m. Mary Turner: (13) Penelope; (14) Polly.

6. Lucretia, b. Aug. 20, 1732; m. Mr. Worseley.
7. George, b. Aug. 29, 1734; d. Mar. 8, 1735.
8. Elizabeth, b. Nov. 16, 1736; d. Tun. 30, 1787.
9. Amelia, b. Nov. 17, 1739; m. Thomas Clark and had issue—Mary, Anne and John.
10. Louisa, b. Nov. 26, 1741; m. Thomas Worley.

[53] Watson, Alan D. *Bertie County, A Brief History*, North Carolina Dept. of Cultural Resources, 1982, p. 65.

[54] Gray Family Papers, Southern Historical Collection, UNC Library, Chapel Hill, North Carolina.

[55] Source:*http://files.usgwarchives.net/nc/martin/obits/r/roulhac-1339nob.text. File contributed for use in USGenWeb Archives by Carolyn Shank Carolynshank@msn.com.*

[56] 13 N.C. 263 (N.C. 1830).

[57] http://blacks.northcarolinahistory.org/encyclopedia/268/entry/.

[58] Ancestry.com. *1850 United States Federal Census* [database on-line]. Provo, UT, USA: Ancestry.com Operations, Inc., 2009. Images reproduced by FamilySearch.

[59] For a contemporary review of Ruffin's role in the development of slave law in the South, see Tushet, Mark V., <u>Slave Law in the American South: State v Mann in History and Literature</u>, (2003).

[60] Ancestry.com. *1820 United States Federal Census* [database on-line]. Provo, UT, USA: Ancestry.com Operations, Inc., 2010. Images reproduced by FamilySearch.

[61] Southern Historical Collection, Library of UNC at Chapel Hill.

[62] Ancestry.com. *1850 U.S. Federal Census - Slave Schedules* [database on-line]. Provo, UT, USA: Ancestry.com Operations Inc., 2004.

[63] http://blacks.gutenberg.org/files/31219/31219.txt.

Endnotes

64. Ancestry.com. *1860 United States Federal Census* [database on-line]. Provo, UT, USA: Ancestry.com Operations, Inc., 2009. Images reproduced by FamilySearch.
65. Ancestry.com. *1870 United States Federal Census* [database on-line]. Provo, UT, USA: Ancestry.com Operations, Inc., 2009. Images reproduced by FamilySearch.
66. Ancestry.com. *1810 United States Federal Census* [database on-line]. Provo, UT, USA: Ancestry.com Operations, Inc., 2010. Images reproduced by FamilySearch.
67. Ancestry.com. *1840 United States Federal Census* [database on-line]. Provo, UT, USA: Ancestry.com Operations, Inc., 2010. Images reproduced by FamilySearch.
68. Ancestry.com. *1840 United States Federal Census* [database on-line]. Provo, UT, USA: Ancestry.com Operations, Inc., 2010. Images reproduced by FamilySearch.
69. Ancestry.com. *1840 United States Federal Census* [database on-line]. Provo, UT, USA: Ancestry.com Operations, Inc., 2010. Images reproduced by FamilySearch.
70. Francis Roulhac Ely, John Gray Roulhac's first cousin, was the sixth largest with 84 slaves cultivating 650 acres of a 1,550 acre plantation.
71. Shofner, *supra*, 118-119.
72. Records of the Bureau of Land Management, http:blacks.glorecords.blm.gov/search.
73. *Book D, p. 136 and Folio 257, 258 & 259, September 4, 1858, Jackson County FL.*
74. Ancestry.com. *1860 United States Federal Census* [database on-line]. Provo, UT, USA: Ancestry.com Operations, Inc., 2009. Images reproduced by FamilySearch.
75. Ancestry.com. *1860 U.S. Federal Census - Slave Schedules* [database on-line]. Provo, UT, USA: Ancestry.com Operations Inc., 2010.

76 Thomas R. Roulhac to his mother, March 13, 1864, in *Ruffin, Roulhac and Hamilton Family Papers*, SHC [Southern Historical Collection].
77 *The Booker T. Washington Papers*, 1901-1902, pp. 221-222. (BTW to R.L. Smith, 10/8/1902, Univ. of IL Press (1977); http://blacks.historycooperative.org/btw/Vol.6/html/221.html.
78 Ancestry.com. *1850 U.S. Federal Census - Slave Schedules* [database on-line]. Provo, UT, USA: Ancestry.com Operations Inc., 2004.
79 Jackson County Estate Records, Book D, p. 136.
80 *Ibid*, p. 78.
81 *Ibid*, p. 190.
82 *Ibid, p. 191.*
83 Ancestry.com. *1850 U.S. Federal Census - Slave Schedules* [database on-line]. Provo, UT, USA: Ancestry.com Operations Inc., 2004.
84 Ancestry.com. *1850 United States Federal Census* [database on-line]. Provo, UT, USA: Ancestry.com Operations, Inc., 2009. Images reproduced by FamilySearch.
85 Ancestry.com. *1850 U.S. Federal Census - Slave Schedules* [database on-line]. Provo, UT, USA: Ancestry.com Operations Inc., 2004.
86 Ancestry.com. *1860 United States Federal Census* [database on-line]. Provo, UT, USA: Ancestry.com Operations, Inc., 2009. Images reproduced by FamilySearch.
87 Ancestry.com. 1860 U.S. Federal Census - Slave Schedules [database on-line]. Provo, UT, USA: Ancestry.com. Operations Inc., 2010.
88 Cox, Dale, *The Battle of Marianna, Florida* (1989 and 2007), pp. 121.
89 Ancestry.com. 1870 United States Federal Census [database on-line]. Provo, UT, USA: Ancestry.com Operations, Inc., 2009. Images reproduced by FamilySearch.

Endnotes

90 Ancestry.com. *1860 United States Federal Census* [database on-line]. Provo, UT, USA: Ancestry.com Operations, Inc., 2009. Images reproduced by FamilySearch.

91 Ancestry.com. *1860 U.S. Federal Census - Slave Schedules* [database on-line]. Provo, UT, USA: Ancestry.com Operations Inc., 2004.

92 Ancestry.com. *1860 U.S. Federal Census - Slave Schedules* [database on-line]. Provo, UT, USA: Ancestry.com Operations Inc., 2004.

93 Ancestry.com. *1860 United States Federal Census* [database on-line]. Provo, UT, USA: Ancestry.com Operations, Inc., 2009. Images reproduced by FamilySearch.

94 His great-grandfather came to Louisiana in charge of a Spanish Colony, and his grandfather, Fernando Morena, from Malaga, Spain, was a mid-shipman in the Spanish Navy and afterwards a surgeon in the Spanish army at Ft. Barrancas. He married Florentina Senac, of New Orleans, a lady of French descent. His maternal grandparents were Nicholas Lopez, from Malaga, Spain, and Victoria Calder, from Paisley, Scotland.

95 For the complete memoir of Francis' early life as set forth in the *Genealogical Memoir of the Roulhac Family in America*, see Appendix 2.

96 Ancestry.com. *1820 United States Federal Census* [database on-line]. Provo, UT, USA: Ancestry.com Operations, Inc., 2010. Images reproduced by FamilySearch.

97 George, Henry, *The History of the Third, Seventh, Eighth and Twelfth Kentucky Regiment of the C.S.A.*, Louisville, 1911.

98 Ancestry.com. 1860 U.S. Federal Census - Slave Schedules [database on-line]. Provo, UT, USA: Ancestry.com Operations Inc., 2010.

99 "Transcript of the Examination of Several Negros Slave respecting a rebellion taken at Windsor, 9 & 1 Jun 1802," Transcripts, Conspiracies, 1803, P.C. 1629.1, North Carolina State Archives, Raleigh. See also Tom Parramore, "*The Great Slave Conspiracy*,"

The State (15 August 1971); Jeffrey 1. Crow, *The Black Experience in Revolutionary North Carolina* (Raleigh: Div. of Archives and History, 1983), pp. 90-94; and Douglas A. Egerton and Thomas C. Parramore, "*A Forum: The Virginia-North Carolina Slave Conspiracy of 1802*," *North Carolina Historical Review* (April 1995): 87-124.

[100] Geraldine N. Phillips, "*Civil War Pension Files in the National Archives: Windows on the Lives of African Americans,*" *Journal of the Afro-American Historical and Genealogical Society* (Spring/Summer 1991), citing John Hope Franklin, *From Slavery to Freedom: A History of Negro Americans* (New York: Alfred A. Knopf, 1966), pp.230-33.

[101] Signed by President Abraham Lincoln 1 January 1863.

[102] According to the 1860 Bertie County Slave Schedule, page 98, line 23, Fanny Roulhac, the only Roulhac listed in the Bertie County schedule, owned 47 slaves--21 males and 26 females. Included were the following males between the ages of 12 and 24: one, 24 years; one, 23 years; one, 22 years; one, 15 years; one, 14 years; one, 13 years; one, 12 years. The 23 year old and the 15 year old were described as "Mulatto."

[103] Two Joseph Rolacks joined the USCT. The first one joined the 2nd Regiment of the USCT on June 23, 1863. The other Joseph, along with his brother David, joined the 36th Regiment on the same day, July 13, 1863.

[104] See Reid, Richard M., *Freedom for Themselves: North Carolina's Black Soldiers in the Civil War Era*, University of NC Press (2008).

[105] The 2nd Regiment was organized at Arlington, Virginia, June 20 to November 11, 1863. Service: Duty at New Orleans, Louisiana and Ship Island, Mississippi, till February 13, 1864. Ordered to Key West, Florida, February 13. Affair at Tampa, Florida, May 5, operation on West Coast of Florida July 1-31. Expedition from Fort Myers to Bayport July 1-4. Expedition from Cedar Key to St. Andrew's Bay July 20-29. Fort Taylor August 21. Station No. 4 February 13, 1865. Attack on Fort Myers February 20. Opera-

tions in the vicinity of St. Mark's February 21 – March 7. East River Bridge March 4-5. Newport Bridge March 5-6. Natural Bridge March 6, duty in District of Florida till January, 1866. Mustered out January 5, 1866. Regiment lost during service three officers and 24 enlisted men killed and mortally wounded and 11 officers and 135 enlisted men by disease. Total 173.

[106] No decisive battles were won by Union troops on Florida soil. Tallahassee was the only southern capital east of the Mississippi River to avoid capture during the war. It was spared by Southern victories at Olustee (1864), where the 35th USCT and the 54th U.S. Colored Regiment fought, and at Natural Bridge (1865). See *A Short History of Florida,* Florida Department of State. The writer wonders whether Joseph Rolack knew that some formerly enslaved Roulhacs, and possibly his relatives, had been brought from North Carolina to Florida in 1830s and 1840s and were living in Marianna, less than a hundred miles from where the Battle of the Natural Bridge was fought.

[107] Ancestry.com. *U.S., Colored Troops Military Service Records, 1861-1865* [database on-line]. Provo, UT, USA: Ancestry.com Operations Inc., 2007.

[108] The 1890 Act allowed Civil War veterans who served at least ninety days to apply for an invalid pension if their partially or totally disabilities were not from vicious habits and prevented them from supporting themselves by manual labor. Widows and dependent children under 16 years of age were also entitled to a pension if the soldier had served more than ninety days.

[109] After the war, Joseph Rolack adopted a new last name that reflected male-line family connections. Joseph and many others discarded their former owners' surnames and adopted their fathers' last names. Before, the war, a slave, if referred to at all by white people by last name, was generally known by his owner's surname, such as Roulhac's Joseph. See Shaffer, Donald R., *After the Glory: The Struggles of Black Civil War Veterans*, Univ. of Kansas Press (2004), p. 100.

[110] For a thorough account of their service, see Reid, Richard M., *Freedom for Themselves: North Carolina's Black Soldiers in the Civil War Era*, University of North Carolina Press (2008).

[111] *Ibid.* 111, 122. Point Lookout, established after the Battle of Gettysburg, was the largest federal prison (capacity of more than 15,000) for captured Confederates, many of whom were or had been slaveholders.

[112] See discussion of Joseph Rolack, Co. C, 36 USCI, following.

[113] The writer wonders whether Jane's son, Nero, was named after Nero Roulhac, born in North Carolina circa 1802, the writer's great-great-grandfather.

[114] It is highly likely that Joseph was born in Bertie County. See the affidavits filed by his mother, Mary Roulhac, in the discussion of Pvt. David Rolack above.

[115] According to the entry placed in the Bible by his mistress Fanny Roulhac and used by his mother Mary in support of a pension for his brother David, Joseph was born in 1836. See Mary Roulhac's deposition above.

[116] See the discussion on Pvt. James Rolack that follows.

[117] Legislation was enacted on 15 June 1864 granting equal pay to Black soldiers. It was made retroactive to 1 January 1864 and to the time of enlistment for those Black soldiers who had been free as of 19 April 1861. See James M. McPherson, *The Negro's Civil War: How American Blacks Felt and Acted During the War for the Union* (New York: Ballantine Books, 1991), p. 206.

[118] See Moss, Juanita Patience, *Battle of Plymouth, North Carolina*, (2004).

[119] Weymouth T. Jordan, Jr., and Gerald W. Thomas, "Massacre at Plymouth: April 20, 1864," *North Carolina Historical Review* (April 1995): 125-197 (176).

[120] *Ibid.* p. 177.

[121] The following entry appears at http://blacks.usgwarchives.org/nc/bertie/wills.html about an unknown sailor that served aboard the USS Southfield: Unknown Bertie County sailor: The muster

roll dated March 31, 1864, for the Southfield (the last muster roll taken before the Southfield was sunk at Plymouth, North Carolina, on April 19, 1864) is torn so that the name of a sailor born in Bertie County is missing. The individual enlisted at Roanoke Island, North Carolina, on February 19, 1863, at the age of 16. His occupation was listed as "contraband." No further specifics are provided for this individual. It is probable that this unknown person is Washington Roulhac.

122 See discussion of Fanny Roulhac above.

123 In October 1932, Fannie modified her application by dropping her claim to be reimbursed for flowers, requested $5.75 for medicine for Pugh Drug Store, and reduced the gravedigger expense to $2 for a total of $202.75. Fannie indicated Lizzie left furniture, a lot, and house worth $525.

124 http://files.usgwarchives.org/nc/bertie/military/colored.txt.

125 Fortune, T. Thomas (1856–1928), an African American journalist and editor, was born into slavery in Marianna, Florida He was the son of a prominent Republican politician during Reconstruction, which enabled him to hold various patronage positions during his adolescence. He studied at Howard University, leaving after a year to pursue a career in journalism. He arrived in New York City in the early 1880s, writing for various black and white publications, most notably as the editor of the *Globe*. He established himself as a militant, prodding African Americans to abandon their unquestioned loyalty to the party of Lincoln. His near-endorsement of Grover Cleveland for president in 1884 led to management conflicts and the demise of the *Globe*, though the paper reemerged first as the *Freeman* and then the *Age*. Under his proprietorship, the *Age* would become the leading black paper of the era, and he would become the "most noted man in Afro-American journalism." As one contemporary observed, "he never writes unless he makes someone wince." http://G.answers.com. Read more at http://GG.rootsweb.ancestry.com/~flgatsaa/Newsletter.html.

[126] *Notes on the State of Virginia*, Query 14, "Laws" The administration of justice and description of the laws?

[127] In 1792, over 1,100 black settlers from Halifax, Nova Scotia, established Freetown, Sierra Leone. The majority were Black Loyalists - ex-slaves freed by the British during the American Revolution and forced to relocate after the British defeat. Other Black Loyalists were evacuated to London, England. Many were among an estimated 300 of the Black Poor of London to establish Granville Town in Sierra Leone in 1787. The colony was abandoned after it was devastated by disease and burned by a neighboring native tribe during a dispute with slave traders. An individual listing of the Black Loyalists is contained in the *Book of Negroes*: blacks.blackloyalist.com/canadiandigitalcollection/documents/official/book_of_Negroes.htm.

[128] *African Repository*, December 1869, p. 367.

[129] The November 11, 1869 emigrants brought to 13,153, the number of emigrants settled in Liberia by the American Colonization Society. *African Repository*, Vol. 46, p. 99 (1870).

[130] *African Repository*, December 1870, p. 373.

[131] *The Price of Liberty: African Americans and the Making of Liberia*, Google Books, (2004), p. 262.

[132] Lawrence Memorial Library, Bertie County, NC, copied August 28, 1987.

[133] See list of emigrants in Appendices 6 and 7.

[134] List of immigrants omitted.

[135] Hurmence, Belinda, *Before Freedom: 48 Oral Histories of Former North and South Carolina Slaves*, Thomas Hall, 81 when interviewed September 10, 1937, Penguin Group, (1990), p.43.

[136] The Red Ball Express was an enormous truck convoy system created by Allied forces to supply their forward-area combat units moving quickly through Europe following the breakout from the D-Day beaches in Normandy. The route was marked with red balls and closed to civilian traffic. The trucks were marked with red balls and given priority when on regular roads. The Red Ball

Express supply plan originated in a 36 hour urgent committee meeting, and was co-designed by Lt. John Bridener Guthrie, Jr. The system, primarily operated and driven by African-American soldiers, lasted only three months, from August 25 to November 16, 1944, when the port facilities at Antwerp, Belgium were opened, some French rail lines were repaired, and portable gasoline pipelines were deployed. http://en.wikipedia.org/wiki/Red_Ball_Express.

[137] Powers, Bernard E., Jr., Black Charleston: A Social History, 1822-1885 (1994); See also Williams, A.B., *The Liberian Exodus: An Account of Voyage of First Emigrants in the Bark "Azor," and Their Reception at Monrovia* (The News and Courier Book Presses, Charleston, S.C., 1778), available at http://docsouth.unc.edu/church/williams/williams.html.

[138] Media coverage: http://query.nytimes.com/mem/archivefree/pdf?res=F30615FA3A5E137B93C0AB178FD85F4C8784F9

[139] G.rootsweb.ancestry.com/~fljackso/MarriagesJE/marrindex.htm.

[140] blacks.rootsweb.ancestry.com/~fljackso/Marriagesje/marrindex.htm.

[141] Source: *The African Repository & Colonial Journal*, Vol. 45.

[142] Source: *The African Repository and Colonial Journal*, Vol 46.

[143] [Source: Ancestry.com. World War I Draft Registration Cards, 1917-1918 [database on-line]. Provo, UT, USA: The Generations Network, Inc., 2005. Original data: U S Selective Service System. World War I Selective Service System Draft Registration Cards, 1917-1918. Washing, D.C.: NARA. M1509, 4,582 rolls. Imaged from Family History Library microfilm; Banks, Ray, comp., WWI Civilian Draft Registrations [database on-line]. Provo, UT, USA: The Generations Network, Inc., 2000. Original data: United States, Selective Service System. Draft Registrations Cards, 1917-1918.].

[144] [Source: NARA. U.S. World War II Army Enlistment Records, 1938-1946 [database on-line]. Provo, UT, USA: The Generations Network, Inc., 2005. original date: Electronic Army Serial Number

Merged File, 1938-1946 [Archival Database]; World War II Army Enlistment Records, Records of the NARA, Record Group 64; National Archives at College Park, College Park, MD.].

[145] Surveyed by: Roy L Roulhac, Willie Hazel Morris, Kenneth Pope and Betty Mae Smith, July 3, 2000, Location: TWP 4N, Rng 10W, Section 16 – South Wynn Street, Marianna, Florida.

Made in the USA
Charleston, SC
18 February 2013